Literacy in African American
Communities

Literacy in African American Communities

Edited by

Joyce L. Harris
University of Memphis

Alan G. Kamhi
University of Oregon

Karen E. Pollock
University of Memphis

LEA
LAWRENCE ERLBAUM ASSOCIATES, PUBLISHERS
2001   Mahwah, New Jersey   London

Lawrence Erlbaum Associates, Inc., Publishers
10 Industrial Avenue
Mahwah, New Jersey 07430

Library of Congress Cataloging-in-Publication Data

Literacy in African American communities / edited by Joyce L. Harris, Alan G. Kamhi,
Karen E. Pollock.
    p. cm.
    Includes bibliographical references and index.
    ISBN 0-8058-3401-X (cloth : alk. paper) — ISBN 0-8058-3402-8 (pbk. : alk. paper)
    1. Afro-Americans—Education.   2. Literacy—United States.   I. Harris, Joyce L.
II. Kamhi, Alan G., 1950-   III. Pollock, Karen E.

  LC2731.L59 2000
  379.2′4′08996073—dc21

                                   99-088717

Printed in the United States of America
10 9 8 7 6 5 4 3 2 1

In homage to the scribes who,
with neither pen nor ink,
wrote on history's pages
and on our hearts
the stories of lives well-lived.

—JLH

Contents

About the Contributors   ix

Foreword   xv
  Shirley Brice Heath

Preface   xxi

Acknowledgments   xxiii

Introduction   xxv

1   Public and Personal Meanings of Literacy   1
  Constance Dean Qualls

2   "Come Sit Down and Let Mama Read": Book Reading
  Interactions Between African American Mothers
  and Their Infants   21
  Carol Scheffner Hammer

3   Spoken and Written Narrative Development: African
  American Preschoolers as Storytellers and Storymakers   45
  David Bloome, Tempii Champion, Laurie Katz,
  Mary Beth Morton, and Ramona Muldrow

4   Emergent Literacy: Home–School Connections   77
  Jerrie C. Scott and Cheryl D. Marcus

5   Literacy in the African Diaspora: Black Caribbean
         American Communities   99
            Sherri L. Horner

6   Reading the Typography of Text   109
            James Hartley and Joyce L. Harris

7   The Path to Reading Success or Failure: A Choice
         for the New Millennium   127
            Alan G. Kamhi and Sandra P. Laing

8   Reading Performance and Dialectal Variation   147
            Julie A. Washington and Holly K. Craig

9   Language Variation and Literacy Acquisition in African
         American Students   169
            Noma R. LeMoine

10   From the Pews to the Classrooms: Influences of the African
         American Church on Academic Literacy   195
            Beverly J. Moss

11   Design and Delivery Issues for Literacy Programs Serving
         African American Adults   213
            Thomas A. Crowe, Marie E. Byrne, and Sue T. Hale

12   Effects of Structure Strategy Instruction on Text Recall
         in Older African American Adults   233
            *Bonnie J. F. Meyer, Andrew P. Talbot, Leonard W. Poon,
            and Melissa M. Johnson*

13   An Age-Related View of Computer Literacy for Adult
         African Americans   265
            Monica M. Huff and Wendy A. Rogers

14   Coming Full Circle: Some Circumstances Pertaining
         to Low Literacy Achievement Among African Americans   277
            John Baugh

Author Index   289

Subject Index   297

About the Contributors

John Baugh is Professor of Education and Linguistics at Stanford University. His research interests include the educational applications of linguistic science, applied linguistics, and African American language. He is the author of *Black Street Speech: Its History, Structure, and Survival* and, more recently, the co-author of *Out of the Mouths of Slaves: African American Language and Educational Malpractice*.

David Bloome is Professor of Education in the Language and Literacy Program at Peabody College of Vanderbilt University. His research focuses on reading and writing as social and cultural practices, with special concern for their relationships among classroom, community, and family settings.

Marie E. Byrne is an Assistant Professor in the Speech-Language Pathology Program at the Mississippi University for Women. She has presented and published research on the relationship between oral and written language for participants in adult literacy programs, especially as those skills relate to the attainment and maintenance of employment.

Tempii Champion is an Assistant Professor in the Department of Communication Sciences and Disorders at the University of South Florida, where she conducts a multicultural literacy program and research on language intervention for African American children. She also teaches classes in African American English and language development.

Holly K. Craig is Professor of Education and Director and Senior Research Scientist in the Communicative Disorders Clinic at the University of Michigan. Her research interests focus on the development of language assessment instruments appropriate for African American children, typical and atypical patterns of language acquisition, and developmental pragmatics.

Thomas A. Crowe is Professor and Chair in the Department of Communicative Disorders and Director of the Center for Speech and Hearing Research at the University of Mississippi. He has presented and published research on the oral and written language of participants in adult literacy programs. His research has included an investigation of the importance of appropriate social communication skills to attaining and maintaining employment for adult literacy learners.

Sue T. Hale is an Instructor and Director of the Speech and Hearing Clinic in the Department of Communicative Disorders at the University of Mississippi. She has presented and published research on the relationship between oral and written language for participants in adult literacy programs. Her research has investigated the relationship of social communication skills to the attainment and maintenance of employment in adult literacy learners.

Carol Scheffner Hammer is an Assistant Professor in the Department of Communication Disorders at The Pennsylvania State University, where her research focuses on language and literacy development in African American and Hispanic preschool children. In particular, she investigates how caregivers construct the literacy learning environment of young children, with emphasis on capturing the variety of behaviors and styles that occur within cultural groups.

Joyce L. Harris is Interim Director of the Office of Diversity and an Associate Professor in the School of Audiology and Speech-Language Pathology at the University of Memphis. She teaches courses in adult neurogenic language disorders and the sociocultural bases of communication. Her print scholarship includes a chapter in *Communication Development and Disorders in African American Children: Research, Assessment and Treatment*, which she co-edited with Alan Kamhi and Karen Pollock. She is also an associate project director of a 4-year Department of Education grant to prepare leadership personnel for communication and literacy in African American children and youth.

James Hartley is Research Professor of Psychology at the University of Keele, Staffordshire, England. His main research interests are in written communication, with special reference to typography and layout. His textbook *Designing Instructional Text* (Kogan Page) is now in its third edition. He is also well known for his research in teaching and learning in the context of higher education, and his latest book in this area, *Learning and Studying: A Research Perspective* (Routledge), has just been published.

Sherri L. Horner is an Assistant Professor of Educational Psychology at the University of Memphis. She received her PhD from City University of

New York, Graduate School and University Center. She has taught at Medgar Evers College, Queens College, and LaGuardia Community College. She did her fieldwork at the Medgar Evers Head Start in Crown Heights, Brooklyn. Her research interests include emergent literacy issues and the sociocultural aspects of literacy development.

Monica M. Huff is a doctoral student at the University of Georgia, where her research interest in computer literacy centers on design improvements and appropriate training. Currently, she is investigating older adults' use of the World Wide Web and developing a bridge between basic cognitive theory and computer interface designs.

Melissa Mapstone Johnson is an Associate Director of a nursing home in Athens, Georgia. She received her training in Life Span Developmental Psychology at the University of Georgia.

Alan G. Kamhi is a Professor and Chair of the Program in Communication Disorders and Sciences at the University of Oregon. His early research focused on linguistic and cognitive abilities of children with specific language impairments (SLI) and mental handicaps. Later research focused on language-learning disabilities, culminating in a book co-edited with Hugh Catts, on reading disabilities from a developmental language perspective. Recent research has focused on language abilities in children with mild-to-moderate hearing loss, phonological awareness and early reading abilities, and differentiating children with SLI from children with nonspecific language impairments. He is also an associate project director of a 4-year Department of Education grant to prepare leadership personnel for communication and literacy in African American children and youth.

Laurie Katz is a Lecturer in Education at Peabody College, Vanderbilt University. She received her doctorate in early childhood and special education from the University of Massachusetts. Her areas of expertise include the integration of special needs and at-risk children into general education settings; the development of collaborative relationships between schools, communities, and families; and the use of ethnographic perspectives in research and program evaluation.

Sandra P. Laing is an Assistant Professor of Speech-Language Pathology in the Department of Communication Disorders at the University of Alabama. Her research interests include child language and reading development and disorders.

Noma R. LeMoine is Director of the Los Angeles Unified School District's Academic English Mastery Program, which has as its primary goal facilitating mastery of school language, literacy, and learning in students whose home language is of a nonstandard variety. She holds master's degrees in Speech-Language Pathology and Audiology and Education and is currently a PhD candidate in Language, Literacy, and Learning at the University of Southern California. She has served over 10 years as an adjunct professor at several California universities.

Cheryl D. Marcus is Activity Director for the Early Start Program at Central State University and Past President of the Xenia (Ohio) Board of Education. Cheryl is completing her doctoral degree in educational leadership at the University of Dayton. Her literacy activities include: coordinator of a church-based literacy program; project coordinator of Central State University's Adopt a School Program and the Ohio African American Read-In Chain; and creator and coordinator of Xenia's Volunteer After-School Enrichment Program.

Bonnie J. F. Meyer is Professor of Educational Psychology at The Pennsylvania State University. As a Fellow of the American Psychological Association and the American Psychological Society, her primary research interests are aging, decision making, reading comprehension and memory, text structure and discourse analysis, and individual differences in interest and verbal ability. She has published two books on text structure and memory for prose as well as numerous articles and book chapters.

Mary Beth Morton is a doctoral student in the Language and Literacy Program in the Teaching and Learning Department at Peabody College, Vanderbilt University. She is currently conducting an ethnographic study of narratives in African American preschoolers.

Beverly J. Moss is an Associate Professor of English at Ohio State University. Her areas of scholarship are in composition and literacy studies, specifically literacy in nonacademic communities, writing instruction, and composition studies. Her research investigates how literacy is defined and how it functions in African American community settings.

Leonard W. Poon is Professor of Psychology, Chair of the Faculty of Gerontology, and Director of the Gerontology Center at the University of Georgia. As a Fellow of the American Psychological Association and Gerontological Society of America, his major research interests are normal and pathological changes in memory and cognition among the aged and contributors to successful adaptation among centenarians.

Constance Dean Qualls is an Assistant Professor in the Department of Communication Disorders at The Pennsylvania State University, where she teaches courses in anatomy and physiology, research methods, and language and cognition in normal and pathological aging. She conducts life-span research on figurative language comprehension and reading practices in adults, and is currently engaged in a study on the readability of health care literature. Her recent publications include "Effects of Familiarity on Idiom Comprehension in African American and European American Fifth Graders" (*LSHSS*, April 1999) and "Written Language Comprehension in Younger and Older Adults" (*JSLHR*, 1998).

Wendy A. Rogers is an Associate Professor in the Department of Psychology at Georgia Institute of Technology. Her primary research interest in literacy has focused on computer literacy in older adults, and has included the development of training programs and design recommendations to help overcome physical and cognitive limitations. A recurrent theme of her research is practically-relevant applied psychology that informs science while improving the lives of older individuals.

Jerrie Cobb Scott is a Professor of Education and the founding Director of the Office of Diversity at the University of Memphis. She has authored and co-authored several publications in the area of literacy, including the forthcoming book *Classroom Environments: Wisdom and Practice* with Jacqueline Royster and Dolores Straker. She has developed literacy programs for elementary schools, colleges, and community organizations, most notably the African American Read-In Chain, a national literacy campaign sponsored by the Black Caucus of the National Council of Teachers of English.

Andrew P. Talbot is a doctoral student in Educational Psychology at The Pennsylvania State University. He also teaches classes in the Psychology Department at Lock Haven University of Pennsylvania. He has published in the areas of reading comprehension, reading rate, and aging.

Julie A. Washington is a Senior Associate Research Scientist in the Communicative Disorders Clinic at the University of Michigan, Ann Arbor. Her research interests focus on language use and development of African American children who are African American English (AAE) speakers, with particular emphasis on the development of dialectal forms, and the impact of language on academic achievement.

Foreword

Shirley Brice Heath
Stanford University

For the landmark volume *Functions of Language in the Classroom*, edited by
Cazden, John, and Hymes (1972), Dell H. Hymes provided an Introduction that has achieved a unique place in the history of this particular
genre. In his opening to a volume which is a classic in several fields—linguistics, anthropology, and language education—Hymes laid out fundamental issues that have since dominated the direction of research in the
field of sociolinguistics. The majority of scholars concerned with language
and education over the past three decades have had to hold their work up
against the norms and standards Hymes set out in that lengthy introduction to a collection of papers that went far beyond discussions of language
use in classrooms. Aside from his co-editors, Courtney Cazden and Vera
John, other central figures in the study of language in social contexts of
home, community, and organizations contributed chapters to that volume. Some of the earliest work on "native speakers" of Black English
appeared, and seminal papers on varieties of narratives and participant
structures for Hawaiian and Native American children were included.

The current volume with its broad representation from researchers in
language-related fields provides the incentive to review the issues Hymes
put forward as "helpful and hopeful" in their fundamental criticism of the
then-current state of language education. Hymes began by chastising linguists for not directly undertaking research on classroom language. In
essence, this same criticism still holds today, but the current volume
reveals that rather than depending on linguists to do studies of classroom

language, scholars in fields such as communication disorders, as well as reading and language development, have undertaken these and related studies. They have often done so after having been trained in linguistics or applied linguistics. Several chapters of this edited collection are informed by theories from areas of linguistics, such as dialectology, historical linguistics, and phonology, while they also demonstrate direct engagement of the authors in classroom research.

This volume represents in additional ways what the years since 1972 have brought within the study of language in society. Hymes makes the point that before the 1970s, linguists and other scholars of language focused on the structures of speaking rather than the uses of language and therefore made no contributions to our understanding of links between language and learning. He argues that "scholars as citizens" (p. xii) have an obligation to move beyond the study of phonology, morphology, or syntax to understand language as it works in matters having to do with access, opportunity, and tools of mobility. He laments the seemingly apolitical stance of linguists and the failure of other scholars concerned with language to see the possibilities for their work to contribute to policy changes.

Since the Ebonics controversies of the late 1990s, numerous linguists—William Labov, John Baugh, and John Rickford most prominently—have repeated and even expanded Hymes' cry for social responsibility by linguists. Contributors to the current volume make obvious their sense of social responsibility. These scholars give their attention not only to education as an institution but also to other critical gatekeeping institutions, as well as to communities from which a growing proportion of students come.

The authors here also appear to take up the implications of Hymes' argument that "authority [also] accrues from mastery of activities and skills, from experience with a variety of language, in a community" (p. xv). The current collection of essays illustrates the importance of locating language varieties within their communities and of respecting the authority of locals over their uses and valuation of these varieties. Again and again these chapters illustrate ways in which speakers draw on a repertoire of genres, styles, and grammatical understandings, while the notion of "standard" relied upon in assessment processes used in formal education ignore range, authenticity, and community validation. Hymes had argued that engaging directly with speakers is the only way to provide the systematic research necessary to make "explicit and objectively systematic what speakers of the language, or members of the community, in a sense already know" (p. xv). Chapters here take this position with respect to topics such as children's narratives (see Bloome et al., chap. 3, this volume), ministers' sermons (see Moss, chap. 10, this volume), and young mothers' book reading events (see Hammer, chap. 2, this volume).

An additional point that Hymes makes—the mutual and reciprocal work of the investigated and the investigator—is also evident in many research reports included here. Parents and teachers work together to understand home–school connections, while scholars listen closely to respondents in order to reshape interview questions so as to reflect as accurately as possible attitudes and beliefs community members may not have previously brought to full consciousness.

Much that Hymes and his co-authors advocated in the 1972 volume has come to be not only the guiding rationale but also the central research methodology used by scholars in the several disciplines that address language in use. The lament made in 1972 that there were far too few scholars with a desire to study classrooms does not apply three decades later. Thousands of doctoral students, mature scholars, and teacher-researchers, as well as students across grade levels, can now be found laying claim to being involved in "language research" as they study the language used in textbooks, the media, and across their commununities. The "democratization of linguistic and ethnographic approaches" (p. xvii) called for by Hymes has come about in many ways and has been led by schools of education who have embraced such approaches wholeheartedly, if not always with acknowledgment of the value of linking these approaches to their mother disciplines. Discourse analysis, ethnographic interviews, and qualitative methods figure centrally in many research studies undertaken by doctoral students in education departments. Numerous series of books lay out in detail the steps of data collection, analysis, and interpretation for those who undertake such studies. We do not lack studies of the kind that Hymes noted as central in the then emerging subfield of "sociolinguistics." The current volume reflects not only this fact but also the far-reaching influence of some of the fundamental work in sociolinguists on language educators in clinical and teaching fields related to language.

However, in spite of the substantial achievements and accumulation of work on language in context over the past three decades, neither the United States nor indeed any system of formal education in the world has managed to leverage sociolinguistic research into educational policy. The notorious cultural lag that standardized tests, textbooks, and teaching practices represent still holds for most classrooms in national and local systems of education. That cognitive and social limits co-occur with the use of languages or dialects, as well as genres, vocabulary choice, and syntactic forms, not sanctioned as "academic" remains the dominant view of educators. The overwhelming evidence that children, and indeed all neurologically normal speakers, have a repertoire of linguistic resources upon which to draw for social meanings has had almost no impact on the artifacts that support classroom teaching and testing. Moreover, in most societies, the public that claims power over formal systems of education hangs onto the view that the variety of language used is a reflection of fundamental character and intelligence. Hymes made the "terrifyingly simple" statement: "If one rejects a child's speech, one probably communicates rejection of the child" (p. xxxiii)—hence tossing away any chance of bringing that student to an understanding of choice and the value of expanding his or her repertoire of language varieties. Hymes did not mince words when he pointed out the racism that lies behind the rejection of Black children—and indeed all children of color—and their language structures and uses.

The current volume echoes many of the same points that Hymes made 30 years ago. This volume like that edited by Cazden, John, and Hymes (1972) is helpful; it is however not hopeful as Hymes claimed the 1972 volume was. But before we explore just why it is not hopeful, let us look at some of its means of providing help.

Several chapters demonstrate the extent to which the study of language in its social context and among users of different identities and definitional attribution has expanded beyond children and students. Particularly welcome in this volume are the chapters on adult learners (see Moss, chap.10; Crowe et al., chap. 11; Meyer et al., chap. 12; Huff & Rogers, chap. 13, this volume) and attention to Black Caribbean communities (see Horner, chap. 5, this volume). This volume also follows through on Hymes' call for scholars to make obvious that which generally lies well outside the consciousness of speakers and readers. Here attention goes to the many ways in which readers take typographic conventions for granted (see Hartley & Harris, chap. 6, this volume), as well as the means by which text structures aid memory of content material (Meyer et al., chap. 12, this volume). Several chapters engage the history and distribution of patterns of literacy, habits of reading, and controversies surrounding the effects of dialectal variation on reading performance.

Now why is it not hopeful? Nearly every page reminds us that many of the problems outlined by Hymes in 1972 remain with us in full force: the refusal to acknowledge the power of repertoires of language varieties, the dominance of simplified notions of literacy, and the continuation of views that denigrate varieties of English spoken by African Americans. Many of the chapters reiterate findings that have appeared in the pages of sociolinguistics journals and in numerous books that have documented the racist basis of negative valuations of varieties of English used by African Americans. Hymes' hopes for greater equity, reforms of educational and other institutions through research findings, and improved incorporation of sociolinguistic principles and practices into teachers' ways of learning have not come about.

Why is this the case? The ready answer comes in broad sweeping, condemning terms—racism, class protectionism, selfishness, and isolationism. But educators and others reading the current volume may find more thought-provoking answers to why there seems an absence of hope these days in another figure from the 1970s—Lawrence Stenhouse. In England in 1970, Stenhouse established the Centre for Applied Research in Education (CARE) with the goal of working with teachers as researchers and as change agents in their schools and communities. Stenhouse believed in the radical power of teacher learning:

> The responsibility of teachers, at all levels, is to free students from the insularity of their own minds, prevent them from lodging in the comfortable branches of the teacher's thought, and to try instead to foster a less cautious and confined exploration of knowledge: one that confers on those who seek it, in a spirit of critical enquiry, the power of its use. (Stenhouse in Rudduck & Hopkins, 1985, p. 3)

Essential to Stenhouse and many of those who followed his ideas in Great Britain over the next decades was the view that society could change only if students could engage with teachers who were themselves constantly learning and staying open to ideas and taking risks in their explorations of attitudes and knowledge. Stenhouse found stagnation and protectionism in each generation to be in large part the result of the focus on "training teachers" and instilling pedagogical practice in education rather than fostering a spirit of "enquiry." He regarded education's push toward encrusting the professional field with tricks of practice and fixed curricula and narrow goals for student learning as resulting in "the reassurance of certainty to ameliorate the agony of responsibility" (p. 127).

We have far to go before the kind of social responsibility Hymes and Stenhouse called for will begin to match the extent of our study of language in social contexts. High-sounding calls for classrooms and schools to reflect common humanity, the pursuit of wisdom, and the rigors of enquiry have been made again and again. They have not brought change nor are they likely to do so in the face of the rigidity of the structures of organizations and belief systems that hold speakers and their languages in hierarchical layers of separation.

This introduction closes with no repeat of such mighty and distant calls. Instead, it turns to a central tenet of linguistics—*meaning*—often termed simply semantics. None of the chapters of this or any other volume on language use and attitudes among African Americans or any other group of speakers of language varieties will reach beyond being *helpful* to enabling us to be *hopeful* without greater attention to meaning. Readers of this and all similar volumes (see, for example, Baugh, 1999; Mufwene, Rickford,

Bailey, & Baugh, 1998; Pollard & Ajirotutu, 2000) must find it in themselves to represent *meanings* about the knowledge given here to other learners through social interaction. Such meanings clearly extend beyond mere semantics to explorations that take up economic, political, and philosophical matters, as well as new considerations of the sociology of organizations to enable understanding relations among knowledge, position, and voice.

REFERENCES

Baugh, J. (1999). *Out of the mouths of slaves*. Austin: University of Texas Press.

Cazden, C. B., John, V. P., & Hymes, D. (Eds.). (1972). *Functions of language in the classroom*. New York: Teachers College Press.

Mufwene, S. S., Rickford, J. R., Bailey, G., & Baugh, J. (Eds.). (1998). *African American English*. London: Routledge.

Pollard, D. S., & Ajirotutu, C. S. (Eds.). (2000). *African-centered schooling in theory and practice*. Westport, CT: Bergin & Garvey.

Rudduck, J., & Hopkins, D. (1985). *Research as a basis for teaching: Readings from the work of Lawrence Stenhouse*. London: Heinemann.

Preface

Justifiably, some might ask: "Why another book on literacy in African Americans?" "Hasn't that subject been aired enough, already?" "Haven't we exhausted all original thoughts on this topic?" "What more can be said about the so-called Black–White literacy gap, America's not-so-secret 'dirty little secret'?" Thoughtful answers to these and similar questions must first accede the existence of an extensive literature exploring issues of language and literacy in African Americans. One must also accede that the intersecting issues of race, culture, history, and literacy produce a juncture of complexity that cannot be easily unsnarled by a single, definitive treatment.

So, in that regard, the creation of another compendium, combining new and formerly expressed ideas on the topic of literacy in African Americans, is entirely appropriate. New scholarship in this area both validates and extends previous work through replication and fresh iteration. One hopes also that readers new to the subject will be enlightened by this late addition to the literature and, further, that the scholars among them will hark back to previous works to arrive at a fuller understanding of past endeavors and to gain a clearer vision of future ones. For knowledge advances in incremental steps, with false starts, dead-ends, and yes, even retraced steps. And so, in pursuit of greater understanding and without further justification, we offer *Literacy in African American Communities*.

At the outset, it is also important to recognize that African Americans are not a homogeneous group. Despite common historical roots and an ethnocultural identity, African Americans make up many communities and experience a variety of social and psychological realities. Age, religion, socioeconomic status, social affiliations, geographic residence, and even language differences comprise variables that define these communities. It was in recognition of the diversity among African Americans that "communities" was included in this volume's title.

In a similar vein, this within-group variability extends to individuals' acceptance, or rejection, of the now widely used term *African American*. Consequently, the interchangeable designations used throughout this volume are not lapses in stylistic consistency; rather, they are a reflection of historical and contemporary preferences for various terms that refer to American-born descendants of enslaved Africans. We request the reader's acceptance of this variability, keeping in mind that such acceptance might be one of many keys to understanding the complexity of African Americans and their collective reality.

— JLH

Acknowledgments

In part, this volume is based on papers presented at the 1998 Memphis Research Symposium: Focus on Communication and Literacy in African Americans, the third in a series of biennial research symposia on communication development and disorders in African American children and youth. The 1998 symposium, chaired by Karen Pollock, was the first of the series to include a life-span focus on communication and literacy. The other members of the committee were Mary Berni, Terry Douglas, Deborah Fletcher, Debra Garrett, Joyce Harris, Sharon Hill, Linette Hinton, Lennette Ivy, Iris Johnson, Alan Kamhi, Sandra Laing, Maurice Mendel, Michele Norman, Constance Qualls, Merlin Taylor, and Rebecca Weaver. We gratefully acknowledge the sponsorship of the School of Audiology and Speech-Language Pathology at the University of Memphis and the Office of Special Education Programs in the U.S. Department of Education.

We would also like to thank Sharon E. Moss, American Speech-Language-Hearing Association, and Violet J. Harris, University of Illinois at Urbana–Champaign, for their reviews and insightful comments during the early development of this project.

Finally, to Naomi Silverman, Senior Editor at Lawrence Erlbaum Associates, for her belief in *Literacy in African American Communities* and for her able guidance through the publication process, we say, "Thank you."

Introduction

In a society that values and rewards sophisticated levels of literacy, African Americans are among those most disadvantaged by low literacy achievement. Consequently, African Americans—irrespective of age or social circumstance—are often the focus of public discourse about literacy in the United States. Existing literature that deals specifically with literacy in African Americans is typically segmented by age (e.g., school literacy, adult literacy), academic discipline (e.g., education, linguistics), or a particular domain (e.g., computer literacy). It is precisely the case that such fragmentation obscures the tenaciously cyclical nature and spreading consequences of this group's endowment of low literacy. Thus, the casual reader never sees the whole picture, leading to stereotypic notions about the intellectual inadequacy of millions of U.S. citizens.

In an attempt to bring the disparate parts of the picture into clearer focus, the chapters in this volume bring together personal, historical, developmental, and cross-disciplinary vantage points from which to view the influences of cultural socialization on literacy values and practices among many African Americans. Such a broadened perspective allows that the literacy issues pertaining to African Americans are as complex and unique as this group's collective history.

Literacy in African American Communities explores both developmental and adult literacy from the perspectives of scholars from education, linguistics, psychology, anthropology, and communication sciences and disorders. The book's opening chapters develop the theme of historical, social, and cultural influences on the literacy experiences of African Americans. In chapter 1, Constance Dean Qualls surveys the objective and affective faces of literacy by discussing the multiple meanings of literacy and presenting the statistical profiles of African Americans' educational and literacy attainment. As a counterpoint, these data are interspersed with the voices of contemporary African Americans who discuss what literacy means to them. The chapter concludes with a presentation of survey data illustrating the reading habits of a sample of African American adults. In chapter 2, Carol Scheffner Hammer compares the book reading interactions of low- and middle-socioeconomic-status mothers and their children. Based on her ethnographic research, Hammer compares her findings with the data from mainstream mother–child book reading literature. She concludes the chapter with specific suggestions for the early literacy education of African American preschoolers.

In chapter 3, David Bloome, Tempii Champion, Laurie Katz, Mary Beth Morton, and Ramona Muldrow discuss the complementary relationship between narrative and social development as observed in African American preschoolers. Illustrative narrative transcripts bolster their discussion of relevant theories of text structure and narrative development. In chapter 4, Jerrie C. Scott and Cheryl D. Marcus discuss home–school connections, pointing out the need for bidirectional exchanges of information. The authors describe two programs that illustrate the effectiveness of the integration of home and school cultures in literacy education.

In chapter 5, Sherri L. Horner discusses one source of value asynchrony between African Americans and Black Caribbean Americans in regard to education and literacy. The chapter points to the need for further research on this growing population of the African Diaspora. Specific directions are provided for increasing our understanding of this population's literacy behaviors and values. In chapter 6, James Hartley and Joyce L. Harris begin with a brief discussion of reading processes, including the interplay between the reader's skills, intent, and the properties of the text. The focus shifts to a discussion of how typographic practices can either hinder or facilitate reading and writing skill development. The chapter contains many illustrative tables and figures, and suggestions for the development of textual materials.

Alan G. Kamhi and Sandra P. Laing, in chapter 7, contrast the literacy experiences of children from low- and high-print homes and discuss how those differences relate to discrepancies between these children during early literacy instruction. The authors review relevant literature and offer suggestions on how to increase the early literacy experience of African American children in order to increase their readiness for early reading instruction. In chapter 8, Julie A. Washington and Holly K. Craig discuss the role of dialectal variation in the development of early reading skills in

African American children. The authors provide a critical review of the literature on dialect and its role in reading development. The chapter concludes with well-reasoned suggestions for future research. In chapter 9, Noma R. LeMoine provides an overview of the historical development of African American language as a backdrop to understanding the educational and literacy issues of contemporary school-age African Americans. The chapter highlights effective instructional activities for enhancing language and literacy education for these students.

The final chapters of the book explore important aspects of adult literacy. In chapter 10, Beverly J. Moss, based on her ethnographic research, looks at the influence of the African American church, a significant cultural institution, on notions of authorship, authority, and literacy. The chapter provides illustrative transcripts and suggests another important home–school linkage. In chapter 11, Thomas A. Crowe, Marie E. Byrne, and Sue T. Hale provide program descriptions of state, federal, and privately funded "literacy training programs" for adolescents and adults. A review of the relationship of speech and language skills to literacy, as demonstrated by language research, is presented.

In chapter 12, Bonnie J. F. Meyer, Andrew P. Talbot, Leonard W. Poon, and Melissa M. Johnson present a description of a study designed to investigate the effectiveness of a reading comprehension protocol in improving the performance of a sample of older African American women. The authors provide a detailed description of the study, transcripts of the participants' responses, and discussion of their impressions and conclusion. In chapter 13, Monica M. Huff and Wendy A. Rogers define computer literacy and discuss the pervasiveness of computer tasks (e.g., word processing, Internet access, electronic banking, online database searching) in the day-to-day lives of adults. They provide a review of literature on computer use by adults, with particular focus on research involving African Americans. After presenting the results of comprehensive surveys of computer use, the chapter concludes with recommendations for future research.

In chapter 14, John Baugh reprises themes heard earlier in the volume, again illustrating sociopolitical, sociocultural, and sociolinguistic influences on literacy and education for African Americans. Baugh closes this volume on a cautionary but optimistic note, suggesting that increased parity in educational resource allocation between society's haves and have-nots can break the cycle of low literacy for African Americans.

– Joyce L. Harris

Chapter 1

Public and Personal Meanings of Literacy

Constance Dean Qualls
The Pennsylvania State University

As we enter the 21st century, literacy has taken on many different meanings in this highly technological, global society. Like the concept of multiple intelligences, multiple interpretations of what it means to be literate are commonplace, creating something of a "literacy renaissance." Diverse terms describing different literacy types support this notion. For example, functional literacy, cultural literacy, academic literacy, computer literacy, scientific literacy, and computational literacy are just some of the ways people talk about literacy. Other descriptive referents include music literacy, figurative literacy, art literacy, biblical literacy, numeric literacy, oral literacy, written literacy, family literacy, and street literacy. Considering these seemingly endless variations on the literacy theme, it is easy to conclude that the connotative meanings of literacy are many and varied. Thus, the implications of literacy are far-reaching.

To accommodate the multiple meanings of literacy, denotative meanings of literacy also have undergone change. For example, *Webster's II New College Dictionary* (1995) defines *literacy* as "the quality or state of being literate," where being *literate* means "one who can read and write; an educated person" (p. 640). The U.S. Congress, in the National Literacy Act of 1991, defined literacy as "an individual's ability to read, write, and speak in English and compute and solve problems at levels of proficiency necessary to function on the job and in society, to achieve one's goals, and to develop one's knowledge and potential." Taking the middle ground, the 1992 National Adult Literacy Survey (NAdLitS) defined literacy as "using printed and written information to function in society, to achieve one's goals, and to develop one's knowledge and potential."

These characteristic references to and definitions of literacy clearly suggest that one must possess a range of skills, including the ability to speak, read, write, calculate, and solve problems, to be considered literate. In addition, one must be able to meet a certain level of proficiency in each of these areas to successfully compete in today's technologically advanced environment. Although the personal, affective meanings of literacy are just as important as literacy proficiency, these dimensions are less frequently explored.

Thus, the primary focus of this chapter is to discuss meanings of literacy that transcend the traditional associations with "reading, writing, and 'rithmetic." Contemporary African Americans share, in their own words, what literacy means to them. These interwoven personal accounts provide a counterpoint to historical references and existing literacy and educational statistics about African Americans. African Americans will reflect on their encounters with today's literacy demands—which include being able to conduct print-based activities of daily living, participate in lifelong learning, engage in adequate health maintenance and management, and, importantly, to provide literacy role models for future generations. Finally, as a preliminary indication of the content and reading frequency engaged in by contemporary adult African Americans, data from the *Reading History and Habits Survey* (RHHS; Harris & Qualls, 1997) are provided.

WHAT DOES LITERACY MEAN?

Meanings of literacy are often qualified based on individual interpretations. Furthermore, the meaning is most likely attributed to the functions of literacy, largely derived from one's own individual experiences and perspective as to what literacy means. For example, one individual may refer to a group of musicians playing jazz as being "musically literate," while another individual might say that they are "jazz literate." In both cases, the individuals provide their own interpretation of the type of literacy proficiency the jazz musicians possess. Of importance is the idea that these are subjective interpretations that may or may not be factual, especially, for example, if the musicians cannot read musical notation, or if they are unable to demonstrate the authentic jazz "feel" in their playing.

In spite of individual interpretations of what literacy means, it is generally agreed that certain common factors, such as education, socioeconomic status, and family dynamics, strongly influence beliefs about the significance and essentiality of literacy. Literacy beliefs, in turn, determine literacy practices. Moreover, these factors cross racial–ethnic and cultural boundaries. Put another way, African Americans, like other racial–ethnic–cultural groups, determine the functional significance of literacy based on their successful negotiation in educational, economic, family, and social contexts. It is not surprising, then, that although anecdotal accounts of what literacy means in African American communities yield a range of introspections, the collective tone of these accounts suggests that literacy is not only important, but is requisite for human existence and "successful" survival. Literacy is powerful—it unifies, separates, liberates.

Literacy Brings People Together . . .

Shortly after I started my doctoral program, I was encouraged to audition for the local symphony chorus. At the time, I wasn't absolutely certain I wanted to make the time commitment, although I hesitantly followed up. Nevertheless, the audition time was set. When my husband and I arrived at the church where rehearsal was being held, the first thing I was told was that they did not need any more voices. Fine, I thought. Even still, after completing a form describing my musical background and experiences, I was hurriedly escorted by the choral director to a small, quiet room with a piano. I was instructed to sing a series of scales and choral melodies, and then the choral director asked me to read some scored music. Without hesitation, I sight-read the song while at the same time thinking to myself, okay, this will be over in a minute and my husband and I can go home. Well, to my surprise, the choral director jumped up and excitedly said, "You can go upstairs and get your music assignment." I said, "Now?" He said, "Now." Then he turned to my husband and said, "You can pick her up at 9 p.m."

Literacy Separates . . .

An example of how literacy separates people can be found in Alice Walker's (1990) *The Color Purple*. Celi, the main character, is separated from her sister not only by distance but also because Celi's husband, Mista', withheld her sister's letters from her. Consequently, Celi assumed that her sister had completely turned away from her, and that they would never see each other again. Later, Celi, with the help of her husband's lover, discovered Mista's cruel deception, and Celi finds the letters from her sister.

Literacy Liberates . . .

Because of the Black press, many Southern Blacks became aware of economic and other opportunities of which they would not have otherwise known (Marks, 1989). By reading newspapers written by and for Blacks, many Southern Blacks became liberated—liberated from the low wages and limited employment opportunities in the South. Black-owned and -operated newspapers used various forms of print materials, including written articles, pictures, cartoons, elaborate advertisements, and written music, to lure Southern Blacks to the North to take advantage of more numerous and better economic opportunities.

LITERACY PROFILE OF AFRICAN AMERICANS: RESULTS FROM THE 1992 NALS

Adult literacy continues as a focus of national attention. Despite the fact that literacy demands continue to change, the national goal is that all adults in the United States will be literate by the year 2000. For example, although the overall level of education in the United States has increased, educational and technological advances impose ever greater literacy demands, to such an extent that more and more people are being left behind. A key issue in this regard is the cycle of low literacy, the legacy of forbidden literacy and poor educational opportunities in some groups of African Americans. Low literacy ensures restricted life chances, restricted access to information, restricted employment opportunities (Qualls & Harris, 1998), and restricted involvement in political decision making vis-à-vis voting (Kernell, 1973).

In 1992, the National Center for Educational Statistics (NCES) of the U.S. Department of Education conducted the first literacy study of its kind ever done in the United States, the NAdLitS (National Center for Educational Statistics, 1993). The literacy skills of more than 26,000 persons age 16 years and older were assessed by either written survey or interview. The population sampled included the general public, persons with disabilities, non-native English speakers, older adults, and prisoners. African Americans and Hispanic Americans were oversampled. Three types of literacy were assessed in the NAdLitS, including prose, document, and quantitative literacy, areas chosen to assess the information-processing skills and strategies used by adults to accomplish a range of literacy goals. Within each literacy type, five proficiency levels (1 = lowest, 5 = highest) were established.

Following is a partial summary of the results from the NAdLitS, with particular emphasis on the literacy status of African Americans. Readers are referred to the executive summary (National Center for Educational Statistics, 1993) for a full report of the survey results.

- Between 40 and 44 million U.S. adults demonstrated proficiencies at the lowest level (Level 1). An interpretation of these results suggests that 21% to 23% of the U.S. population is functionally illiterate.

- African American adults, along with other diverse groups (e.g., Native Americans, Hispanic Americans, etc.), were more likely than Whites to perform in the two lowest levels, a finding that was generally explained by lower levels of education in these groups compared to Whites.
- Adults with lower levels of education were more likely to perform in the lower literacy levels compared to those who had completed high school or who had some postsecondary education. The reported mean educational level for African Americans was 11.6 years.
- With the exception of African Americans, individuals born in the United States outperformed those who were not. In other words, the African Americans surveyed demonstrated proficiencies similar to non-American-born individuals (e.g., individuals born in Spanish-speaking countries).
- Adults in prison were far more likely to demonstrate lower levels of proficiency than individuals in the general population. The significance of this finding is that the incarcerated adults surveyed tended to be younger, less well educated, and from minority backgrounds (approximately 65%). When sex, race–ethnicity, age, and level of education were controlled, overall differences between the prison and household populations were attributed to demographic make-up and educational status (Haigler, Harlow, O'Connor, & Campbell, 1993).
- Adults demonstrating higher levels of literacy were more likely to be employed, worked more, and had higher wages than individuals demonstrating lower levels of proficiencies.
- Compared to middle-aged and younger adults, older adults demonstrated limited literacy proficiency, regardless of race–ethnicity, a finding partially explained by lower levels of education in adults 65 years and older.
- Nearly half (41%–44%) of the adults in the lowest proficiency level were living in poverty, compared with only 4% to 8% of those in the two highest levels. According to the National Center on Education and the Economy (1990), the poverty rate for African American families is about three times that of White families.
- Overall, adults demonstrating higher levels of proficiency were far more likely to vote than were those in the lower levels. Race–ethnicity as a factor in voting was not reported.

The results of the NAdLitS indicate relations between literacy and education level, and between literacy and socioeconomic status. Based on their literacy profiles, some African American adults experience a lower quality of life, have limited employment opportunities, and are less likely to participate in the political process. Interestingly, many of the adults who demonstrated low literacy proficiency indicated that they read and write English well (National Center for Educational Statistics, 1993). For older African Americans, in particular, a literacy disadvantage has profound implications for health care and health maintenance.

Illiteracy rates in African Americans have declined dramatically over the past 100 years. Contemporary interpretations of illiteracy are based on the concept of functional literacy—that is, the impact of educational attainment on literacy requirements dictated by society (Snyder, 1993). Functional illiteracy continues as a threat to some individuals in the African American community, particularly because literacy is measured by academic standards. Furthermore, technological advances create new forms of illiteracy that frustrate and isolate individuals and groups of individuals. Here are some comments on automatic teller machines (ATMs) and computerized digital music recording:

> I can't use those stupid bank machines [ATMs]. They talk to me and I try to understand what to do, but I just get confused. (72-year-old African American female, retired, Washington, DC)

> I don't use them [ATMs] . . . I let my wife fool with the damned things. I don't know what I'll do when she's gone. (67-year-old African American male, retired, Tennessee)

> The language of MIDI [musical instrument digital interface] sequencing and other forms of computer-generated music is a type of literacy. But, to participate successfully in the recording industry today, you must educate yourself in the language of the business, especially before spending lots of hard earned money. (54-year-old African American male, recording studio owner, Pennsylvania)

EDUCATION PROFILE OF AFRICAN AMERICANS: THEN AND NOW

Literacy is intimately linked to education, and, therefore, any discussion of literacy must take education into account. In 1993, the NCES published a document chronicling 120 years of education in America. Based on a review of historical data, this publication reports education statistics on just about every aspect of America's educational system from 1869 to 1990. According to the NCES report, fluctuations in birth rates and shifts in the population (e.g., resulting from migratory trends) have a profound impact on society as birth cohorts move through school, workforce adulthood, and retirement. Following are only those educational statistics relevant to African Americans. Readers are referred to Snyder (1993) for a full report.

- Prior to the emancipation of Southern Blacks, school enrollment for Blacks largely was limited to only a small number of Blacks in Northern states.
- After the Civil War, enrollment rates for Blacks rose from 10% in 1870 to 34% in 1880, remaining unchanged over the next 20 years.
- The beginning of the 20th century brought sustained increases in enrollment rates for Blacks and Whites; during this period, the difference in enrollment rates between Blacks and Whites narrowed significantly.
- By the early 1970s, school enrollment rates for Blacks had risen to 90%; by 1991, 93% of 5- to 19-year-olds were enrolled in school.
- Between 1960 and 1970, the mean number of years of school completed by young Blacks rose from 10.5 to 12.2, with no change between 1970 and 1991.
- The average educational attainment for the entire population continued to rise as more highly educated younger cohorts replaced older Americans who had fewer educational opportunities. This was in sharp contrast to the 1940s, when more than half the U.S. population had completed no more than an eighth-grade education.
- In 1991, about 70% of Blacks had completed high school. A much smaller change (12% to 18%) was seen in the number of Blacks who completed 4 or more years of college during the period between 1980 and 1991.

While these data show dramatic increases in the mean educational level of African Americans over the last 100 years, educational opportunities for African Americans continue to be encumbered by issues related to access and quality, factors that directly impact on literacy. Notably, many African American children receive their education in inner-city schools. Urban school systems are often overwhelmed by a host of problems, some of which include outdated books, high student-to-teacher ratios, limited or no computers, low-quality instruction, and a less-than-adequate learning environment (e.g., no heat or air conditioning, leaky ceilings, unkempt bathrooms, discipline problems, low expectations and indifference; Kozol, 1991). As a consequence, some of these students graduate from high school lacking the basic skills necessary to gain entry into college, largely evident by low scores on college entrance exams compared to their White counterparts. Furthermore, many of these individuals who are admitted to colleges or universities require remedial work in basic reading, writing, and math and, often, are faced with having to learn to operate a computer for the first time. The problems these individuals face are usually insurmountable, and often lead to failure. Thus, it is not only important to provide access to educational opportunities, but the quality of the educational experience is paramount in ensuring adequate literacy skills for one to compete in today's society.

UNIQUE CHARACTERISTICS OF AFRICAN AMERICAN LITERACY

All human communities strive to maintain their cultural identity through customs, values, beliefs, literature, social practices, religion, family traditions, and language (including linguistic content and style). The oral tradition, a legacy brought to these shores by enslaved Africans, is integral to the Black identity and continues to be employed by African Americans to maintain cohesiveness within their communities. Van Keulen, Weddington, and DeBose (1998) suggested that the oral tradition embodies the emotional, psychological, and cultural tone of the Black ethos. Essential to the oral tradition is high oralcy or high oral–verbal literacy. Thus, verbal agility is a highly valued skill in African American culture, and is marked by the use of figurative language during various culturally based speech acts such as sounding, calling out, rapping, loud talking, and signifying (Smitherman, 1977).

Signifying, a form of verbal posturing, is a culturally approved style of talking disparagingly about someone. Often used by African Americans to verbally insult or to entertain (Smitherman, 1977), signifying is an indirect way for one to make a point while maintaining social contact. Thus, motivation to use figurative expressions is rooted in social necessity. Many African Americans use nonliteral expressions to convey intentions and underlying motivations while moderating the impact of disagreeable situations (Qualls, 1998). Consider the statement, "Sure, I'll be here when you get back—um-hm." Although this statement appears reasonable in the literal sense, the implied meaning, or intent, is in opposition to what was said. That is, in truth, the speaker will be gone when the listener returns. Examination of these types of interactions clearly suggests that the oral tradition maintains at least two literacy prerequisites: verbal and nonliteral, or figurative. Verbal literacy and figurative literacy are central to the conveyance and comprehension of messages in the oral tradition. Limited proficiency in either or both will cause a breakdown in communication.

> Literacy means being competent in a given area . . . being literate is not limited to just reading the words, there must be a deeper understanding of what the words mean. (57-year-old African American female, executive director, Bible institute, Virginia)

Historically, African Americans have relied on implicit language, multiple meanings, and ambiguity as an important means of communication. As a consequence of their social condition, Africans in America, or *slaves*, were forced to develop a form of communication to *effectively* interact with each other and with their oppressors. Through trial and error mostly, the slaves developed an oral–verbal communication system that served both of these purposes. Multiple meanings, ambiguity, coded messages, body language, and song were used to convey messages to each other, while at the same time these messages appeared nonthreatening to the slaveowners. Ironically, the slaves' secret messages were often conveyed through music with biblical themes that seemed to express their own wretched condition.

For example, the song "Steal Away" instructed listeners to prepare for escape, "I Go to The Rock" instructed listeners to assemble at a predetermined landmark for passage, and "Sometimes I Feel Like a Motherless Chile" expressed longing for the mother country, Africa (Smitherman, 1977; Van Keulen et al., 1998). Because the slaves were proficient in their use of double meanings, one might ask, would this communicative device be as well developed in African Americans were it not for their having been exposed to the conditions of slavery? The answer to this question is far from straightforward. However, if one contends that enslavement is the primary condition under which double-coded messages are used, then the answer might be "no." On the other hand, if one argues that language difference, not necessarily the conditions of slavery, is the basis for developing an alternative form of communication, the answer might be "yes." It is more likely that both the conditions of slavery and language barriers among the enslaved Africans necessitated their becoming adept at double-coding messages. This communication ploy enabled them to negotiate their environment using "linguistic creativity." Thus, the slaves were skilled at using their language skills to create exclusive communication environments.

> During my childhood, my brother and sister and I created our own way of communicating. Originally, we began using pig Latin, thinking that no one knew what we were saying. Eventually, our parents, uncles, and aunts figured out our code so we made some changes, thus, creating VKS language, our own unique way of communicating. No one but the three of us are literate in VKS language, therefore empowering us in a way that no powerful position or prestigious award could. We still get a big kick out of speaking in a way that no one else can understand. (32-year-old African American female, computer specialist, Maryland)

African Americans have used and continue to use the oral tradition and figurative language as a means of survival in the face of adverse sociopolitical practices such as slavery and economic oppression. Today, some

African Americans continue to value conveyance of the message verbally to a greater extent than through the written word. Based on established literacy standards and practices in the United States, however, it appears that verbal literacy is not as highly valued as is the ability to read and write. Consequently, this divergence of thinking on the relative importance of learning and using certain literacy types will restrict some individuals' life chances academically, occupationally, and politically. Nevertheless, many African Americans continue to employ the oral tradition for entertainment, to initiate and maintain social contacts, for self-esteem and community approval, and to promote within-group self-identity (Van Keulen et al., 1998). It is likely that the degree to which the oral tradition is employed by individual African Americans will depend on their level of acculturation—that is, the degree which they have adopted the beliefs and practices of mainstream Americans.

PERSONAL IMPACT OF LITERACY

Family and Community Literacy

Family and community literacy practices often dictate what individuals will consider as important, as well as those practices an individual will adopt. In other words, reading becomes important in a community of readers. Furthermore, when family, church, and other community members serve as literacy role models, or when they emphasize the importance of reading and writing, so will the children in the community.

> Literacy is a thirst for knowledge that was instilled in me from the womb. Continued education is my parents' legacy to me . . . as my father would say, "You will never have complete literacy." Literacy opens many doors and I am *always* ready, willing, and able to enter. (58-year-old African American female, diversity consultant, Ohio)

In her study on the promises and challenges of family literacy, Connors (1994) found that when adult participants had positive attitudes toward education and demonstrated literacy acts (e.g., completed homework assignments with their children), the children demonstrated improved use of literacy skills. To determine the influence of the home environment on children's reading skills, Campbell (1996) contrasted family factors between first graders who scored in the highest quartile and those who scored in the lowest on the Woodcock–Johnson tests of reading. She found that children who did well in reading were from smaller families, had better educated mothers, and were healthier. Campbell concluded that children's learning is heavily influenced by home environment.

Literacy means you can read and write . . . I used to preach to my son, "Education is important because you can't go anywhere without it." (69-year-old African American female, retired, Tennessee)

Individual differences in literacy behaviors and expectations in the family and community literacy practices of African Americans profoundly influence the literacy behaviors of its members. Consider the following personal account:

Hazel Locker: A Case for Literacy

"Hazel, get off the floor!" "IONTOO." [Hazel pouting]. "Keba (Keva), Baumi."

Had this dialogue been in Standard English it might have sounded like this: "Hazel, get off the floor." "I don't want to." "Keva, stop bothering me." This is the kind of dialogue I often heard from my half-sister, Hazel Locker, and if you can't pinpoint the language she is speaking, don't despair. Hazel, afflicted with Down syndrome (DS) at birth, and diagnosed with mental retardation (MR), invented her own language for communication with me and her other family members. Was Hazel a literate person? Growing up with Hazel shaped my ideas and beliefs about literacy and its dimensions of intellect, language, and communication. My experience with Hazel helped me to form a particular definition of literacy, which means: "Any combination of intelligible, verbal and/or nonverbal communication that permits meaningful participation in human activities." If we ascribe validity to this definition, then any reasonable person who knew Hazel would conclude that she was rather literate.

It was our mother's loving kindness, nurturing, and natural gifts that probably had the most dramatic impact on Hazel's development. Our mother made three strategic decisions that would forever shape Hazel's destiny. First, she decided to "de-institutionalize" Hazel from confinement in a children's center in Laurel, Maryland. Second, she "mainstreamed" Hazel into our family life without granting any special consideration or privileges to Hazel. Third, our mother decided to provide opportunities for Hazel to interact with her peers in nurturing situations and environments. Each of these decisions affected Hazel's ability to attain and sustain a reasonable level of literacy and consequent quality of life.

If we start with the idea that intelligence is a component of literacy (which I believe it is), we have to ask: Was Hazel intelligent? No matter which perspective about intelligence you accept, whether classical, revisionist, or radical, intelligence is generally held to mean "the ability to learn and to generalize what is learned" (Herrnstein & Murray, 1994). Did Hazel demonstrate the ability to learn and to generalize what she learned? I argue that Hazel was able to learn. For example, she learned to dress herself and take care of her personal hygiene and wants, discuss her feelings, play and win games (she was a Blue Ribbon winner in the Special Olympics), and establish effective social relations with others. Therefore, according to the general definition, we can say that Hazel was intelligent.

Regarding language, Hazel (against conventional medical wisdom about mental retardation) appropriated many of the linguistic conventions of American English to develop her own unique dialect. You could say that while her vocabulary and conversational style were extremely limited, they were, nevertheless, practical and rather effective in facilitating normal social activity within the context of her family and social life. Samples of Hazel's language, compared to certain words and clauses found in American English, include "Ginson" (Give me some), "Wegon" (Where are you going?), "I like peanu' bula" (I like peanut butter), "Okay," and "Mama."

Hazel had a unique opportunity to establish and hone her language and communication skills because of our family environment. The constant dialogue in our household constituted a form of the "emergent" method of language learning for Hazel. Our childhood household was a virtual "soundstage," with family members constantly convincing, debating, expressing, and imploring each other. There was perpetual negotiating and posturing for shares of limited resources, respect, rank, and favor, occasionally interrupted by periods of brief silence and listening (usually during prayers and recitals). Participation in musical activities was a source of both enjoyment and influence on Hazel's ability to create and use language. Each of us was challenged to learn and understand a variety of messages conveyed in a variety of mediums. This environment enabled us to understand Hazel and for her to understand each of us. Hazel's written communications, however, could be described as primitive. Hazel's nonverbal communication abilities were manifested foremost in her body language (i.e., hand signaling, gesturing, and particularly dancing).

Hazel was constantly interacting with family members who possessed more than ordinary capability in music, technology, literature, and public speaking. This exposure had a profound effect on Hazel's ability to grasp the concepts she needed to function effectively in her environment.

In closing, I can think of no clearer example of what literacy means to me than that found in Hazel Locker. My mother's leadership and gifts as a poet, storyteller, prolific reader, pianist, playwright, songwriter, and music educator stands as the prominent catalyst for Hazel's development as a literate person. Our family setting enabled Hazel to achieve a degree of literacy not found in most individuals with DS. By being exposed to "normal" family life, Hazel was able to appropriate language to express her feelings, desires, and outlook through both her own brand of language and forms of nonverbal communication that enables one to enjoy the benefits of family and social life that all human beings deserve. Because of this, her actions and behaviors satisfy all of the components of my definition of literacy. Therefore, Hazel Locker must be counted among those of us who call ourselves literate. (49-year-old African American male, a[2] Renaissance Arts, Washington, DC)

Hazel's case highlights several interesting points. First, literacy perceptions and expectations are often formed based on the family in context. Thus, subjective interpretations of the boundaries of literacy, functional literacy, and illiteracy are formulated early in one's life, and are shaped by certain life events. Second, Hazel's case speaks to the importance of language stimulation in emerging literacy, regardless of the ultimate level of literacy proficiency attained. Third, family practices in literacy are dynamic and evolving, once again, mediated by the family in context. Furthermore, expectations are differentially realized, dependent on one's role within the family context.

Intergenerational Issues in Literacy

Literacy is continuously changing. In other words, literacy is an activity that is shaped by cultural and community beliefs about the price of education and rewards of learning (Gadsden, 1993). From an intergenerational perspective, the educational legacies of elderly African American adults are enacted through interpretations and translations of literacy, which evolve over the life span (Gadsden, 1992). These interpretations and translations have implications for shaping the literacy beliefs of younger generations.

> I am literate because I can read, write, and understand. My grandmother had me write an article for the church newsletter about interesting characters and events in the Bible. I was able to do that because she makes me read for an hour every Saturday before watching television. She is very strict but I have learned so much from reading my Bible storybook and writing. I will use my literacy to be a famous artist, writer, and veterinarian when I grow up. (11-year-old African American female, 5th-grade student, Ohio)

Literacy helps individuals continue to learn new things, regardless of their age. Literacy allows older individuals to read for pleasure, to be informed about the world and their communities, to handle everyday tasks, and to take care of their own needs. Literacy also makes it possible for older persons to remain in or rejoin the workforce, and to contribute to other generations through volunteerism, civic participation, and family support (Brown, Prisuta, Jacobs, & Campbell, 1993). More importantly, older adults who are literate are able to share literacy experiences with younger generations, thus providing important literacy role models.

Functional and Health Literacy

Many adults with limited literacy proficiency conceal this aspect of their lives from significant others, primarily because of shame (Parikh, Parker, Nurss, Baker, & Williams, 1996). Of the 58 patients who demonstrated low functional health literacy on the Test of Functional Health Literacy in

Adults (TOFHLA), Parikh et al. found that 67.2% had never told their spouses of their reading difficulties, 53.4% had never told their children, and 19% had never told anyone. Patients who demonstrated low literacy were more likely to be male, have less than a high school education, and be over the age of 60. This finding has important implications for some individuals in the African American community (e.g., some African American males) because revealing their limited literacy ability to their family and friends can have a devastating effect on their self-esteem.

> Literacy is a passport . . . without literacy, we are prisoners with only limited ability to move about in the world, and those who can't read are normally unwilling to venture too far from the safety net of familiarity. Most illiterate and limited readers are defensive, unsure of themselves, and are most often easily taken advantage of. Literacy is liberation, freedom . . . it is the opportunity to make choices, even if the choices are mistakes . . . literacy helps us to know what to erase. (53-year-old African American female, computer administrator, Maryland)

Some members of the African American community demonstrate low tolerance for those who cannot read and write, while others are far more accepting. Tolerance or lack of tolerance of low literacy is seen in all racial and cultural groups and is by no means unique to African Americans. Nevertheless, in some instances, spouses or other family members dismiss an individual's limited literacy skills as a consequence of some other psychological or behavioral condition. It is not uncommon that those individuals who demonstrate this type of acceptance often engage in compensatory behaviors, essentially covering up the loved one's literacy problems.

Individuals with limited literacy proficiency are skilled at avoiding situations in which they are required to openly demonstrate their literacy skills. For these individuals, seeking employment or medical assistance will be problematic because of the requirement to complete forms. In some cases, the individual with low literacy will request that someone else complete the form or application for them because they are too busy. Statements such as "You are better at this than I am" or "I don't have the patience for this . . . it won't take you no time to do it" are just a few other examples of avoidance behaviors used by individuals with low literacy. In the meantime, they have accomplished the task without doing it themselves, and the person completing the task may be none the wiser.

Limited literacy skills present a barrier to receiving adequate health care, especially for adults with limited English proficiency and older adults. To determine the ability of patients to complete basic reading and numeracy tasks required for health care settings, Williams et al. (1995) surveyed 2,659 predominantly indigent and minority patients in two urban public hospitals using the TOFHLA, including 767 patients who were Spanish speakers.

Their results revealed that a high proportion of the patients were unable to read and understand written basic medical instructions, including comprehending directions for taking medications (41.6%), understanding information regarding their next appointment (26%), and understanding the informed consent document (59.5%). Thirty-five percent of the English-speaking patients and 62% of the Spanish-speaking patients had inadequate or marginal functional health literacy. Among the elderly, 81.3% of the English-speaking patients and 82.6% of the Spanish-speaking patients demonstrated inadequate or marginal functional health literacy. Williams et al. concluded that many patients seen in acute care facilities do not possess adequate health literacy skills to negotiate the health care system and obtain access to high-quality health care. These findings suggest that in addition to academic and computer literacy, adult literacy training programs include aspects of health care.

DATA ON AFRICAN AMERICAN ADULTS' READING PRACTICES

Adult attitudes, notions, and practices of literacy influence the attitudes and behaviors of children. At present, however, we have little knowledge as to what literate African American adults typically read to lend understanding in this regard. During the past decade, there has been a renaissance of African American novelists, an indication that there is definitely more than academic literacy being practiced among African Americans. African American adults are also reading for pure aesthetic pleasure or for self-improvement and encouragement. However, more information is needed about the types of literacy practiced in homes on a daily basis. Thus, the RHHS (Harris & Qualls, 1997) was constructed as a starting point. Knowledge of reading practices can inform adult education and literacy programs, social workers, and health care professionals. Just as important, this information can tell us what literacy behaviors we can expect to see in future generations.

> Literacy is the door to the world . . . it is through reading that you can visit other countries, learn about different cultures and religions, and learn languages. Through reading literature, you can escape from the troubles of the world. Literacy is a foundation upon which many aspects of our lives rest. (21-year-old African American female, college student, Maryland)

The RHHS (Harris & Qualls, 1997) was established as a measure of *participatory* literacy that provides an indication of the type and frequency of reading that adults engage in on a daily basis. The RHHS consists of two parts. Part I contains 52 items from nine print-media categories and requires the participant to rate the frequency with which they read each item type based on a 5-point rating scale (0 = *never*; 1 = *hardly ever*; 2 = *once in a while*; 3 = *on a regular basis*; 4 = *often*). Part II consists of 11 open-ended questions about reading history, current reading practices, and the use of reading tools. Part II was designed to evoke information regarding the individual's judgment of the relative importance of reading.

Fifty-six healthy African American adults ages 17 to 87 years (39 females, 17 males) completed the survey. Participants were grouped by decade. Seventy-nine percent of the participants reported they were high school or college graduates, 14% had some high school, and 7% reported they had less than 12 years of schooling. Twenty-one percent were students, 49% were employed at the time of testing, and 30% reported they were retired.

Results of a multivariate analysis of variance (MANOVA) showed a significant main effect of age group, $F(1, 54) = 1.661, p < .05$, on the RHHS. Tukey's HSD post hoc analysis revealed that significant differences in reading frequency on correspondence, $F(1, 49) = 2.621, p < .05$; e-mail, $F(1, 49) = 2.254, p < .05$; forms, $F(1, 49) = 2.338, p < .05$; and pamphlets/brochures, $F(1, 49) = 3.695, p < .01$, contributed to the main effect. Pairwise comparisons indicated significant differences between the following groups: 17–19- and 40–49-year-olds on correspondence; 40–49- and 70–90-year-olds on e-mail; 17–19- and 60–69-year-olds on forms; 17–19- and 30–39-year-olds, 17–19- and 50–59-year-olds, and 17–19- and 60–69-year-olds on pamphlets/brochures.

The results of multiple paired t tests revealed significant differences between the reading types, with the exception of the following: books–correspondence; books–newspapers/magazines; books–references; correspondence–newspapers/magazines; correspondence–recreation; e-mail–recreation; newspapers/magazines–references; and pamphlets/brochures–references.

To determine the predictive value of the reading habits (e.g., library visits) and reading tools (e.g., magnifying glass) on reading frequency, a regression analysis was conducted. Results showed a significant main effect ($p < .001$), revealing that responses on three factors predicted reading frequency, including visiting a flea market, borrowing books from family/friends, and owning a reading light. The relation between these factors and reading frequency was negative, suggesting that those who read more do not visit flea markets, do not borrow books from friends or family members, and do not own a reading light. Here is a summary of the results:

- Significant differences were found between type and frequency of reading.
- Overall, compared to individuals in the other age groups, the youngest and the oldest adults in this sample engaged in fewer reading activities.

- Labels are read more frequently than all other reading types in this group of individuals.
- The use of electronic media is restricted in these individuals, especially for the oldest adults.
- Only three reading practices (habits or tools) predicted reading frequency.

These results suggest that African Americans read a variety of materials with varying amounts of frequency, depending on age. These findings also suggest that reading frequency is not necessarily related to the reading practices an individual employs. Of particular interest is the restricted use of electronic media in this population. These data support other reports of limited computer use among African Americans (see Huff & Rogers, chap. 13, this volume), suggesting low levels of computer literacy in this population. These preliminary findings provide an important first step in understanding what African American adults read, including the frequency and type, as well as their reading habits. Certainly, additional studies are needed. By surveying large numbers of individuals from different regions of the country, we can get a better picture of the reading history and habits profile of a cross section (e.g., different ages, gender, socioeconomic status, health status, etc.) of African American adults. Information gained from these studies can yield useful information for health care, adult literacy programs, and computer education programs. Finally, there is a need for similar research that will more directly investigate the connotations (affective, aesthetic, emotional meanings) of reading by contemporary African American adults—young and old—and children.

> Literacy means power . . . reading enables us to do the very basic things in life. . . . Literacy is exciting because it opens up new avenues, like how to do new and different things. Literacy gives you a sense of accomplishment and self-esteem . . . literacy allows you to be creative. (35-year-old African American female, entrepreneur, California)

SUMMARY

When considering the current state of literacy in African Americans, one must acknowledge the impact of historical and social events that uniquely shape the literacy profile of this population. Readers are referred to Anderson (1995) for a detailed account of literacy and education in the African American experience. Manguel (1996) provides an elegant exposé on how the African slaves in America were forbidden, by law, to read, although many found ways to learn in spite of the law. African Americans have continued to struggle for equal access to education, and thus equal access to literacy, from the time the first slave boat landed on American soil until the present day. Early Blacks attempting to vote were required to pass illegal and grossly unfair literacy tests while local registrars, who themselves had questionable literacy in many cases, waived the literacy requirement for Whites (McMillen, 1977). Remnants of these historical events continue to adversely impact literacy and education for some African Americans. Despite these difficulties, however, many African Americans have achieved high levels of literacy, and are "successful" in their social, educational, and occupational pursuits.

National efforts are targeting literacy and education as a priority, as evidenced by the 1992 national literacy survey, national read-in chains, celebrity advertisements about reading and writing, and an increase in literacy councils across the country. Community-based organizations such as churches, schools, and libraries contribute greatly to increasing literacy among their members by sponsoring reading programs and providing reading tutors. Many of these programs concentrate on reading, however, often overlooking the importance of writing and other types of literacy (e.g., computational and computer literacy). Nevertheless, there is an ever-increasing number of resources available to adults who are interested in honing their reading, writing, computational, and computer skills and, thus, improving their overall quality of life.

This chapter has explored the public and personal meanings of literacy. Public accounts of literacy reflect the denotative meanings of literacy as the ability to read, write, calculate, and solve problems, skills necessary to successfully function and compete in today's society. To convey the true spirit of the meanings of literacy from a personal perspective, several contemporary African Americans, representing a range of educational, economic, and social (age, gender, geographic location) backgrounds, shared their thoughts on what literacy means. It is through these and other stories like these that the meanings of literacy in African American communities will be more fully understood.

REFERENCES

Anderson, J. D. (1995). Literacy and education in the African-American experience. In D. A. Wagner (Ed.), *Literacy among African-American youth* (pp. 19–37). Cresskill, NJ: Hampton Press.

Brown, H., Prisuta, R., Jacobs, B., & Campbell, A. (1993). Executive summary of literacy of older adults in America. In *Adult literacy in America: A first look at the results of the National Adult Literacy Survey*. Washington, DC: National Center for Education Statistics.

Campbell, F. A. (1996, June). *Family factors associated with high and low reading and mathematics scores in children from low income families*. Paper presented at the Head Start national research conference, Washington, DC.

Connors, L. J. (1994). *Small wins: The promises and challenges of family literacy* (Center on Families, Communities, Schools and Children's Learning Rep. No. 22). Washington, DC: U.S. Department of Education, Office of Educational Research and Improvement.

Gadsden, V. L. (1992). Giving meaning to literacy, intergenerational beliefs about access. *Theory Into Practice, 31*, 376–385.

Gadsden, V. L. (1993). Literacy, education, and identity among African-Americans: The communal nature of learning. *Urban Education, 27*, 352–369.

Haigler, K. O., Harlow, C., O'Connor, P., & Campbell, A. (1993). Executive summary of literacy behind prison walls: Profiles of the prison population from the National Adult Literacy Survey. In *Adult literacy in America: A first look at the results of the National Adult Literacy Survey*. Washington, DC: National Center for Educational Statistics.

Harris, J. L., & Qualls, C. D. (1997). *Reading History and Habits Survey*. Memphis, TN: University of Memphis.

Herrnstein, R. J., & Murray, C. (1994). *The bell curve: Intelligence in class structure in American life*. New York: The Free Press.

Kernell, S. (1973). Comment: A re-evaluation of Black voting in Mississippi. *American Political Science Review, 67*, 1307–1318.

Kozol, J. (1991). *Savage inequalities: Children in America's schools*. New York: HarperCollins.

Manguel, A. (1996). *A history of reading*. New York: Penguin.

Marks, C. (1989). *Farewell, we're good and gone: The great Black migration*. Bloomington: Indiana University Press.

McMillen, N. R. (1977). Black enfranchisement in Mississippi: Federal enforcement and Black protest in the 1960s. *Journal of Southern History, 43*, 351–372.

National Center for Educational Statistics. (1993). *Adult literacy in America: A first look at the results of the National Adult Literacy Survey*. Washington, DC: Author.

National Center on Education and the Economy. (1990). *America's choice: High skills or low wages!* (Report of the Commission on the Skills of the American Workforce). Washington, DC: Author.

Parikh, N. S., Parker, R. M., Nurss, J. R., Baker, D. W., & Williams, M. V. (1996). Shame and health literacy: The unspoken connection. *Patient Education & Counseling, 27*, 33–39.

Qualls, C. D. (1998). *Figurative language comprehension in younger and older African Americans*. Unpublished doctoral dissertation, University of Memphis, Memphis, TN.

Qualls, C. D., & Harris, J. L. (1998, June). *What do African American adults read?* Paper presented at the third biennial Memphis research symposium: Focus on Communication and Literacy in African Americans, Memphis, TN.

Smitherman, G. (1977). *Talking and testifyin'*. Boston: Houghton Mifflin.

Snyder, T. (Ed.). (1993). *Excerpts from chapter 1 of 120 years of American education: A statistical portrait*. Washington, DC: U.S. Department of Education, National Center for Educational Statistics.

Van Keulen, J. E., Weddington, G. T., & DeBose, C. E. (1998). *Speech, language, learning, and the African American child*. Boston: Allyn & Bacon.

Walker, A. (1990). *The color purple*. New York: Pocket Books.

Webster's II New College Dictionary. (1995). Boston: Houghton Mifflin.

Williams, M. V., Parker, R. M., Baker, D. W., Parikh, N. S., Pitkin, K., Coates, W. C., & Nurss, J. R. (1995). Inadequate functional health literacy among patients at two hospitals. *Journal of the American Medical Association, 274*, 1677–1682.

"Come Sit Down and Let Mama Read": Book Reading Interactions Between African American Mothers and Their Infants

Carol Scheffner Hammer
The Pennsylvania State University

The emergent literacy experiences of young children have been studied for over two decades. What this research has told us about infants' early book reading experiences is that mothers establish routines which help to support their children's participation in the interaction (Ninio & Bruner, 1977; Senechal, Cornell, & Broda, 1995; Sulzby & Teale, 1991). These early routines typically consist of four types of utterances: an attentional vocative (e.g., "Look"); a query (e.g., "What's that?"); a label (e.g., "It's a dog"); and an utterance that provides feedback to the child based on his or her response (e.g., "Yes, it's a dog"). These routines are illustrated in the following excerpt:

Mother:	Look!
Child:	*Touches picture.*
M:	What are those?
C:	*Vocalizes.*
M:	Yes, they are rabbits.
C:	*Vocalizes.*
M:	Yes, rabbits.

(Ninio & Bruner, 1977, pp. 6–7)

The research also informs us that mothers ask questions they think their children can answer, draw parallels to their children's experiences, and that act out what is happening in the story (DeLoache & DeMendoza, 1987). In addition, mothers of infants label and comment on the pictures, rarely reading complete sentences from the text (DeLoache & DeMendoza, 1987; Martin, 1998; Ninio & Bruner, 1977).

This research is limited, however, because it is based on the interaction styles of White, middle-class mothers and infants, which most likely does not describe the book reading styles of mothers and children from other cultures. We cannot ignore the early literacy experiences of children from multicultural groups for at least two reasons. First, literacy is more than a simple decoding task. It is a social and cultural experience that begins very early in children's lives (McLane & McNamee, 1990). Because the social context varies from culture to culture, literacy experiences of children from different cultural backgrounds will be mediated differently depending on their family's culture (Westby, 1995). Second, mismatches between children's home and school literacy experiences may place children who are not from the mainstream culture at a disadvantage at school. This is not to say that their literacy styles are deficient, rather that they may differ from the mainstream style. Therefore, we need to know more about the experiences of children from other cultures so that we can integrate the book reading styles they encounter at home into their school reading experiences. By incorporating familiar experiences into their school environment, it is hypothesized that children will be more successful in school.

Few studies have examined the emergent literacy experiences of African American children, leaving our knowledge of how mothers and children construct early book reading experiences rather limited. Heath (1982, 1983) studied working-class African American families in the Piedmont Carolinas. While living in the community, she found that caregivers provided their children with early literacy experiences that differed greatly from those they were exposed to in school. For example, the children heard no bedtime stories or stories beginning with the phrase "Once upon a time . . ." Instead, the children's community valued different social experiences, which required children to become proficient tellers of "fictionalized, true stories" (Heath, 1983).

Anderson-Yockel and Haynes (1994) built on Heath's work by performing quantitative comparisons of the book reading behaviors of working-class White and African American mothers and their 18- to 30-month-old children. These researchers found that the groups were more similar than different in their behavior. The African American mothers, however, asked their children fewer questions, and their children produced more spontaneous verbalizations compared to White children whose verbalizations were in response to questions.

Teale (1986) conducted a study that involved African American, White, and Hispanic mothers and children between 30 and 42 months of age from low-income homes. In general, Teale observed a wide range of variation within these three groups. Families within each group differed in how frequently they read to children, how often adults engaged in literacy activities, and how available literacy materials were to children.

I conducted research that extended this line of research to African American mother–infant dyads of low and middle socioeconomic status (SES; Hammer, 1996, 1997). The research was undertaken for two reasons. First, I wanted to learn about African American children's early experiences with books, experiences that set the foundation for later literacy skills. Second, I wanted to capture the styles of the dyads. In particular, I was interested in learning about the interaction styles of low- and middle-SES mothers and children. Although we have limited knowledge about low-SES dyads, we have even less information on African American families from middle-income backgrounds. Given a common cultural background, I anticipated that there would be similarities between these two groups. My aim was to determine their commonalities as well as to capture their differences. Simply comparing the means and standard deviations of observed behaviors between different communities can obscure the rich variations in behavior that occur within communities.

BOOK READING INTERACTIONS OF AFRICAN AMERICAN MOTHER–INFANT DYADS

The Mothers and Their Children

Twelve mothers and their infants living in a large Southern City took part in this investigation. Six of the mothers and their infants were of low SES and six were of middle SES, as determined by the Two-Factor Index of Social Position (Hollingshead & Redlich, 1958). For most of the dyads, I used information on the mother's education and occupation to calculate their social position, except when the father lived with the family. When the father resided in the same house, I calculated the social position of the dyad by using information about the parent with the higher educational and occupational levels.

In general, the mothers in the low-SES group averaged 11.8 years of education, and the mothers in the middle-SES group completed an average of 14.7 years of schooling. The dyads in the low-SES group all had incomes that fell below the poverty level. The median salary range for the middle-SES group was $30,000–$40,000. Table 2.1 contains demographic information about the mothers.

TABLE 2.1
Demographic Information About the Mothers

Name	Age	Marital Status	Education (in years)	Employment Status	Job Title	Annual Income ($)
Low-SES Group						
Sheryl	20	Single	13	Part time	Student/nursing intern	< 10,000
Thelma	25	Married	11	Not employed	Homemaker	10,000–15,000
Simone	27	Single	12	Full time	Waitress	10,000–15,000
Lisa	33	Single	12	Full time	Shirt presser	< 10,000
Pamela	37	Married	12	Full time	Maid	< 10,000
Deborah	28	Living with child's father	11	Not employed	On disability/homemaker	15,000
Middle-SES Group						
Anita	23	Single	13.5	Full time	Secretary	15,000–20,000
Nitoya	31	Married	16	Full time	Equipment auditor	30,000–40,000
Marilyn	32	Married	18	Full time	Teacher	>50,000
Jacklyn	32	Separated	16	Full time	Nurse	30,000–40,000
Julie	37	Single	14	Full time	Tax examiner	30,000–40,000
Tausha	22	Married	12	Full time	Medical records clerk	20,000–30,000

Note. SES = socioeconomic status.

All the mothers had normally developing infants between the ages of 13 and 18 months. This meant that the infants (a) were born no earlier than 36 weeks gestational age; (b) passed the Denver Developmental Screening Test II (Frankenburg & Dodds, 1990); (c) scored within normal limits on the Sequenced Inventory of Communication Development (Hedrick, Prather, & Tobin, 1984); (d) communicated through some single-word utterances as documented by their mothers on the Language Development Survey (Rescorla, 1989); and (e) had no parental concerns about hearing. Information about the infants is summarized in Table 2.2. There were no significant differences between the two groups in terms of their language abilities. The low-SES group consisted of four boys and two girls, and the middle-SES group consisted of five boys and one girl.

Reading to Children

The mothers and their infants participated in two to three 15-minute play sessions. All the sessions occurred in a large, carpeted preschool classroom and were videotaped. The mothers and infants played with three sets of toys. These included cause-and-effect toys, symbolic play toys, and books. The set of books included both picture books without a narrative (e.g., object-naming books, a counting book, books containing pictures of basic actions) and books with text (e.g., simple story books containing a basic plot). I asked the mothers to play with each set of toys during each session and permitted them to determine how long they and their children played with each set. In addition, I completed a questionnaire with the mothers that targeted how often they and their children engaged in a variety of behaviors including looking at books. This chapter focuses on the mothers' and children's behaviors during book reading.

TABLE 2.2
Infants' Ages and Language Abilities

Variable	Low-SES Group		Middle-SES Group	
	M	SD	M	SD
Age (in months)	16.3	1.75	16.8	0.75
SICD receptive language age (in months)	17.3	3.27	18.7	2.10
SICD expressive language age (in months)	18.7	3.27	18.7	2.10
Number of words in expressive vocabulary	40.5	38.22	24.0	20.35

Note. SES = socioeconomic status; SICD = Sequenced Inventory of Communicative Development.

HOW MOTHERS AND CHILDREN STRUCTURE THEIR BOOK READING INTERACTIONS

Interactions of Low- Versus Middle-SES Mothers and Infants

A previous analysis of the mothers' and infants' book reading interactions revealed many similarities between the two groups (Hammer, 1996, 1997). The dyads in the low- and middle-SES groups spent equal proportions of time engaged in book reading during their play sessions (U' = 22, p = .52). The mothers in both groups spent approximately 20% of their play sessions reading books to their children. In terms of the mothers' language behaviors, the mothers' behaviors were more similar than different. Specifically, the low- and middle-SES mothers directed the same amount of speech toward their children, averaging 22 and 26 utterances per minute, respectively. In addition, the mothers generally shortened their utterances (i.e., produced approximately three words per utterance) and used a similar variety of words when talking about the books, as measured by type–token ratios (see Table 2.3). One mother in the middle-SES group, however, differed from this pattern. She averaged more than 4.5 words per utterance. This mother read the text from the books word-for-word, which resulted in her using longer and more complex utterances. With regard to the mothers' production of various grammatical categories, no differences occurred in the number of nouns and verbs the mothers produced per utterance.

In terms of the communicative acts used, the mothers in both groups produced a similar percentage of statements, questions, responses to their children's vocalizations, and play-based utterances (e.g., "Moo," "Beep beep"). Also, they read a comparable number of sentences directly from books (see Table 2.4 for a description of the communicative acts coded;

TABLE 2.3
Maternal Language Behaviors

Behavior	Low-SES Group		Middle-SES Group	
	M	SD	M	SD
Utterances per minute	21.6	8.03	25.7	7.85
Mean length of response	2.94	.36	3.20	.08
Type–token ratio	.40	.05	.44	.06
No. of nouns per utterance	.57	.12	.73	.27
No. of verbs per utterance	.72	.16	.74	.26
No. of modifiers per utterance*	.10	.43	.28	.25

Note. SES = socioeconomic status.
*p = .01

TABLE 2.4

Maternal Communicative Acts Coded

Communicative Act	Definition
Statements	
Label for object	Utterances in which an object or attribute was named, e.g., "Ball."
Names person	Utterances in which an individual was named, e.g., "Granddad."
Comment	Utterances describing objects/observable events, e.g., "That's a big ball."
Statement	Utterances that evaluated, provided mental reports or rules that were not observable directly, e.g., "This doesn't go here."
Disagreement	Utterances that suggested a refusal to comply with a request or inferred that the mother did not agree with the child's behavior, e.g., "Uh uh."
Speaks for child	Utterances said in the first person that were an interpretation of what the child might think in a given situation, e.g., "Say, Oh mama. I like this."
Directives	
Requests for attention	Utterances that attempted to gain the child's attention, e.g., "Look."
Requests of action	Utterances that asked a child to perform an action, e.g., "Get the ball."
Requests for information	Questions that were designed to elicit information from the child, e.g., "Where's Tausha?"
Play Based	
Exclamation	Expressions that suggested surprise, dismay, etc., e.g., "Oh oh!"
Greeting	Utterances that opened or closed a conversation, e.g., "Hello."
Toy sound	Vocalizations/words that sounded like noises produced by toys or objects, e.g., "Bonk."
Performatives	Jokes, teases, protests, warnings, and claims that were achieved when produced, e.g., "There you go."
Responses to child's vocalizations	
Responses to requests for action	Responses to the child's attempts to perform an action, e.g., "You want that?" after the child pointed to a desired toy.
Responses to requests for information	Responses to the child's question, e.g., "I don't know."
Responses to requests for attention	Responses to a child's attempt to obtain the mother's attention, e.g., "Yes."
Responses to child's communication	Responses to the child's vocalizations or gestures that did not fall into an above category because the child's communicative intent was unclear, e.g., "Yeh" produced after the child vocalized.
Praise	Utterances or vocalizations that served to reinforce the child's behavior, e.g., "Big girl."
Imitations	Repetitions of the child's vocalization or utterance, e.g., "Ball" said after the child said "Ba."
Requests for clarification	Questions that sought clarification from the child about a vocalization or utterance, e.g., "Huh?," "What?"
Sentences read from the book	Text read directly from the book.

Note. Based on Fey (1986).

see Table 2.5 for the specific results). In general, the groups used directives and statements most frequently. Further exploration of the data revealed that four mothers in each group produced directives more frequently than any other category. In fact, two mothers in the low-SES group produced more directives than the combined number of statements, questions, and sentences read from books.

Consistent with the current literature on African American mother–child book reading interactions, the mothers in both groups included a small percentage of questions when reading books to their children. Questions characterized 9% and 15% of the low- and middle-SES mothers' utterances, respectively. Only one mother in each group used questions more than 20% of the time.

Contrary to the literature on book reading interactions of White, middle-class dyads, 11 of the 12 African American mothers read sentences directly from the books to their children. For 8 of these mothers, sentences from books comprised 12% or less of the utterances they produced. However, 20% of the utterances of 2 mothers from the low-SES group and 50% of the utterances of 1 mother from the middle-SES group fell into this category.

With regard to the children's speech, no differences were found (see Table 2.6). The children produced a similar number of vocalizations, averaging approximately seven vocalizations per minute. In addition, the children did not differ with respect to the proportion of spontaneous or imitated words and phrases produced. Thirty-one percent of the low-SES children's and 18% of the middle-SES children's vocalizations consisted of spontaneous words and phrases. Thirteen percent and 10% of the vocalizations of the children in the low-SES and middle-SES groups, respectively, were imitated words or phrases.

TABLE 2.5
Maternal Communicative Behaviors

Communicative Acts	Low-SES Group		Middle-SES Group	
	M	SD	M	SD
Sentences from books	.10	.10	.14	.18
Questions	.09	.08	.15	.08
Statements	.26	.14	.26	.28
Responses	.05	.03	.06	.03
Play	.10	.05	.06	.04
Directives*	.38	.09	.27	.05

Note. SES = socioeconomic status.
*p = .03.

TABLE 2.6
Children's Communicative Behaviors

	Low-SES Group		Middle-SES Group	
Behavior	M	SD	M	SD
Vocalizations per minute	6.56	3.47	6.94	1.75
Proportion of spontaneous words/phrases	.31	.37	.18	.14
Proportion of imitated words/phrases	.13	.13	.10	.11

Note: SES = socioeconomic status.

Despite these similarities, I observed three differences between the two groups. The first involved differences in the dyads' book reading at home. The mothers in the middle-SES group reported reading more frequently to their children on a daily basis than did the mothers in the low-SES group. Specifically, five of the six mothers in the middle-SES group indicated that they read books daily to their children, whereas only two mothers in the low-SES group reported doing so. This difference approached the level of significance ($\chi^2 = 3.1$, $p = .08$).

Second, the mothers differed in the use of modifiers in their utterances. Specifically, the middle-SES mothers produced significantly more modifiers in their utterances than did the mothers in the low-SES group ($U' = 33.5$, $p = .01$). The middle-SES mothers incorporated a modifier in an utterance in close to one third of their utterances, whereas the low-SES mothers included a modifier in approximately 10% of their utterances.

Third, although both groups of mothers frequently produced directives, the mothers in the low-SES group used significantly more directives ($U' = 32$, $p = .025$) than did the mothers in the middle-SES group. It may be that the low-SES mothers used more directives in order to attract their children's attention to the activity, because looking at books was a less common occurrence in these children's homes.

Although this discussion of the dyads' behaviors during book reading gives us some understanding of how they structure their interactions around text, the analysis does not capture the rich variety of styles that the dyads displayed. Therefore, I conducted a qualitative analysis of the mothers' and infants' interactions that better illustrates the complex and varied nature of young children's emergent literacy experiences.

Variations in Book Reading Styles

After careful and repeated viewing of the videotapes and transcripts of the book reading interactions, I identified four styles that I labeled as follows: modeling, different styles for different book genres, text reading, and limited periods of joint attention. I describe each of these styles in the following sections and provide excerpts from the transcripts to provide the reader with evidentiary support for my conclusions.

Modeling Style.   Two low-SES mothers used a modeling style that was characterized by the mothers presenting a verbal model for their children to imitate. In general, the established routine used by both mothers consisted of a presentation of a model followed by a pause. The children usually filled the pause with a vocalization or word approximation. Having obtained a response from their children, the mothers then presented another model. Both mothers employed this style with both picture books and books with text. Each mother, however, provided her child with different types of models as is demonstrated in the following examples.

Pamela, a mother who read books to her child several times a day, employed verbal models that consisted of one-word utterances that were used to label a picture. Following her model, she paused to allow her child an opportunity to imitate her. Occasionally, she commented about the picture and provided her child with feedback when he imitated her model by vocalizing "um hmm." She asked only a few *wh-* questions (5% of her utterances were questions), such as "What's this?" The following excerpt illustrates Pamela's style.

Pamela:	Come on. Sit down. We gonna do a little lesson. Come on. Sit right here (*pulling a chair out for Emil*). We do a little lesson.
P:	OK. I'm gonna turn you around (*as she puts him in the chair*). Gonna do a little lesson here.
P:	OK. Book (*holding the book out in front of him*). A book. There's a book.
P:	What's that? (*pointing to the picture.*) What's that? Look (*pointing*). Ball.
Emil:	A ba (*as he points to the picture*).
P:	Um hmm. Ball.
E:	A ba (*pointing*).
P:	Um hmm.
E:	Da (*reaching for the book as his mother turns the page*).
P:	Duck (*pointing*). Duck. Duck. Look. Duck.
P:	He go quack quack quack. Come on. Duck (*continuing to point*).
E:	Hee (*pointing to another picture*).
P:	Duck. Look. Look (*pointing*).

E:	Da (*pointing as he turns to his mother*).
P:	Dog (*pointing*). Woof woof. Dog. Woof woof.
E:	A da (*pointing*).
P:	Woof woof.
E:	A da.
P:	Woof woof, woof woof, woof woof. Sit down. Look. Duck.
E:	Da.
P:	Quack quack.
E:	Da.
P:	Dog. Woof woof. Dog.

Simone, on the other hand, encouraged her child to imitate her models by saying, "Say __," a more direct prompt. She included a relatively high percentage of questions (23%), which she appeared to produce for different purposes. In the beginning of an interaction, she used questions to establish or maintain her child's attention. Once her child's attention to a book was established, she often produced questions that tapped her child's receptive language abilities (e.g., "Where's Barney?"). Like Pamela, Simone provided little feedback to her child through the form of affirming utterances. Generally speaking, she presented a new model to her child after he attempted to imitate her model. Simone's style is demonstrated through the following excerpt during which Simone and her son, Jordan, were looking at *Barney's Farm Animals* (Kearns, 1993), a book with text.

Simone:	Look what I got Jordan (*showing him the book*). There go Barney. Look. There go Barney.
Jordan:	Ah da.
S:	That say Barney.
J:	Da ba (*looking at his mother*).
S:	You want mama to read to you a story? Hmm? Or just wanna see the pictures?
S:	Look at that pig (*pointing*). He say oink oink. Jordan, see the pig? (*Jordan turns the page*).
S:	The cat.
J:	Da ba.
S:	Hmm?
S:	Say cat.
J:	Ga (*as he turns the page*).
S:	Good.

J:	Ga.
S:	Say . . . (*Jordan closes the book*).
J:	Uuu.
S:	What'd you see? Come on. Let's see what we can find in the Barney book.
J:	Da da (*opening the book*).
S:	Hmm?
J:	Ba ba ba (*holding up the book*).
S:	Oh, you got it. OK, you look at it (*as Jordan sits down with the book*).
J:	Gaga.
S:	OK.
J:	Ga. Ga (*as he touches the book*).
S:	You see Barney? That Barney (*pointing*).
J:	Ha. Ba.
S:	You know him?
J:	He.
S:	Say hen (*pointing*).
J:	Ga.
S:	Say hen.
J:	Ga.

Simone indicated that she looked at books infrequently with her child. However, she had an established style for engaging her child in books.

Different Styles for Different Book Genres. Unlike Pamela and Simone who used a modeling style when looking at different genres of books, one mother from the low-SES group and four mothers from the middle-SES group employed different styles when looking at picture books and books with text. In general, when looking at picture books, the mothers labeled the pictures and encouraged their children to imitate their models. When looking at books with text, they combined reading the texts with models. As expected, variations were noted in the mothers' styles.

Sheryl was the mother from the low-SES group who changed her style depending on the type of book. When looking at picture books, Sheryl employed a modeling style. For example, when looking at books with pictures of objects, Sheryl labeled the object and paused to allow her child an opportunity to imitate the model. If her child did not repeat the model, she prompted her child for a response. When looking at books in which actions were illustrated through pictures, Sheryl labeled the action and then acted out the verb. In the following excerpt, Sheryl and her daughter, Breana, were looking at a counting book.

Sheryl:	Look chairs. The baby's in the chair. See that chair. She's in the chair.
S:	Five trucks. Let's count 'em (*as she takes Breana's finger and points to each of the trucks*). One, two three, four, five. Five trucks.
S:	Six blocks. Look at the blocks. Let's count 'em (*as she points to each block using Breana's finger*). Saay Oone, two, three, four, five, six (*pointing with Breana's finger to each block*).
S:	Look. Seven dinosaurs. What's that? Say dinosaur.
Breana:	Or (*as she points to the picture*).
S:	Can you count 'em? Let's count 'em. Say one.
B:	One.
S:	Two (*as the mother and child are pointing to each one*).
B:	Two.
S:	Three.
B:	Dee.
S:	Four, five, [six.]
B:	[Six.]
S:	Seven. Yeaaahh! (*as she claps*).
B:	Yeah!
S:	She got eight crayons. Don't mark on the floor. Can you count 'em? Let's count 'em. Let's count (*as she points to the crayons as she counts*).
B:	Ka.
S:	One.
B:	Two.
S:	Three. Say Three.
B:	Three.

However, when reading *Barney's Farm Animals* (Kearns, 1993), the same book read by Simone, Sheryl primarily read the text with few comments about the pictures or story, as is shown in the following dialogue. All words in quotation marks indicate excerpts that were read directly from the text.

S:	Let's read the Barney book. Look.
B:	Bani.
S:	Can you say, " 'Cock-a-doodle-doo,' says the Rooster."

B: Bani (*points to the picture*).

S: "Barney says, 'Good morning.' "

B: Bani.

S: " 'Moo moo' says the cow."

B: Moo moo moo moo.

S: "The cow gives us milk to drink." " 'Cluck cluck cluck cluck,' says the hen." "Barney helps the mother hen."

B: Ba.

S: " 'Ma ma,' says the goat."

B: Barney.

S: Do you see Barney feeding the apple to the goat? Look. See the apple. Barney's feeding the goat.

As indicated earlier, several middle-SES mothers adjusted their styles according to the type of book that they and their children were reading. The following example is of Julie looking at an object book with her daughter. Like the mothers I described in the modeling style section, Julie occasionally commented on a picture and gave her daughter feedback; however, she most commonly produced a model after which she provided her child an opportunity to imitate her utterance.

Julie: Look.

Linda: Ah ba.

J: Look at this.

L: Ah di.

J: Look at the ball. Woof woof. Dog.

L: Uu uu doggie.

J: Dog. (*Turns the page.*)

J: Birthday. (*Linda turns back to the previous page.*)

J: You like the one with the dog?

L: Ah doggie.

J: Woof woof. Dog.

L: Doggie.

J: Dog.

L: Uu. Dog.

J: Yes. Dog. (*Turns the page.*) Ball. See the ball? See the . . .

L: Ah ba.

J: (*Turns the page.*) Chairs.

L:	(*Turns the page.*) Ha.
J:	Truck. Truck.
L:	Tuck.
J:	Box. Blocks. (*Turns the page.*) Dinosaur.
L:	UU. Wa dinosa (*pointing*).
J:	(*Turns the page*). Crayon.

When reading books with text, Julie changed her style. Her style is depicted in the following excerpt during which Julie is reading *Barney's Farm Animals* (Kearns, 1993) to her daughter:

J:	"Barney says good morning." Say good morning.
L:	Da da (*pointing to the picture*).
J:	Say good morning. (*She turns the page.*) " 'Moo', says the cow." Say cow. (*She pauses.*)
L:	Aow.
J:	Cow.
L:	(*Points to the picture.*) Moo moo o mo dow.
J:	"The cow gives us milk to drink." Okay. " 'Cluck cluck,' says the hen."
L:	Duk duk (*turning the page*).
J:	Wait a minute. "Barney helps the mother hen."
J:	Goat. Bahaahaah. " 'Maa,' says the goat."
J:	"Barney feeds the apple to the goat." (*She turns the page.*)
L:	Mama dada (*pointing to the picture*).
J:	The apple.
L:	A apa.
J:	" 'Meow. Meow,' says the cat. Barney saves the cat." See the cat?
L:	A dat.
J:	Cat. (*She turns the page.*)
J:	" 'Oink oink,' says the pig. The pig rolls in the mud." See the pig?
L:	A ba.
J:	Pig.

As illustrated, Julie read the lines of text. She also provided models, commented on the pictures, and responded to her daughter's vocalizations. One mother, however, read the text of the book extensively as will be discussed in the following section.

Text Reading Style.   Anita, a mother from the middle-SES group, read the text of the books word for word when reading to her child. She typically only interrupted her reading of the text when her child was not attending to the book. During those times, she interjected questions or pointed to and labeled pictures on the pages until her son attended once again. At that time, she resumed reading the text. Anita reported that she read to her children every night before they went to bed. When reading to her son during this project, she set up the activity by sitting him in her lap while commenting, "like if we go to bed."

Anita:	"Once upon a time there was three bears." "There was the father bear" (*pointing to the picture*). "The mother bear" (*pointing*).
Michael:	Ah ah ah ah.
A:	"Mother bear was a medium-sized bear."
M:	Do.
A:	"And baby bear was a wee-tiny bear."
M:	Wo bo.
A:	"One day mother bear cooked porridge for breakfast."
M:	Ah. An da bo.
A:	Yeh. "The porridge was too hot to eat."
M:	Ah yea yea.
A:	"The bears took a walk in the woods while it cooled." "While they were gone a little girl named Goldilocks came into their house."
M:	Ga (*as he reaches for a toy that is close by*).
A:	Look at Goldilocks. "She looked into the door and didn't see anyone there."

Because Anita read regularly to her child, Michael was accustomed to this style and attended to the books for extended periods of time. The dyads discussed in the next section, however, established joint periods of attention for shorter periods of time, the reasons for which I propose in the discussion that follows.

Limited Periods of Joint Attention.   Three mothers from the low-SES group and one mother from the middle-SES group spent little time (12% or less) reading books with their children. When the mothers and their children looked at the books, the mothers typically labeled the objects for their children. Occasionally, they commented on objects and read the text from the books. None of the mothers incorporated many questions into their interactions (less than 10% of their utterances). However, what made these dyads unique was that the mothers spent much of their time attempting to recruit their children's attention to the books. I propose two reasons why these four mothers needed to prompt their children to look at the books. First, two of the mothers did not look at books very often with their children at home. Thelma reported looking at books a few times a week and Deborah did not look at books with her child. In fact, when Thelma's child first picked up a book, her comment to him was, "You can't read no story." Therefore, I suggest that the mothers needed to spend their time directing their children to the task because the children were not accustomed to looking at books regularly. The following interaction between Thelma and her daughter, Lakesha, supports this hypothesis.

Thelma:	Come on. Bring the chair. Let's look in the book. Come on. Sit right.
Lakesha:	(*Lakesha is on the other side of the room*).
T:	Come on. What mama to read to you?
L:	(*Walks toward her mother.*)
T:	Sit in the chair.
L:	(*Sits in the chair.*)
T:	"Look What I Found" (*the title of the book*). The big bird.
L:	Ba ee.
T:	Big Bird.
L:	Ba ba.
T:	"Look what I found in the orchard."
T:	That's Ernie.
L:	(*Reaches for the book.*)
T:	"Look what I found in the canyon."
L:	(*Takes the book from her mother.*)
T:	She don't want me to read it to her (*said to the investigator. The book reading session ends.*)

The second proposed reason relates to the remaining two dyads, in which both children tended to set the agenda. For example, Lisa, a mother from the low-SES group who looked at books daily with her child, attempted to gain her child's interest in books, but spent less than 10% of their time looking at books during the play sessions. Lisa and her son, Jamal, established brief periods of joint attention. Typically, Jamal attended to a book for a short period of time. After briefly attending to the book, he selected another book. His mother switched her attention to the new book; however, Jamal quickly moved on to another book. This is demonstrated in the following interaction during which Lisa and Jamal are looking at *Barney's Farm Animals* (Kearns, 1993).

Lisa:	There go Barney. Look at Barney and the goat. Barney feeding the goat. You see him?
Jamal:	(*Looks at the pictures.*)
J:	Woo woo.
L:	Woo woo. That's Barney.
J:	(*Closes the book.*)
L:	Let me see (*as she opens the book*). Look at that. There goes the kitty cat. Kitty cat.
L:	There go Barney. Barney talkin' to the kitty cat.
J:	(*Turns the page.*)
L:	(*Turns the page.*)
J:	(*Looks at the other books.*)
L:	That's Barney man (*putting down her book*).
J:	(*Picks up a different book.*)
L:	There go baby (*as she picks up a book and holds it for Jamal to see*). Baby.
J:	(*Pulls the basket of books towards him.*)
L:	Look. Look.
J:	*Holds up the basket.*
L:	That's what you do. (*Jamal is not attending.*) Beat on the pots and pans.
L:	(*Looks at the book.*)
J:	(*Picks up another book and turns the page.*)
L:	(*Looks at Jamal and picks up another book.*)
J:	Woo woo woo.
L:	(*Looks at his book.*)

Marilyn, a middle-SES mother, also read to her children several times a day. She commented that her 3-year-old daughter loved to look at books; however, Samuel, her 17-month-old son, typically attended briefly to her numerous attempts to entertain him with books.

Both Jamal and Samuel controlled whether or not they engaged in book reading despite their mothers' repeated attempts to interest them in books. Thus, both the children's interest and the maternal styles contributed to the style of the book reading interactions developed by the mother–child dyads.

CONCLUSIONS AND FUTURE DIRECTIONS

Book Reading Interactions of African American Mother–Infant Dyads

The aim of this study was to determine how African American mothers and infants of low and middle SES structured their book reading interactions. In general, the dyads displayed more similarities than differences. The mothers in both groups engaged their children in book reading activities for similar periods of time. When talking to their children, the mothers shortened their utterances, used a relatively low percentage of different words, and produced a similar number of nouns and verbs in their utterances. Similarly, their children vocalized with the same frequency and produced similar proportions of spontaneous and imitated words and phrases.

These results are not surprising. Bus, van Ijzendorn, and Pelligrini (1995) also found that the frequency of book reading experiences provided to children was not related to mothers' SES. In addition, since the mothers are from the same cultural group, are living in the same city, and were educated through an educational system based on the mainstream culture, I would not expect that the manner in which they construct their book reading interactions would be vastly different.

The reader is cautioned that, given the small number of dyads, the failure to find statistically significant differences does not allow me to conclusively say that no differences existed between the two groups in terms of the aforementioned behaviors.

The two groups of dyads, however, differed with respect to three behaviors. First, the middle-SES mothers tended to look at books with their children more frequently. I assert that if the sample size had been larger, this difference may have been significant. Second, the middle-SES mothers included more modifiers in their utterances than did the mothers in the low-SES group. Thus, the middle-SES mothers added a level of complexity to their language by including modifiers in close to one third of their utterances. Third, the mothers varied with regard to the communicative intentions they produced. The low-SES mothers produced more directives than their middle-SES counterparts, who used an equal percentage of directives and statements. Given the small sample size, these findings can be considered particularly robust. This is due to the fact that small samples have reduced statistical power that makes the detection of significant differences more difficult.

The differences between the behaviors of the low-SES and middle-SES mothers are best explained by the mothers' level of education. Recall that the mothers in the middle-SES group averaged 3 more years of education than the mothers in the low-SES group. I hypothesize that the mothers with a higher educational level are more likely to read to their children, emphasize descriptors more, and produce fewer directives because these behaviors are valued in schools. As a result, the mothers may have incorporated these behaviors into their routines in order to prepare their children for school.

Book Reading Styles of Low- and Middle-SES Dyads

Capturing and describing the interactional styles of the dyads during book reading was my second goal. As anticipated, the findings indicated that a single book reading style did not exist. Similar to a study by Teale (1986), variations occurred in the mothers' and children's behaviors, with four styles being identified. Two mothers in the low-SES group used a modeling style regardless of the type of book they engaged their children in. Another group of mothers that included mothers from both SES levels employed different styles depending on the type of book they and their children were reading. When looking at books with pictures, these mothers used a modeling style. When looking at books with text, they combined reading the text (more complex language) with providing models for their children to imitate. This result was similar to that of DeLoache and DeMendoza (1987), who discussed how both low- and middle-SES mothers used more elaborate language with more complex books. It may be that books with text (even basic narratives found in books for infants) serve to elicit more complex language and more varied language models from this subgroup of mothers than do books with pictures. As a result, these mothers used picture books as an opportunity to teach vocabulary items (Peralta de Mendoza, 1995). Books with text provided them with an opportunity to expose children to more complex language as well as a chance to teach vocabulary items.

One mother from the middle-SES group employed a text-reading style. This style is not discussed in any of the literature reviewed and, in fact, was a vastly different style than I expected from a middle-SES mother.

A small group of mothers from both SES levels engaged in book reading activities for brief amounts of time. During this time, they used their language to direct their children to the task. I suggest two possible reasons for this behavior. First, some dyads were not accustomed to looking at books together, which resulted in the mothers spending time drawing their children's attention to books. It is important to note that the two mothers who did not look at books with their children regularly had the lowest educational levels. Other researchers have observed this behavior in White, middle-class mothers when they introduce books to their infants who were younger than the infants who participated in this study (Senechal, Cornell, & Broda, 1995). Therefore, I assert that this is not an atypical pattern. It simply may be a style used when mothers and children first look at books together. Second, some children did not demonstrate an interest in joint book reading. As pointed out by Panofsky (1989), children play a large role in determining their literacy experiences. They can choose whether or not to look at books as well as when and for how long. The children in this investigation clearly chose not to interact with their mothers around books for an extended period. This reminds us that when observing parent–child interactions, we cannot automatically assume that the mother is in control of what occurs during an interaction. Instead, the children may have considerable influence over their mothers' behaviors (Bates, Bretherton, & Snyder, 1988).

Because of the implicit assumption in the literature that the routines employed by White, middle-class mothers represent the "ideal" framework for reading books to young children, I believe it is necessary to discuss the findings in relation to the literature on the mainstream population.

Comparisons to White, Middle-Class Dyads

The African American mothers who participated in this study resembled White, middle-class mothers in that they simplified their speech and established routines when looking at books with their children. The routines they provided their children, however, varied greatly from the middle-class style that was discussed at the beginning of the chapter (DeLoache, 1984; Ninio & Bruner, 1977). One primary difference was that the mothers in this study employed a variety of styles. A second is that none of the observed styles involved a question-asking routine that is characteristic of White, middle-class mothers. A growing body of evidence suggests that African American mothers do not use a large number of questions when interacting with their children (see, e.g., Anderson-Yockel & Haynes, 1994; Heath, 1983). However, their styles promoted responses and labels from their infants. In other words, the mothers were skilled at providing and eliciting language from their children. Third, nearly all the mothers read portions of the text written on the pages of the books. It is generally assumed that White, middle-class mothers skip or simplify the text, choosing to label or talk about pictures on the pages (DeLoache & DeMendoza, 1987; Martin, 1998). These differences have important implications for professionals and school personnel who work with African American families.

Implications and Future Directions

As demonstrated by this study and others reported in the literature, families from African American cultures appear to interact differently around books than do families from the White, middle-class culture. This is because cultures differ in terms of their views of the functions of literacy and how one becomes literate (Westby, 1995). These differences, however, place African American children at risk for school failure, because the literacy styles observed in educational programs (from birth through adulthood) closely resemble those used by White, middle-class families. As a result, children from mainstream families typically transition into an educational setting with relative ease. However, African American children who are provided with different early literacy experiences may find the transition to a school program more difficult, because they need to learn the style of interaction used in school as well as the "content" and "skills" that are being taught through that interaction style. In addition, because teachers are not familiar with the style African American children have been exposed to at home, they do not always respond to children in a manner that is consistent with the children's experiences. As a result, opportunities for "teachable" moments may be missed (Vernon-Feagans, 1996).

One solution to this potential problem would be to ask the families to change their style to the mainstream style. However, because literacy is a social task mediated through one's culture (McLane & McNamee, 1990; Westby, 1995), we, as professionals, cannot expect families from other cultures to bear the responsibility for "fixing the problem." As stated by Ochs and Schieffelin (1984), the behaviors observed in parent–child interactions extend beyond and are embedded in a broader context. To request changes to occur within an interaction impacts greatly on how a family organizes itself (Teale, 1986). As a result, professionals and educators need to be knowledgeable about the early literacy experiences that African American children bring to preschools and schools, because there is no one correct way to become literate. By incorporating home book reading styles into children's educational experiences, professionals have the potential to minimize the home–school mismatch that children often encounter when they attend preschool and elementary school programs. I and other researchers hypothesize that, as the result of encountering familiar interaction styles, children will experience greater success in engaging in literacy activities in school (Hammer, 1998).

REFERENCES

Anderson-Yockel, J., & Haynes, W. (1994). Joint picture-book reading strategies in working-class African American and White mother–toddler dyads. *Journal of Speech, Language, and Hearing Research, 37,* 583–593.

Bates, E., Bretherton, I., & Snyder, L. (1988). *From first words to grammar: Individual differences and dissociable mechanisms.* New York: Cambridge University Press.

Bus, A., van Ijzendorn, M., & Pelligrini, A. (1995). Joint book reading makes for success in learning to read: A meta-analysis of intergenerational transmission of literacy. *Review of Educational Research, 65,* 1–21.

DeLoache, J. (1984). What's this? Maternal question in joint picture book reading with toddlers. *Quarterly Newsletter of the Laboratory of Comparative Human Cognition, 6*(4), 87–95.

DeLoache, J., & DeMendoza, O. (1987). Joint picturebook interactions of mothers and 10-month-old children. *British Journal of Developmental Psychology, 5*, 111–123.

Fey, M. (1986). *Language intervention for young children.* Austin, TX: ProEd.

Frankenburg, W., & Dodds, J. (1990). *Denver Developmental Screening Test II.* Denver, CO: Denver Developmental Publications.

Hammer, C. S. (1996). *Guiding language development: How African American mothers and their infants structure play.* Unpublished doctoral dissertation, University of Iowa, Iowa City.

Hammer, C. S. (1997, November). *Book reading behaviors of African-American mothers and their infants.* Paper presented at the American Speech, Language, and Hearing Association convention, Boston.

Hammer, C. S. (1998). Toward a 'thick description' of families: Using ethnography to overcome the obstacles to providing family-centered services. *American Journal of Speech-Language Pathology, 9*, 5–22.

Heath, S. B. (1982). What no bedtime story means: Narrative skills at home and school. *Language and Society, 11*, 49–76.

Heath, S. B. (1983). *Ways with words.* New York: Cambridge University Press.

Hedrick, D., Prather, E., & Tobin, A. (1984). *Sequenced Inventory of Communication Development.* Seattle: University of Washington Press.

Hollingshead, A., & Redlich, F. (1958). *Social class and mental illness* (pp. 387–397). New York: Wiley.

Kearns, K. (1993). *Barney's Farm Animals.* Richardson, TX: Lyrick Studios.

Martin, L. (1998). Early book reading: How mothers deviate from printed text for young children. *Reading Research and Intervention, 37*, 137–160.

McLane, J., & McNamee, G. (1990). The beginnings of literacy. *Zero to Three, 12*(1), 1–8.

Ninio, A., & Bruner, J. (1977). The antecedents of labelling. *Journal of Child Language, 5*, 1–15.

Ochs, E., & Schieffelin, B. (1984). Language acquisition and socialization. In R. Shweder & R. Levine (Eds.), *Culture theory* (pp. 276–320). New York: Cambridge University Press.

Panofsky, C. (1989). The functions of language in parent–child book reading events. *Theory Into Practice, 28*, 120–125.

Peralta de Mendoza, O. (1987). Developmental changes and socioeconomic differences in mother–infant book reading. *European Journal of Psychology of Education, 10*, 261–272.

Rescorla, L. (1989). The Language Development Survey. *Journal of Speech and Hearing Disorders, 54*, 587–599.

Senechal, M., Cornell, E., & Broda, L. (1995). Age-related differences in the organization of parent–infant interactions during picture-book reading. *Early Childhood Research Quarterly, 10*, 317–327.

Sulzby, E., & Teale, W. (1991). Emergent literacy. In R. Barr, M. Kamil, P. Mosenthal, & P. Pearson (Eds.), *Handbook of reading research* (Vol. 2, pp. 727–757). Hillsdale, NJ: Lawrence Erlbaum Associates.

Teale, W. (1986). Home background and young children's literacy development. In W. Teale & E. Sulzby (Eds.), *Emergent literacy: Writing and research* (pp. 173–206). Norwood, NJ: Ablex.

Vernon-Feagans, L. (1996). *Children's talk in communities and classrooms.* Cambridge, MA: Blackwell.

Westby, C. (1995). Culture and literacy: Frameworks for understanding. *Topics in Language Disorders, 16*(1), 50–66.

Chapter 3

Spoken and Written Narrative Development: African American Preschoolers as Storytellers and Storymakers

David Bloome
Vanderbilt University

Tempii Champion
University of South Florida

Laurie Katz
Middle Tennessee State University

Mary Beth Morton
Vanderbilt University

Ramona Muldrow
Tennessee State University

In this chapter, we present findings from an ongoing study of young African American children's spoken and written narrative development. Our findings, combined with those of other recent studies, suggest that children (a) adopt and adapt extant stories and recounts of experiences to accomplish a broad range of in situ social goals, and (b) develop a repertoire of narrative styles and structures. These two findings are consistent with calls for reconceptualizing spoken and written narrative development (Champion, 1995, 1998; Champion, Seymour, & Camarata, 1995; Dyson, 1991). The linkage of narrative development and literacy is based on our findings and recent research that has linked narrative development with reading and writing development (e.g., Dombey, 1995; Mardell, 1996; Rooks, 1998; Roth, Froma, Speece, Cooper, & De La Paz, 1993; Tallant, 1992).

Our study is informed by recent theory and research associated with anthropological and sociolinguistic studies of narrative and literacy. We begin by describing our theoretical perspective, then we present the study and its findings.

THEORETICAL PERSPECTIVE

Our research is grounded in sociolinguistic ethnography (e.g., Gumperz, 1986; Gumperz & Hymes, 1986; Hymes, 1974) and related approaches to the study of language as a social and cultural phenomenon (e.g., Bauman & Sherzer, 1974; Gee, 1990; Rowe, 1994; Schieffelin & Ochs, 1986; Wells, 1986). Of special use has been the concept of *language practices*, social and cultural practices involving the use of language.[1] The construct of language practices builds on Hymes' (1974) construct of speech event, Heath's (1982a) construct of literacy event, and Street's (1995) definition and use of literacy practices. In our view, there are socially established practices for the use of spoken and written language in particular situations. Thus, within a speech community, there are similarities in the use of spoken and written language over time and across different people engaged in a particular type of event.

One of the problems with the term language practices is that it may give the impression that the practices are static or deterministic. There certainly may be efforts to stabilize a set of language practices. The people in the event may hold each other accountable for using language in a particular way. However, people are continuously modifying established language practices, adapting them to new situations, and, at times, straightforwardly challenging and sabotaging established language practices. Therefore, rather than view language practices as a static set of situated ways of using spoken and written language, it may be more useful to think of language practices as an evolving and dynamic set of social practices that are always at a nexus of social change, stability, and struggle. Although we view spoken and written language as intimately related and inseparable, for convenience and clarity we occasionally discuss them separately.

Narrative as Text and Performance

Our approach to narrative development builds on two different research approaches: narrative as text (e.g., Labov, 1972) and narrative as performance (e.g., Bauman, 1986; Bauman & Briggs, 1990). Across diverse

---

[1]Almost all social and cultural practices can be viewed as language practices because almost all involve the use of language. Some social and cultural practices highlight the use of language, such as storytelling practices or reading practices; however, we do not limit our use of "language practices" to such practices. Our use of the term *language practices* signals a research intent to focus on language issues within a set of social and cultural practices.

disciplines, most research on children's narrative development has defined a narrative as a text and has studied narrative development through the analysis of the structure of texts over time. Approaches to the study of narrative as text include high point structure analysis (e.g., Labov, 1972), story grammar analysis (e.g., Johnson & Mandler, 1980), conversational analysis (e.g., Jefferson, 1978; Sacks, 1972), critical discourse analysis (e.g., Fairclough, 1995), and propositional analysis (e.g., Frederiksen, 1989). Whether spoken or written, texts are part of the material conditions that people encounter and must address in their everyday lives, and children are frequently confronted with a broad range of narratives in their academic activities. Whether one views the structural aspects of texts as inherent to narratives or given to them by traditions of practice, researchers' attempts to articulate textual aspects of narratives provide insight into what people may have to address in their creation and use of narratives.

Narrative texts do not exist alone or in isolation, they exist only in the event in which they are "performed."[2] As Bauman (1986), citing Jakobson (1971) and Benjamin (1969), pointed out, "Narratives are keyed both to the events in which they are told and to the events that they recount, toward narrative events and narrated events" (p. 2). Bauman made a distinction among text, narrated event, and narrative event, although he viewed them as an "indissoluble unity" (p. 7). Part of the importance of Bauman's conception of narrative is to link narratives and storytelling in ways that shift the analysis of narratives from solely a literary task to a sociolinguistic and ethnographic task, similar to the implicit work that participants in a storytelling event must do. Bauman's examples primarily involve narratives that would traditionally be recognized as oral stories, but the analytic framework he provides can be used with a much broader conception of narrative and storytelling, including the use of written language.

Building on Bauman's framework, Solsken and Bloome (1992) made a distinction among story, narrative, and storytelling event, although they viewed the three as inseparable.

> A story is an abstraction of history realized in narrative within a storytelling event. . . . A story is a chronological sequence of events abstracted from experience. That is, experiences are not inherently packaged as stories with beginnings, middles and ends nor do experiences necessarily provide coherent relationships between events. Rather, story transforms experience into events and imposes boundaries, a chronology, and a set of coherent

---

[2]Although not discussed in this chapter, see also Rosen (1986), Toolan (1988), and Cortazzi (1993) for other discussions of narratives as occurring in and as part of an interactional event.

relationships on experiences. This is axiomatically so regardless of whether story-construction occurs in a reflective mode (constructing a story of past experience) or in real-time (constructing story during experiences as they occur), whether a group or individual is involved. . . . When people construct a story they are constructing an abstraction that, by itself, has no realization. Rather it is realized in narrative. A narrative is the text of the story. The text may or may not present the story chronologically. The narrative may go beyond the story by including what Labov (1972) has called evaluations. . . . Narratives do not exist by themselves. They exist only in storytelling events. Storytelling events can involve several people or one individual, they can be formally labeled storytelling events (e.g., show and tell) or embedded in events with other labels. In a storytelling event people act and react to each other while producing the narrative. That is, there are always at least two simultaneous activities in a storytelling event—the telling of a story (or stories) and the making of the storytelling event itself. (pp. 5–6)

One implication of definitions of narrative given by Bauman (1986) and Solsken and Bloome (1992), among others with similar views (see Atkinson, 1991; Beach & Phinney, 1997; Cortazzi, 1993), is that narratives must be analyzed within the context of the social events in which they occur.

Part of this implication is that storytelling can be viewed as a way in which people socially define and position themselves with regard to others, social institutions, and so forth. A narrative is not simply a result of what the speaker or writer has produced, but the result of a sort of co-authorship between the speaker/writer and listeners (Ochs, 1997). Children make sense of others and the world in which they live through jointly constructed narratives. Ochs suggested that "how we think about ourselves and others is influenced by both the message content of jointly told narratives and the experience of working together to construct a coherent narrative" (p. 185). Thus, part of the analysis of storytelling and part of the exploration of narrative development is an exploration of how children use storytelling to affiliate with their friends, families, and teachers, and how they use storytelling to define themselves. A second implication is that narratives (storytelling) need to be placed in historical time, that is, as a part of what has come before and what will, or is anticipated to, come later (cf. Bakhtin, 1935/1981). But placing a narrative in historical time is not as much an empirical matter as it is a socially constructed matter that often remains indeterminate (cf. Bloome, 1993).

The warrant then for the analysis of narratives and for the exploration of narrative development is to redefine (or perhaps more accurately to relocate) what is traditionally taken as narrative instead as a storytelling event, and to view children as storytellers engaged in social events, with all the complications and complex social goals and dynamics that are involved in any social event.

Narrative Development as the Acquisition of a Repertoire[3]

In our view, theories of narrative development have not adequately provided a basis for evaluation of the narrative development of children who speak African American Language (AAL). Focusing primarily on narratives as texts, Champion (1995, 1998) found that the narratives produced by a small group of AAL-speaking children were characterized as both topic-centered and topic-associated (for definitions and additional discussion, see Hyon & Sulzby, 1994; Michaels, 1981, 1986; Michaels & Collins, 1984). Based on high point structure analysis, the captured narratives fit within a range of maturity levels. This was so within individuals and across the group. These findings both confirmed and extended then-current research (e.g., Applebee, 1978; McCabe & Peterson, 1991). The extension was that the children produced a range of different types of narratives, and that various factors, including the prompts given, the situation, personal relationships, and so forth, influenced the nature of the narrative structures they produced. Perhaps more important, Champion (1995) found that some narratives that did not fit neatly within high point analysis nonetheless were well formed. She found that these narratives could be described as moral-centered, performance-centered, or dispute narratives. In generating these additional types of narrative structures, she did not attempt to create a definitive narrative structure taxonomy. Rather, she sought to broaden the ways in which narrative structures are characterized and to expand the notions about narrative development. She speculated that children, both AAL-speaking children and others, might better be described as developing a repertoire of narrative structures and styles (see also Preece, 1987).

Borrowing from anthropological studies of cross-cultural contact and culture change (Street, 1993a), two processes—adoption and adaptation—seem likely to be involved in the development of a repertoire of narrative structures and styles. Adoption would include children's mimicking and reproduction of narratives in the ways that they experienced them (e.g., they may attempt to tell "The Three Little Pigs" in the same manner in which they were told the story). Adaptation would include various hybridizations and transformations of extant narratives (cf. Bakhtin, 1953/1986), sometimes overt and sometimes subtle, that might merge cultures and their language practices, subvert one or the other, or create directions for new practices. The adaptation or adoption of storytelling practices needs to be viewed as a component of children's attempts to accomplish various social goals. For example, in order to establish group membership with other students, a child might insert a rainbow into her

---

[3]Parts of the text in this section are borrowed from Sheridan, Street, and Bloome (2000).

story as the other children have done; in so doing, the narrative and storytelling would also change to accommodate the rainbow.

Literacy Development[4]

Our approach to the study of children's reading and writing development builds on our approach to narrative development. Our approach, which we associate with social–cultural approaches (and more specifically with what has been called the New Literacy Studies; see Street, 1993b), differs from traditional approaches to reading and writing development.[5] Traditional approaches seek to identify a series of decontextualized psychological and/or linguistic processes (or skills) that constitute reading and writing. Having so defined reading and writing, researchers and educators can define development as *the* sequence in which children acquire (or develop) the requisite processes (or skills). Researchers may debate which processes constitute reading and writing, and they may debate the sequence in which they are acquired; regardless, underlying the debate is a shared assumption that there is a relatively stable set of processes that define reading and writing, and that reading and writing development is relatively stable and unilinear. Given such a view, researchers and educators can ask questions about children such as "What processes does the child have? What processes does the child not have?" "How does the child compare to others with regard to developmental progress?" From this tra-

---

[4]Although our research has focused on spoken narratives and the writing of narratives (and not on the reading of stories, for example), in this section we include discussion of reading, because the issues we raise pertain to it as well.

[5]There are numerous theories regarding reading, writing, and language development. Given the limitations of space, we have heuristically divided approaches into those that assume that reading, writing, and language are a set of decontextualized psychological processes and that reading, writing, and language development follow a relatively stable and unilinear progression (similar to what Street, 1997, described as the autonomous model) versus those approaches that assume that reading, writing, and language are a diverse set of social and cultural practices and that development is primarily a process of socialization and enculturation (similar to what Street, 1995, described as the ideological model). We label the first set of approaches *traditional approaches* and the second *social–cultural*. However, we recognize that there are important differences among different theories within each of the two sets of approaches we have heuristically defined, and we recognize that in some cases the division obfuscates some complexities. Further, we recognize that the labels we have chosen reflect our perspective as educational and communication disorders researchers. In our fields, social–cultural approaches to reading, writing, and language are relatively recent, although social–cultural approaches have a long history; similarly, some of the approaches that would fall under the "traditional" label are relatively recent. Nonetheless, for the purposes of this chapter, we find the heuristic distinction between "traditional" and "social–cultural" approaches useful.

ditional perspective, questions can be asked about which instructional practice is most effective in providing a child with the needed processes and in promoting that child's development along the predetermined sequence. In our view, such questions inherently create a deficit model of children's reading, writing, and narrative development, and the application of this view to broader populations defined by, for example, race, culture, gender, or class inherently creates a deficit view of that race, culture, gender, or class.[6]

We take a different approach. We define reading and writing as a diverse and evolving set of language practices that involve the use of written language (e.g., Baker & Luke, 1993; Bloome, 1987; Green, 1990; Street, 1995). As we discussed at the beginning of this chapter, language practices are social and cultural practices that are enacted and transformed by people interacting in specific events. In any specific situation, people will have shared expectations—a shared cultural model—about what is an appropriate use of written language, how the written language should be interpreted (what interpretative framework should be brought to bear on the writing), who should play what role in the writing event, and the implied social positions and relationships created among the people in the writing event. Literacy practices are socially established and shared ways of using written language within a specific type or set of events. In brief, what constitutes reading and writing is what people in interaction with each other make reading and writing to be. From this point of view researchers and educators ask questions such as "What ways of using written language are embedded in which literacy practices, with what implications for the intellectual, social, and cultural work that needs to be done to participate appropriately in such practices?" "How do children learn what literacy practices are appropriate in which situations?" "What social positions and social relationships are embedded in a particular set of literacy practices?" "What rights and obligations are embedded in particular literacy practices, and how are these rights and obligations distributed across participants?" "What social organizations are implicated by particular literacy practices? and vice versa." "How can participants adapt and transform extant literacy practices and transpose literacy practices from one setting into another?" "What conflicts are involved in which literacy practices? in the transformation of which literacy practices? with what consequences?"

---

[6]It is important to note that deficit models vary greatly from each other, depending on the explanation for the deficit. Although deficit models that assume a genetic explanation of racial group differences are, by definition, racist, deficit models are not necessarily racist, classist, or sexist (e.g., an explanation of a deficit model that focused on oppressive relationships between a dominant group and a subordinate group).

THE RESEARCH STUDY

Although it began in a preschool program in a community center and has now moved to a preschool program that is part of the public schools, the research project has remained pretty much the same. Both schools have a long history of service to low-income African American communities. While the students in the community center preschool were all African American, in the public school (preschool and kindergarten) the students were all African American with the exception of one white child. In both settings we conducted various language and speech assessments so that we would have some data on what these traditional assessments suggested about the children's speech and language. It is important to note that in both settings we met frequently with the teachers, and in both settings the teachers were instrumental in shaping how the research project was designed, how it changed, and so on.

Data Collection

The Corpus of Data.   One of our major goals was to establish a large corpus of narratives created by African American children that would allow other researchers and us opportunities for an in-depth study of narrative. We are still in the process of creating this database. To date, the corpus of data includes over 2,000 recorded stories and over 1,000 written stories.

The Storytelling Program Context.   The data were collected within the context of a storytelling program.[7] Twice a week, the research team went to the preschool. Students gathered on the rug area. While everyone was getting ready for the activity, the children were asked to tell about what they did over the weekend, what they were doing in school, or a story they had written (the requests varied between reports, stories, and other genres). One of the members of the research team told or read a story. By design, the stories differed in mode (told and read) and genre (e.g., folktales, modern chil-

---

[7]The dilemma that we and other language researchers face is that there is no such thing as narrative performance outside of a context; furthermore, there is no such thing as children learning to use language over time without those uses and experiences being embedded either in a formal or informal educational context. Thus, the question is not whether one prejudices the data but rather being aware that children are always in educational contexts (in school or at home) and that one needs to understand the specific educational contexts within which children's narrative performances are being captured. Further, it is important to note that the purpose of the storytelling program was not to research and develop an instructional program but rather to learn about children's narrative development. We make no claims about the relation of instructional features of this particular instructional program to writing, reading, or narrative development.

dren's stories, personal stories). All stories were either traditional African American or African stories (e.g., folktales), about African or African American life, or personal stories by the African American members of the research team. On occasion, one of the children's parents came into the classroom to read or tell a story. Parents chose a book from home or from the classroom. Sometimes it was the child's favorite story.

After the storytelling, students volunteered and were selected to tell a story. Next, students went to the table area where they wrote and drew stories in their *author books*.[8] As the students were writing and drawing stories, the teachers and researchers circulated among the students, dating the children's pages and writing each child's dictated story in standard orthography.

After about 20 minutes, the students returned to the rug area where they volunteered to "read" or "tell" their stories. Several times during the year, students were asked to select one of their stories from their author book (or to write another) for publication. The story was dictated to a member of the research team, who typed, printed, and bound the book with spiral binding. The students drew pictures to go with the words. The storytelling activity is designed to provide data on the students' telling and creating stories in both spoken and written modes. All of the storytelling was recorded.

Data Analysis

The data analyses reported in this chapter focused on (a) the variety of narrative structures employed; (b) the content of the students' narratives; (c) uptake in student narratives of content and structures from stories heard in the classroom, on television, and from other sources; (d) transformation and variation in students' narratives from the adapted narratives; (e) students' self-identification within their narratives; and (f) the use of the storytelling for social purposes (e.g., to acknowledge friendships). The written narratives were submitted to comparable analysis. However, we were also interested in (g) the use and nature of written language (e.g., letters used) and (h) the relation of letters and words to other symbols in the written story.[9]

---

[8]During the 3rd year, based on what the teachers suggested, the pages of the author books had a horizontal line added about a third of the way up from the bottom. We asked the students to write the story below the line and draw above the line. Some paid attention to that request and some didn't. We did not enforce it.

[9]Future analyses will examine the frequency of the narrative structures, content, use of letters, and so forth found in our study, as well as the occurrence of these features over time within cases. However, we do not believe that we have a sufficient database yet to conduct such analyses.

FINDINGS

First, we report findings in four major sections: textual structure, uptake and transformation, uptake of other children's stories and transformation, and construction of social identities and social relationships. The findings apply to both spoken and written narratives/storytelling. Next, we report findings that focus on storytelling and literacy in three areas: writing objects and static representations, uptake and hybridization in written stories, and differentiating stories and non-narrative writing.

Textual Structure

Sara's[10] story that follows is an example of how an experience, such as going to the store, is structured into narrative. Although Sara's story is sequential, it is structured around a "high point" (lines 20–21) which is approached by a series of building events and recycling through a series of moral dilemmas that build on each other. She begins the narrative by identifying the character and the setting (an orientation), and then she provides the plot. (For transcription conventions see the Appendix.)

01	S:	This little
02		This little girl
03		was goin to the store to go buy some candy
04		and when she was going to the store
05		when she got to the store
06		she say
07		why
08		why don't I get some fruit to eat
09		to eat
10		den she got some fruit when she went to the fruit store
11		She say it was very good
12		but the fruit store I ask my mom can I have some more stuff
13		well she say
14		next morning she went to school and said
15		mom
16		can I ask you something
17		and mom said
18		yes dear

---

[10]All of the names used are pseudonyms.

19   Well mom I need a couple books for my project

20   and she said

21   Ok

22   and the mom went to the store and got her some books for the project

23   den that's the end

24   T: Awlright very good excellent

Sara's story begins with a language form that signals a story: "This little girl was goin' to the store to go buy some candy." The story is not about her. Going to the store is a highly valued activity, as is buying candy. Sara begins the use of dialogue. The little girl no longer wants candy but some fruit. Perhaps Sara has picked up this line from her parents who may have told her to get some fruit instead of candy. Perhaps she is using the line here to redefine the little girl as someone more mature than a child who would get candy. The little girl has gone to the fruit store. There are a small number of fruit stores in the city, so it is possible that she did indeed go to a fruit store. At the fruit store, the story stops being about the little girl and switches into the first person, and the story becomes about Sara and her mom. The dialogue may be a repetition of a conversation she had with her mother, or it may have been constructed from bits of conversation with her mother and with others. It shows that her mother is responsible, that the child and her mother have a loving relationship, and that her mother will buy things for her if it is for school. This may be the moral of the story (fruit instead of candy, and books instead of stuff). It also reveals the loving relationship between her and her mother.

Structurally, the story appears to simulate prototypical high point structure, although imperfectly so. Sara establishes orientation (the setting and characters), followed by rising action establishing a complicating action (the child asks for something but the mother must approve the request), then a resolution (the child makes the appropriate request and the mother buys the requested item), and then the story ends. There are no evaluations or comments about events or characters in the story.

However, analysis of the structure on another level suggests that there are three moral dilemmas in the story: (a) buying candy versus buying fruit, (b) buying more stuff, and (c) buying books for a school project. The mother plays the role of the moral authority, buying books but not stuff. Cyclical action and repetition occur frequently in children's stories. For example, in "Goldilocks and the Three Bears," there are multiple cycles of the bears and their porridge, chairs, and beds. The popular and widely used *Brown Bear, Brown Bear* (this book was in all the classrooms in this study) uses the same textual pattern over and over. Also, many of the stories we told or read had multiple cycles of activity in them. Sara could have borrowed the concept of cyclical action from any or all of them. Although she may have been recounting an actual event, it is likely that she transformed what occurred to fit with the structure of cyclical action, and it is likely that she modified the pattern of cyclical action to fit the content of her story.

Sara's story also illustrates, although at an abstract level, another aspect of narrative structure that was recurrent in our data. Her story, like many in Champion's (1995, 1998) studies and our corpus of data, focused on moral issues. The implicit moral was constructed around an issue that the child assumed the audience was aware of. The moral theme of Sara's story appears to be something like: There are things worthwhile asking to spend money on (fruit, books) and things that you should not ask to spend money on (candy, stuff). If you ask your mother to buy you the right things, she will get them for you. You should not ask her to get you the wrong kind of things. Rather than organizing a story around the solution of a problem, which is fundamental to the assumption of high point analysis, stories may be organized around the presentation or working-out of a moral issue. The question to ask about a story such as Sara's is not the degree to which features of the narrative structure matched an ideal model of high point structure or a predetermined story grammar, but rather how the story foregrounded the moral issues that gave it purpose and coherence.

Sara's story could be viewed as a moral-centered story, but other stories might be centered on other purposes, such as acknowledging friendship or family, gaining social status in the peer group, claiming a social identity, or entertaining. Stories could have multiple purposes and those purposes could shift during the storytelling.

Uptake and Transformation

In one of the classrooms, almost all the students for 4 months told nothing but "Goldilocks and the Three Bears" or "The Three Little Pigs," sometimes getting the pigs, the bears, and Goldilocks mixed into the same story. However, after looking carefully at the transcripts of those storytelling events, we discovered subtle changes in the telling that suggested that students were playing off each other and making social connections with each other through storytelling.

For example, consider the following spoken narratives.

31   T: O.K. Jimmy
32   Nice and loud Jimmy so Ms. (*name of teacher in the back*) can
            hear you

33		O.K. everybody quiet
34	J:	This a story about the three little pigs.
35		The first little pig
36	T:	Shhhhh
37	J:	The first little pig says his house out of 'traw
38		it was out of 'traw and the wolf came and said knock, knock let me in.
39		The frighten pig cried no, no, no not by hair of my chinny, chin, chin
40		and it huff and puff and blow the house down
41		and den he went to the second little pig house
42		and the second little pig's house was made out of
43	Sx:	straw
44	J:	sticks
45	Sx:	straw
46	J:	sticks
47	Sx:	straw
48	T:	O.K. this is Jimmy's story O.K.
49	Sx:	(*undecipherable comment*)
50	J:	It wasn't very strong
51	T:	It might change a little
52	J:	and the wolf came and said knock, knock let me in
53		and it said no, no, no not by the hair of my chinny, chin, chin
54		and he huff and puff and blow the house down
55		and he
56		and the wolf run all the way to the third little pigs house
57		and the third little pig made his house out of bricks
58		It was very strong and the wolf came and said knock, knock let me in
59		and the frighten pigs cried no, no, no
60		not by the hair of my chinna, chin, chin
61		den I huff and puff and blow your house down
62		den den he didn't blow the house down
63	Ss:	(*clapping starts*)
64	J:	that's the end
65	T:	Awl right

| 66 | Sx: | Can I read one[11] |
| 67 | T: | Very good version of three little pigs |

On lines 43 to 47 there is a brief argument about whether the house was made out of straw or sticks, until the teacher stepped in and stated that it was Jimmy's story and that he could change the story if he wanted. Notice that the children's right to transform stories also was reinforced by the teacher in line 67. Shortly thereafter, another child engaged in telling about the three little pigs.

81	R:	my story about the three little pigs
82	T:	O.K. but very louder they're not going to be able to hear you
83	R:	my
84		my story about the three little pigs.
85		the first pig made it out of straw
86		no, no not by hair of chinny, chin, chin, I'll huff and puff and blow your house down
87		and den the second pig came
88		he build his house with sticks
89		and his
90		and it wasn't real strong
91		and
92		and
93		and the wolf came
94		knock, knock let me in
95		(*undecipherable*)
96		say no, no, no
97		not by the hair of my chinny, chin, chin
98		and the pig
99		and the last one build his with bricks
100		and it was strong
101		and and the
102		and the wolf came knock, knock let me in

---

[11]Line 66 is an interesting comment by a child who is bidding for a chance to tell a story. The students have not get gone to their tables for storywriting. It may be that the child views the storytelling as similar to what the teacher did previously (read a book), or has generalized "reading" to include storytelling, or has confused the storytelling at that time with the storytelling they do after their storywriting, which is occasionally described as reading their stories from their author books.

103	and he say not by hair of my chin, chin, chin, den I'll huff
104	and a puff and I'll blow your house down
105	and he didn't blow the house down

This second telling of "The Three Little Pigs" can be viewed as a response to the argument that occurred during the first telling. It can also be viewed as building on the first version, and therefore not needing to be as elaborate. Notice that there is no disagreement about the materials used to make the houses. Perhaps the argument has been resolved or perhaps the children have either agreed that there are multiple versions of the story or that they are not to interrupt another child's rendition.

But the uptake is not limited to content. Both children stylized several lines. We use *stylized* here as might be used in reference to jazzing up a melody, using intonation and rhythm to highlight the lines and to render them in a different way. Especially stylized were "I'll blow your house down" and "not by the hair of my chinny chin chin." The second child stylized "and he didn't blow the house down" so that the storytelling appears to be more about stylizing the performance than about the story content. Stylizing builds across the two storytellings and from the version played by the teacher at other times during the class on the phonograph. The point is that stories play against preceding stories and events, but the event played against is contested and negotiated, not a given.

Using Other Children's Stories and Transformation

Especially during storywriting, when the children were at the tables, next to each other, writing and talking with each other, they often monitored what each other was doing, helped each other (e.g., by drawing a motorcycle if requested), and built on each other's stories and storytelling. The series of dragon stories that follows is one example. Thomas was working at the table when one of the adults came by.

111	T:	Wow look at what you've got here, this is what
112	Th:	A blue dragon
113	T:	A blue dragon, this is a great story
114	Th:	It's a story on it
115	T:	It's a story on it
116		great
117		What's your name
118	Th:	Thomas
119	T:	Ok Thomas

120		Can you tell me the story that goes with the blue dragon
121	Th:	Fire come ou' his mouth
122	T:	Fire coming out his mouth
123		wow
124		Is there anything else come out in this
125	Th:	Nope
126	T:	Well that's a great dragon
127		A great story

Reggie was sitting near Thomas, and he overheard the preceding conversation. Reggie had looked at what Thomas was writing and drawing, and they had talked about their dragons.

131	T:	Hi Reggie
132		you've done a lot today haven't you
133		Can you tell me about these
134	R:	Dats da story
135	T:	Can you tell me the story
136	R:	Dats abou' abou' is abou' a dragon
137	T:	About a dragon huh
138	R:	Dats da dragon
139		an' dats da daddy dragon
140		dats mama dragon
141	T:	Thats the dragon
142		thats the daddy dragon
143		thats the mommie dragon
144		Ok
145		and Thomas says he has a big dragon too
146		great

Reggie has made the dragon into a family. Thomas was listening. Later, when the children came to the rug area to tell the stories they had written, Thomas told the following story using the same page he had been writing and drawing on.

150	T:	What's your name
151	Th:	Da dragon go fire in his mouth
152		he went over dere in night dire
153		everywhere in the whole city

154		den he blow all all da city wa' on fire
155		an' got fire on it
156	T:	Wow
157	Th:	An' da ambulance wa' tryin to put everybody in the hospital up
158	T:	Great
159	Th:	An' da dragon wa'
160		(*makes a roaring dragon sound*)
161		on da streets
162		an' when da dragon wake up he hears some noise
163		it was some people talkin real loud so he blowed them people down in da fire cause dem were (*indecipherable*)
164		so the ambulance come ge'
165		so the dragon was tryin to get da ambulance
166		an' put it in his mouth an' blow em down out of his mouth
167		an' go back to his friend's house
168		he wa' goin to sleep an' goin to sleep
169		till to stop an' wa' night time
170		dats all da story
171	T:	That's a wonderful story

Thomas cannot wait to tell his story and ignores the request to say his name. His storytelling is energetic and in his excitement he sometimes stumbles over words. He looks at the page as an aid to prompt his storytelling. His story has gotten longer. The dragon has fire in his mouth and destroys the city. He includes ambulances and hospitals. The dragon does not act capriciously but only because he was awakened from his sleep by people talking, perhaps another version of a moral-centered story.

Although there is nothing lexically specific in Thomas' story that builds on Reggie's story, they are embellishing their stories in response to each other by adding layers of story value and excitement (blowing up the city, ambulances, etc.) and plot. Thomas may have built on Reggie's creation of a dragon family. At the end of Thomas' story he has the dragon go back to bed as if waking up the dragon was a cause for the dragon's fiery behavior, perhaps a scenario he associates with family (other children did note in their stories family members sleeping and being awakened). Thomas and Reggie are not finished with dragons yet. On subsequent days they continue to write about dragons.

Part of what is important to note regarding how Thomas and Reggie played off of each other is that they created opportunities and encouragement for each other to expand their stories. Thus, playing off each other's stories is not just a matter of borrowing or building on lexical, grammatical, or textual aspects, but of creating a social space and time for textual play (in this case, expansion of the narrative).

Construction of Social Identities and Social Relationships

The children "experimented" with narrative style, structure, and content, to create social relationships, affiliations (e.g., with their family, with a peer group), and social identities. These social relationships and identities can be conceptualized in three domains: family, themselves (e.g., gendered identities), and people in the classroom (teachers and classmates). Social relationships and social identities are claimed both in the narrative (text) and in the nature of the storytelling.

Family.   Often the children included family members—mothers, fathers, sisters, brothers, grandmas, grandpas, and cousins—in their storytelling. Mothers were the most emphasized family member, as illustrated in this short story:

```
201    Me and my momma went to the store
210    Me and my momma went rolling
211    and den she started going back home and eat
212    and den
213    and den we went over my grandma's house and help her
214    we went over to Chuckie Cheese
215    and that's the end
```

Going to the store was a highly valued activity, and going to the store with one's mother showed that the child had a good relationship with and was loved by his or her mother (see also Sara's story earlier). Although the children frequently showed that they were loved by their parents and family, only rarely did the children directly state that they were loved, such as in this story:

```
220    This is my mom writing a letter about she loves me.
```

Grandmothers were often included and held special value for the children, often above mothers and fathers.

```
230    My Grandmama is trying to pick me up.
231    She is trying to find my school.
```

This story is a report of an actual event as the child had been picked up at the preschool by his grandmother, who had trouble finding it. However, the primary question to ask about this story may not be about its accuracy, but rather about how the story locates and defines the child socially. One interpretation is the story as a signal of an important relationship with his grandmother and the importance of being picked up by his grandmother (the event).

Family stories can also reposition family members in relation to each other. For example:

240   me and my brother
241   I was in my car
242   I took
243   my brother to the store
244   we went home.

The brother is a baby and so he does get taken places, but the story positions the storyteller as taking the brother to the store, giving the storyteller a more adultlike status. The story is given additional meaning by the locating of the story in the store and in the home. Both locations, especially the store, have high value for the children. Brothers and sisters can also have special value.

Claiming Social Positions and Social Identities for Themselves. Children wrote about themselves as part of social groups. The children established themselves within these groups in several ways: (a) by explicit naming; (b) by using relational terms such as momma, daddy, cousin, and so on, in their stories; (c) by using icons and pictorial representations; and (d) by describing the story's setting—home, store, Chuck E. Cheese, mall, car, park, water, and so forth. Some settings seemed to hold more status than others and sometimes played an implicit role in the construction of moral narratives. For example, good behavior was rewarded with a trip to the store or mall to buy something, or with a treat such as going to Chuck E. Cheese.

The children signaled their gender through descriptions of themselves—what they did or what they drew (e.g., motorcycles and hearts)—and through descriptions of others. For example, they wrote about what they wore, about their hair (e.g., braids), going to the barber shop, getting a skirt or dress, and they wrote about their characters in similar ways, with their characters usually having the same gender as themselves. For example, Michael, who was sitting near Johnny, wrote (this is his rendering of what he wrote):

250 I'm gonna *race* Johnny with these *cars*.
251 And then we're gonna start *racing*
252 I'm gonna *beat* Johnny
253 We're gonna *shoot water guns* at each other
254 I got a *trophy*.

Each of the italicized items mentioned in Michael's story is an item associated with being a boy. None of the stories in our corpus of data told or written by girls have included any of the items in Michael's story.

Two of the icons associated with the girls were hearts and rainbows, and this was so across both research sites. Leslie's story that follows shows her use of these icons and inclusion of her mother. She had been working on a story during storywriting and had drawn a hen; then the girls at her table started drawing rainbows and she included rainbows in her written (drawn) story, and on the opposite page she created rainbows and hearts. The following is the story she told while holding and looking at the story she created in her author book.

261 L: One time a hen came outside
262   then two rainbows was up in the sky an den
263   um
264   a little girl
265   she came outside an saw
266   two rainbow
267   an she
268   an she went back in the house an said
269   mama mama I saw two rainbow
270 T: look at that
271 L: I can see the two rainbows
272 T: can you see the two rainbows
273 Sx: Yeah
274 Sx: I can't
275 T: Well let's come over here
276 Sx: I can't
277 Sx: I can
278 Sx: Oooooo
279 Sx: I can
280 Sx: Oooooo
281 Sx: two rainbows

282		(*undecipherable comments*)
283	T:	wonderful
284		is that it
285	L:	no I got (*undecipherable*)
286	T:	There's more to the story
287		There's
288		O.K. let's hear the next story from Leslie
289	L:	One time
290	T:	Shhhh
291	L:	another little girl came outside
292		she saw another rainbow
293		then
294		a hen came outside
295		and a heart
296		and a heart
297		and a
298		and
299		it was another rainbow came
300		and the another girl ran in the house an said
301		mama mama I saw a heart

Social Relationships With People in the Classroom.   Children included family in their storytelling before they included people in the classroom. This sequencing is an observation, not necessarily a developmental trend. But as time went on, we teachers' names appeared in the children's stories. One day a former teacher visited the classroom with his wife and new child. Afterward, one of the children included the teacher's name in his story. The teachers were surprised when they first observed the children including their names in their stories. The following example shows the use of location, naming, and familial relationships to give the teacher included in the story high status.

400   Ms. Meridian going to church and then her grandmother came

The teacher had discussed both her grandmother and going to church, so it is possible to interpret the story as a report rather than the creation of social status for the teacher. However, since the two events were selected from a broad range of events and since these two events (church and grandmother) hold high value among the children (based on our conversations with them), the story can also be interpreted as allocating status.

Later, children included other classmates. Sometimes the children they included were sitting next to or across from them, and other times they were at different tables. The following is an example of *explicit naming* by Brian to claim social relationships with two friends. He gave value and status to that friendship by locating them in a valued activity, coloring. He drew pictures and then told us what his story was:

410 Jonathan, Darron, Me
411 We are all coloring.

The accuracy of the stories as a report or recount of events appeared not to be important. For example, in this story, according to April's father, the girls had never actually gone to each other's house.

420 Leslie went over April's house

Nonetheless, both the activity and the location had high value for both girls and, in our opinion, was a strong sign of declared friendship. Similarly, the following story written by April (as April told it to us):

430 One time this heart
431 It went to Leslie's house
432 We went to pick up Leslie and then we went to my house.

This story is filled with highly regarded icons—heart and going over someone's house to play.

CONNECTING STORYTELLING AND LITERACY

Although not reported here, our findings support those of others (e.g., Ferreiro & Teberosky, 1982) who have noted that (a) children's early writing is closely connected to their use and understanding of a broad range of semiotic symbols and systems (e.g., drawing, pictures; see also Dyson, 1989, 1991, 1993); (b) children's early writing connects writing to meaning rather than to grapho–phonemic relationships (see also Kato, Ueda, Ozaki, & Mukaigawa, 1998); and (c) young children may often assume that the part (e.g., a drawing of a person) stands for the whole[12] (e.g., what the person is doing). The findings we present here focus on how the chil-

---

[12]This may be a type of metonymy, although it may also reveal limitations in children's understanding of how much they can assume is shared knowledge (an issue for many writers at all ages).

dren incorporated various narrative features into their written stories, how they used letters and words as part of their stories, and how they differentiated written stories from other writing activities. We are also interested in how they used nonalphabetic symbols to create narratives.

Writing Objects and Static Representations

Picture 1 shows a "story" written by Robert in October at the very beginning of the storytelling program. When asked about his story he said, "This is my hand and my name." The letters at the bottom are his name and they are either from his name or similar to letters in his name. For

example, although there is no "P" in his name, there is an "R" and the "P" looks like an incomplete "R." The hand is static; there is no plot or action.

One must be careful not to infer that letter play and static representations are a "stage" in written narrative development. Letter play and static representations occur throughout our data, across the two grade levels. We suspect that letter play is related to a particular curiosity or interest the children have, prompted by events in the classroom such as when they are first learning to write their names and are signing in on a daily basis; when they begin word or letter study with their teacher; when they study days, months, or seasons; when they "discover" the power of putting their name on the list for playing in a center; or when they "discover" how writing someone else's name can influence social relationships. Static representations, such as hands, or like those in Picture 2 by Leslie, communicate values and aspects of identity. Alternatively, static representations may be drawing practice (drawing a motorcycle or dragon) or they may be physical fun (which may best describe tracing one's hand). Leslie's rainbows and hand are sometimes static representations and sometimes characters in a story (see lines 261–301 earlier). The use of a static representation as a story may represent an early stage of written narrative development, but it may also reflect the books that have been read to the children. Most children's books, for example, consist of pictures and words. In some families, while reading books to

children, parents ask children to name the pictured objects (Bloome, 1985; Heath, 1982b). In brief, it is not clear whether static representations are simply a choice about how to make a "story," a genre borrowed from extant "stories," or a stage in written narrative development (or a stage in apprenticeship). Such representations may be all of these.

Uptake and Hybridization in Written Stories

Picture 3 shows a story created by Cheryl on November 20, 1997. The page on which she created her story had a line drawn about three quarters of the way down. The teachers said that these lines were drawn to encourage students to "write" below the pictures as shown in story books.

Cheryl's picture shows her writing below the line with some recognizable letters and some letterlike symbols. She has also placed writing in the picture itself, part of which is her name (lower left), while the rest appears to be letter play. It was not unusual for the children to combine various genres such as a story (with a plot), static representations, and letter play. When we asked Cheryl to tell us what she wrote, she said the following:

> A bow-n-arrow. I learned how to catch deer and rabbits. I'm going to cook it. I cooked it already. My momma came in and whupped me because she told me to catch two. I said she had no business whupping me because I did nothing wrong.

The deer and rabbits were characters in stories recently told to the class. However, neither cooking nor a mother's punishing her daughter were part of the story about deer and rabbits. Cheryl has combined stories she has heard with a personal experience and an imagined scenario. She has transformed the story through a process of hybridization, a process that occurred frequently in the children's written and spoken stories.

Differentiating Stories and Non-Narrative Writing

Picture 4 shows a story that Cheryl wrote at the end of January. She told us that the letters said, "Once upon a time, there was a house." There may be some correspondence between the words and the letters she wrote, as she had received instruction about sounds and letters since the beginning of the year. The instruction was part of a broader literacy program that included reading books to the children and language experience activities. Sometimes Cheryl's written stories were extensive and complex (as was Sara's story earlier) and sometimes brief, as the story in Picture 4.

However, a few children differentiated story writing from other types of writing. For example, Picture 5 created by Cheryl on February 11, 1998, shows that Cheryl is differentiating between two written language practices: story writing and homework. Cheryl and many of the students occasionally created homework. Doing homework was a valued activity that indicated maturity and being a good student. When asked to describe the homework, students called out the names of the letters and numbers. They did not provide a narrative or describe an object or static representation. Homework was writing letters and numbers, not creating meaning, narrative, or storytelling.[13]

---

[13]This finding may reflect Street and Street's (1991) differentiation of school language and literacy practices versus nonschool language and literacy practices.

FINAL COMMENTS

One of the major goals of our research was to examine the narratives produced by young African American children in order to better understand one aspect of their language development. As Champion (1995, 1998; Champion, Seymour, & Camarata, 1995) wrote, narrative developmental research traditionally had focused on white children. The findings were often assumed applicable to other populations, including African American children. One result has been that the frameworks often used to assess, instruct, and research the narrative development of African American children have not been grounded in a substantial corpus of data of African American children's narratives, raising questions about their validity. Although our corpus of data has flaws, it does provide a degree of ethnolinguistic validity for the study of African America children's narratives.

However, our findings are not necessarily specific to African American children. Clearly, there are culturally specific aspects of narratives that vary across cultures (e.g., Gee, 1985; Gutierrez-Clellen & Quinn, 1993; Heath, 1983; Schieffelin & Ochs, 1986; Scollon, 1988). Yet, the findings and issues that have emerged from our research appear to have applicability, at least to some degree, especially for reframing how children's narratives and narrative development might be approached.

Our research, to date, supports Champion's (1995, 1998) thesis that children develop a repertoire of narrative structures. Our findings suggest that children may take up, adapt, and transform the narrative styles, structures, and content that are made available to them. The sources available to students to take up various narrative styles, structures, and content include formal instruction, informal instructional contexts, family contexts, and others. The range of available sources provides the possibilities out of which a repertoire of narrative styles, structures, and content develop.

Our findings also suggest that children make themselves into storytellers given the material resources and opportunities to do so through interactions with adults and peers (see also Schieffelin & Ochs, 1986). In stating the claim in this manner, we emphasize the process as a collective and collaborative one. The existence of human and material resources, including people, storytelling events and texts, and props, are provided by and through social institutions in a manner based on assumptions about what should happen at a particular time and place. Storytelling as a social process occurs within a variety of formal and informal situations used to establish identities and relationships and accomplish other social goals. Perhaps not surprisingly, we found that the children were learning to differentiate various spoken and written language forms. Creating a written narrative was distinguished from doing homework, for example. That children are able to differentiate language genres at an early age suggests that they will continue to employ the resources of various language practices to create textual worlds and social affiliations.

ACKNOWLEDGMENTS

Another version of this chapter was originally presented at the Third Biennial Memphis Research Symposium: Focus on Communication and Literacy in African Americans, University of Memphis, Memphis, TN. The research reported herein was funded, in part, by a grant from the National Council of Teachers of English Research Foundation. The opinions and statements reported in this chapter do not necessarily reflect the policies or positions of the National Council of Teachers of English Research Foundation.

APPENDIX
Transcription Conventions

Line length: We used Green and Wallat's (1981) *message unit* as the unit of analysis. Each line represents one message unit. Green and Wallat define a message unit as the smallest unit of conversational meaning. They are identified primarily by prosodic markers. We have not included the prosodic markers in the transcript in order to make the transcript easier to read. We have only included prosodic cues when important to an issue discussed in the data analysis.

Sx = unidentifiable students.
Ss = many students.
T = any adult.

Phonological variations: Phonological variations from standard English (e.g., when "th" is pronounced "d") are only shown in the transcript when they were prominent and easily identified in the recording.

REFERENCES

Applebee, A. (1978). *The child's concept of story*. Chicago: University of Chicago Press.

Atkinson, P. (1991). *The ethnographic imagination*. London: Routledge.

Baker, C., & Luke, A. (Eds.). (1993). *The critical sociology of reading pedagogy*. Amsterdam: John Benjamins.

Bakhtin, M. (1981). Discourse in the novel. In M. Holquist (Ed.) & C. Emerson & M. Holquist (Trans.), *The dialogic imagination* (pp. 259–422). Austin: University of Texas Press. (Original work published 1935)

Bakhtin, M. (1986). The problem of speech genres. In C. Emerson & M. Holquist (Eds.), & V. McGee (Trans.), *Speech genres and other late essays* (pp. 60–102). Austin: University of Texas Press. (Original work published 1953)

Bauman, R. (1986). *Story, performance and event*. Cambridge, England: Cambridge University Press.

Bauman, R., & Briggs, C. (1990). Poetics and performance as critical perspectives on language and social life. *Annual Review of Anthropology, 19*, 59–88.

Bauman, R., & Sherzer, J. (Eds.). (1974). *Explorations in the ethnography of speaking*. Cambridge, England: Cambridge University Press.

Beach, R., & Phinney, M. (1997). Framing literary text worlds through real-world social negotiations. *Linguistics and Education, 9*(3), 159–198.

Benjamin, W. (1969). *Illuminations*. New York: Schocken Books.

Bloome, D. (1985). Bedtime storyreading as a social process. *Thirty-fourth yearbook of the National Reading Conference*. Rochester, NY: National Reading Conference.

Bloome, D. (1987). Reading as a social process in a middle school classroom. In D. Bloome (Ed.), *Literacy and schooling* (pp. 123–149). Norwood, NJ: Ablex.

Bloome, D. (1993). Necessary indeterminacy: Issues in the microethnographic study of reading as a social process. *Journal of Reading Research, 16*(2), 98–111.

Champion, T. (1995). *A description of narrative production and development in child speakers of African American English*. Unpublished doctoral dissertation, University of Massachusetts, Amherst.

Champion, T. (1998). "Tell me somethin' good": A description of narrative structures among African-American children. *Linguistics and Education, 9*(3), 251–286.

Champion, T., Seymour, H., & Camarata, S. (1995). Narrative discourse among African American children. *Journal of Narrative and Life History, 5*(4), 333–352.

Cortazzi, M. (1993). *Narrative analysis*. London: Falmer Press.

Dombey, H. (1995). *Interaction at storytime in the nursery classroom* (Report No. PS 023829). Brighton, England: University of Brighton. (ERIC Document Reproduction Service No. ED 389 452)

Dyson, A. (1989). *Multiple words of child writers: Friends learning to write*. New York: Teachers College Press.

Dyson, A. (1991). Toward a reconceptualization of written language development. *Linguistics and Education, 3*(2), 139–162.

Dyson, A. (1993). *Social worlds of children learning to write in an urban primary school*. New York: Teachers College Press.

Fairclough, N. (1995). *Critical discourse analysis*. London: Longman.

Ferreiro, E., & Teberosky, A. (1982). *Literacy before schooling*. Exeter, NH: Heinemann.

Frederiksen, C. (1989). Text comprehension in functional task domains. In D. Bloome (Ed.), *Classrooms and literacy* (pp. 189–232). Norwood, NJ: Ablex.

Gee, J. (1985). The narrativization of experience in the oral style. *Journal of Education, 167*(1), 9–35.

Gee, J. P. (1990). *Social linguistics: Ideology and discourses*. London: Falmer Press.

Green, J. (1990). Reading is a social process. In J. Howell, A. McNamara, & M. Clough (Eds.), *Social context of literacy* (pp. 104–123). Canberra, Australia: ACT Department of Education.

Green, J., & Wallat, C. (1981). Mapping instructional conversations—A sociolinguistic ethnography. In J. Green & C. Wallat (Eds.), *Ethnography and language in educational settings* (pp. 161–207). Norwood, NJ: Ablex.

Gumperz, J. (1986). *Discourse strategies*. New York: Cambridge University Press.

Gumperz, J., & Hymes, D. (Eds.). (1986). *Directions in sociolinguistics: The ethnography of communication*. Oxford, England: Basil Blackwell.

Gutierrez-Clellen, V. F., & Quinn, R. (1993). Assessing narratives of children from diverse cultural/linguistic groups. *Language, Speech, and Hearing Services in Schools, 24*, 2–9.

Heath, S. (1982a). Protean shapes in literacy events: Ever shifting oral and literate traditions. In D. Tannen (Ed.), *Spoken and written language: Exploring orality and literacy* (pp. 91–117). Norwood, NJ: Ablex.

Heath, S. (1982b). What no bedtime story means: Narrative skills at home and school. *Language in Society, 11*, 49–76.

Heath, S. (1983). *Ways with words*. Cambridge, England: Cambridge University Press.

Hymes, D. (1974). *The foundations of sociolinguistics: Sociolinguistic ethnography*. Philadelphia: University of Pennsylvania Press.

Hyon, S., & Sulzby, E. (1994). African American kindergartners' spoken narratives: Topic associating and topic centered styles. *Linguistics and Education, 6*(2), 121–152.

Jakobson, R. (1971). Shifters, verbal categories, and the Russian verb. In R. Jakobson, *Selected writings* (Vol. 2, pp. 130–147). The Hague, Netherlands: Mouton.

Jefferson, G. (1978). Sequential aspects of storytelling in conversation. In J. Schenkein (Ed.), *Studies in the organization of conversation* (pp. 219–248). New York: Academic Press.

Johnson, N., & Mandler, J. (1980). A tale of two structures: Underlying and surface forms in stories. *Poetics, 9*(1), 51–86.

Kato, Y., Ueda, A., Ozaki, K., & Mukaigawa, Y. (1998). Japanese preschoolers' theories about the "Hiragana" system of writing. *Linguistics and Education, 10*(2), 219–232.

Labov, W. (1972). *Language in the inner city*. Philadelphia: University of Pennsylvania Press.

Mardell, B. (1996). *Helping preschoolers become better storytellers: A teacher's perspective* (Report No. PS 024646). Cambridge, MA. (ERIC Document Reproduction Service No. 400 101)

McCabe, A., & Peterson, C. (Eds.). (1991). *Developing narrative structure*. Hillsdale, NJ: Lawrence Erlbaum Associates.

Michaels, S. (1981). "Sharing time": Children's narrative styles and differential access to literacy. *Language in Society, 10*(3), 423–442.

Michaels, S. (1986). Narrative presentations: An oral preparation for literacy with first graders. In J. Cook-Gumperz (Ed.), *The social construction of literacy* (pp. 94–116). Cambridge, England: Cambridge University Press.

Michaels, S., & Collins, J. (1984). Oral discourse styles: Classroom interaction and acquisition of literacy. In D. Tannen (Ed.), *Coherence in spoken and written discourse* (pp. 219–244). Norwood, NJ: Ablex.

Ochs, E. (1997). Narrative. In T. A. Van Dyjk (Ed.), *Discourse as structure and process* (pp. 184–204). London: Sage.

Preece, A. (1987). The range of narrative forms conversationally produced by young children. *Journal of Child Language, 14*, 353–373.

Rooks, D. (1998). Can I tell you my story? How storytelling contributes to pupils' achievements in other aspects of speaking and listening and to their understanding of how language works. *Reading, 32*, 24–28.

Rosen, H. (1986). The importance of story. *Language Arts, 63*(3), 226–237.

Roth, S., Froma, P., Speece, D., Cooper, D., & De La Paz, S. (1993). Unresolved mysteries: How do metalinguistic and narrative skills connect with early reading. *Journal of Special Education, 30*, 257–277.

Rowe, D. (1994). *Preschoolers as authors: Literacy learning in the social world of the classroom.* Cresskill, NJ: Hampton Press.

Sacks, H. (1972). On the analyzability of stories by children. In J. Gumperz & D. Hymes (Eds.), *Directions in sociolinguistics* (pp. 325–345). New York: Holt, Rinehart & Winston.

Schieffelin, B. B., & Ochs, E. (Eds.). (1986). *Language socialisation across cultures.* Cambridge, England: Cambridge University Press.

Scollon, R. (1988). Storytelling, reading, and the micropolitics of literacy. In J. E. Readence & R. S. Baldwin (Eds.), *Dialogues in literacy research: Thirty-seventh yearbook of the National Reading Conference* (pp. 15–34). Chicago: National Reading Conference.

Sheridan, D., Street, B., & Bloome, D. (2000). *Writing ourselves: Mass-observation and literary practices.* Cresskill, NJ: Hampton Press.

Solsken, J., & Bloome, D. (1992, April). *Beyond poststructuralism: Story and narrative in the study of literacy in the everyday world.* Paper presented at the meeting of the American Educational Research Association, San Francisco.

Street, B. (Ed.). (1993a). *Cross-cultural approaches to literacy.* Cambridge, England: Cambridge University Press.

Street, B. (1993b). The new literacy studies: Guest editorial. *Journal of Research in Reading, 16*(2), 81–97.

Street, B. (1995). *Social literacies.* London: Longman.

Street, B., & Street, J. (1991). The schooling of literacy. In D. Barton & R. Ivanic (Eds.), *Writing in the community* (pp. 143–166). London: Sage.

Tallant, C. (1992). *Telling with, not telling to: Interactive storytelling and at-risk children* (Report No. CS 508105). Chicago: Speech Communication Association Convention. (ERIC Document Reproduction Service No. ED 355 574)

Toolan, M. (1988). *Narrative: A critical linguistic introduction.* London: Routledge.

Wells, G. (1986). *The meaning makers: Children learning language and using language to learn.* Portsmouth, NH: Heinemann.

Chapter 4

Emergent Literacy: Home–School Connections

Jerrie C. Scott
University of Memphis

Cheryl D. Marcus
Central State University

Much has changed since the days when preparation for school-based literacy was referred to as *reading readiness* and consideration was given primarily to the kindergarten period. The term *emergent literacy* has replaced not only the old term reading readiness, but also older views about preparation for school literacy. As Cooper (1993) explained:

> Emergent literacy is the idea that children grow into reading and writing with no real beginning or ending point, that reading and writing develop concurrently, interrelatedly, and according to no right sequence or order. Instead, learners are always emerging. Moreover, this process begins long before children enter school—through the activities and experiences in their everyday lives and through their interactions with peers and adults. Literacy learning involves all elements of the communication process— reading, writing, speaking, listening, and thinking. (p. 9)

The wide acceptance of the view that the process of acquiring literacy begins "long before children enter school" has made connections between home and school a major area of concern for educational practitioners, researchers, and theorists. All children come to school with language and literacy experiences. The language that children bring to school serves as the foundation for all learning, and the literacy experiences that they bring emerge most naturally and efficiently as an extension of home-based literacy experiences. Whether admitted or not, this is the package

of prior knowledge that school literacy programs build upon. The problems are that not all spoken varieties match the language base on which
the school tries to build and not all literacy practices in the home are con-
gruent with the literacy practices of the school. This leaves us with the situation of discontinuities between home and school language patterns and
literacy practices. There is much evidence that home–school discontinuities account partially for difficulties that nonmainstream students have
emerging through the various phases of literacy acquisition (Campbell,
1996; Cazden, 1986); yet, we can say that the bridge between nonmainstream homes and school remains more unidirectional (school to home)
than bidirectional, despite evidence that a two-way bridge would have a
much greater yield (Corno, 1989; Irvine, 1990; Marcus, 1996).

In this discussion, we argue for a two-way connection between nonmainstream homes and school. Beginning with a review of some of the
evidence of discontinuities between the language and literacy of nonmainstream homes and school, we suggest that this work has begun to
build a knowledge base from which to build a two-way bridge between
nonmainstream homes and school. Second, we discuss some of the barriers that block fuller use of existing knowledge in developing school literacy and parent training programs. Third, we provide descriptions of two
programs that attempt to build a two-way bridge between home and
school, ending with research questions that have evolved from our own
practical experiences with the two programs that we developed, as well as
from the work of others.

DISCONTINUITIES

O. Taylor and Garrett (1996) described the chronology of research on the
language of African Americans and other nonmainstream groups. The
1960s and 1970s focused on language structure. The 1980s shifted to
meaning and the use of language. The 1990s heightened interest in the
discourse patterns of African American and other communities. In each
of these eras, home–school discontinuities have been identified as potential factors accounting for the failure to adequately develop literacy competencies among nonmainstream groups (Wolfram, 1991). Regarding the
chronology of research on literacy, the 1960s focused on language socialization, creating the framework for a plethora of deficit-oriented literacy
models (Bernstein, 1964). Focus shifted from debates over language
socialization and learning to debates over orality and literacy (Hirsch,
1987). By the late 1980s and early 1990s, researchers had begun to provide more detailed accounts of the literacy practices in both the home and
school environments (Bloome, 1989; Moss, 1994).

Language Structure

Differences between the language forms acquired in nonmainstream homes and standard English provided the first evidence of possible discontinuities between home and school. During the early stages of research, attention was directed almost exclusively toward dialect features and the potential ways that nonstandard dialects interfered with the development of reading, writing, and speaking competencies. The hypothesis that features of the spoken dialect would be transferred to the reading and writing of text or to the speaking of standard English came to be known as the *dialect interference* hypothesis. Researchers set out to test the hypothesis, usually with a focus on surface features of low-prestige dialects and their reproduction in the decoding of text (reading), the encoding of text (writing), or the recoding of speech forms (speaking). Many researchers concluded that the differences between dialect forms and standard English forms in speech failed to account precisely for deviations from standard English found in the decoding and encoding of written texts or the recoding of spoken text. For example, J. Scott (1979) found that African American children in the first grade sometimes superimposed dialect features in their reading of sentences written in standard English, and they also superimposed standard English forms in their reading of sentences written in dialect. Similar findings by others led to the conclusion that however speech forms are used in decoding texts, the process is far more complex than could be accounted for by the dialect interference hypothesis (Goodman, 1965; J. Scott, 1979).

Many resolved that instructional intrusion caused greater problems to African American students than did the structural linguistic variants (Morrow, 1990; J. Scott, 1992). Instructional interference comes in several forms: persistent corrections of pronunciation during oral reading, which amounts to confusing the teaching of reading with the teaching of standard English phonology (Goodman, 1965); and the teaching of phonics skills out of context and without regard for phonological differences across dialects, making it difficult for nonmainstream dialect speakers to develop confidence in their decoding strategies (J. Scott, 1992). In short, the assumption that speakers of nonmainstream dialects would transfer their spoken language patterns to reading and experience difficulty in reading structures where the spoken language and written texts differed was not supported. Similar results were found for writing. Interestingly enough, research shows that African American children move through the same stages as non–African Americans in their move from invented spelling to conventional spelling (Sulzby, 1985). This would indicate that the speech forms of African Americans enter into the stages of literacy development in the same orderly way that speech forms of other dialects do. However, the transition toward conventional spellings are likely greater for African American English speakers than for White mainstream speakers (C. Scott & Rogers, 1996). Factors related to the delivery of reading and writing instruction are perhaps more influential than the dialect itself. As a general principle, it can be said that an overemphasis on form over meaning results in ineffective instructional practices not only in reading but in writing.

Language Functions

As linguistic studies progressed beyond the sentence, it became clearer that differences between the discourse patterns of nonmainstream homes and school represented another area of discontinuities. Focusing on communicative competencies, Campbell (1996) theorized that participation in the educational process requires most African American children to acquire a second set of cultural and communication norms:

> Rules regarding who may speak to whom, when to talk and how much to say, what can be talked about, when to be silent, who is allowed to speak first, and what words and structures may be used are all examples of ways of speaking that children must understand and in which they must demonstrate cultural proficiency. (p. 80)

Looking at variations in the ways that language functions in homes and school, Morrow (1997) suggested that the "acquisition of language, reading, and writing seems to follow a pattern: children seem to be more interested in the functions of literacy first, then the form, and later the conventions" (p. 141). Questions and narratives are examples of discourse patterns that function differently in nonmainstream homes and school and potentially affect literacy acquisition.

Didactic questions, which are used more to get respondents to display knowledge and understanding than to elicit information, are frequently used in school and in some mainstream homes. Heath (1983) found that in African American homes, children were more accustomed to answering questions that called less for a display of knowledge than for metaphorical or descriptive information, as story starters, or defense explanations ("What's that on your pants?"). In the former, the person asking the question knows the answer, whereas in the latter, the questioner is actually eliciting unknown information.

Much has been said about the differences in narratives learned at home and those expected in school. J. Scott (1990) showed that the narratives of African American students fit a common narrative structure used by African Americans. The narrative structure of African Americans, as described by Labov (1972), consists of four parts: an abstract (a summary of the main point), orientation (contexts of time, place, person, activities, situations), story events, and coda (shows the effects of the event on the narrator). In her analysis of narratives used by African American children during sharing time (or show-and-tell), Michaels (1981) distinguished between topic-centered and topic-changing, or topic-associating, narratives. Topic-centered narratives, which are preferred in the school, are developed around a central theme and contain factual information and explicit cohesion forms, such as conjunctions and transition words. Topic-associating narratives are found in many nonmainstream homes, including African American homes. A series of personal anecdotes without an overall theme characterizes these narratives, which rely on the use of prosodic cues rather than explicit semantic and syntactic forms, such as conjunctions and relative clauses, for thematic cohesion. Smitherman (1977) explained:

> This meandering away from the point takes the listener on episodic journeys and over tributary rhetorical routes, but like the flow of nature's rivers and streams, it all eventually leads back to the source. Though highly applauded by blacks, this narrative linguistic style is exasperating to whites who wish you'd be direct and hurry up and get to the point. (pp. 147–148)

Michaels and Cazden (1986) suggested that the exasperation of teachers is manifested in teachers' responses:

> The result of this study showed that black and white adults responded differently to topic associating narratives. White adults were more likely to find these stories hard to follow, or bad stories, and they were more likely to infer that the child telling the story was a low-achieving student. Black adults were more likely to evaluate positively both topic associating and topic-centered stories—noticing differences, but seeming to appreciate both. (p. 152)

The different discourse strategies found in questions and narratives are important because they may limit access to quality instruction. Teachers are better at expanding and extending patterns with which they are familiar, resulting in more of the collaborative, or scaffolding, support for users of the topic-centered narratives and respondents to the didactic questions. As Michaels and Cazden (1986) pointed out:

> Improving teacher/child collaboration can increase these children's opportunities to learn by increasing their access to the kind of quality instruction that they need and that teachers intend to provide. If these extended discourse activities are truly key situations influencing children's access to literacy instruction, then in the service of equity and improved educational practice, we must try to understand and improve conversational engagement and collaboration between teachers and children of all backgrounds. (p. 153)

In the interest of bridging home and school language functions, it is important to remember that in homes, function takes precedence over form and convention.

Literacy Functions

Literacy functions in homes and school differ in a variety of ways, including styles of transmitting knowledge (D. Taylor & Dorsey-Gaines, 1988). There are parallels between the ways of transmitting literacy in homes, including nonmainstream homes and communities, and what is now called *constructivist pedagogy*. For example, research on Native American and Hawaiian children has shown that in these families, children are accustomed to learning from each other, not in a one-on-one situation with adults (Phillips, 1972). Likewise, in African American homes, literacy is transmitted through "playing school," a practice that is often overlooked in major reports, such as *Becoming a Nation of Readers* (Anderson, Hiebert, Scott, & Wilkinson, 1985), that set forth the parameters for home environments that are supportive of literacy development (J. Scott, 1988). Peer-to-peer learning is among the strategies associated with constructivist pedagogy.

In the African American families studied by Heath (1983), communicative rules around reading and writing involved collaborative efforts, including the decoding of unclear words, gathering information, and spontaneous storytelling in response to ideas conveyed in written text. Heath noted that African American children from Trackton and low-income White children from Roadville were less practiced at reading and writing as an end and more practiced at reading and writing as a means to an end. Several researchers have identified ways in which the means-to-ends practices work in nonmainstream homes. This type of collaboration is encouraged in various models of cooperative learning, where literacy acquisition and the learning of content are represented not by solo performance, but by shared meaning taking and meaning making. Apprenticeship learning is still another delivery strategy advocated in constructivist pedagogy. Phillips (1983) pointed out that Native American parents rarely verbally instruct children. Instead, these parents demonstrate the task and children practice the task privately, making their performance public only after achieving competence.

It appears that some of the same ways of transmitting knowledge in natural settings may be adapted for use in classrooms. Certainly this would reduce discontinuities between teaching and learning styles in homes and school. Successful intervention programs, designed specifically to utilize home-based patterns in designing instructional programs, provide evidence that consideration of home–school discontinuities has positive effects on literacy development. For example, Delain, Pearson, and Anderson (1985) found that the use of sounding, playing the dozens, capping, and other discourse patterns found in African American communities had a positive effect on African American children's understanding of figurative language in literature. As well, the collaborative "talk story" narrative form, used as a basis for restructuring reading instruction, improved Hawaiian children's reading success (Tharp, 1982). When teachers were informed that their didactic questions might be unfamiliar to some children and that they should use some of the more open-ended question forms familiar to Black children, the children's functioning in the classroom improved. Focusing on the home, Levenstein's (1983) parent-training project was able to reduce home–school discontinuities by training parents in some of the techniques that teachers typically use, such as didactic questions, demands for display of knowledge, and demands for lexical specificity.

All of the aforementioned suggests that a two-way bridge can be built between nonmainstream homes and school with results that greatly increase the literacy success of children. With respect to language structure, an important bridging principle is that an overemphasis on textual forms can impede instructional effectiveness. With language functions, it is important for teachers to be aware that structures such as narratives and question can vary in their functions from one cultural group to another, sometimes limiting conversational engagement and access to learning. With literacy functions, bridging may come more readily through the use of constructivist pedagogical practices that accommodate a variety of learning styles, including those associated with nonmainstream homes. Not to be overlooked is the fact that this work on discontinuities is building a knowledge base from which to bridge literacy development in nonmainstream homes to literacy development in the school. An important question to ask, then, is why there are not more programs that take the language and literacy resources of nonmainstream homes into account.

BARRIERS

With the work that has evolved, many different instructional models have been developed. Some are directed toward changing classroom operations, whereas others are focused on parent training. Unfortunately, too many continue to operate from the premise that where differences between school and nonmainstream homes exist, there is no positive transfer value from home to school. That is, the "difference" must be corrected rather than utilized in schools. In her discussion of the 1997 Ebonics controversy, J. Scott (1998) identified three major barriers to the building of bidirectional bridges between home and school. First, negative attitudes toward the language and culture of nonmainstream groups prevent the broader public from even considering African American English, or any other low-prestige variety of English, for use as the foundation upon which to broaden and enhance literacy development. Second, resistance to elevating the status of low-prestige groups prevents reasoned and reasonable conversations about how language of the home can be used to enhance learning. It appears that a validation of the language, even for the purpose of enhancing learning, might also validate the low-prestige group, empowering the group to become more successful. Resistance to elevating the status of low-prestige groups is driven partially by an interest in maintaining the power and privileges of high-prestige groups. Third, limited numbers of exemplary models exist, for reasons having also to do with negative attitudes and resistance. Moreover, ethnocentrism and stereotyping erroneously lead to the belief that the culturally based behaviors of high-prestige groups are behavioral universals. As successful programs are developed and used in experimental contexts, such attitudes and resistance often result in the programs' dismantling, thereby disallowing true tests of their efficacy. As Baugh (1981) suggested, to remove such barriers it is important for school personnel to become less ethnocentric and more ethnosensitive.

Campbell (1996) identified five barriers to successful collaboration with families: (a) ethnocentrism and stereotyping, (b) one-way notions of differences, (c) unidirectional relationship (typically children from diverse backgrounds have borne the strain of changes), (d) assumptions about knowledge of school, and (e) hierarchical authority with parents expected to defer to professionals (hierarchical relationships ignore the adult-to-adult nature of parent–teacher relationships and the wealth of knowledge and information that can be shared):

> Oftentimes professionals erroneously assume that the underlying assumptions of parent-training programs, which are based on white, middle class studies of parent–child interactions, are acultural or universal, revealing natural, rather than culturally learned, behaviors and that the resulting goals are appropriate for all families. (p. 88)

Campbell concluded that when working collaboratively with families, professionals must be prepared to "encounter a variety of family structures, cultural traditions, gender role and status expectations, communication styles and norms, child-rearing practices, values, beliefs, attitudes, goals, and aspirations" (p. 86). And we would add that bidirectional bridging requires that parents also understand more about what they can do to facilitate school-based literacy learning.

TOWARD BIDIRECTIONAL BRIDGING
OF HOME AND SCHOOL

How do we differentiate between unidirectional and bidirectional relationships between home and school in the development of literacy? While a unidirectional model provides knowledge to students by both homes and school, it does not allow for the valuable exchange of information needed to build cultural synchronization between nonmainstream homes and school. The lack of cultural synchronization operates from the position that when teachers do not understand the cultural capital of students in their classrooms (e.g., the language, values, home environment, or learning styles of students), they fail to capitalize on the strengths of the acquired modalities that are brought from home.

Irvine (1990) suggested that cultural synchronization mediates the interaction of teacher and student: "When teachers and black students are in tune culturally, it can be expected that communication is enhanced, instruction is effective, and positive teacher affect is maximized" (p. xx). She went on to explain that "cultural misunderstandings between teachers and students result in conflict, distrust, hostility, and possible school failure for black students. The conflict is exaggerated because of cultural inversion and cultural aversion" (p. 26). Cultural inversion is demonstrated through the unwillingness of African American students to forgo certain cultural behaviors; cultural aversion is demonstrated by teachers' and administrators' reluctance to discuss race and race-related issues.

The unidirectional models for home–school linkages provide a one-way feed into the knowing, using, and expressing domains of the child by home and school. Functioning separately, each institution provides its level of support as best as it can. Too often, especially where schools serve diverse communities, home and school develop polar ideologies that send children mixed messages about expectations and values (Comer, 1980; van Kleeck, 1994). The literacy development of children suffers, as the children must attempt to mediate the conflicting ideologies and negotiate a space of comfort for operating effectively in the two environments. Thus, a unidirectional model places the child in the center with home ideologies and school ideologies feeding the literacy development from different and sometimes conflicting perspectives. A bidirectional relation allows for the exchange of ideas, a respect for different orientations to literacy, and a dialogic link between home and school that clearly articulates expectations and support for the child, the home, and the school or community (Marcus, 1996). A bidirectional model should bridge home and school ideologies by providing a transitional passage for children that makes linkages between the expectations, literacy activities, and literacy goals of the home and school. Cultural synchronization (rather than cul-

tural dissonance) undergirds the literacy of the child, and cultural synchronization serves as a filter that allows the appropriate convergence, or
separation, of home and school ideologies. Of special importance here is
the recognition that although not all home and school literacy functions
are the same, both play important roles in the emergent literacy of the
child. The gains will come in the belief that home and school must work
together, each understanding and respecting the shared as well as different values, roles, and responsibilities. As expressed by Campbell (1996),
"Families transmit and shape cultural attitudes, behaviors, and patterns.
Effective home–school partnerships allow for the construction of a bridge
to better meet the needs of the child, family, and school" (p. 86). Figure
4.1 shows the distinction between unidirectional and bidirectional home–
school connections.

UNI-DIRECTIONAL MODEL

BI-DIRECTIONAL MODEL

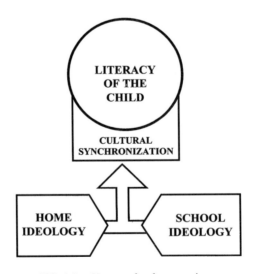

FIG. 4.1.   Home–school connections.

The next question is, how do we move toward building a two-way bridge between home and school in the development of literacy? We provide here two examples of training programs designed to provide bidirectional bridging between home and school.

Parents as Expert Teachers (PET): Creating a Dialogic Link

This training program was developed with a view toward recognizing parents as expert teachers and creating a dialogic link between home and school, capable of enhancing the understanding of the roles, responsibilities, and activities of home and school in the development of literacy. The program is informed by research that reports the value of strong home–school partnerships for enhancing literacy acquisition (Irvine, 1990; McGillip & Michael, 1994; Strickland, 1985). Of special concern are the young nonmainstream language users, whom teachers devalue because of their nonstandard language, their use of unfamiliar discourse patterns, and their use of home-based literacy practices that are neither recognized nor accepted as a basis for learning and participating as full members of the learning community.

The training provides for three modules—one for parents, one for teachers, and a final one for both parents and teachers. The parent module is designed to elicit information from parents to develop a primer of culturally relevant activities that occur naturally in the home and that support school-based literacy activities. The teacher module is designed to elicit information from school personnel to develop a primer of school-based policies, strategies, and activities that will enable parents to be knowledgeable about, and more supportive of, school-based literacy practices. The parent–teacher module is designed to communicate the organizational structure of schools to parents, to inform teachers of the cultural values operating in homes, and ultimately to develop a home–school partnership plan that will enable school and home to better work together in the enhancement of children's total literacy development. The goals, objectives, and sample activities of the three modules are shown in Table 4.1.

Different parts of the modules have been presented to parents in various settings, but much work, empirical as well as practical, remains to be done. For example, a modified version of the PET program was presented during a back-to-school rally at a church in August 1997. As president of her local district's board of education, the second author accepted the invitation to work with parents in the church and presented select activities from the parent-training module. The four areas most frequently mentioned in the open-ended evaluative responses of parents were: (a) they gained information that would allow them to actively support the dis-

TABLE 4.1

Parents as Expert Teachers: Creating a Dialogic Link

Goals	Objectives	Sample Activities
I. Parent Training Goal: To assemble a primer of home-based skills, strategies, and activities.	1. To identify what parents know and do in the home to support children's learning. 2. To describe what is known by experts about home-based literacy practices that support school learning. 3. To describe what homes expect the schools to do to support home-based values and family literacy practices. 4. To develop a chart of skills and strategies used in homes. 5. To examine home-based skills and strategies described in the literature. 6. To gain a commitment to use the information to provide more home-based support of school-based literacy practices. 7. To assess the knowledge gained about what parents already do and what others do. 8. To develop skills, strategies, and activities that can be used to support the literacy goals of homes.	1. View and discuss the film "Why Parental Support Is Needed" by James Comer. 2. Administer the Parent as Expert Teacher (PET) Survey developed by Marcus. 3. Engage parents in responding to questions about their expectations for schools to support values of homes. 4. Classify the skills and strategies identified in the PET Survey by literacy areas: reading, writing, listening, speaking. 5. Expand the lists of skills and strategies by adding those reported in the literature. 6. Develop individual action plans and identify shared actions for inclusion in the primer. 7. Compare individual action plans to those recommended in the state and/or district's parent involvement plans. 8. Compile information from workshops into a document—Primer for Parents.
II. Teacher Training Goal: To assemble a primer of school-based skills, strategies, and activities for homes to support schools and schools to support homes.	1. To determine what the school wants parents to do. 2. To identify what experts say are successful models of home–school partnerships.	1. View and discuss film "Why Parental Support Is Needed" by Comer. 2. Administer the Survey of Effective Practices of Home–School Partnerships developed by Marcus.

3. To compare practices and expectations used for giving assignments so that homes can more easily support school literacy requirements.
4. To adopt skills and strategies that can be used to influence the content and pedagogy of literacy instruction.
5. To gain a commitment to use the information to make policies that better fit the expectations of schools.
6. To select the knowledge gained about what teachers know and do and what others do.
7. To share skills, strategies, and activities by grade level that support the literacy learning of children.

III. Parent–Teacher Training

Goal: To develop a home–school partnership plan for enhancing literacy.

1. To recall and present the information discovered in Module I (parents) and Module II (teachers) workshops.
2. To define the school policy, rules, structures, and teacher expectations of parents' support for learning.
3. To explain the parents' expectations of schools for the successful literacy development of their children.
4. To agree to be respectful and embrace the knowledge gained in both the home and school workshop.

3. Identify literacy assignments that teachers believe can be implemented effectively at home.
4. Review experts' descriptions of home-based literacy activities that have been shown to have positive transfer value for supporting school-based literacy skills.
5. Describe the "best fit" strategies and activities that can be used as a guide for homework assignments.
6. Write policy statements that dignifiably enable homes to support schools and schools to support homes and list standard activities for use in making homework assignments.
7. Using information from workshops, compile into a Primer of Policy and Practices that make for good home–school connections.

1. View and discuss video "Connecting Families and Schools: Building Partnerships That Work."
2. Teachers present the Primer of Policies and Practices to parents.
3. Parents present the Primer for Parents to teachers.
4. Parents and teachers engage in dialogue about parents' expectations for teachers and teachers' expectations for parents.

(Continued)

TABLE 4.1 (*Continued*)

Goals	Objectives	Sample Activities
	5. To edit and refine home-based support strategies so that they are in concert with school policies, practices, and rules.	5. Parents and teachers edit the primers.
	6. To agree to support the new structure and expectations of teachers in school-based activities.	6. Parents and teachers create pledge cards.
	7. To agree to support the knowledge gained indicating parent expectations and home-based activities that can be used to enhance the instructional strategies in aiding students' literacy learning.	7. Compile information into a Partnership Plan, modeled on the Family–School Compact for Learning. Arrange for policy adoption.
	8. To compose a new inclusive structure and plan by combining the home and school primers into one document, forming a dialogic link from homes to schools and from schools to homes.	8. Arrange for policy adoption and dissemination of partnership plan.

trict's goal of strengthening home–school partnerships; (b) their aware-ness of school policies and practices gave them an increased sense of empowerment; (c) their understanding of the literacy-related and cultur-ally diverse activities found in the homes increased their confidence; and (d) by examining the policies of the school that articulated behavioral expectations for children at the elementary and secondary levels, parents enhanced their ability to talk to teachers and administrators. Marcus con-tinues to refine the modules and to frame empirical methods for testing the efficacy of the underlying assumption that two-way bridges between homes and school will have a greater impact on literacy development than the one-way bridge that currently dominates programs that seek to reduce discontinuities between nonmainstream homes and school.

BET on Learning: The Home–School Connection

This program evolved from a partnership between an urban literacy research and development center at a small historically and predomi-nantly African American institution and Black Entertainment Television (BET). Both authors of this chapter played key roles in developing the lit-eracy center. BET's education director, Rosaland Doaks, engaged the ser-vices of the literacy center to design a program designed to increase the utilization of its educational programs in classrooms across the country. The center's major objective was to create innovative ways of enhancing literacy among nonmainstream groups. Television, often criticized for its negative impact on children's learning, could become a powerful educa-tional tool and a meaningful family literacy event, offering what we saw as a mechanism for improving linkages between homes and school. Thus, the partnership provided an opportunity to devise an innovative approach to positive uses of television.

The partnership was extended to five schools and involved training pro-grams that focused on homework, the most frequently used method of engaging parents in children's learning. By using literacy-based homework assignments, centered on issues treated on the BET *Teen Summit* program, it was possible to fulfill the functional interest that parents have in transmitting their value systems to their children. BET's *Teen Summit* airs for general pub-lic viewing as well as for educational purposes, the latter giving teachers the opportunity to view the program and plan appropriate homework assign-ments. The regular public viewing gives students and parents the opportu-nity to view the program together and to respond to teachers' homework assignments. Homework assignments were designed to foster an apprecia-tion for the uses that can be made of television viewing as a family literacy activity and for encouraging parents to view the education of their children as a shared home–school responsibility. In preparation for viewing the program and completing the homework, workshops were conducted for teachers and for groups of parents, children, and teachers. The goals, objectives, and major topics of the workshops are given in Table 4.2.

The key resources for instructional development were the *Teen Summit* television program and *Young Sisters and Brothers* (*YSB*) magazine, which was used by teachers as a guide for discussions of topics presented on the *Teen Summit* television program. Using *YSB* magazine as a supplement to the *Teen Summit* show enhanced the quality of lessons planned and added exciting possibilities for expanding literacy skills.

Perhaps the most telling dimension of linkages between home and school literacy is the homework assignments. Homework assignments were designed to utilize a variety of reading, writing, and speaking activities. For example, for a *Teen Summit* show on gangs, homework assignments required

TABLE 4.2
BET on Learning: The Home–School Connection

Teacher Workshops	*Parent–Teacher–Student Workshops*
Goal: Teachers develop at least one home–school connection lesson, utilizing at least two types of homework assignments for full development over the 4 months of program implementation.	Goal: The creation of a Profile of Parent Literacy Activities and the development of strategies for supporting children's literacy acquisition and development.
Objective:	Objectives:
To establish a framework for developing literacy-focused in-school lessons and homework assignments that meet standards of effectiveness as set forth in current literature and the criteria identified for attaining maximal success with homework.	To enhance parents' conscious awareness of literacy activities that occur in homes that support school literacy.
	To make explicit teachers' perceptions of the types of homework assignments that are most productive for fulfilling the values of both the home and school.
	To involve students as active participants in the framing of the project.
Major topics:	Major topics:
1. Characteristics of successful homework assignments.	1. Characteristics of supportive responses to homework assignments.
2. Major types of homework assignments.	2. Most and least preferred types of homework assignments.
3. How to align different types of homework with learning purposes.	3. How to strengthen home support of school homework.
4. How to align in-class assignments with natural home-based literacy events.	4. How to align homework assignments with family literacy practices.
5. How to maximize parent involvement.	5. How to use the *Teen Summit* television program and *YSB* magazine to foster closer relations with children and the school.
6. How to use the *Teen Summit* television program and *YSB* (*Young Sisters and Brothers*) magazine in the development of in-class lessons and homework assignments.	

students to ask their parents to recount their experiences with gangs and to produce an essay on differences between gangs of the past and of today. Students were given essay writing assignments on a topic that required students to interview their parents and describe changes that have occurred in America over time. In response to a program that treated educational issues, students were asked to describe the importance of education, as reflected by the views of their parents as well as by their experiences as students. To arrive at such a description, students were assigned interviewing, reading, and writing tasks. A standard activity was oral and written definitions of concepts such as long-term and short-term planning, citizenship, responsibility, drug abuse, teen parenting, and voting. Also frequently used were consciousness-raising questions (e.g., What makes you feel a kinship, loyalty, responsibility to America, to schools, or to families?) Ongoing projects for work with parents included assignments such as designing books for siblings or friends, tape-recorded and transcribed collections of parents' stories, and comparisons of meanings derived by parents and children of remade versions of popular songs. It should be noted that we hoped to encourage family literacy activities through this program. Therefore, assignments were geared toward reviving some of the literacy practices that seem to be disappearing, notably the oral storytelling tradition of African Americans. The culminating exercise was a mock *Teen Summit* with parents and students participating as posse members and as audience, thereby creating a dialogue between students and parents. Such an activity might be carried out in local community centers, schools, or homes; however, because of our collaborative work with the BET network, the mock *Teen Summit* was staged with props and a BET technical crew, along with the host of the televised *Teen Summit*. The mock *Teen Summit* replicated the actual *Teen Summit* except that parents and teens served as the "posse."

Benefits of the program as reported by teachers, parents, and students were encouraging. Teachers were pleased about the greater involvement of parents in students' literacy development. They spoke of their previous lack of awareness and insensitivity to the literacy practices in students' homes. Parents stressed the importance of using the television programs to create neutral grounds for discussing values and problems confronting today's youth. Students were most impressed by the opportunities afforded them to ask parents questions that were of special interest, but that tended to surface only in contentious situations, such as correcting an existing problem.

For the program designers, this program served as an experiment in creating home–school connections. In essence, we learned that helping parents to use television as a home-based literacy event and helping teachers design naturalistic homework yielded benefits not only for reading the *word*, but also for reading the *world*. It is as Freire (1970) suggested, reading the word is a means to the more pragmatic end of reading the world. In this sense, we see then the importance of bridging home to school in the development of literacy, for it is this bridge that will allow us to reach the true meaning of emergent literacy—the idea that we grow into literacy without real beginning or end points.

Throughout this chapter we have been theorizing, not from research but from practical experiences, explorations of how to build two-way bridges between nonmainstream homes and school. We turn finally to the question of research. What are the implications of our practical experiences for research? The following discussion focuses not on implications of research for practice, but implications of practice for research. Three basic questions have emerged from our practical experiences with attempts to bridge two-way bridges between home and school.

The first question is, under what conditions do language functions in nonmainstream homes resemble those of school? Following the work of Moss (1994), as well as our own experiences and observations, we suspect that didactic questions are used in a wide range of school-like literacy activities that occur outside the school. More research needs to be conducted in settings that represent schooling outside the formal school environment.

A second practice-based question is, how do ways of eliciting narratives affect the way that respondents structure stories? Here we note so-called literate strategies in the narratives of both the students and parents. Of special interest is the distinction between topic-centered narratives of White children and topic-associated narratives of African American children. Do the types of questions that are used in homework assignments have a tendency to elicit more topic-centered narratives? Do school-like tasks trigger more school-like uses of language, including topic-centered narratives? Our practical experiences with the training programs tell us that we need to examine more closely the entire range of narrative structures that are used in nonmainstream homes. We wonder if and how much the search for differences influences the type of data collected, the research setting, and the type of participants selected for study. It is easy to fall into a kind of dichotomy-mania when there is an interest in describing differences among groups. Further study is needed to more fully describe the range of narrative styles used in various social contexts in both African American and non–African American communities.

Third, we have begun asking questions about the value of attempting to make common practices in the home (e.g., television viewing) into family literacy events. We are inclined to believe that the supplanting of the admonishment "No Television" with "Know Television" provided the kind of functional basis for home literacy practices that has led many researchers to conclude that function precedes form and convention. Based on responses of parents, the functional value of "knowing" television is that values and experiences can be transmitted in conversations about television programs. The empirical question is whether conscious use of television as a family literacy event can enhance conversational interactions in homes relevant to school literacy and simultaneously address parents' interest in using television viewing as a means to their more noble goal of transmitting cultural values to their children.

Finally, directions for research are suggested in the preceding discussion of discontinuities. Language and literacy functions should represent a continuum of language use that extends from home to school. What we do not understand well enough is how, or if, forms of literacy transmission in homes, such as peer mentoring, apprenticeship learning, and cooperative learning, differ as they move from the home to the school setting. Home practices that appear to be similar to school practices might look and feel very different when they are used in the delivery of instruction in classrooms. For example, do students who come from homes where literacy problems are solved cooperatively rather than as solo performance experience the cooperative arrangements in classrooms as being like those which happened at home? Children may not experience as similar those events that appear parallel from the perspective of educators. It might be possible to conventionalize the familiarity out of home-based literacy practices when these practices are structured for classroom use. There is clearly a need for more research on how the forms that occur naturally in the home environment can be reconfigured to fit the teaching and learning settings of classrooms.

In raising these research questions, we hope to emphasize that the search for ways to reduce discontinuities between nonmainstream homes and school needs to be continued. As in our own work, we believe that research questions that evolve from practice can help to clarify research questions that need to be addressed. In our case, explorations with designing and implementing programs that seek to create a two-way bridge between home and school have resulted in a strong commitment to formalize research on how to create a dialogic link between teachers and parents. Also, we are committed to investigating ways to turn naturally occurring events in the home into family literacy events. These areas hold great promise for learning more about the particularities of emergent literacy and home–school connections.

REFERENCES

Anderson, R., Hiebert, E., Scott, J., & Wilkinson, I. (1985). *Becoming a nation of readers: The report of the Commission on Reading*. Washington, DC: National Institute of Education.

Baugh, J. (1981). Design and implementation of writing instruction for speakers of non-standard English: Perspectives for a national neighborhood literacy program. In B. Cronnell

(Ed.), *The writing needs of linguistically different students* (pp. 17–41). Los Alamitos, CA: SWRL Research and Development.

Bernstein, B. (1964). Elaborated and restricted codes: Their social origins and some consequences. *American Anthropology, 66,* 55–69.

Bloome, D. (1989). Beyond access: An ethnographic study of reading and writing in a seventh grade classroom. In D. Bloome (Ed.), *Classrooms and literacy* (pp. 53–104). Norwood, NJ: Ablex.

Campbell, L. (1996). Issues in service delivery to African American children. In A. Khami, K. Pollock, & J. Harris (Eds.), *Communication development and disorders in African American children* (pp. 73–94). Baltimore: Brookes.

Cazden, C. B. (1986). Classroom discourse. In M. C. Wittrock (Ed.), *Handbook of research on teaching* (3rd ed., pp. 432–463). New York: Macmillan.

Comer, J. (1980). *School power.* New York: The Free Press.

Cooper, J. D. (1993). *Literacy: Helping children construct meaning.* Boston: Houghton Mifflin.

Corno, L. (1989). What it means to be literate about classrooms. In D. Bloome (Ed.), *Classrooms and literacy* (pp. 29–52). Norwood, NJ: Ablex.

Delain, M., Pearson, P., & Anderson, R. (1985). Reading comprehension and creativity in Black language use: You stand to gain by playing the sounding game. *American Educational Research Journal, 22,* 155–173.

Freire, P. (1970). *Pedagogy of the oppressed.* New York: Seabury Press.

Goodman, K. (1965). Dialect barriers to reading comprehension. *Elementary English, 42,* 853–860.

Heath, S. (1983). *Ways with words: Language, life and work in communities and classrooms.* New York: Cambridge University Press.

Hirsch, E. (1987). *Cultural literacy: What every American needs to know.* Boston: Houghton Mifflin.

Irvine, J. (1990). *Black students and school failure: Policies, practices and prescriptions.* New York: Greenwood Press.

Labov, W. (1972). *Language in the inner city: Studies in the Black English vernacular.* Philadelphia: University of Pennsylvania Press.

Levenstein, P. (1983). Implications of the transition period for early education. In B. M. Godlinkoff (Ed.), *The transition from prelinguistic to linguistic communication* (pp. 46–84). Hillsdale, NJ: Lawrence Erlbaum Associates.

Marcus, C. (1996). *Forming connections between homes and schools: The dialogic link.* Unpublished master's thesis, Central State University, Wilberforce, OH.

McGillip, J., & Michael, M. (1994). *The home–school connection: Guidelines for working with parents.* Portsmouth, NH: Heinemann.

Michaels, S. (1981). Sharing time: Children narrative style and differential access to literacy. *Language in Society, 10,* 423–442.

Michaels, S., & Cazden, C. (1986). Teacher–child collaboration as oral preparation for literacy. In B. Schieffelin & P. Gilmore (Eds.), *The acquisition of literacy: Ethnographic perspectives* (pp. 132–154). Norwood, NJ: Ablex.

Morrow, L. (1990). *Literacy development in the early years: Helping children read and write.* Boston: Allyn & Bacon.

Morrow, L. (1997). *Motivating reading and writing in diverse classrooms: Social and physical contexts in a literature-based program.* Urbana, IL: National Council of Teachers of English.

Moss, B. (1994). Creating a community: Literacy events in African American churches. In B. Moss (Ed.), *Literacy across communities* (pp. 147–178). Cresskill, NJ: Hampton Press.

Phillips, S. (1972). Participant structures and communicative competence: Warm Springs in community and classroom. In C. Cazden, V. John, & D. Hymes (Eds.), *Functions of language in the classroom* (pp. 370–394). New York: Teachers College Press.

Phillips, S. (1983). *The invisible culture: Communication in classrooms and community on the Warm Springs Indian Reservation*. New York: Longman.

Scott, C., & Rogers, L. (1996). Written language abilities of African American children and youth. In A. Khami, K. Pollock, & J. Harris (Eds.), *Communication development and disorders in African American children* (pp. 307–332). Baltimore: Brookes.

Scott, J. (1979). Black dialects and reading: Which differences make a difference? In R. Shafer (Ed.), *Applied linguistics and reading* (pp. 51–62). Newark, DE: International Reading Association.

Scott, J. (1988). Nonmainstream groups: Questions and research directions. In J. L. Davidson (Ed.), *Counterpoint and beyond: A response to Becoming a Nation of Readers* (pp. 27–32). Urbana, IL: National Council of Teachers of English.

Scott, J. (1990). The silent sounds of language variation in the classroom. In S. Hynds & D. Rubin (Eds.), *Perspectives on talk and learning* (pp. 285–297). Urbana, IL: National Council of Teachers of English.

Scott, J. (1992). Deficit theories, ethnic dialects, and literacy research: When and why recycling is not cost efficient. In C. Kinzer & D. Leu (Eds.), *Literacy research, theory, and practice: Views from many perspectives* (pp. 49–63). Chicago: The National Reading Conference.

Scott, J. (1998). The serious side of Ebonics humor. *Journal of English Linguistics, 26*(2), 137–155.

Smitherman, G. (1977). *Talking and testifyin': The language of Black America*. Boston: Houghton Mifflin.

Strickland, D. (1985). Early childhood development and reading instruction. In C. Brooks, J. Scott, M. Chaplin, D. Lipscomb, W. Cook, & V. Davis (Eds.), *Tapping potential: English and language arts for the Black learner* (pp. 88–101). Urbana, IL: Black Caucus of the National Council of Teachers of English.

Sulzby, E. (1985). Children's emergent reading of favorite storybooks: A developmental study. *Reading Research Quarterly, 10*, 458–481.

Taylor, D., & Dorsey-Gaines, C. (1988). *Growing up literate: Learning from inner-city families*. Portsmouth, NH: Heinemann.

Taylor, O., & Garrett, D. (1996). Foreword. In A. Khami, K. Pollock, & J. Harris (Eds.), *Communication development and disorders in African American children* (pp. ix–xii). Baltimore: Brookes.

Tharp, R. (1982). The effective instruction of comprehension: Results and description of the Kamehameha Early Education Program. *Reading Research Quarterly, 17*, 503–527.

van Kleeck, A. (1994). Potential cultural bias in training parents as conversational partners with their children who have delays in language development. *American Journal of Speech-Language Pathology, 31*, 67–78.

Wolfram, W. (1991). The community and language arts. In M. C. Wittrock (Ed.), *Handbook of research on teaching* (3rd ed., pp. 470–476). New York: Macmillan.

Chapter 5

Literacy in the African Diaspora: Black Caribbean American Communities[1]

Sherri L. Horner
University of Memphis

> The Caribbean is defined here as the archipelago stretching 2,500 miles from the Bahama Islands and Cuba in the north to Guyana, Suriname, and French Guiana in northern South America, and also including Belise on the Caribbean coast of Central America. These 22 islands and four mainland political entities share geographic proximity and related cultural and historical experiences.
>
> —Segal (1987, p. 44)

Literacy is more than a conglomeration of reading and writing skills: It also encompasses attitudes, behaviors, and symbolic meanings of what it is for an individual to be literate. "*Becoming* and *being* literate are processes

---

[1]There are several terms that are used to refer to people from the Caribbean, and each of these terms has various meanings, depending on individual definitions and personal preferences. Some authors use *West Indian* to refer only to people of African descent, and their descendants, from the English-speaking Caribbean, whereas others include the French- (or Creole-) speaking Caribbean also. Other authors and many people from the Caribbean living in New York City most often use the term *Caribbean*. The Caribbean diaspora includes people of African, Hispanic, and East Indian origins, with many Caribbeans being both Black and Hispanic. Because of the focus of this chapter, I use the terms *Caribbean*, *Black Caribbean*, and *Caribbean American* interchangeably to refer to people of African descent from the Caribbean, and their descendants, regardless of language spoken. When referring specifically to English-speaking and French-speaking Caribbeans, the term *West Indian* is used. For this chapter, I use the term *African American* to refer to North Americans of African descent. The term *Black*, unless otherwise noted, is used to refer to *all* peoples of African descent, of both Caribbean and North American origin.

that can vary across individuals and groups and are shaped and given meaning by society" (Ferdman, 1990, p. 181). For instance, in the Central African Republic (CAR), several of my Gbaya friends could quote, verbatim and at length, French stories that they had learned years before in school, but they could not tell me what they meant. For them, understanding the passages was not important but relating them was. However, for my Muslim friends in CAR, literacy meant being able to recite long passages of the Koran. In modern American society, neither of these activities would be considered literate behaviors because they do not include the ability to decode and comprehend unfamiliar written passages. Scribner and Cole (1981) also found literacy behaviors in the Vai of West Africa that differed from traditional American literacy behaviors.

Heath (1982, 1983) and Reder (1987) delineated ways in which people from different cultural backgrounds contrast in their beliefs, attitudes, and behaviors toward literacy. African American churchgoers define and practice literacy in distinct ways (Moss, chap. 10, this volume), and Scott and Marcus (chap. 4, this volume) detail differences in literacy between the homes of African American schoolchildren and schools. The meaning of literacy and what is defined as a literacy event depend on the cultural background of the people participating in the event and also on the context or setting of the event. The purpose of this chapter is to explain, according to Ogbu's (1981, 1992) cultural–ecological theory, why African American and Caribbean American communities differ in their beliefs, attitudes, and behaviors about literacy and schooling. My examination of the differences in these communities will be both impressionistic and empirical—based on personal observations and on the literature.

BACKGROUND ON CARIBBEANS AND IMMIGRATION

Caribbeans have immigrated to the United States in several distinct movements (Foner, 1987; Kasinitz, 1992; Marshall, 1987). The first wave came at the turn of the 20th century and lasted about three decades. In 1900, the U.S. Census recorded 20,336 foreign-born Blacks[2]; by 1920 these numbers had risen to 73,803 (Kasinitz, 1992). Because of the Immigration Act of 1924, which instituted national quotas, the number of Caribbean

---

[2]Until the 1980 census, researchers used the number of "foreign-born" Blacks as a proxy for West Indians (including Haitians). However, with the more recent influx of Africans into the United States, this can no longer be used (Kasinitz, 1992). Of course, any measurement has some inherent difficulties. For instance, most denote Hispanic as a distinct category although there are many Black Hispanics in the Caribbean and elsewhere.

immigrants was greatly reduced in the following two decades. There was a smaller second wave of Caribbean immigrants during World War II when migrant workers were needed due to shortages in important industries (Marshall, 1987). The largest wave, which continues today, began in 1965 with the passage of the Hart–Cellar Immigration Reform Act. From 1965 to the present, more Caribbeans came to the United States than in the previous 70 years combined (Kasinitz, 1992). As of 1990, there were 229,000 Haitians, 343,000 Jamaicans, and 119,000 people from Trinidad and Tobago residing in the United States (O'Hare, 1992). Unlike earlier migrations when the vast majority of immigrants were men, more of the new immigrants are female (56%; Pessar, 1990). They come from all socioeconomic backgrounds and all regions of the Caribbean.

The vast majority of Black Caribbeans migrate to urban areas. For instance, over half of all Barbadians (70%), Dominicans (76%), Haitians (57%), Jamaicans (50%), and Trinidadians and Tobagians (60%) live in the New York–New Jersey area (Kraly, 1987). Black Caribbeans (excluding Black Hispanics) make up 19% of the New York City Black population and 3% of the U.S. Black population (Kasinitz, 1992).

A CULTURAL–ECOLOGICAL THEORY

Ogbu (1981, 1990, 1992) has developed a cultural–ecological theory to aid our understanding of why different minority groups adapt differently to school and other institutionalized settings, achieve at different rates, and acquire literacy and numeracy differently. Ogbu (1981) delineated two types of minority groups: immigrant, or voluntary, and nonimmigrant, or involuntary. Although his theory has implications for many minority groups in the United States and other countries (e.g., Maori in New Zealand, Burakumin and Koreans in Japan; see Gibson & Ogbu, 1991), this chapter deals only with Black Caribbeans residing in the United States.

Immigrant or voluntary minorities are those groups who have chosen to migrate to the host country, usually because of a belief that they, or their children, will have greater opportunities for success than in their native country. Note that Ogbu (1992) does not consider refugees as immigrant minorities; therefore, some Haitians and other Caribbeans may not be considered immigrant minorities because they are political refugees. However, most Black Caribbeans would be considered immigrant minorities because they have chosen to emigrate to the United States.

During many informal conversations, Caribbean parents of preschoolers at a Brooklyn Head Start Center said that they had moved to New York City so their children could receive a better education and have more career opportunities. Although they were nostalgic for their homelands and they and their children returned to visit as often as possible, most were quite adamant that they would raise their children in the United States to increase their chances economically.

The second group of minorities are nonimmigrant or involuntary (Ogbu, 1981). These are people whose ancestors were brought into their present society by force, either through slavery (African Americans), conquest (Native Americans and many Mexican Americans in the Southwest), or colonization (Puerto Ricans).

Although both immigrant and involuntary minorities experience prejudice and discrimination from the White majority, these groups respond differently because of their distinct histories and cultural backgrounds. Several ways in which these groups of minorities differ are in their frames of reference, folk theories of getting ahead, cultural and language differences, and the degree of trust or acquiescence toward the dominant group (Ogbu, 1991).

Immigrants have a dual frame of reference in that they compare their present living conditions either with their conditions before they emigrated or with the conditions of friends and relatives back home. Because they have chosen, usually for economic reasons, to emigrate, most voluntary minorities have positive dual frames of reference. Therefore, even though they may be in menial jobs and encounter many economic, political, and social difficulties, they still maintain an optimistic view of their, and their children's, future. This contrasts with the beliefs of involuntary minorities. Because they have no "homeland" to compare with their present situation, they make comparisons to the situations of the dominant White group. Because of racism and discrimination in the United States, they develop a negative frame of reference in that they are worse off than the dominant group.

In my college courses on special education, students of both African American and Caribbean backgrounds would discuss the overrepresentation of Blacks in special education classrooms and other forms of discrimination in U.S. school systems. However, the Caribbean students also would compare and contrast the options available to students with disabilities in New York versus their home islands. Several students whose children were disabled actually emigrated because better resources were available for their children in the United States than in the homeland.

One reason for the optimism of immigrant minorities is their folk theory of getting ahead. Although these immigrants may be excluded from the better jobs and have limited career options, they attribute this to being "foreigners," not speaking English well enough, or not being educated in American schools (Ogbu, 1991). In spite of finding barriers, they still believe that a good education will increase their, or their children's, chances of being competitive in the American job market. For instance, many Caribbean parents at a Brooklyn Head Start Center were having their 4- and 5-year-olds tested for giftedness in the hopes of increasing their chances of a good public school education.

Michael (1990) detailed the results from interviews of six Caribbean teenagers. While these parents stressed education to their children, they themselves worked in blue-collar jobs, mostly in private household services. "The parents of these children have ambitions for them—ambitions defined by the American Dream, the histories of past generations of immigrants, and the West Indian folk belief that everyone can succeed" (pp. 250–251). The children themselves also had ambitions: They wanted to become white-collar workers such as lawyers, doctors, and teachers.

Involuntary minorities "often express the wish that they could get ahead through education and ability as members of the dominant group do, but they know that they cannot" (Ogbu, 1991, p. 14). Their folk theory therefore differs from the dominant group and voluntary minorities. Their folk theory tends to stress collective effort, and because they believe that the rules for self-advancement do not work for them, they try to change the rules.

According to Ogbu (1991, 1992), immigrant minorities have primary cultural and language differences; the differences between Caribbean and dominant cultures existed before the immigrants emigrated. Immigrant minorities will continue their beliefs and practices to some extent. However, for those practices they interpret as barriers standing in the way of achieving the goals of their emigration, they attempt to overcome them without interpreting such behaviors as giving up their own culture and language.

Involuntary minorities have secondary cultural and language differences, because these differences developed after they became an involuntary minority (Ogbu, 1991). They perceive their cultural system as not only different but in opposition to the cultural system of their oppressors. Therefore, they do not interpret these differences as barriers they must overcome but rather as "symbols of identity to be maintained" (p. 15).

The final element that distinguishes immigrant minorities and involuntary minorities is the degree of trust and acquiescence they have toward the dominant group, including the institutions they control. In correspondence with their folk theories, immigrants tend to see the prejudice and discrimination against them as due to their immigrant status, not their race or ethnicity. Therefore, they see it as changeable and are willing to acquiesce in order to achieve the goals of their emigration. On the other hand, involuntary minorities see the prejudice and discrimination as due to their race or ethnicity, institutionalized and long lasting. Therefore, they do not trust the dominant group or the institutions run by the dominant group.

One way of documenting these differing views toward the dominant institutions is to investigate school retention rates. According to Rong and Preissle (1998), approximately 90% of 17- and 18-year-old Caribbeans had either graduated from high school or still were in school. This percentage is equal to that for all native-born Americans. The U.S. Census Bureau (Dervarics, 1998) reported that approximately 75% of African Americans age 18 to 24 had attained at least a high school or equivalent degree. Therefore, approximately 15% more Caribbean youths have high school diplomas than do African Americans.

Caribbean students also are accelerated at a higher rate than all native-born Americans. For instance, 29% of Caribbean students have finished elementary school (fifth grade) by age 10 whereas only 19% of all native-born students have done so (Rong & Preissle, 1998). By secondary school, the gap has closed but Caribbeans are still ahead of native-born students: 13% of Caribbeans graduate at age 17 but only 6% of native-born Americans do.

"The cultural models resulting from these differing theories and frameworks are learned by the children of the respective minority types, and these shape the attitudes, knowledge, and competencies the children bring to school" (Ogbu, 1991, p. 17). Individual members of ethnic groups will vary both in the extent of their identification with the group and in the degree to which their behavior is based on the group's cultural norms.

Waters (1994), in an ethnographic study of 83 first- and second-generation Caribbean American teenagers, described three different ways in which these youths identified with their cultural heritage and how their behaviors and attitudes differed accordingly. Those students who took on a Black American identity (42%) tended to develop an oppositional frame of reference. "These teens tend to adopt a peer culture of racial solidarity and opposition to school authorities" (p. 812). They also believed that racial discrimination would prevent them from reaching their goals. These youths would fit the pattern of behavior more similar to involuntary rather than voluntary minorities.

Those youths who developed an ethnic American identity (e.g., Caribbean American, Jamaican American; 30%) tended to attempt to distance themselves from Black Americans. "They specifically see their ethnic identities as keys to upward social mobility, stressing, for instance, that their parents' immigrant values of hard work and strict discipline help them to succeed in the United States when Black Americans fail" (Waters, 1994, pp. 814–815).

The third type of student identified with their immigrant status (28%). These students were usually more recent arrivals and had Caribbean accents and mannerisms; therefore, they identified themselves as Jamaican or Haitian rather than American. The teenagers who identified themselves either ethnically or as immigrants tended to do better in school than those who identified themselves as Black American. As Michael (1990) states, "In the final analysis, in spite of the multiple pressures facing the children of the new wave immigration, most are able to take advantage of opportunities which they never had in their homeland. And, with the will to persist and struggle, many in the end outdo their Black American counterparts" (p. 251).

CONCLUSION

In summary, according to Ogbu's (1981, 1992) cultural–ecological theory, Caribbean Americans, because they chose to immigrate to the United States, have different beliefs, attitudes, and behaviors toward literacy and schooling than do African Americans. Research (Michael, 1990; Rong & Preissle, 1998; Waters, 1994) has begun to document some of these differences; however, studies on Caribbean students in the United States are still very limited.

As this population continues to grow, especially in urban areas such as New York and Miami, researchers need to investigate similarities and differences among Black Caribbean, African American, White American, and other immigrant communities and their literacy behaviors, attitudes, and beliefs. Unfortunately only a handful of studies (Michael, 1990; Rong & Preissle, 1998; Waters, 1994) have looked at Caribbean Americans and their schooling. None have investigated literacy specifically. Therefore, several suggestions for future research are delineated here:

1. Rong and Preissle (1998) documented high school graduation and acceleration rates for different ethnic groups of Americans. However, more researchers need to investigate achievement levels of Caribbean Americans.
2. Heath (1982, 1983), Taylor (1983), and Teale (1986) all documented an array of literacy behaviors within African American communities. Similar ethnographic research needs to be done within Caribbean American communities.
3. To support or refute Ogbu's theory, researchers should develop studies that compare behaviors, attitudes, and beliefs toward literacy of Black Caribbean Americans to those of African Americans, White Americans, and other immigrants.
4. The Caribbean is a very diverse region with immigrants coming from many different islands and socioeconomic backgrounds. They also have had varied educational experiences in their homelands

and in America. Therefore, researchers should also investigate differences and similarities within Caribbean American communities.

5. Another area of interest would be generational differences. Do first, second, and previous generations of Caribbean Americans interact differently in schools and within literacy contexts?

6. Finally, future research should investigate how teachers and other educators can utilize knowledge about Caribbean Americans to help in their literacy development and schooling.

ACKNOWLEDGMENTS

I would like to express my gratitude to Stephen Pape and Merrill Morris for their helpful comments on an earlier draft of this chapter.

REFERENCES

Dervarics, C. (1998). Graduating from school more common among Whites than Blacks or Hispanics. *Population Today, 26*(12), 3–4.

Ferdman, B. M. (1990). Literacy and cultural identity. *Harvard Educational Review, 60*, 181–204.

Foner, N. (1987). Introduction: New immigrants and changing patterns in New York City. In N. Foner (Ed.), *New immigrants in New York* (pp. 1–33). New York: Columbia University Press.

Gibson, M. A., & Ogbu, J. U. (1991). *Minority status and schooling: A comparative study of immigrant and involuntary minorities*. New York: Garland.

Heath, S. B. (1982). What no bedtime story means: Narrative skills at home and school. *Language in Society, 11*, 49–76.

Heath, S. B. (1983). *Ways with words: Language, life, and work in communities and classrooms*. New York: Cambridge University Press.

Kasinitz, P. (1992). *Caribbean New York: Black immigrants and the politics of race*. Ithaca, NY: Cornell University Press.

Kraly, E. P. (1987). U.S. immigration policy and the immigrant populations of New York. In N. Foner (Ed.), *New immigrants in New York* (pp. 56–67). New York: Columbia University Press.

Marshall, D. (1987). A history of West Indian migrations: Overseas opportunities and "safety-valve" policies. In B. B. Levine (Ed.), *The Caribbean exodus* (pp. 15–31). New York: Praeger.

Michael, S. (1990). Children of the new wave immigration: An exploration. In A. W. Bonnett & G. L. Watson (Eds.), *Emerging perspectives on the Black diaspora* (pp. 239–256). Lanham, MD: University Press of America.

Ogbu, J. U. (1981). Origins of human competence: A cultural–ecological perspective. *Child Development, 52*, 413–429.

Ogbu, J. U. (1990). Minority status and literacy in comparative perspective. *Daedalus, 119*, 141–168.

Ogbu, J. U. (1991). Immigrant and involuntary minorities in comparative perspective. In M. A. Gibson & J. U. Ogbu (Eds.), *Minority status and schooling: A comparative study of immigrant and involuntary minorities* (pp. 3–33). New York: Garland.

Ogbu, J. U. (1992). Adaptation to minority status and impact on school success. *Theory Into Practice, 31*, 287–295.

O'Hare, W. P. (1992). America's minorities: The demographics of diversity. *Population Bulletin, 47*(4), 2–47.

Pessar, P. R. (1990). Dominican international migration: The role of households and social networks. In R. W. Palmer (Ed.), *In search of a better life: Perspectives on migration from the Caribbean* (pp. 91–114). New York: Praeger.

Reder, S. M. (1987). Comparative aspects of functional literacy development: Three ethnic American communities. In D. Wagner (Ed.), *The future of literacy in a changing world* (pp. 250–270). Elkins Park, PA: Franklin.

Rong, X. L., & Preissle, J. (1998). *Educating immigrant students: What we need to know to meet the challenges.* Thousand Oaks, CA: Corwin Press.

Scribner, S., & Cole, M. (1981). *The psychology of literacy.* Cambridge, MA: Harvard University Press.

Segal, A. (1987). The Caribbean exodus in a global context: Comparative migration experiences. In B. B. Levine (Ed.), *The Caribbean exodus* (pp. 44–64). New York: Praeger.

Taylor, D. (1983). *Family literacy: Young children learning to read and write.* Portsmouth, NH: Heinemann.

Teale, W. H. (1986). Home background and young children's literacy development. In W. H. Teale & E. Sulzby (Eds.), *Emergent literacy: Reading and writing* (pp. 173–206). Norwood, NJ: Ablex.

Waters, M. C. (1994). Ethnic and racial identities of second-generation Black immigrants in New York City. *International Migration Review, 28*, 795–820.

Chapter 6

Reading the Typography of Text

James Hartley
Keele University

Joyce L. Harris
University of Memphis

Reading is a multicomponent cognitive task whose complexity is largely hidden from the consciousness of most readers. However, every reader—irrespective of age, ethnicity, or skill level—must encounter and then decipher graphic symbols, the essence of written language and print literacy. This chapter, therefore, does not purport to address issues that are unique to readers who are African American. Rather, we believe that a discussion about typography and text organization has a rightful place in any treatment of print literacy. We also believe that the frequent omission of such discussion can best be attributed to the human tendency to overlook the obvious. Moreover, the dizzying array of fonts, font sizes, font styles, special effects, and color options—once available only to typesetters—now pose an almost irresistible lure for designers of computer-generated print materials. Thus, we believe that informed consideration of the organization and appearance of print materials will improve the design, or selection, of features that facilitate decoding and reading comprehension. It is likely that such accommodations will prove especially beneficial to beginning and low-literacy readers.

In this chapter, we begin by making some general comments about reading that have relevance for the typographic setting of text in print and text on computer screens. We then move on to suggest how the typographic design of text either can support, or be manipulated to support, different reading skills. Finally, we consider how writing instruction, particularly using word-processing technology, can help individuals better "read" (i.e., understand) the typography of text.

The perceptual–cognitive task at the molecular level of text processing involves discriminating between symbolic marks and deciding whether or not these marks are meaningful. Typically, skilled readers carry out this process unconsciously as they pursue the more global objectives of searching for ideas and meaning. For example, most readers are unaware of their visual fixations, saccades, and regressions during reading (Huey, 1908; Manguel, 1996). Likewise, they are unconcerned with the laborious grapheme-to-phoneme conversions that so distract beginning and low-literacy readers. Nor, indeed, are most readers aware of having learned the conventions of text organization, layout, and typography that are so basic to deciphering written language. Nonetheless, all of this unconscious processing by skilled readers is far from unconscious for beginning readers. Thus, what may seem to skilled readers to be only small typographic details (e.g., concerning typefaces, typesizes, spacing, etc.) are actually important concerns for beginning or low-literacy readers (see Box 6.1).

Ann Henshaw asked 5-year-old children to explain to her why we had periods or "dots" at the end of sentences. Following is a sample of the replies.

"Well...the ones with dots on *should* have dots on. It's the words... Well sometimes you *don't* need one. When you've had enough of doing dots you don't do one 'cos then it won't make your arm ache."

"Some words need them. Some words don't."

"It's for if you go off the page and go on to the desk...you stop...you don't start again...you start again after a minute or two."

"It's to tell you when they've finished."

"When they have to finish a page of writing they have them...if there's no room and you have to go on to another page they put a [period] there. Then the put a picture...then they go to another page...then a picture."

"I stops you from doing writing."

"It's at the end of your work you put one. You get told off if you don't."

"It's to finish a sentence. If you don't put a {period} and you write a letter people might think you've forgotten to [mail] the other half."

"Look," (reading aloud) "Then it is the [period]. See?...I miss out a bit of my voice and I start again."

BOX 6.1.   An illustration of how the smallest of typographic conventions has to be learned. From "The Fullstop," by A. Henshaw, 1983, *Times Educational Supplement, 15.7.83*, p. 17. Adapted with permission of the author and the *Times Educational Supplement*.

Consider, for example, how the order of the letters can have a profound effect on meaning (compare *god* with *dog*), and so too can spacing (compare *the rapist* with *therapist*) and grouping (compare *to let* with *toilet*). Punctuation also plays a part (compare *Give experience with dates* with *Give experience, with dates*), and so too does prior knowledge (consider what you need to know to understand the sentence *The young man the jumps*). Clearly, the conventions of written language, unconsciously processed or not, are an important issue in a broad discussion of literacy.

Skilled readers read texts for many different purposes. They may be following instructions, searching for something that they have read somewhere before, or looking for something new. They may be skimming the text to get the gist of an argument, or they may be reading deeply so that they can recall and use the information in some forthcoming task. They may be reading for pleasure, or because they are bored. Skilled readers use different strategies as appropriate when they deliberately search text, look for section headings, pause to reread things that are difficult, and stop to question themselves about their understanding of the content (Brown & Pressley, 1994).

Not only do skilled readers read for different purposes but they, themselves, differ in their interests, motivations, reading proficiency, and cognitive styles (Jonassen & Grabowski, 1993). Some readers are more visualizers than verbalizers, some read more deeply than others, some might be visually impaired, and some, if not all, will adjust their reading methods to match the task at hand. And all, conceivably, are more skilled at reading some kinds of texts than others, owing to various levels of domain-specific knowledge. Readers, therefore, are as diversified as are the sundry reasons and texts that they peruse.

TYPOGRAPHY AND READING

In this section we discuss how the typography and layout of a text can help or hinder skilled and beginning readers. Under the headings Typography, Layout, Typographic Cueing, and Access Structures (devices used to help readers gain access to the text), we consider how this can be done. Moreover, we argue that typographic detailing assists with the molecular, or unconscious, processing described previously, and that layout and access devices facilitate more global, or conscious, aspects of reading.

Typography

Typesizes. For historical reasons the measurement systems used in typography for print are varied and complex (see Manguel, 1996; Schriver, 1997). Clearly, there are many different typefaces and typesizes, but for all practical purposes, most publishers are likely to choose between one or two typefaces and one or two typesizes for a particular text. Typesizes generally vary in practice from about 6 point to around 14 point, but sizes of 8, 9, 10, 11, and 12 point are considered the most effective (see Fig. 6.1). One point, in fact, measures approximately 0.014 of an inch, and the typesize refers to the depth of space required by one line of type set "solid" (i.e., with minimum line-to-line space). Larger typesizes are typically used for headings and posters.

When discussing typesize, however, it is important to note that the size of the image conveyed by the same point size in different typefaces actually differs according to the typeface (see Fig. 6.2). Furthermore, in advocating a particular size, commentators appear to forget that most readers can compensate for differences in typesize by adjusting their focal depth. Choosing a typesize is therefore not an exact science, and any particular choice has to be related to other issues—such as typeface, line length, and interlinear spacing (Hartley, 1994; Schriver, 1997).

Nonetheless, it is possible to make some recommendations. Typesize considerations, for example, are important in print when using narrow column widths. Larger typesizes mean fewer words per line (as shown in Fig. 6.1) and this may break the sense of the text, thereby reducing comprehension. This is an important factor to bear in mind when producing books for young children, low-literacy readers, the visually impaired, and possibly older people (Hartley, 1994; Schriver, 1997).

8 point typesize affects line length as well as letter height.

10 point typesize affects line length as well as letter height.

12 point typesize affects line length as well as letter height.

FIG. 6.1.   Different typesizes affect line length as well as letter height.

This line is written in 12 point Arial.

This line is written in 12 point Times Roman.

This line is written in 12 point Bookman.

This line is written in 12 point Century Schoolbook

FIG. 6.2.   The same typesize in different typefaces produces different effects.

Typefaces.   Typefaces can be divided into many different categories, but the two main ones are serif and sans serif faces. *Serif* typefaces have small finishing strokes at the top and bottom of each letter. (Sans serif, as shown in this sentence, do not.) There is a great deal of debate about the supposed virtues of each kind of face. Some researchers believe that serifs help to guide the reader's eye along each letter and word (especially at the top), but there is little conclusive proof for such assumptions (Hartley, 1994; Schriver, 1997). Nonetheless, our particular preference is generally for a serif face, largely because we think that serifs make the letters more evenly spaced, and hence more legible. Indeed, words such as *illicit* can look very odd in a sans serif typeface.

Perhaps the most important difference, however, lies in how these different kinds of typefaces can be used. It is now becoming common practice, for example, to present tables, or figure and table captions, in a sans serif typeface to differentiate this information from the main body of the text, if this is printed in a serif typeface. Sans serif often is used also to represent the printed letters of beginning writers.

Different typefaces, too, carry different connotations, or emotional meanings, to skilled readers (Harrison & Morris, 1967; Lewis & Walker, 1989). For example, we are familiar with the use of italic letters on wedding invitations to convey a sense of formality and solemnity. In Great Britain, Gothic letters might appear on funeral announcements, whereas in the United States, they might appear in reference to Halloween and on playbills for horror movies. Times Roman, on the other hand, is typically used in academic prose, where it conveys an academic flavor to readers. Accordingly, typefaces should be chosen with regard to what seems most appropriate for the task at hand (Schriver, 1997). Typically, it is safest to follow the traditional practices of the literate culture.

Layout

The layout of a text is just as important, if not more so, than the typeface chosen to print it. Indeed, layout considerations drive the choices of typeface and size (Hartley, 1994). Importantly, style and layout can create a welcoming, reader-friendly impression, an important consideration for many beginning and low-literacy readers (Doak, Doak, & Root, 1996).

Page-size.   The first major decision with printed text is to decide on what size page to print it. This choice is determined by how the text is to be used and by the components in the content. Text that consists of little more than run-on prose, like chapters in a novel, poses few problems and constraints. Conversely, text that is made up of instructions, diagrams, illustrations, lists, footnotes, and other such materials, is much more problematic. Thus, the layout of a child's junior high school science book, with its numerous lists, boxes, and illustrations to facilitate comprehension and learning, presents more production considerations than does, for example, an undergraduate philosophy textbook.

Hartley (1994) described how pages can be arranged vertically (in portrait style) or horizontally (in landscape). For each arrangement, the pages can be bound on the left or at the top (in notebook style). With larger pages a decision has to be made about the number—one, two, three, or more—of columns of print to use. In addition, the amount of space allotted to margins and to gutters between the columns must be determined. It is here that choices about typesizes and faces are made. Even small details, such as where to put the page numbers, are constrained by these earlier decisions. Whatever choices are made, they must be adhered to consistently throughout the text, as it confuses the reader to find format changes from page to page.

Spacing the Text. Letter spacing, word spacing, and line spacing are all important issues in clarifying text in print and on screen. Spacing that is too narrow can make it difficult to discriminate between the letters, the words, and the lines. And, as we see later, reading is easier when word and line spacing are consistent throughout a text (see Fig. 6.3).

In Fig. 6.4, the designer has used horizontal justification in the top illustration; that is to say, the text has straight left- and right-hand margins. In books, the print on each page begins and ends at the same point; this is called vertical justification. This balanced, rectangular approach is achieved by varying the amount of space between the words (or between the letters in narrow columns) and between the lines (especially if different heading levels are used on a single page).

An alternative approach is to use equal word and line spacing, or unjustified text. Here the spacing between the words is consistent, producing a ragged right margin, and the spacing above and below the lines and the elements in the headings, subheadings, captions, and so on, can be decided on in advance and used consistently throughout the text.

Justified text does not pose many problems for skilled readers while reading text that is relatively simple, typographically speaking (Schriver, 1997). But in our view, unjustified text is more appropriate for texts that are typographically more complex. The lower half of Fig. 6.4 provides an illustration. In addition, some researchers suggest that unjustified text is more suitable than justified text for young children learning to read, and for older readers (see Hartley, 1994).

Space and Structure. Finally, in this section, we need to consider one other feature of space and how it can be used to convey the underlying structure of a piece of text. Spacing is important, because it is used to sep-

In this paragraph the text is set solid, that
is, there is no extra space set between the   *12 point set solid*
lines. Large amounts of such text would
be difficult to read.

In this paragraph the lines are separated

by a one and a half-line of space. This   *12 point with 1.5 spacing*

spacing improves the legibility of the text.

In this paragraph the lines are separated

by a 'double-space'. This is thought of as

the optimum amount of line space for   *12 point double-spaced*

submitting articles for publication, but it is

probably too much for normal reading.

FIG. 6.3.   The effects of interline spacing.

arate letters, words, lines, paragraphs, section headings, and chapters
from each other. When the appropriate amount of space is used *consistently*
at each of these junctures, this white space can enhance the reader's
understanding of complex materials (Hartley, 1994). Effective spacing
also helps readers to know where they should go next, as it conveys structure and sequence at a glance (see Fig. 6.4). Inappropriate spacing is confusing.

Typographic Cuing

Typographic cues are devices used by authors and printers to enhance
both the textual and spatial components of text, thus addressing the
author's concern for the readers' comprehension and the printer's for leg-

Now the sons of Jacob were twelve. The sons of Leah: Reuben,
Jacob's firstborn, and Simeon, and Levi, and Judah, and Issachar, and
Zebulun. The sons of Rachel: Joseph and Benjamin. And the sons of
Bilhar, Rachel's handmaid: Dan and Naphtali. And the sons of Zilpah,
Leah's handmaid: Gad and Asher. These were the sons of Jacob,
which were born to him in Padanaram.

Now the sons of Jacob were twelve.

>   The sons of Leah:
>   Reuben, Jacob's firstborn, and
>   Simeon, and Levi, and Judah, and
>   Issachar, and Zebulun.

>   The sons of Rachel:
>   Joseph and Benjamin.

>   And the sons of Bilhar, Rachel's handmaid:
>   Dan and Naphtali.

>   And the sons of Zilpah, Leah's handmaid:
>   Gad and Asher.

These were the sons of Jacob, which were born to him in Padanaram.

FIG. 6.4.   The effects of line spacing. Top: original text, justified. Bottom:
the same text, unjustified, and with regular units of line space to show the
underlying structure of the content.

ibility. We believe that the spatial cues previously discussed are more
important, but we accept that they can be enhanced by the addition of
typographic cues. Thus, headings may stand out more clearly if they are
signified in capital letters, bold type, color, or italics. Young children, and
readers with low literacy skills, of course, need to have these changes in
word images explained to them (Moore & Scevak, 1997), as such conscious awareness may lead to greater self-efficacy when they encounter
various reading tasks. One cannot assume that the significance of typographic cues is apparent to all.

Capital Letters.   Words printed in uppercase letters have less distinc-
tive information per unit of space than do words set in lowercase letters
(Hartley, 1994). This makes paragraphs of text set in capital letters—as,
for example, in some warning notices—difficult to read. Writers often also
use capital letters to emphasize a particular word or phrase (e.g., DO
NOT . . .). This may be acceptable, but the same wording in **bold lowercase** letters would probably do as well.

Italicized Letters. Whole passages set in italics are more difficult to read than passages set in normal type (Hartley, 1994). Another problem is that typesetters use italicized letters to signify several different things, and this might be confusing for less experienced readers. For example, italics might indicate a book title ("In *The Biology of the Bean*, the author . . ."), provide a subheading (*Feeling the Bean*), introduce a technical term ("What color is the seed coat, or *testa?*"), draw attention to something (e.g., "How are the seeds *attached* to it?"), or particularize ("Can the testa be removed easily with a *dissecting* needle?").

Color. Color is a major typographic cue that is used in text for a number of different purposes. Color can be used decoratively for motivational and aesthetic reasons, and color can be used functionally to aid the reader's ability to follow and understand the text. Most people seem to agree that color illustrations are desirable from a *motivational* point of view, although the research suggests that the motivational effect of color illustrations varies greatly with the age, intelligence, and education of the reader. Younger children and less able readers pay more attention to illustrations than do older, more able readers (Hartley, 1994).

Some researchers, however, have gone so far as to suggest that the primary function of most color illustrations in textbooks is to make the product more marketable. They argue further that, in children's books, particularly picture books for very young children, much of the pictorial material is designed more to reflect adult tastes than the learning requirements of children.

Most tourists will agree that good examples of the functional use of color are provided by the maps in the London and Paris subway systems in Europe and the Washington, DC, system in the United States. Several different colors are used, and each one denotes a different route. The Paris system has the added advantage that each route is also numbered, which provides support for the colorblind, a significant subgroup of adult readers (discussed later). The use of color is a helpful addition to line drawings and illustrations, particularly technical ones (Dwyer, 1978, 1987).

In specifying the use of color in texts (or on screen) it is important to bear in mind the following:

- About 8.5% of males and 0.5% of females are colorblind to some extent.
- If reference is made to a particular color in the text, then that color must have a name in the language of the reader.
- A pale color, visible when seen in a large area, may be almost invisible when used to print a word or a fine line.

- A dark color will appear almost black when it is used to print a word or a fine line.
- Colors disappear when they are photocopied using black and white.
- Legibility is impaired when black is printed on a strongly colored background.
- Legibility is impaired when pale colors are used on pale backgrounds.
- Legibility is severely impaired when text is printed over color illustrations or photographs.
- Legibility is improved when dark colors are used on pale backgrounds (black on white or yellow is best) and when light colors are used on dark backgrounds.

Multiple Cuing.   It is clear from this discussion that there are many ways of cuing important words or phrases and, indeed, people are tempted to use more cues than are necessary. We might well ask, for example, if a heading is printed in lowercase bold, does it need to be larger, in italic, and in a different color as well?

The scant amount of research on this topic suggests that multiple cuing can be confusing. Hershberger and Terry (1965), for example, concluded their article by saying, "Simple typographic cuing significantly enhances the ratio of important to unimportant content learned without reducing the total amount learned," but "complex typographic cuing (distinguishing five categories of lesson content) does not appear to benefit the reader in the least" (p. 59).

Today's printed texts are undoubtedly more colorful than they used to be (LaSpina, 1998), and screen-based text can often be a riot of color, with many different colors used on many different-colored backgrounds. Readers prefer such colorful texts to black-and-white ones, even if this color has no measurable effects on reading comprehension. What printers and screen designers have to be on guard against, however, is the (mis)use of color that makes the text more difficult to read (Keys, 1993; Woods, Johannesen, & Potter, 1993).

Access Structures

The term *access structure* was coined by Waller (1979) to describe devices that help the reader access and read text in a variety of ways. Access structures use both spatial and typographic cues to group relatively large chunks of text and to sequence them appropriately. Knowledge about various texts' access structures and informational organization aids comprehension and learning at all skill levels and ages (Doak, Doak, & Root, 1996; Ellis, 1991).

In this section we briefly consider four kinds of access structure: summaries, headings, numbering systems, and lists. We need to note here, of course, that there are many others, such as footnotes, contents pages, indexes, boxed asides, running heads (at the tops of pages), and different ways of signaling new paragraphs. Hartley (1994) reviewed the research on the design of these additional features.

Summaries. Summaries help readers to recall salient information, but there is some debate about whether they do this better if they are placed at the beginning or end of a piece of text (Murray & McGlone, 1997). Some authors, of course, distinguish between and use different kinds of summaries. Hartley (1994), for example, used beginning *overview* summaries, for each of his chapters, to provide a description in general terms of what was to follow; partway *interim* summaries to summarize the text so far; and concluding *review* summaries to summarize the chapter overall. Often, review summaries include more technical vocabulary, introduced in the chapter itself, than would be appropriate in a beginning summary.

Headings. Headings help readers to perceive the overall structure of a text and aid its recall (Lorch, Lorch, & Inman, 1993). In addition, headings aid search and retrieval (Hartley & Trueman, 1985). There is some discussion over the optimum frequency for headings, their length, their position (marginal or embedded), their style (e.g., questions vs. statements), and their quality, because, for example, poorly conceived headings can mislead. Some investigators have suggested that, for less able readers, headings written in the form of questions are more suitable than those written in the form of statements. However, so far, the research has not supported this idea (Hartley & Trueman, 1985). Others have indicated that headings are particularly helpful for readers with high prior knowledge (Wilhite, 1989).

Numbering Systems. Some writers use numbering systems to help sequence their text. Government reports, technical materials, and even some book chapters have sections and paragraphs numbered 1.00, 1.01, 1.02, 2.00, and so on. Some numbering systems, intended to aid retrieval, can be confusing. This is especially true when there are references in the text to other numbering systems, or when the system is extremely detailed—2.01.03, for example. Waller (1977) and Smith and Aucella (1983) provide examples.

Lists. In many texts the content, although presented in continuous prose, is in reality a list. Figure 6.5 shows an example. It is often helpful to separate the items in the list, using either numbers or bullets (as in Fig.

Five devices that aid the reader are (i) skeleton outlines for each
chapter, (ii) headings in the text, (iii) an end summary, (iv) a glossary
for new technical terms, and (v) a comprehensive index.

Five devices that aid the reader are:
  (i) skeleton outlines for each chapter,
  (ii) headings in the text,
  (iii) an end summary,
  (iv) a glossary for new technical terms, and
  (v) a comprehensive index.

Five devices that aid the reader are:
• skeleton outlines for each chapter,
• headings in the text,
• an end summary,
• a glossary for new technical terms, and
• a comprehensive index.

Five devices that aid the reader are:
    • skeleton outlines for each chapter,
    • headings in the text,
    • an end summary,
    • a glossary for new technical terms, and
    • a comprehensive index.

FIG. 6.5.   Different ways of sequencing list material.

6.5). Designers suggest that it is best to use numbers when the items in the
list have a particular order, and bullets when it really does not matter
which item comes first.

Tables of contents, bibliographies, and indexes are all examples of different kinds of lists. Each consists of a string of main entries, all of which
contain a number of sub-elements. The task of the designer is to display
both the main elements and the sub-elements clearly, because different
people will want to use the list in different ways. Printers and screen
designers typically do this by using different typographic cues when, in
our view, a more judicious use of spacing, perhaps with one or two typographic cues, would be preferable. Figure 6.6 provides an example, and
additional examples can be found in Hartley (1994).

TYPOGRAPHY AND WRITING

The typographic conventions that we have discussed so far all have to be
taught to beginning readers. One way to teach these conventions is to
ensure that children use them in writing their own texts. In fact, we think
that all that we have said so far has implications for writing instruction.

Burnhill, P. Hartley, J. & Davies, L. (1980). Lined paper, legibility and creativity. In J. Hartley (Ed.), *The psychology of written communication* (pp. 82-91). London: Kogan Page.

Dwyer, F. M. (1978). *Strategies for improving visual learning.* Box 784, State College, Pennsylvania: Learning Services.

Fowler, R. L. & Barker, A. S. (1974). Effectiveness of highlighting for retention of text material. *Journal of Applied Psychology, 59,* 358-364.

Hartley, J. (1994). *Designing instructional text* (3rd edition). East Brunswick, N.J.: Nichols.

Burnhill, P. Hartley, J. & Davies, L. (1980).

    Lined paper, legibility and creativity.

    In J. Hartley (Ed.), *The psychology of written communication* (pp. 82-91).

    London: Kogan Page.

Dwyer, F. M. (1978).

    Strategies for improving visual learning.

    Box 784, State College, Pennsylvania: Learning Services.

Fowler, R. L. & Barker, A. S. (1974).

    Effectiveness of highlighting for retention of text material.

    Journal of Applied Psychology, 59, 358-364.

Hartley, J. (1994).

    Designing instructional text (3rd edition).

    East Brunswick, N.J.: Nichols.

FIG. 6.6. Spatial versus typographic cuing in lists. Top: references set in the traditional manner, using mainly typographic cues to separate authors, titles, and places of publication. Bottom: references set in a more readable manner, using mainly spatial cues to separate these elements.

Our earlier discussion about serif and sans serif faces, for example, has implications for reading and for writing. It might appear that when children are learning to write individual letters, a sans serif face would be the best style to copy. But it might be wise to think about joining letters from the start when learning to write. So serif faces in children's reading books might be more appropriate. Indeed, in the United Kingdom there is interest in a new family of typefaces called Sassoon Primary that makes such a link between handwriting and reading (see Sassoon, 1993). Figure 6.7 gives an example.

Our discussion about the spacing of the text also has clear relevance for writing instruction, as children need to learn about the spacing between letters, words, sentences, paragraphs, and headings. Some current conventions in this respect need closer examination.

Children, for example, are often taught to use a "finger space" between words when learning to write. The resulting product is likely to suffer from too large a space between the words, making the text difficult to read. Furthermore, children are often encouraged to write on unlined paper. The consequences of this can be seen in Fig. 6.8. It is hard for children to keep physical control without guidance (Burnhill, Hartley, & Davies, 1980). Aligned text is especially critical in writing arithmetic calculations, for example.

These examples suggest that we need to think more about the use of lined paper, and possibly squared (i.e., grid) paper, for enabling children to grasp the conventions of typography. Most exercise books and notebooks in Europe, but not England, have squared paper. In our view, lined

Sassoon Sans

He was right out of the water and away from the waves and he lay still. He rolled on to his back, and lay very still. He lay there for a long time. He blew and puffed, and lay there on the sand. And as he lay there, the wind blew more softly and the clouds began to blow away. There was a little blue sky. The sun began to shine a little.

FIG. 6.7. A typeface (Sassoon Primary) developed to make a link between handwriting and reading. (Excerpt reproduced with permission of Rosemary Sassoon.)

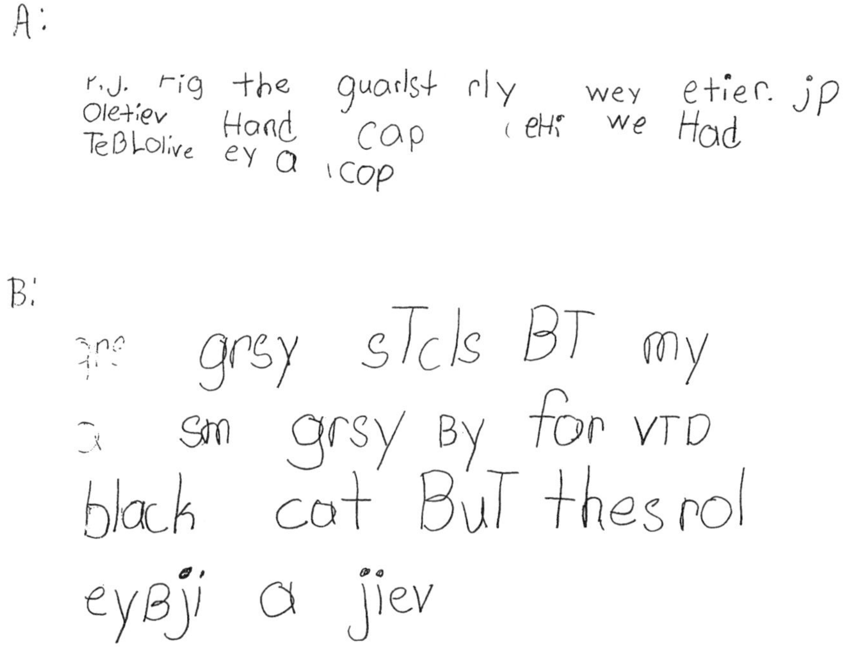

FIG. 6.8.   Examples of a child's writing on unlined and lined paper.

paper is extremely helpful, but we are not so sure about squares or grids for writing. Different words with the same number of letters have different widths (compare *difficulties* with *commensurate*), so writing in a grid is not a natural practice for most of us. Perhaps what is needed is paper with a set of (say three) vertical lines, the first to indicate the starting point (or left margin), the next to indicate the start of an indent, and the third to indicate the starting point for a double indent, for a list or outline.

Perhaps the best way to teach children the conventions of typography, however, is to allow them to explore these conventions for themselves by using word processors to produce written documents of their own. Certain groups of children, however, have limited, or no, access to computers (see Huff & Rogers, chap. 13, this volume), and greater efforts to provide other opportunities for generating texts should be made on their behalf. In either case, young writers will have to consider the audience for their texts (other children? teachers? parents? politicians?); the kinds of texts they want to produce (story? informational text? poster? directory?); and the page size, typesizes and styles, and kinds of typographic cuing to be employed. Examples of good (and poor) writing samples can be collected, discussed, evaluated, and copied. Mock-ups and actual texts can be produced. One of the key benefits of word-processing technologies is that they allow writers to experiment, to try out different solutions, and to make modifications before settling on a final version. Furthermore, working in pairs or small groups necessitates discussion about the most appropriate solution and why that solution seems to work. Such an approach honors and motivates students (Teel, Debruin-Parecki, & Covington, 1998).

CONCLUSION

In this chapter we have sought to explain how current typographic practice can make texts easier or harder to read, and how every reader, regardless of age, ethnicity, or skill level, can benefit from informed text design. In a similar vein, we have suggested that the conventions of typography and access to written materials can be taught to the benefit of beginning readers, as well as learners of every age and description. Many examples of poor typographic practice, as catalogued by Hartley (1998), exist; however, additional research is needed to reveal to what extent readers of different skill levels are affected by poorly designed textual materials. In the absence of sufficient empirical evidence, as yet, it would seem that beginning and low-literacy readers will have more difficulty than others comprehending poorly designed texts. Word-processing technologies offer a virtually penalty-free way to experiment with writing conventions, and this potential advantage, alone, should urge increased advocacy for equity in computer access in educational settings.

Finally, if we want readers and writers to become fully literate, we must not only expose them to well-designed texts, but we must also teach them to "read" the conventions of texts and to recognize these conventions as essential elements of the message. As stated previously, we believe that integrated reading and writing instruction will facilitate such understanding. No doubt, as we move further into the 21st century, new technologies will play a greater role than ever before in literacy acquisition and use. However, as before, we must concede that the clarity of the message rules—not over and above—but with the assistance of technology.

REFERENCES

Brown, R., & Pressley, M. (1994). Self-regulated reading and getting meaning from the text: The transaction strategies instruction model and its ongoing validation. In D. H. Schunck & B. J. Zimmerman (Eds.), *Self-regulation of learning and performance* (pp. 155–179). Hillsdale, NJ: Lawrence Erlbaum Associates.

Burnhill, P., Hartley, J., & Davies, L. (1980). Lined paper, legibility and creativity. In J. Hartley (Ed.), *The psychology of written communication* (pp. 82–91). London: Kogan Page.

Doak, C. C., Doak, L. G., & Root, J. H. (1996). *Teaching patients with low literacy skills* (2nd ed.). Philadelphia: Lippincott.

Dwyer, F. M. (1978). *Strategies for improving visual learning.* (Available from Learning Services, Box 784, State College, PA)

Dwyer, F. M. (1987). *Enhancing visualized instruction—Recommendations for practitioners.* (Available from Learning Services, Box 784, State College, PA)

Ellis, D. B. (1991). *Becoming a master student* (6th ed.). Rapid City, SD: College Survival, Inc.

Harrison, C., & Morris, C, D. J. (1967). Communication theory and typographic practice. *Journal of Typographic Research, 1*(2), 115–124.

Hartley, J. (1994). *Designing instructional text* (3rd ed.). East Brunswick, NJ: Nichols.

Hartley, J. (1998). Return to sender: Why written communications fail. *The Psychologist, 11,* 477–480.

Hartley, J., & Trueman, M. (1985). A research strategy for text designers: The role of headings. *Instructional Science, 14,* 99–155.

Hershberger, W. A., & Terry. D. F. (1965). Typographical cueing in conventional and programmed texts. *Journal of Applied Psychology, 49,* 55–60.

Huey, E. B. (1908). *The psychology and pedagogy of reading.* New York: Macmillan. (Reissued in 1986 by MIT Press)

Jonassen, D. H., & Grabowski, B. L. (1993). *Handbook of individual differences, learning, and instruction.* Hillsdale, NJ: Lawrence Erlbaum Associates.

Keys, E. (1993). Typography, color and information structure. *Technical Communication, 40,* 638–654.

LaSpina, J. A. (1998). *The visual turn and the transformation of the textbook.* Mahwah, NJ: Lawrence Erlbaum Associates.

Lewis, C., & Walker, P. (1989). Typographic influences on reading. *British Journal of Psychology, 80,* 241–258.

Lorch, R. F., Lorch, E. P., & Inman, W. E. (1993). Effects of signaling topic structure on text recall. *Journal of Educational Psychology, 85,* 281–290.

Manguel, A. (1996). *A history of reading.* New York: Viking.

Moore, P. J., & Scevak, J. (1997). Learning from texts and visual aids: A developmental perspective. *Journal of Research in Reading, 20,* 205–223.

Murray, J. D., & McGlone, C. (1997). Topic overviews and the processing of topic structure. *Journal of Educational Psychology, 89,* 251–261.

Sassoon, R. (1993). Through the eyes of a child—Perception and type design. In R. Sassoon (Ed.), *Computers and typography* (pp. 150–177). Oxford, England: Intellect.

Schriver, K. A. (1997). *Dynamics in document design: Creating text for readers.* New York: Wiley.

Smith, S. L., & Aucella, A. F. (1983). Numbering formats for hierarchic lists. *Human Factors, 25,* 343–348.

Teel, K. M., Debruin-Parecki, A., & Covington, M. (1998). Teaching strategies that honor and motivate inner-city African-American students: A school/university collaboration. *Teaching and Teacher Education, 14,* 479–495.

Waller, R. H. W. (1977). Notes on transforming: No. 4. In J. Hartley (Ed.), *The psychology of written communication* (pp. 145–153). London: Kogan Page.

Waller, R. H. W. (1979). Typographic access structures for instructional text. In P. A. Kolers, M. E. Wrolstad, & H. Bouma (Eds.), *Processing of visible language* (pp. 175–187). New York: Plenum.

Wilhite, S. C. (1989). Headings as memory facilitators: The importance of prior knowledge. *Journal of Educational Psychology, 81,* 115–117.

Woods, D. D., Johannesen, L., & Potter, S. S. (1993). The sophistry of guidelines: Revisiting recipes for color use in human–computer interface design. In *Proceedings of the Human Factors and Ergonomics Society 36th Annual Meeting, 1992.* Santa Monica, CA: Human Factors and Ergonomics Society.

Chapter 7

The Path to Reading Success or Failure: A Choice for the New Millennium

Alan G. Kamhi
University of Oregon

Sandra P. Laing
University of Alabama

The path to proficient reading begins well before children receive formal reading instruction in school and continues until they can recognize words accurately and with little effort. Most normally developing readers develop accurate, effortless word recognition skills in the first few years of elementary school. The period of time before formal reading instruction has come to be known as the period of emergent literacy. From birth until the beginning of formal education (age 5 or 6 in the United States), children growing up in literate cultures accumulate knowledge about letters, words, and books. How much literacy knowledge children acquire during this period depends on how much exposure they have to literacy artifacts and events as well as their interest and facility in learning. At one end of the continuum are children from low-literacy homes who have little exposure to literacy artifacts and events, as well as children who have language-learning problems. These children begin school without much literacy knowledge. At the other end of the continuum are children from high-literacy homes who have the linguistic and cognitive skills to soak up knowledge about spoken and written language. Particularly precocious children may enter kindergarten with relatively proficient word recognition skills.

In this chapter, we begin by considering the types of knowledge children from high-literacy homes acquire during the emergent literacy period. In the second part of the chapter, studies are reviewed that compare the early literacy experiences of children raised in high- and low-literacy families. In the final part of the chapter, we consider other factors that contribute to reading failure, as well as the kinds of programs and changes in teacher education necessary to prevent and reduce reading failure in this country.

EARLY LITERACY EXPERIENCES

From birth until the beginning of formal education, children growing up in high-literacy families are exposed to a variety of literacy artifacts and literacy events. The term *literacy socialization* has been used to refer to the social and cultural aspects of learning to read. Van Kleeck and Schuele (1987) discussed three specific areas of literacy socialization: (a) literacy artifacts, (b) literacy events, and (c) the types of knowledge children gain from literacy experiences. Children growing up in high-literacy families are surrounded by literacy artifacts from the time of birth. Characters from nursery rhymes decorate walls. Sheets and crib borders often have pictures and writing, alphabet blocks and books might be on the shelf, and T-shirts often have slogans or city names printed on them. In addition to the child's own possessions, homes are filled with books, newspapers, magazines, mail, pens, crayons, and writing pads. Many homes will also have at least one computer.

Homes that contain lots of literacy artifacts inevitably have adults who frequently use these artifacts and want their children to use them as well. Children raised in high-literacy families are thus exposed to many literacy events from which they can learn not only the purposes of print, but also specific information about the sounds, letters, and words that make up texts. The most frequent literacy event in which children participate is joint book reading. In 1985, the Commission on Reading of the National Institute of Education called joint book reading "the single most important activity for developing the knowledge required for eventual success in reading" (p. 23). In high-literacy homes, parents begin reading to their children as soon as they are born. In some families, mothers may even begin reading to their children before birth. Reading to infants and young toddlers does not teach them to read, but it does teach children that books are important to the adults in their world and that lots of talk surrounds books. They may also realize that their parents work hard to get and keep their attention on these curious objects and delight in their slightest attempts to participate. Before babies can even talk, they may be turning pages of books and spending considerable time looking at pictures in books, and, even with babies, parents label pictures, actions, and events and relate the information in the book to the child's life (van Kleeck, 1995).

As infants get older, parents gradually introduce input that is more cognitively demanding. For example, Snow and Goldfield (1981) showed that parents decreased their labeling and increased discussion of events as their children got older (2;6 to 3;6). As children mature, they are also expected to play more of an active role in the book-reading activity. One way children become more active is their ability to respond to so-called test questions. Heath (1982), for example, found that there were three kinds of information children learned to talk about during book-reading routines: (a) what explanations, (b) reason explanations, and (c) affective explanations. Learning to respond to these kinds of questions prepares children for the types of questions they will encounter from teachers and on tests once they enter school.

Children from high-literacy families often have a lot of help in learning to respond to test questions and provide various kinds of explanations about what they read. Parents who are attuned to their child's developmental level will provide questions and answers that the child can understand. As children get older, the process of "sense making" becomes more of a shared enterprise (Heath, 1982; van Kleeck, 1995). One important characteristic of this shared enterprise is that children learn how to ask questions about the texts they are reading. The answers they receive to their questions are a key source for the development of conceptual knowledge and reasoning skills during the preschool years. Another important source for conceptual and reasoning skills is the books themselves, which become more sophisticated and complex as children get older.

Joint book reading not only fosters conceptual and reasoning skills, it also exposes children to specific components of print and book conventions (see Hartley & Harris, chap. 6, this volume). This exposure often leads to children wanting to learn more specific information about print, such as letter names and the sounds associated with them. In some cases, the literacy artifacts and joint book-reading activities may lead preschoolers to the discovery of the underlying alphabetic principle—that words consist of discrete sounds and that these sounds are represented by letters in print.

Caveat

Despite the commonsense appeal of the importance of joint book reading, there is some controversy in the literature about the actual impact that joint book reading has on early reading ability. The controversy was set in motion by Scarborough and Dobrich's (1994) review of 3 decades of research on the influence of joint book reading on language and literacy development. The observed effects in this research were quite variable within and between samples. Indeed, preschool joint book-reading experiences accounted for only 8% of the variance in young school-aged children's literacy skills. Based on these findings, Scarborough and Dobrich

suggested that demographic, attitudinal, and skill differences in preschoolers made stronger direct contributions to early reading success than
joint book reading.

Scarborough and Dobrich's (1994) conclusions have been challenged
by several researchers. Lonigan (1994), for example, made the point that
the small direct effects of reading to preschoolers may have larger long-
term consequences on children's reading abilities. In other words, earlier
exposure to print will likely result in more language and literacy experiences that will foster the development of a range of cognitive and linguistic skills that in turn will lead to more advanced reading achievement. In
support of this claim, Lonigan cited a study by Jorm, Share, Maclean, and
Matthews (1984) in which two groups of kindergarten children were
matched on measures of verbal intelligence and sight word reading but
differed in phonological skills. At the beginning of first grade, the group
that had better phonological skills was 4 months more advanced in reading than the other group and 9 months more advanced by the beginning
of second grade.

Scarborough and Dobrich's (1994) findings were also challenged by
Bus, van Ijzendoorn, and Pellegrini (1995). Using a quantitative analysis
to review a more extensive body of studies, these investigators found evidence that joint book reading does have a direct impact on learning to
read. There were hardly any studies with negative effects. Although book
reading only explained about 8% of the variance in the outcome measures, the effect size of .59 was fairly strong. The effects were not dependent on the socioeconomic status (SES) of the families. Even in low-SES
families with low levels of literacy, book reading affected literacy skills.
Because book reading seems to make the start of school easier, it is particularly important for children from low-SES families.

It is not surprising that there is not a linear relationship between joint
book reading and early reading ability. There must be a point or threshold where more joint reading has little additional impact on reading ability. As Scarborough and Dobrich (1994) noted, "It might matter a great
deal whether a preschooler experiences little or no shared reading with a
responsive partner, but beyond a certain threshold level, differences in the
quantity or quality of this activity may have little bearing" (p. 285).

Another possible confounding factor in joint book-reading studies is
children's interest or facility in literacy activities. A child (typically a boy)
who does not want to sit still may get little out of joint book-reading activities. For such children, it is conceivable that too much shared reading
might have some negative consequences because they may develop a negative attitude toward reading and other literacy events. The possibility of
the negative effects of book reading is an intriguing one. Scarborough and
Dobrich (1994) used the analogy of eating broccoli to illustrate the possi-

ble consequences of a negative attitude. Will serving broccoli to a child who dislikes it turn the child into a broccoli lover, or will it serve to reinforce and solidify the child's negative attitude? There is some evidence that a negative attitude can impact early reading ability. Wells (1985), for example, found that 11% of preschoolers did not like being read to. He also found that preliteracy knowledge scores at age 5 were strong predictors of subsequent reading achievement at ages 7 and 10 (Wells, 1985, 1986). These preliteracy scores were significantly correlated with parental reports of the child's perceived interest in literacy ($r = .45$), as well as the degree of concentration exhibited when engaged in literacy experiences ($r = .56$) and the amount of time spent on literacy activities ($r = .65$).

A positive attitude and motivation to read play an important role in how much preschool children learn about the form of printed language. Most parents would probably not go out and buy phonics workbooks for their preschool children or play phonological awareness games unless their children enjoy these activities. There must be a basic interest in language and literacy for children to seek out these activities. This interest is sustained, however, by the ability to achieve high levels of success in these activities.

Acquiring Specific Literacy Knowledge

As previously noted, exposure to literacy artifacts and joint book-reading activities contributes to and facilitates the learning of letter names, shapes, and sounds. Letter recognition accuracy and speed have been shown to be significantly related to early reading ability (Adams, 1990). Letter recognition speed and accuracy are important for reading because the more time one spends identifying letters, the more difficult it will be to learn sound–letter correspondences and to decode novel words. Learning sound–letter correspondences depends on solid knowledge of letters. Individuals who continue to have difficulty recognizing letters will inevitably have decoding problems, which, in turn, will lead to comprehension difficulties and frustration with the whole reading process.

Exposure to a variety of literacy artifacts, frequent joint book reading, and various experiences with letter names and sounds may lead some preschoolers to the discovery of the alphabetic principle. The insight that letters stand for individual sounds in words requires knowing something about letters (e.g., their names, shapes, and sounds) and the awareness that words consist of discrete sounds. Phoneme awareness, or more generally, phonological awareness, has received considerable attention in the last 15 years (cf. Adams, 1990; Blachman, 1989, 1994; Torgesen, Wagner, & Rashotte, 1994).

The important role phonological awareness plays in learning to read has sparked interest in identifying early indications of phonological sensitivity. Children as young as 2 years old begin to show some appreciation of the sound system (e.g., van Kleeck & Schuele, 1987). This awareness is seen in children's spontaneous speech repairs, rhyming behaviors, and nonsense sound play. At the same time children are playing with sounds, they are also learning to recognize letters. Interest in sounds and letters inevitably leads to interest in learning the correspondences between sounds and letters. Much of this learning occurs in informal learning situations or in the context of word games, such as naming all the words that begin with a particular letter. The same children who enjoy these kinds of games are also likely to enjoy writing and doing worksheets filled with exercises about letters, sounds, and their correspondences.

There is no question of the significant role phonological awareness plays in learning to read. Unfortunately, sometimes the importance of phonological awareness obscures the role more general language and cognitive abilities play in becoming a proficient reader. Recent studies (e.g., Catts, Fey, Zhang, & Tomblin, 1999) indicate that general language abilities play a more important role in early reading ability than previously thought. The significant influence that language and cognitive abilities have on reading performance after the third grade has never been in doubt (e.g., Hoover & Gough, 1990).

Summary

It should be apparent that children who grow up in high-literacy homes can learn a great deal about literacy during the emergent literacy period. It is not uncommon for these children to enter kindergarten with the ability to recite the alphabet, recognize letters, use a typewriter or a computer, write their name and a few other words, and sight-read a dozen or more written words. It is also not uncommon for a precocious child who enjoys literacy activities to enter school with fairly sophisticated decoding skills.

Children raised in high-literacy homes also acquire considerable knowledge about language through their exposure to print. Frequent experiences with print expose children to the more formal written-language patterns. Although Standard American English spoken in mainstream homes may be closer to written language, the differences between spoken and written language are not trivial (see Kamhi & Catts, 1999). For children who grow up speaking a dialectal variation of Standard American English, early exposure to print should minimize the possible impact dialect differences may have on learning to read. Early literacy experiences not only expose children to a wide variety of language forms and structures, they also increase the children's knowledge base and reasoning abilities.

Children who begin school with such extensive knowledge about literacy obviously have a considerable advantage over children who enter school without this knowledge and experience. Reid Lyon (1998), the chief of the Child Development and Behavior Branch of the National Institute of Health and Human Development, estimated that about 5% of children enter school reading, and 20% to 30% learn to read relatively easily in any classroom regardless of the particular type of instruction. For the remaining 60%, reading is a much more formidable task, and at least 20% to 30% of these children will have difficulty learning to read. Not coincidentally, many of the children in this latter group come from low-literacy homes.

EARLY LITERACY EXPERIENCES OF AFRICAN AMERICAN CHILDREN

It is common knowledge that failure to read adequately is much more likely in poor, non-White, and non-native speakers of English (Lyon, 1998). Lyon cited figures from the National Assessment of Educational Progress (1994, cited in Lyon, 1998) showing that in California, 59% of fourth-grade children had little or no mastery of the knowledge and skills necessary to perform reading activities at the fourth-grade level. When this figure was broken down into ethnic–racial groups, 71% of African Americans, 81% of Hispanics, 44% of Whites, and 23% of Asians were reading below basic levels. Data such as these support the general notion that all children who are Black and poor will have limited early literacy experiences and be poor readers. A couple of landmark ethnographic (Taylor & Dorsey-Gaines, 1988) and descriptive (Teale, 1986) studies sought to dispel this notion.

Taylor and Dorsey-Gaines (1988) went into the homes of five low-SES families whose children were successful in school and recorded the literacy events that occurred. They found that the children engaged in a variety of literacy events, and the parents did as well. In a more descriptive study, Teale (1986) documented the numerous ways in which low-SES families used print. Teale found that some children had considerable literacy experiences in the home, whereas other children had relatively few. Purcell-Gates, L'Allier, and Smith (1995) noted that these studies have often been interpreted by educators as evidence that all children from low-SES homes experience varied uses of print in their daily lives. This position is just as untenable, however, as the widely held notion that all low-SES children have limited early literacy experiences.

Further evidence was apparently needed to support Teale's (1986) initial findings, so Purcell-Gates (1996) set out to obtain this evidence by recording the uses of print in the homes of 20 low-income families over a 1-year period. Ten of the families were African American, 7 were White, 2 were Hispanic, and 1 was Asian. Researchers were present throughout the day, from the time the children woke up until they went to bed. The families were told that the researchers were interested in the ways in which young children learn in the home-family context before they had formal schooling. Nothing was said about the specific interest in literacy. All literacy materials and instances of print were noted, and all uses of print by everyone in the home were recorded. Samples of children's reading and writing were also obtained. The focal children ranged in age from 4 to 6. Following is a comparison of two African American families, a low-literacy one and a high-literacy one.

Low-Literacy Family. Mrs. Williams was a 33-year-old African American mother of four children living in a one-bedroom public housing apartment that belongs to her mother. She dropped out of school at 11th grade. Her husband graduated from high school, but was now living in another state. The focal child, Tina, was 4. She attended a preschool program. Mrs. Williams' sister and her two children also lived in the apartment. All of the adults were unemployed. Neighbors and other family members often visited, so conversation was a major activity in the home as was television.

The apartment contained few literacy materials. There were 10 children's books and a children's dictionary, but no one was ever observed reading these books. There were no examples of children's schoolwork displayed in the apartment. Adult reading material was limited to *TV Guide* and one women's magazine. On two occasions when Mrs. Williams wanted to write something, she borrowed a pencil and piece of paper from the researcher.

There was approximately one literacy event for every 3 hours observed. The most typical one was reading the cable TV listing as it scrolled across the screen. There were few other literacy events.

High-Literacy Family. Ms. Augustine was a 32-year-old single African American mother of five children, ranging in age from 4 to 13. She graduated high school and attended business college for 8 months. Her main source of income was public assistance. The family lived in a 3-bedroom public housing apartment. Print material was present in every room of the apartment. There were over 100 books, including children's storybooks, adult novels, Bibles for a variety of ages, cookbooks, and schoolbooks. There were also newspapers, magazines, and comic books. Children's schoolwork as well as drawings and poems were displayed on the refrigerator and a bulletin board in the kitchen. Homework was the major activity in the household. Late evening was designated as homework time, but the children also went to the homework room in the housing complex. The room was run by the parents association of the complex. Ms. Augustine was an active participant in the association. Two public school teachers volunteered to help children with their homework while parents read stories to the younger children and helped the older children with various arts and crafts projects.

Ms. Augustine read to her youngest child every day. The older children read newspapers, magazines, and comic books. The family engaged in 2.5 literacy events every hour. Literacy events were not just tied to homework, but were also included during entertainment activities, such as writing names and captions on drawings. Television viewing was limited and tended to be a planned activity.

The findings from this study clearly demonstrate that there is wide variation in the degree to which print permeates the lives of inner-city children, in both the extent to which family members use print and the types of print being written and read. Comparing a high- and a low-literacy family can give the false impression that there is an equal number of low-SES families at each end of the continuum. This is not the case, as Purcell-Gates (1996) reported in considering data from all 20 families. These families averaged less than one instance of actual reading and writing (0.76) per hour, indicating that literacy was not an important aspect for most of the families. In addition, the text read and written in these homes was usually at the phrase and clause level (as opposed to the discourse level) because cereal boxes, flyers, coupons, and TV notices were being read rather than books, newspapers, and magazines.

Another important finding emerged from this study. When the children began learning to read in school, all of the parents increased the level of involvement in their children's literacy learning. Parents explicitly taught letters and words, read to their children, and interacted more directly with their children around print. The increase in parent involvement does not, however, minimize the differences between the families. The more literacy experiences children had in the home, the more literacy knowledge they had when they entered school. The children in high-literacy families were thus at a much higher level when they entered school than children in low-literacy homes, and the increased parent involvement served to maintain the advantage these children had over their peers from low-literacy families.

Purcell-Gates (1996) cautioned that the picture she presents of low-SES families may be brighter than the one that truly exists. This is because the families who agreed to participate in the study were probably not representative of the typical low-SES home. All of the families in the study were interested in their children's learning and were comfortable enough with themselves as people and parents to let the researchers into their homes. Many parents were also enrolled in literacy programs for themselves, thus showing an interest in improving their own literacy skills.

Even if the picture Purcell-Gates (1996) paints of the early literacy experiences of low-SES families is overly optimistic, it still reflects the range of experiences encountered by inner-city African American children. Perhaps there are fewer literacy events in the average low-SES home and fewer high-literacy families than the study would have us believe, but we do not need additional studies to tell us that the more literacy experiences children have before they get to school, the more easily they will learn to read. This does not necessarily mean that children from high-literacy homes will perform comparably to mainstream children on measures of reading achievement. Performance on fourth-grade reading achievement tests, the data cited earlier by Lyon (1998), is influenced by many other factors besides the frequency and type of early literacy experiences. Some of these factors are considered in the next section.

Other Factors That Impact on Reading

Why do African Americans consistently have higher rates of reading failure than Whites and Asians, and reading levels similar to Hispanics? Having limited experiences with print before school certainly contributes to low literacy levels, but the nature of the relationship between early literacy experiences and early reading ability is not straightforward. This is because a number of other factors are more directly related to early reading. Lyon (1998), for example, identified four factors that hinder reading development irrespective of SES and ethnicity: (a) deficits in phoneme awareness and the development of the alphabetic principle, (b) deficits in acquiring and using reading comprehension strategies, (c) interest and motivation in reading, and (d) the inadequate preparation of teachers. Limited early literacy experiences can account for problems in the first three areas. The problems caused by inadequate preparation of teachers and the poor instruction that results clearly have no relation to early literacy experiences.

Phoneme Awareness. As mentioned earlier in this chapter, there is a wealth of research showing the strong relationship between phoneme awareness and early reading ability (cf. Torgesen, 1999). Measures of phonemic awareness skills assessed in kindergarten and first grade can predict with 80% to 90% accuracy who will become good readers and who will have difficulty learning to read (Lyon, 1998). This means that most poor readers have poor phonological awareness skills, and because a large proportion of poor readers are low-SES minority children, these children would be expected to perform poorly on measures of phoneme awareness. Few studies have looked specifically at phonological awareness in African American children. An interesting study by Chaney (1994), however, found that the quantity of family literacy experiences for 43 three-year-old children was significantly related to measures of general language development, metalinguistic awareness, and knowledge about print. African American children from the two lowest income groups made up 35% of the sample. The low-SES African American children were more likely to have lower language levels than the high-SES White children, but when income level was controlled, race had no impact on the quantity of family literacy experiences.

Chaney's (1994) study points out the close relationship between early literacy experiences, general language ability, and metalinguistic awareness. The metalinguistic measures included five tasks that evaluated phonological awareness, five that evaluated word awareness, and two that assessed structural awareness. The relationship between early literacy experiences, language, and phoneme awareness was examined more closely in a recent study by Senechal, LeFevre, Thomas, and Daley (1998). These investigators examined whether storybook exposure and the amount of specific literacy teaching were related to oral and written language skills. Oral language skills included receptive vocabulary, listening comprehension, and phoneme awareness, whereas written language skills included concepts about book reading, alphabet knowledge, reading CVC words, and invented spelling. Parents of 110 four- to 6-year-old children completed an extensive questionnaire that included questions about their children's experiences with storybook reading and the frequency of teaching behaviors. The principal finding of the study was that storybook reading only predicted oral language skills whereas parent teaching only predicted written language skills.

Taken together, the findings of Senechal et al. (1998) and of Chaney (1994) indicate that the relationship between early literacy experiences, language, phoneme awareness, and, ultimately, reading ability is not as straightforward as some researchers make it appear (e.g., Lyon, 1998). This does not diminish the importance of phoneme awareness abilities on early reading ability, but it raises questions as to whether early literacy experiences lead directly or indirectly (mediated by more general language knowledge) to phoneme awareness. These points notwithstanding, it is clear that children raised in low-SES homes are more likely to have fewer literacy experiences and lower levels of performance on measures of language and phoneme awareness.

Reading Comprehension Strategies. Reading comprehension depends heavily on language comprehension abilities and world knowledge. Word recognition skills can be excellent, but if children have limited vocabulary and background knowledge and have difficulty making inferences and integrating information, they will surely experience reading difficulties. There is no shortage of studies showing that a disproportionate number of African American children perform below the mean on measures of language and reasoning (cf. Kamhi, Pollock, & Harris, 1996; Labov, 1995).

Motivation.   Motivation and interest are significant factors in aiding or limiting the amount of improvement a child makes in reading (Lyon, 1998). Children who experience difficulty learning to read often attempt to avoid reading, but proficient reading depends to some extent on the amount of reading one does. The less a child reads, the less opportunity there will be for improving reading skills. Prevention and early intervention programs are critical to counter the predictable decline in motivation that occurs as children get older (Lyon, 1998).

Inadequate Preparation of Teachers.   As we have learned more about the factors that influence reading, it has become clear that the inadequate preparation of teachers is one of the major reasons many children raised in low-SES homes never achieve normal reading levels. Most teachers receive little formal training in reading development and disorders. According to Lyon (1998), surveys of the few reading courses teachers take indicate that (a) the coursework is superficial and unrelated to teaching practice, (b) supervision of student teaching is fragmentary and inconsistent, and (c) there is little opportunity to observe instructional reading methods. Teachers also have little or no background in language development, phonetics, and cognitive development and thus have little knowledge of the importance of phonemic awareness, language abilities, and reasoning skills for reading. As a result, when children experience difficulty learning to read, teachers are not able to identify the sources for this difficulty. Teachers may incorrectly assume that the child just isn't working hard enough or is not paying attention, when the real problem may be that the child needs some direct instruction in basic literacy knowledge (e.g., letter names, phoneme awareness, sound–letter correspondences, vocabulary, etc.).

SUMMARY

There are many diseases, disorders, and handicaps where the causes are unknown, or if they are known, there is little to do about them. This is not the case for reading problems. We know the kinds of knowledge and skills children need to learn to read. We know that children raised in high-literacy homes will rarely have difficulty learning to read. We know that language knowledge, particularly phonological knowledge, is a significant determiner of early reading ability. We also know that most teachers and

special educators do not have the knowledge or training needed to significantly reduce the high rate of reading failure in the schools. The fact
that we know so much about reading means there is no shortage of ideas
about how to prevent and reduce reading failure. A sampling of these
ideas is presented in the next section.

Preventing Reading Failure

When the cause of a problem is known, prevention becomes a possible
goal. If we know that a toxic substance causes a particular disease, there
are two ways to prevent the disease: inform people that they must avoid
the toxic substance or eliminate the toxic substance from the environment. Preventing the disease in this case is relatively simple, but what if
prevention involves doing something rather than not doing something?
We know that certain lifestyles and diets increase the risk of heart disease.
Reducing the risk of heart disease does not simply involve avoiding certain foods or stressful situations, it requires a change in lifestyle that will
include regular exercise and a low-fat diet. Preventing heart disease is
much more difficult than preventing a disease caused by a toxic substance
because people must do something to reduce the risk of heart disease.

Reading failure is a lot like heart disease because it requires doing
something different to reduce the risks. Children need to have frequent
early literacy experiences in the home and preschool and have knowledgeable teachers once they enter school. To improve family literacy
experiences, families not only must be convinced of the important link
between literacy experiences and reading achievement in school, they
must also be shown how to provide these experiences to their children.
This is not a trivial task, as Gadsden and others have shown (Edwards,
1995; Gadsden, 1994). It may be relatively easy to enhance the content of
parent–child interactions and increase the literacy experiences in the
home, but these changes do not always lead to noticeable improvements
in children's language or reading levels (cf. DeBaryshe, 1992; Morrow,
O'Connor, & Smith, 1990). Gadsden (1994), in her review of family literacy research, found that few studies addressed the relative impact of family literacy programs. Most of the programs have provided "how-to" information rather than information about whether the child and their
families considered the programs effective, useful, or appropriate. Gadsden argued that family literacy should be conceptualized broadly as a lifelong activity that may change as needs change. An inherent component of
this broad view is that the family is an educational community in which
shared learning occurs. Gadsden is optimistic that effective family literacy programs can be developed if these programs move beyond focusing
on the purposes and functions of literacy and provide intensive instruc-

tion and support as well as address broader issues about the role of literacy in the home, schools, workplace, and community.

Improving teachers' knowledge and skills in reading instruction is no less daunting than changing family literacy practices. The educational community recognizes the need for change, but bringing about such change has proven to be very difficult. In order for teachers to have the necessary coursework in language and reading, teacher certification requirements will have to change. In most states, the certification offices do not have formal or collaborative relationships with academic departments or colleges of education. This means that the requirements for a college degree may have little relationship to the requirements for a teaching certificate (Lyon, 1998). Even more problematic is that university and state department of education teacher requirements do not include coursework in language and reading or the practicum experiences necessary to develop the skills needed to teach children to read.

Improving the preparation of teachers requires a major change not only in the education curriculum and requirements, but also in the preparation and skills of the professors who teach the language and reading courses. The preparation of professors can be improved by having them take the language and reading courses taught in departments of psychology, linguistics, speech-language pathology, and English. Certification requirements need to be more flexible to allow students at all degree levels to take advantage of high-quality non-education courses in language and reading.

Reducing Reading Failure

Although prevention of reading failure should be the primary goal of any long-range program, for many children it is already too late to prevent reading failure. The combination of being raised in a low-literacy family and having poor instruction is too much to overcome. For these children, reducing the magnitude and extent of reading failure is the best we can do. Numerous programs have been developed to improve reading levels of at-risk children. The U.S. Department of Education and the National Institute of Child Health and Human Development have been funding projects for over 30 years that have proven to be effective in improving reading levels of at-risk children.

Beginning in the Johnson era, considerable money was spent to develop programs to improve academic performance in low-SES children. Most of the efforts involved highly structured, isolated skills instruction in reading, with little attention given to writing (Strickland, 1994). Although basic skills instruction improved standardized test performance, it placed an unintended ceiling on learning. Rising test scores began to level off and children appeared to actually stop learning. The problem with basic skills learning became clear. Children might be able to perform well on tests that measured discrete skills, but they were unable to use the information they had learned to solve other problems, think for themselves, or critique their own work.

In recent years, literacy programs have focused on improving early literacy experiences, family literacy practices, and teaching specific literacy knowledge, such as phoneme awareness (e.g., Carnine, Silbert, & Kameenui, 1997; Edwards, 1995; Lindamood & Lindamood, 1998). The success of these programs suggests that it is possible to reduce the current high rate of reading failure. Although no two programs are exactly alike, there are some basic principles that should underlie efforts to reduce reading failure. A few years ago, Strickland (1994, pp. 331–335) provided an excellent list of such principles and recommendations to improve the literacy of African American children and other at-risk populations. A sampling of these recommendations is provided here.

1. Provide literacy programs with an emergent literacy perspective that values children's knowledge and recognizes that, like all children, African American children come to school eager to learn and please teachers.

2. Use instructional strategies and observational techniques that allow children to demonstrate what they know. Use this information to increase linguistic awareness and knowledge of the world.

3. Initiate family literacy programs in which adults and children treat reading as a cooperative social experience. At the very least, these programs should make books and other materials available to parents to use with their children.

4. Start coordinated school and social service intervention programs to prevent reading failure.

5. Encourage accelerated achievement for high-achieving children.

6. Use literacy programs that build on and expand children's language and culture.

7. Encourage the use of Standard American English (SAE) through exposure to a variety of oral and written texts and oral language activities. Use of SAE should be viewed as language expansion and enrichment of the students' home language.

8. Give incentives to attract and keep the very best teachers and provide ongoing professional development for teachers to learn about the growing body of literature that provides new ways to raise the literacy levels of low-SES African American students and other at-risk populations.

To this list, we can add a few suggestions from Lyon (1998, p. 12) that deal more specifically with improving reading performance.

9. Preschool children should be able to name, recognize, and write the letters of the alphabet and spell words they hear without concern for accuracy.

10. Kindergarten children should be able to recognize and print both upper- and lowercase letters with reasonable ease and accuracy, become familiar with the basic purposes of reading and writing, and develop age-appropriate language comprehension skills.

11. Beginning reading programs should contain adequate instructional time to teach phoneme awareness skills, sound–letter correspondences, fluent decoding, and the development of comprehension strategies.

A Story in Search of an Ending

We clearly have the knowledge to teach most children to read. In many places throughout the country this knowledge is being put to use to reduce reading failure and improve literacy levels of at-risk children. Most of the other developed countries have higher literacy rates than the United States. Hirsch (1996) attributed higher literacy rates to the use of a core curriculum and preschool programs that make sure that disadvantaged children begin school with the same knowledge and skills as advantaged children. Hirsch, like many other educators, feels that reading failure could be eliminated in this country if we use our knowledge and resources to make sure that every child is reading by the end of first grade. Since our crystal ball is not working too well at the moment, here are two endings to the story, a happy and a not-so-happy one.

The Happy Ending. One day in the distant future, the ozone layer will no longer have large holes, major diseases will have been genetically eliminated, high-speed computers will translate thoughts to spoken words or print, and literacy problems will no longer exist in most societies. In the early part of the 21st century, voice recognition software will become widely available in homes, schools, and workplaces. The availability of computers that readily translate speech to written text has all but eliminated the need to learn how to write or spell. Children still need to learn to read, but the proliferation of family literacy programs, high-quality preschools, and well-trained language and reading teachers ensure that reading difficulties are limited to children with specific developmental disabilities or other handicapping conditions.

The Not-So-Happy Ending.   Major diseases have been eliminated and technological advances have had a significant impact on life in developed countries, but global warming has led to extreme climatic and geographical changes in the world that have forced mass migrations from highly populated coastal regions. With all of these changes, the division between haves and have-nots has become even greater than it was at the end of the 20th century. The level of literacy needed to function in the middle of the 21st century is attained by only the most advantaged children. As the criteria for functional literacy continued to rise because of increasing technological advances, it was finally acknowledged that narrowing the gap between advantaged and disadvantaged children was an unrealistic and unattainable goal. Education efforts and monies were redirected to programs that were career-oriented from programs that attempted to improve basic skills such as reading. As a result, children raised in disadvantaged homes usually end up in low-paying career tracks where the literacy demands are not that stringent.

Coda.   From our vantage point as we enter the 21st century, each of these scenarios seems plausible. There are, of course, other plausible scenarios that fall in the middle of these two scenarios. Like most people, we prefer happy endings and, as clinicians and educators, we will do all that we can to make the happy ending a reality. One should expect no less from us, for any teacher who is not committed to improving reading levels should find another profession. Yet, despite our inherent optimism, there is the gnawing sense that reading failure will continue to be a significant problem in this country because major changes will not occur in the preparation of teachers, and family literacy programs and high-quality preschools will remain unavailable to most disadvantaged children.

REFERENCES

Adams, M. (1990). *Beginning to read: Thinking and learning about print*. Cambridge, MA: MIT Press.

Blachman, B. (1989). Phonological awareness and word recognition: Assessment and intervention. In A. Kamhi & H. Catts (Eds.), *Reading disabilities: A developmental language perspective* (pp. 133–158). Boston: College-Hill.

Blachman, B. (1994). What we have learned from longitudinal studies of phonological processing and reading, and some unanswered questions: A response to Torgesen, Wagner, and Rashotte. *Journal of Learning Disabilities, 27,* 287–291.

Bus, A., van Ijzendoorn, M., & Pellegrini, A. (1995). Joint book reading makes for success in learning to read: A meta-analysis on intergenerational transmission of literacy. *Review of Educational Research, 65,* 1–21.

Carnine, D., Silbert, J., & Kameenui, E. (1997). *Direct instruction reading* (3rd ed.). Columbus, OH: Merrill.

Catts, H., Fey, M., Zhang, X., & Tomblin, B. (1999). Language basis of reading and reading disabilities: Evidence from a longitudinal investigation. *Scientific Studies of Reading, 3*, 331–361.

Chaney, C. (1994). Language development, metalinguistic awareness, and emergent literacy skills of 3-year-old children in relation to social class. *Applied Psycholinguistics, 15*, 371–394.

Commission on Reading. (1985). *Becoming a nation of readers: The report of the Commission on Reading.* Washington, DC: National Institute of Education.

DeBaryshe, B. (1992). *Early language and literacy activities in the home* (U.S. Department of Education Field Initiated Studies Program Grant R117E00044). Greensboro: University of North Carolina at Greensboro, Department of Human Development & Family Studies.

Edwards, P. (1995). Connecting African-American parents and youth to the school's reading curriculum. In V. Gadsden & D. Wagner (Eds.), *Literacy among African-American youth: Issues in learning, teaching, and schooling* (pp. 261–279). Cresskill, NJ: Hampton Press.

Gadsden, V. (1994). *Understanding family literacy: Conceptual issues facing the field* (NCAL Tech. Rep. TR94-02). Philadelphia: University of Pennsylvania, National Center on Adult Literacy.

Heath, S. (1982). What no bedtime story means: Narrative skills at home and at school. *Language in Society, 11*, 49–76.

Hirsch, E. D. (1996). *The schools we need and why we don't have them.* New York: Doubleday.

Hoover, W., & Gough, P. (1990). The simple view of reading. *Reading and Writing: An Interdisciplinary Journal, 2*, 127–160.

Jorm, A. F., Share, D. L., Maclean, R., & Matthews, R. (1984). Phonological recoding skills and learning to read: A longitudinal study. *Applied Psycholinguistics, 5*, 201–207.

Kamhi, A., & Catts, H. (1999). Language and reading: Convergences and divergences. In H. Catts & A. Kamhi (Eds.), *Language and reading disabilities* (pp. 1–22). Boston: Allyn & Bacon.

Kamhi, A., Pollock, K., & Harris, J. (Eds.). (1996). *Communication development and disorders in African American children: Research, assessment, and intervention.* Baltimore: Brookes.

Labov, W. (1995). Can reading failure be reversed? A linguistic approach to the question. In V. Gadsden & D. Wagner (Eds.), *Literacy among African-American youth* (pp. 39–68). Cresskill, NJ: Hampton Press.

Lindamood, P., & Lindamood, P. (1998). *The Lindamood phoneme sequencing program for reading, spelling, and speech.* Austin, TX: Pro-Ed.

Lonigan, C. (1994). Reading to preschoolers exposed: Is the emperor really naked? *Developmental Review, 14*, 303–323.

Lyon, G. R. (1998, April). *Overview of reading and literacy initiatives.* Paper presented to the Committee on Labor and Human Resources, Washington, DC.

Morrow, L. M., O'Connor, E. M., & Smith, J. K. (1990). Effects of a story reading program on the literacy development of at-risk kindergarten children. *Journal of Reading Behavior, 22*, 255–275.

Purcell-Gates, V. (1996). Stories, coupons, and the TV Guide: Relationships between home literacy experiences and emergent literacy knowledge. *Reading Research Quarterly, 31*, 406–428.

Purcell-Gates, V., L'Allier, S., & Smith, D. (1995). Literacy at the Harts' and Larsons': Diversity among poor, inncity families. *The Reading Teacher, 48*, 572–578.

Scarborough, H., & Dobrich, W. (1994). On the efficacy of reading to preschoolers. *Developmental Review, 14*, 245–302.

Senechal, M., LeFevre, J., Thomas, E., & Daley, K. (1998). Differential effects of home literacy experiences on the development of oral and written language. *Reading Research Quarterly, 33*, 96–117.

Snow, C., & Goldfield, B. (1981). Building stories: The emergence of information structures from conversation. In D. Tannen (Ed.), *Analyzing discourse: Text and talk* (pp. 127–141). Washington, DC: Georgetown University Press.

Strickland, D. (1994). Educating African American learners at risk: Finding a better way. *Language Arts, 71*, 328–336.

Taylor, D., & Dorsey-Gaines, C. (1988). *Growing up literate*. Portsmouth, NH: Heinemann.

Teale, W. H. (1986). Home background and young children's literacy development. In W. H. Teale & E. Sulzby (Eds.), *Emergent literacy: Writing and reading* (pp. 173–206). Norwood, NJ: Ablex.

Torgesen, J. K. (1999). Assessment and instruction for phonemic awareness and word recognition skills. In H. Catts & A. Kamhi (Eds.), *Language and reading disabilities* (pp. 128–153). Boston: Allyn & Bacon.

Torgesen, J. K., Wagner, R. K., & Rashotte, C. A. (1994). Longitudinal studies of phonological processing and reading. *Journal of Learning Disabilities, 27*, 276–286.

van Kleeck, A. (1995). Emphasizing form and meaning separately in prereading and early reading instruction. *Topics in Language Disorders, 16*(1), 27–49.

van Kleeck, A., & Schuele, C. (1987). Precursors to literacy: Normal development. *Topics in Language Disorders, 7*(2), 13–31.

Wells, G. (1985). Preschool literacy-related activities and success in school. In D. Olson, N. Torrance, & A. Hildyard (Eds.), *Literacy, language, and learning: The nature and consequences of reading and writing* (pp. 229–255). New York: Cambridge University Press.

Wells, G. (1986). *The meaning makers*. Portsmouth, NH: Heinemann.

Chapter 8

Reading Performance and Dialectal Variation

Julie A. Washington
Holly K. Craig
University of Michigan

Learning to read is at once the most fundamental and the most significant literacy skill acquired by school-age children. There is extensive evidence suggesting that children who read well experience academic success, and those who do not read well fare poorly academically. This latter group of poor readers has also been identified as contributing significantly to the overall numbers of school dropouts, single parents, juvenile delinquents, and imprisoned adults (Maguin, Loeber, & LeMahieu, 1993; Nettles & Perna, 1997; Singham, 1998). In addition, children who do not acquire functional levels of literacy constitute a significant percentage of the undereducated and underemployed adults in the United States (Koretz, 1987; Singham, 1998; Smith, 1984; U.S. Department of Commerce & U.S. Bureau of the Census, 1997). Slavin, Karweit, Wasik, Madden, and Dolan (1994) reported that the likelihood of a child graduating from high school can be reliably predicted by his or her reading skill level at the end of third grade.

A recent report by the National Research Council's Committee on the Prevention of Reading Difficulties in Young Children (Snow, Burns, & Griffin, 1998) identified several variables that place children at high risk for reading difficulties. Children who are poor, African American or Hispanic, and educated in urban schools are at great risk for poor reading outcomes. By implication, children who are not members of these large and growing minority groups, who are middle to upper income, and are educated in suburban schools have good reading outcomes, comparatively (Snow et al., 1998). These demographic disparities have been the subject of much discussion and concern, but currently are not as well understood as they need to be.

The reading difficulties experienced by African American children in particular are of longstanding concern and have received considerable attention in the literature. The extant literature is replete with studies and essays detailing the gap in achievement between African American children and their White peers (Allingtion & Walmsley, 1995; Bankston & Caldas, 1997; Baratz-Snowden, 1987; Delpit, 1995; Entwisle & Alexander, 1988; Fishback & Baskin, 1991; Singham, 1998; University of Michigan, 1989). This achievement gap reportedly appears prior to entry into kindergarten and persists into adulthood (Jencks & Phillips, 1998b). As a consequence of the attention and the variety of explanations explored, the nature and magnitude of the problem have been well articulated. However, the gap in reading achievement, mathematics, and science that exists between African American children and their White peers persists, with little progress made toward resolution in the past decade (National Assessment of Educational Progress [NAEP], 1997). It will be important for future work in this area to focus on providing solutions that can be acted upon by the classroom teachers charged with teaching African American children to read.

This chapter provides a review of the literature on reading and achievement difficulties experienced by African American children. It is impossible to separate the reading problems experienced by these children from the widely referenced "Black–White achievement gap" that exists between African American and White students. The interrelationships between reading difficulties and overall achievement outcomes is undeniable. A brief overview of the factors that have been implicated as critical influences is presented, with specific attention to the possible relationship of dialectal variations to the reading problem. Finally, important future directions for research on language and reading with this population are discussed.

DISCREPANCIES IN READING PERFORMANCE

The Black–White achievement gap is not new. One of the earliest documented reports of the disparity between the reading abilities of African American children and their White peers was recorded in 1910 as a part of a report to the general assembly in the state of Georgia (Fishback & Baskin, 1991). This early report described a "literacy gap" between African American and White children characterized primarily by difficulty in learning to read, and overall underachievement of African American students. Although the gap has narrowed somewhat over the past 8 decades, it continues to be a matter of concern among educators today. In its most recent annual report, *The Condition of Education*, the National Center for Education Statistics (NCES) charted trends in reading proficiency by age (9, 13, and 17 years old) and race (White, African American, and Hispanic) from 1971 to 1994 as measured by the NAEP (1997). The NAEP report indicated that the reading performance of African American students was significantly higher in 1994 than in 1971. Between 1971 and 1988 the scores of African American students on many standardized tests improved at a pace that was much faster than that of their White peers. However, this positive performance trajectory was not sustained into the 1990s for African American 13- and 17-year-old students, and the reading performance of 9-year-olds has plateaued since the late 1980s. The scores for 13- and 17-year-old students declined significantly in the late 1980s, with an upward trend apparent by the mid-1990s. These scores have not regained the peak levels achieved in the 1980s (NAEP, 1997; Nettles & Perna, 1997).

After many years of steady progress, the reasons for this decline and subsequent increase in reading performance remain unclear. In 1987, Baratz-Snowden cautioned that the upward trends in achievement reported by the NAEP and other longitudinal surveys would not be sustained without dramatic changes in the educational opportunities for African American children. She suggested that several variables that characterize the life circumstances of urban African American children, especially high rates of poverty and its correlates (e.g., single female heads of households and teenage parenting), were increasing and would have a negative impact on the long-term achievement gains of African American students. Baratz-Snowden predicted further that a decline in overall achievement for African Americans would occur unless targeted interventions were established to reverse these negative social trends. Although these factors alone have not proven to be the cause of this decline, Grissmer, Flanagan, and Williamson (1998) suggested that socioeconomic and educational gains resulting from the civil rights movement likely contributed significantly to the gains reported in the 1980s. Unfortunately, in the 1990s, African American children are still two to three times as likely to be raised in poverty as their White peers (Brooks-Gunn, Klebanov, & Duncan, 1996; Entwisle, Alexander, & Olson, 1997; Nettles & Perna, 1997), and by implication the hardships represented by an impoverished environment may be reflected in their poor academic performance.

The increases in academic performance in the 1980s reported by the NAEP have been widely presented as evidence that progress is being made toward closing the literacy/achievement gap. However, Baratz-Snowden (1987) appropriately noted that these gains have been modest at best and that the rate of change suggests an alarmingly low probability of closing the gap before the mid 21st century. Specifically, even with these gains in performance the 1996 median score on the NAEP for African American students in reading, science, and math remains disturbing at the 20th to 25th percentile compared to White students who participated in the assessment (Grissmer et al., 1998).

Contributing Factors

Six broad factors have been presented as critical influences on the poor reading and overall academic performance of African American children, as follows:

Factor 1:   Unequal opportunities historically because of racial segregation.
Factor 2:   Low socioeconomic status (SES) and its correlates, specifically income and level of education of the primary caregiver.
Factor 3:   Low cognitive skills.
Factor 4:   Poor home literacy environments.
Factor 5:   Low teacher expectations.
Factor 6:   Interference of African American English (AAE) dialect in the reading process.

No single one of these factors has been determined to entirely explain the literacy gap, but each is widely accepted as important for understanding the gap. The sixth factor, dialect interference, is discussed at length following a brief discussion of the other five factors. The section on future research needs focuses on the interactions between dialect and reading as well.

Factor 1: Unequal Opportunities.   Prior to its inception in the 1960s and 1970s, desegregation of the nation's public schools was widely expected to be one of the most important, positive influences on the reading achievement of African American children. Accordingly, the gap in reading scores that had come to characterize the performances of African American children when compared to their White peers was expected to disappear when equal opportunities for obtaining a quality education were achieved through public school desegregation.

We now know that desegregation of public school classrooms has failed to close the gap in the reading skills of African American children and their White peers. Racial differences in reading skills are evident even in desegregated schools, and the racial mix of a school does not appear to have a sustainable impact on the reading scores of African American children (Jencks & Phillips, 1998b; Phillips, Crouse, & Ralph, 1998). In an interesting statistical reanalysis of the data presented in 1910 by the Georgia Department of Education, Margo (1987) manipulated variables associated with unequal educational access such as poor or absent textbooks in an effort to neutralize the impact of segregated education. He found that equalizing these school inputs would have eliminated only 40% to 50% of the considerable gap in achievement between African American and White students. Subsequent investigations have supported this finding. These investigations indicate that only one third to one half of the variance in academic achievement can be explained by factoring in desegregation (Fishback & Baskin, 1991; Orazem, 1987). Although this is a considerable percentage of the variance, it leaves a significant portion of the variance unexplained. Theoretically, desegregation represented equal access to educational resources. In reality, segregation was not the only barrier to obtaining equal opportunities, and desegregation as a single solution was not sufficient to erase the achievement gap.

Factor 2: Socioeconomic Status. Children from low-SES backgrounds are at high risk for academic failure. Low-SES children perform below established norms in literacy on national, state, and school assessments, and these performance differences increase as they progress to later grades in school (Chall, Jacobs, & Baldwin, 1990; Entwisle et al., 1997). African American children are impoverished at more than two to three times the rate of their White peers (Brooks-Gunn et al., 1996; Entwisle et al., 1997; Nettles & Perna, 1997). Since African American children are disproportionately represented among the nation's poor, poverty is an oft-cited explanation for poor reading performance and the related academic difficulties encountered in this population.

In an investigation of 2nd, 4th, and 6th-grade readers who were low-income, Chall et al. (1990) reported a disturbing trend in the development of reading. Specifically, the reading skills of their low-income subjects evidenced marked deceleration with increasing grades. Around 4th grade, when schools shift away from teaching the basic skills of reading and expect students to use reading to acquire new knowledge, a rapid deceleration in reading performance began and continued through the 11th grade, the upper grade level examined in this investigation. Others have observed this phenomenon as well. Nettles and Perna (1997) presented similar findings in their report on the educational status of African American preschool, elementary, and secondary school children. They determined that with each increasing grade the performance of African American children who are low-income drifts further away from the performance of their middle-SES peers. By implication, at 4th grade, when reading becomes the vehicle for learning new information, performance in subject areas such as math, science, and social studies that depend on the strength of a student's reading skills for mastery are adversely affected as well. Indeed, in our own research program at the University of Michigan we compared the math and science scores of a sample of 55 middle- and low-SES African American 1st and 3rd graders to their reading scores on the Metropolitan Achievement Test (MAT). The MAT is a nationally used standardized assessment instrument that is administered to all children in Metropolitan Detroit beginning in 1st grade. A logistic regression analysis revealed that for these normally developing subjects, 47% of the unique variance in math and 17% of the unique variance in science could be explained by the students' reading levels.[1]

Although SES is frequently represented as a difference in income status, when income alone is used as a predictor variable for language and/or reading it seldom yields informative results. It is the social status factors that covary with poverty that have been determined to be most informative, and of these factors educational level of a child's parents or primary caregiver often has proved most revealing (Fazio, Naremore, & Connell, 1996; Margo, 1987; Washington & Craig, 1999). This variable continues to be implicated as one that critically differentiates children who are poor readers from those who will be good readers (Chall et al., 1990), and those with poor or good vocabulary skills compared to agemates (Washington & Craig, 1999). Vocabulary skills, both receptive and expressive, have been identified as important component skills for good readers.

Although SES and its covariates are important for understanding differences in literacy rates for children of all races, further examination of data obtained from African American children reveals that African American children who are middle SES are experiencing measurable academic and reading difficulty as well. Middle-SES African American children exhibit higher rates of reading success than African American children from low-income homes, but a significantly higher rate of reading failure than White children from comparable socioeconomic backgrounds (Singham, 1998). Singham examined the performance of African American children in Shaker Heights, Ohio, a middle- to upper-middle-class suburb of Cleveland. He concluded that despite the resources available to all of the children in this community, African American children from middle-SES homes performed considerably below their White peers on standardized reading tests. Regardless of income, African Americans historically are overrepresented in the bottom tail of composite test score distributions and underrepresented in the upper tail (Hedges & Nowell, 1998). The underachievement of African American children from middle-SES homes has been most difficult to explain. If SES was the predominant variable impacting the reading performance of African American children, by virtue of their middle-SES status and the assumption of increased resources and higher parental education associated with that status, mid-

---

[1]MAT Math/Reading: $F(46) = 27.54, p = .000$; MAT Science/Reading: $F(46) = 3.98, p < .05$.

dle-SES children should be performing at comparable levels with their White peers. Why are African American children from middle-SES homes not faring better? This will be an important question to address for future reading research with African American children.

Factor 3: Low Cognition. The overrepresentation of African Americans in the lower tails of standardized distributions and underrepresentation in the higher tails characterizes not only academic testing but extends to tests of cognition as well. These disparities in performance by race have decreased over time in the lower tail, but not in the upper tail of cognitive or academic distributions (Hedges & Nowell, 1998). Unfortunately, Herrnstein and Murray (1994) and others have used these performance differences on normative distributions to argue that African Americans are genetically predisposed to be less intelligent than their White counterparts. According to this viewpoint, the low-average and below-average performance that has been described for African American students should be expected and accepted. The human costs of this viewpoint are that our attempts to impact the SES, educational, and environmental contexts of our African American students will be perceived as futile and will not even be attempted.

Acceptance of the now infamous claim of Herrnstein and Murray (1994) rests on the assumption that instruments designed to measure IQ are culturally appropriate, and that they provide a valid index of an individual's innate ability. After decades of empirical testing, most African Americans and Whites discount the racial differences identified through cognitive testing as a reflection of the racial or cultural bias inherent in these instruments (Jencks, 1997). Furthermore, most generally agree that IQ tests measure learned rather than innate abilities (Jencks, 1998; Jencks & Phillips, 1998; Nisbett, 1998), making an individual's performance vulnerable to environmental and cultural influences. Thus, it is now widely accepted that cognitive inferiority is not the basis of performance differences for African American children, and most current cognitive scores underestimate the IQs of African American children.

Factor 4: Home Literacy Environment. Is there a mismatch between the practices of the school and those of the African American community that contributes in some significant way to the difficulties encountered when teaching African American children to read? It is widely agreed that the home literacy environment contributes significantly to the poor reading outcomes of African American children, yet its specific contribution has not been measured adequately. Allen and Boykin (1992) cited differences in SES combined with cultural differences as the most significant contributors to this mismatch. They claimed that differences in the sociocultural belief systems of African American families creates a cultural discontinuity between the school and the child's culture that significantly impacts performance, and that this was especially true for children from low-SES homes. Nichols (1977) asserted that African American families and schools ascribed differential value to reading, affecting the personal motivation of the African American child learning to read.

The value placed on reading in African American homes has been indexed most often using parent surveys that seek information regarding the number of books present in the home and the frequency with which the caregiver reads to a child. Using this methodology to investigate the home literacy environment as a possible predictor variable for reading achievement, Chall et al. (1990) determined that two of the strongest predictors of both reading and vocabulary knowledge were the literacy environment in the home and the mother's educational level. African American children who had more books and were read to at home performed better on reading assessments than those children who had few books and were not read to at all or were read to infrequently (Chall et al.).

Most authors agree that the home literacy environment is important for understanding and impacting the reading performance of any child. However, research with African American families is complicated by the failure to distinguish between cultural values and practices. Clearly, a parent's wish for his or her child to perform well in school is not a value that is exclusive to any one community. The desire to have children experience academic success and attain reading proficiency can be assumed to be shared values by most parents in both the African American and White communities. What we cannot assume is that these shared values are manifested as shared practices. For example, the frequency of book reading experiences and the availability of a large number of books in the home represent practices that have been demonstrated to reflect the value placed on the development of reading skills in middle-class, White homes. Book reading time and number of books may not be valid indicators for African American families. In the families participating in our research program at the University of Michigan, for example, we have noted that our African American parents tend to purchase educational toys and aids such as flash cards and workbooks in order to encourage development of literacy skills in their young children. This anecdotal observation suggests that perhaps the literacy focus in these families would not be accurately captured by counting the numbers of books purchased or read. Literacy practices that represent culturally appropriate indicators of the value placed on reading achievement in African American families need to be addressed.

Factor 5: Low Teacher Expectations.   The current Secretary of Education (Riley, 1999) assailed the "tyranny of low teacher expectations" when discussing low student achievement in America's schools. Although he was not talking about African American children in particular, low teacher expectations have been implicated in the literature repeatedly as an important influence on the poor reading skills of African American children. Chall et al. (1990) identified the "extent of challenge" presented by the teacher for his or her African American students to be the most potent variable influencing vocabulary gain and comprehension in children learning to read. Entwisle and Alexander (1988) investigated the role of teacher expectations on African American student performance and found that students for whom teachers have high expectations are held to stricter standards, called on more, and more often pressed for answers, thus improving classroom performance. Students for whom expectations are low are subjected to more managerial behaviors, contributing little to improvement in performance. Ferguson (1998) presented evidence that teachers' beliefs about student ability affected African American students more than they affected Whites.

There have been many explanations offered concerning child- or teacher-centered variables that might elicit low expectations for African American students by their classroom teachers. These variables include some that have been discussed in the preceding sections, namely, the student's SES and perceived cognitive ability. One of the most frequently cited variables, however, is the student's use of a cultural dialect that differs from Standard Classroom English (SCE).

Most African American children speak African American English to some extent, regardless of SES (Washington & Craig, 1994, 1998). Goodman and Buck (1973) described AAE as a low-status dialect that puts African American children at risk for reading failure because of rejection of the dialect by teachers. Markham (1984) cited informed teachers with positive attitudes toward linguistic diversity as an essential component of successful literacy instruction. The tendency on the part of teachers to correct dialectal miscues in reading more frequently than nondialectal miscues has been documented repeatedly and cited as evidence of low teacher acceptance of dialectal variations (Barnitz, 1980; Cunningham, 1976–1977; Goodman & Buck, 1973; Markham, 1984). For example, Cunningham reported that during oral reading, teachers corrected dialectal miscues 78% of the time. In contrast, nondialectal miscues were corrected only 27% of the time. When asked to explain when correction was offered versus when it was not, these teachers indicated that miscues resulting in changes in meaning and those that were deemed grammatically unacceptable were targeted. The AAE features used by the children during oral reading exercises seldom resulted in meaning changes from the text read. By implication, grammatical unacceptability was the primary reason for correction. It is the belief of many teachers and researchers that the use of AAE interferes with both reading and writing instruction, but, as discussed in the next section, empirical support for this view is mixed.

Factor 6: Dialect Interference.   Historically, discussions of the relationship between AAE and reading skill development closely paralleled those
presented in the early literature on AAE dialect. Early linguists investigating the characteristics and use of AAE engaged in considerable debate
about the integrity of the dialect. Proponents of the *deficit hypothesis* considered AAE a deficient form of Standard American English (SAE) that over-
simplified the grammatical rules of English, resulting in incorrect productions (Bereiter, 1966). Conversely, linguists supporting the *difference
hypothesis* contended that AAE was a systematic, rule-governed variation of
English that was rich in both form and content (Fasold & Wolfram, 1970;
Labov, 1970, 1972; Wolfram, 1971; Wolfram & Fasold, 1974). Ultimately,
the difference hypothesis received the most empirical support, was accepted widely, and governs our thinking currently about AAE.

Parallel discussions about AAE were taking place in the reading literature
as educators sought to understand the source of the reading difficulties documented for African American children. In this early work, the question
most frequently explored was whether AAE provided the strong oral foundation necessary to support reading, or whether it was a deficient form of
English that did not support learning to read. Cunningham (1976–1977)
succinctly presented three prevailing views that characterized most investigations in the late 1960s and 1970s, and the implications of each, as follows:

1. AAE is a deficient form of English that provides an inadequate language base for development of written language skills. Thus, it is
   important to teach SAE to African American children.
2. AAE is linguistically different from SAE. The difficulty encountered
   with reading is due to a mismatch between oral language and the
   language of instruction, making a union of the two desirable.
3. AAE is a low-status dialect, and teacher attitudes toward the dialect
   negatively impact reading development. Changes in teacher attitude would have a profound effect on efforts to teach African American children to read.

Mounting evidence in the linguistic literature of the systematic nature
of the dialect and the rules governing its use, combined with reading studies designed to establish linguistic competence (Torrey, 1983), quickly
silenced those who supported the view that use of AAE provided insufficient language structure to support reading. An alternative explanation
that gained widespread acceptance and continues to be implicated was the
concept of *dialect interference*.

Goodman (1965) and Baratz (1969) hypothesized that there would be
a direct relationship between dialect divergence and reading success.
They suggested that AAE speakers presented with SAE text were faced

with an additional transformation involving translation from one language system to the other that interfered with reading comprehension and fluency. Subsequent investigations of the role of dialect were inconclusive, however, with some supporting the dialect interference hypothesis and others challenging its validity. These investigations focused primarily on the influence of the phonological and morphosyntactic features of AAE on reading comprehension or production.

Melmed (1970) and Rystrom (1973–1974) examined selected phonological features of AAE for their effect on the comprehension of words containing these features represented in SAE phonology. Both investigations determined that comprehension was unaffected by the presence of AAE phonological variations. Hart, Guthrie, and Winfield (1980) also determined that AAE phonology did not interfere significantly with their first-grade subjects' ability to learn sound–symbol correspondences. These low-income children performed comparably to their White peers on this phonemic task. Other studies focused on the phonology of AAE have also failed to find significant evidence of dialect interference in reading (Gemake, 1981; Harber, 1977).

Investigations of the influence of morphosyntactic features of AAE and reading have found significant influences. Bartel and Axelrod (1973) investigated the relationship between low reading achievement and the extent of use of AAE syntax and morphology in African American ninth graders. The participants were asked to read aloud a series of sentences from the Gray Oral Reading Tests (Wiederholt & Bryant, 1992), which were audiorecorded and analyzed for the presence of AAE features. The findings of this investigation indicated that participants who used the most dialect during reading also had the lowest reading levels, supporting the dialect interference hypothesis. Steffensen, Reynolds, McClure, and Guthrie (1982) examined the performance of African American third, sixth, and ninth graders on reading comprehension tasks using cloze procedures. They determined that their AAE-speaking subjects produced significantly more verb errors compared to SAE speakers and concluded that differences in AAE verb morphology interfered with comprehension of verb forms in SAE. Ames, Rosen, and Olson (1971) and Baratz (1969) reported similar findings in studies of oral reading with low-SES African American children, concluding that the interference of the dialect significantly reduced overall reading skills in their subjects.

Notable exceptions to these findings of dialect interference in reading include Nolen (1972), who reported that the reading performance of 156 African American second- and fourth-grade children who were speakers of AAE did not seem to be affected by their use of AAE. Even when reading materials were presented in AAE rather than SAE the performance of these subjects was unaffected. The White children in the control group read significantly better than the African American children overall, but Nolen concluded that dialect did not appear to contribute to this outcome. These findings have been supported by others (Simons & Johnson, 1974; Troutman & Falk, 1982). Further, in a reexamination of Goodman's (1965) original dialect interference hypothesis, Goodman and Buck (1973) performed a miscue analysis on passages read aloud by AAE-speaking children assigned to a high- and a low-proficiency reading group. They concluded that there was no cause-and-effect relationship between increased dialect involvement and low reading proficiency. Students in the low-proficiency group as well as those in the high-proficiency group both tended to do some dialect shifting in their miscues. Goodman and Buck hypothesized that it was in fact the rejection of the dialect by teachers that interfered with the natural process of learning to read and undermined the confidence of the reader, rather than direct interference of the dialect in the reading process. Dummett (1984) also supported this nonlinguistic factor as the most likely explanation for the reading problem experienced by African American children.

Overall, the role of dialectal variations remains unclear. Many studies have focused primarily on the phonological features of AAE because of their perceived importance for attaining phonological awareness skills. Although they are far from conclusive, most of these studies agree that the phonological variations that characterize AAE probably contribute very little to the reading problem. This outcome is not surprising. Phonological awareness is centrally a metalinguistic skill, whereas the phonological features of AAE are motor patterning rules. Articulation differences such as those represented by many regional dialects across the United States have not been implicated in reading deficits, so the phonological features of AAE may be of minor import to the reading difficulties experienced by African American children.

The impact of the morphological and syntactic features of AAE seems less clear. Current discussions of reading skill development continue to suggest that dialect affects reading in African American children in some way, even if it is not well understood (Delpit, 1995). Most would agree with Goodman and Buck (1973) that there is no direct cause–effect relationship between reading deficits and AAE, but that the child's linguistic differences seem to have some measurable influence on the attainment of reading proficiency.

It is notable that most of the studies investigating the relationship of AAE and reading were written more than 15 years ago, with the majority appearing in the 1970s. Although no clear answer emerged from these studies, the question of the contribution of linguistic diversity to reading problems was essentially abandoned as researchers explored explanations in other domains. Cook-Gumperz and Gumperz (1992) suggested that researchers became impatient with the search for sociolinguistic explanations because no direct cause-and-effect link was apparent. Like the other factors presented in the preceding sections, dialectal variation likely contributes to the variance in reading performance, but does not provide a single, clear-cut explanation for the difficulty with reading experienced by African American children. Perhaps more than any of the other factors, investigations of dialect interference have raised as many questions about its influence as have been answered. The remaining questions and paucity of answers suggest that this line of research is worthy of continued pursuit.

FUTURE RESEARCH DIRECTIONS

As we enter a new millennium and the perceived "reading crisis" continues, discussions of reading as a largely linguistic task driven by the strength of a child's oral language skills, including vocabulary, sentence structure, and word knowledge, have increased (Chall et al., 1990; Snow, 1995; Snow et al., 1998). The time is right to reexamine the link between the African American child's linguistic and reading skills. Research examining the achievement gap appears to be the subject of renewed interest (Delpit, 1995; Jencks & Phillips, 1998a; Singham, 1998). Many important questions have been left unanswered and should be revisited. Furthermore, it will be important that attempts to answer these research questions be informed by past studies, avoiding some of their methodological shortcomings.

The major questions that seem to warrant further exploration are as follows:

1. Do the morphosyntactic characteristics of AAE contribute to reading difficulties for African American children? If so, How? When? and Which ones?

The possible contribution of morphosyntactic features of AAE to the reading problem is an open question. AAE apparently affects all domains of language including semantics, pragmatics, and phonology, but those that affect word formation and grammatical relationships have been of special interest for understanding literacy because of their potential to impact reading outcomes. However, the extent to which these features are influential is still unclear. In addition, if these dialectal variations do impact reading it is equally unclear at what point in the reading process that dialect becomes important. For example, in our own research program we calculated the density of dialect[2] used by 50 African American children at Time 1 (preschool or

_____

[2]*Dialect density* was defined as the number of dialect tokens produced in a 50 C-unit corpus divided by the total number of words produced. Language samples were collected during a free-play interaction involving the child and an African American female examiner (Craig, Washington, & Thompson-Porter, 1998).

kindergarten) and Time 2 (fourth grade) and compared it to reading ability in third and fourth grades as measured by the MAT. The preliminary data suggest that the density of dialect used during preschool and kindergarten was a strong predictor of reading outcomes at third and fourth grades. These data suggest that examining dialect use in African American children during the emergent and pre-emergent stages of reading may be informative. Finally, we (Washington & Craig, 1994, 1998) found differential use of dialect features by young children such that some features (zero copula/auxiliary and subject–verb agreement) were used by most children regardless of income status, whereas others were used infrequently. It is possible that not all child AAE features have the potential to interfere with reading, but only a circumscribed set really matters. If future research can determine which features are most likely to impact reading outcomes, reading instruction and reading outcomes may be improved.

2. What additional factors contribute uniquely to low reading performance in African American children?

Unlike AAE, which uniquely characterizes African American children, many of the factors identified as potential barriers to reading development would influence reading outcomes in any child regardless of ethnic background. For example, poverty, home literacy environment, parental education, and teacher expectations for performance are important influences on achievement for all children. It is not clear how or why these variables impact the African American child in ways that are different from children of other races. Research indicates that the reading skills of low-SES African American children are significantly lower than for low-SES White children, yet it is not clear why this is true. Ferguson (1998) reported that low teacher expectations affect the performance of African American children more than White children. Why? Is there some critical interaction of factors that uniquely characterizes African American children learning to read that is not present for other children? Or alternatively, are there variables that have not been examined that are unique to African American children and that when combined with these identified variables interfere with reading development?

3. Why aren't middle-SES African American children reading better than they are?

Singham (1998) and others have expressed concern about the reading skills of middle-SES African American children, whose average reading performance reportedly is comparable to that of low-SES White children and significantly below the level of their middle-SES White peers. The reading problems experienced by middle-SES children seem important to understand in any attempt to identify barriers to reading that may be unique to African American children. The confounding effects of poverty, low parental education, and reading levels are presumably absent in this population. Despite the resources available to these children, however, they often struggle with learning to read and frequently do not attain reading proficiency at the rate or levels of their middle-SES White counterparts. Although the outcomes for low-SES African American children may not be generalizable to middle-SES children, the reverse may not be true. If factors exist that influence reading outcomes for African American children that are specific to this ethnic group, then identifying these factors for middle-SES children, whose performance will not be influenced by poverty and its covariates, should be informative for understanding the barriers to reading proficiency for all African American children.

Obtaining answers to these three broad questions should provide important new information about reading skill development in African American children. As we pursue these questions, however, it will be important to avoid the methodological shortcomings of some of the early work on this topic. Several major methodological concerns are identified and discussed briefly next.

1. The full set of AAE features have not been the focus of systematic inquiry.

Specific AAE features may affect reading whereas others may not be important for reading achievement. The extant literature includes research focused on only a small set of AAE features, with decidedly mixed results. Perhaps more important, these studies were conducted at a time when we knew very little about the use of AAE by children, necessitating the use of adult forms of the dialect to study children. Only recently have the AAE forms used by children been understood. Children generally use the same types of AAE as adults, but the use of these features differs by age, and the surface structure realizations of these features may be different than the adult's usage (Washington & Craig, 1994, 1998). For example, in our child corpus, remote past *been* ("I been knowin' how to do that") was not apparent until approximately 7 years of age, and double modals took the form of double copulas and auxiliaries, "I'm am" or "I'm is" rather than "might could," as has been identified for adults. The absence of developmental information for earlier investigations may not have allowed these forms to be identified as dialectal in nature. Instead they may have been discounted as ungrammatical.

In addition, the child's ability to code-switch from the use of AAE to SAE is neglected in the reading literature. Children decrease AAE production in school contexts across the early elementary grades. Research designs need to ensure that statistics comparing dialect production and reading aloud are not really tapping failure to develop code-switching skills and reading aloud. For example, Bartel and Axelrod (1973) interpreted negative correspondences between use of AAE when reading aloud and reading skill levels as support for the dialect interference hypothesis. As their subjects were ninth graders, this correspondence may have mirrored the students' skills at code-switching or failure to develop code-switching skills, rather than anything basic about the dialectal forms themselves. The impact of code-switching on reading skill development in African American children seems important to consider.

2. Low SES and AAE are confounded in the literature.

With few exceptions the results of most studies focused on reading skills and use of AAE have examined performances of low-SES African American children. The results of these investigations have been generalized to the entire population, regardless of socioeconomic background. There is a paucity of research focusing specifically on middle-SES African American children despite indications that these children are at risk for reading failure and use AAE to a lesser extent than low-SES peers. It is possible that knowledge gained about children from one SES group will be informative for understanding the other, but until that has been demonstrated empirically it will be important to study these two groups separately. It will be important also to confirm for low-SES children the poverty covariates that exert the most influence on reading development and how to manage them in the classroom.

3. The contribution of reading test bias has not been widely explored.

Although a small number of studies have suggested that reading tests may be biased for use with African American children (Jencks & Phillips, 1998b; Hamill & Wiederholt, 1971), test bias has been largely overlooked as at least a partial possible explanation for the magnitude of the gap in performance on standardized tests between these children and their White peers. This is somewhat surprising as many other standardized testing instruments, including college admissions, cognitive, and language tests, have been identified as biased for use with African American children and youths (Baratz-Snowden, 1987; Jencks, 1998; Washington, 1996; Washington & Craig, 1999). The bias identified for cognitive and language tests seems particularly relevant, as cognition and language are both major component skills of reading. As administration of standardized group assessments becomes routine at both the national and state levels, establishing the validity of these instruments for use with African American children will be particularly important. Performance on these instruments is being used to decide everything from classroom placements to readiness for high school graduation. If these instruments are simply highlighting performance differences by race rather than tapping true reading competence, the reading abilities of many African American children will be underestimated. The consequences of this underestimation may be significant. Jencks (1998) appropriately noted that the gap in reading test scores cannot be explained entirely by test bias, however. The skill differences identified on these tests are very real and affect the academic performance of many African American children.

4.   The tasks used in many reading studies do not seem to be clear tests of reading competence and may disadvantage African American students.

Miscue analysis is used frequently in studies of dialect interference to examine the degree to which use of AAE interferes with oral reading of SAE text. Participants are asked to read a passage aloud while the examiner identifies reading "errors" that can be characterized as dialectal in nature. The frequency of occurrence or proportion of these "miscues" in the reading sample is used to estimate the relative degree to which dialect interferes with reading. Burke, Pflaum, and Knafle (1982) found that scoring AAE productions as miscues resulted in significant underestimation of African American children's reading abilities. This methodology seems particularly inappropriate in its characterization of dialect-based differences from print as miscues, which in this literature seems simply to be a euphemism for errors.

In studies of oral language we have found that it is possible to identify language impairments by assessing an African American child's nondialectal productions, avoiding altogether the potential influences of dialect until we better understand the rules governing dialect production in children (Craig, 1996; Seymour, Bland-Stewart, & Green, 1998). It also seems preferable for reading assessments to explore those assessments that avoid dialectal variations at this point in our understanding.

Additionally, reading studies do not discuss the potential confound presented by using verbal output to represent the child's reading abilities. If the African American child is "translating" from AAE to SAE during reading as Goodman (1965) and Baratz (1969) suggested, then reading aloud seems to require an additional transformation that is not required for silent reading, potentially confounding the outcomes. It is with this final transformation that the child's ability to code-switch from the use of AAE to SAE in oral language seems critical. Experience in our research program suggests that most children the ages of the participants in many of these studies (e.g., fourth and sixth graders) have begun to code-switch in conversational contexts with an examiner. For children who have difficulty reading, the stress represented by reading may be compounded by the cognitive and linguistic demands to code-switch while reading aloud. Currently, we do not know enough about code-switching processes in young children to assess their potential impact on attempts to read aloud. This will be an important line of inquiry to pursue.

SUMMARY

In many ways, the course of reading research involving African American children continues to parallel studies of oral language with this population. In particular, the importance of assessing the potential impact of dialectal variations on assessment and achievement outcomes for African American children is critical for studies of both written and oral language. Both genres will benefit considerably from increased knowledge of dialectal processes such as code-switching, knowledge of the developmental course of the dialect, and information concerning the culture-specific influences of social status variables such as gender, SES, caregiver education, and environmental inputs. In addition, outcomes in both language and reading suggest interpretive caution is necessary when using standardized tests.

Reading skills have their roots in language skill development. Future reading research would be positively informed if knowledge gained about oral language skills could be transferred to the study of reading. In concert, language research would benefit if the impact of language on academic skills such as reading were routinely considered when devising assessment and/or intervention alternatives for African American children.

ACKNOWLEDGMENT

This work was supported by the Center for Improvement of Early Reading Achievement (CIERA) at the University of Michigan—U.S. Department of Education, Office of Educational Research and Improvement, Grant R305R70004.

REFERENCES

Allen, B. A., & Boykin, A. W. (1992). African American children and the educational process: Alleviating cultural discontinuity through prescriptive pedagogy. *School Psychology Review, 21*, 586–596.

Allington, R. L., & Walmsley, S. A. (1995). *No quick fix: Rethinking literacy programs in America's elementary schools*. New York: Teachers College Press.

Ames, W. S., Rosen, C. L., & Olson, A. V. (1971). The effects of nonstandard dialect on the oral reading behavior of fourth grade children. In A. V. Olson (Ed.), *Teaching reading skills in secondary schools* (pp. 63–70). Scranton, PA: Intext Educational Publishers.

Bankston, C. L., III, & Caldas, S. J. (1997). The American school dilemma: Race and scholastic performance. *Sociological Quarterly, 38*(3), 423—429.

Baratz, J. C. (1969). *Teaching black children to read*. Washington, DC: Center for Applied Linguistics.

Baratz-Snowden, J. (1987). Good news, bad news: Black performance on standardized tests. *Change, 19*, 50–54.

Barnitz, J. G. (1980). Black English and other dialects: Sociolinguistic implications for reading instruction. *The Reading Teacher, 33*(6), 779–786.

Bartel, N. R., & Axelrod, J. (1973). Nonstandard English usage and reading ability in Black junior high students. *Exceptional Children, 38*(8), 653–655.

Bereiter, C. (1966). *Teaching disadvantaged children to read*. Englewood Cliffs, NJ: Prentice-Hall.

Brooks-Gunn, J., Klebanov, P. K., & Duncan, G. J. (1996). Ethnic differences in children's intelligence test scores: Role of economic deprivation, home environment, and maternal characteristics. *Child Development, 67*, 396–408.

Burke, S. M., Pflaum, S. W., & Knafle, J. D. (1982). The influence of Black English on diagnosis of reading in learning disabled and normal readers. *Journal of Learning Disabilities, 15*(1), 19–22.

Chall, J. S., Jacobs, V. A., & Baldwin, L. E. (1990). *The reading crisis: Why poor children fall behind*. Cambridge, MA: Harvard University Press.

Cook-Gumperz, J., & Gumperz, J. (1992). Changing views of language in education: The implications for literacy research. In R. Beach, M. Green, M. Kamil, & T. Shanahan (Eds.), *Multidisciplinary perspectives on literacy research* (Vol. ISBN: 0-8141-3219-7, pp. 212–229). Urbana, IL: National Council of Teachers of English.

Craig, H. (1996). The challenges of conducting language research with African American children. In A. Kamhi, K. Pollock, & J. Harris (Eds.), *Communication development and disorders in African American children* (pp. 1–17). Baltimore: Brookes.

Craig, H. K., Washington, J. A., & Thompson-Porter, C. (1998). Average c-unit lengths in the discourse of African American children from low-income, urban homes. *Journal of Speech, Language and Hearing Research, 41*, 433–444.

Cunningham, P. M. (1976–1977). Teachers' correction responses to Black-dialect miscues which are non-meaning-changing. *Reading Research Quarterly, 12*(4), 637–653.

Delpit, L. (1995). *Other people's children: Cultural conflict in the classroom*. New York: The New Press.

Dummett, L. (1984). The enigma—The persistent failure of Black children in learning to read. *Reading World, 24*, 31–37.

Entwisle, D. R., & Alexander, K. L. (1988). Factors affecting achievement test scores and marks of Black and White first graders. *The Elementary School Journal, 88*, 449–472.

Entwisle, D. R., Alexander, K. L., & Olson, L. S. (1997). *Children, schools, and inequality*. Boulder, CO: Westview Press.

Fasold, R. W., & Wolfram, W. (1970). Some linguistic features of Negro dialect. In R. W. Fasold & R. W. Shuy (Eds.), *Teaching standard English in the inner city* (Vol. 6, pp. 41–86). Washington, DC: Center for Applied Linguistics.

Fazio, B. B., Naremore, R. C., & Connell, P. J. (1996). Tracking children from poverty at risk for specific language impairment: A 3-year longitudinal study. *Journal of Speech and Hearing Research, 39*, 611–624.

Ferguson, R. F. (1998). Teacher's perceptions and expectations and the Black–White test score gap. In C. Jencks & M. Phillips (Eds.), *The Black–White test score gap* (pp. 273–317). Washington, DC: Brookings Institute.

Fishback, P. V., & Baskin, J. H. (1991). Narrowing the Black–White gap in child literacy in 1910: The roles of school inputs and family inputs. *Review of Economics and Statistics, 73*(4), 725–728.

Gemake, J. S. (1981). Interference of certain dialect elements with reading. *Reading Improvement, 18*(2), 183–189.

Goodman, K. S. (1965). Dialect barriers to reading comprehension. *Elementary English, 42*(8).

Goodman, K. S., & Buck, C. (1973). Dialect barriers to reading comprehension revisited. *Reading Teacher, 27*(1), 6–12.

Grissmer, D., Flanagan, A., & Williamson, S. (1998). Why did the Black–White score gap narrow in the 1970's and 1980's. In C. Jencks & M. Phillips (Eds.), *The Black–White test score gap* (pp. 182–226). Washington, DC: Brookings Institute.

Hamill, D., & Wiederholt, J. L. (1971). Appropriateness of the Metropolitan Tests in an economically deprived, urban neighborhood. *Psychology in the Schools, 8*(1), 49–50.

Harber, J. R. (1977). Influence of presentation dialect and orthographic form on reading performance of Black inner-city children. *Educational Research Quarterly, 2*(2), 9–16.

Hart, J. T., Guthrie, H. T., & Winfield, L. (1980). Black English phonology and learning to read. *Journal of Educational Psychology, 72*(5), 636–646.

Hedges, L. V., & Nowell, A. (1998). Black–White test score convergence since 1965. In C. Jencks & M. Phillips (Eds.), *The Black–White test score gap* (pp. 149–181). Washington, DC: Brookings Institute.

Herrnstein, R. J., & Murray, C. (1994). *The bell curve: Intelligence and class structure in American life.* New York: Simon & Schuster.

Jencks, C. (1998). Racial bias in testing. In C. Jencks & M. Phillips (Eds.), *The Black–White test score gap* (pp. 55–85). Washington, DC: Brookings Institute.

Jencks, C., & Phillips, M. (1998a). *The Black–White test score gap.* Washington, DC: Brookings Institute.

Jencks, C., & Phillips, M. (1998b). The Black–White test score gap: An introduction. In C. Jencks & M. Phillips (Eds.), *The Black–White test score gap* (pp. 1–51). Washington, DC: Brookings Institute.

Koretz, D. (1987). *Educational achievement: Explanations and implications of recent trends.* Washington, DC: Congressional Budget Office.

Labov, W. (1970). *The study of nonstandard English.* Champaign, IL: National Council of Teachers of English.

Labov, W. (1972). *Language in the inner city.* Philadelphia: University of Pennsylvania Press.

Maguin, E., Loeber, R., & LeMahieu, P. G. (1993). Does the relationship between poor reading and delinquency hold for males of different ages and ethnic groups? *Journal of Educational and Behavioral Disorders, 1*(2), 88–100.

Margo, R. (1987). Accounting for racial differences in school attendance in the American South, 1900: The role of separate-but-equal. *Review, 69*, 661–666.

Markham, L. (1984). De dog and de cat: Assisting speakers of Black English as they begin to write. *Young Children, 39*(4), 15–24.

Melmed, P. J. (1970). *Black English phonology: The question of reading interference* (Monographs of the Language-Behavior Research Laboratory 1). Berkeley: University of California.

National Assessment of Educational Progress. (1997). *Trends in academic progress: Achievement of U.S. students in science, 1969–1994; mathematics, 1973–1994; reading, 1971–1994; writing, 1984–1994, 1996.* Washington, DC: U.S. Department of Education, National Center for Education Statistics, National Assessment of Educational Progress.

Nettles, M. T., & Perna, L. W. (1997). *The African American education data book* (Vol. 2. Preschool through high school). Washington, DC: Frederick D. Patterson Research Institute of the College Fund/UNCF.

Nichols, P. C. (1977). A sociolinguistic perspective on reading and Black children. *Language Arts, 54*(2), 150–157.

Nisbett, R. E. (1998). Race, genetics, and IQ. In C. Jencks & M. Phillips (Eds.), *The Black–White test score gap* (pp. 86–102). Washington, DC: Brookings Institute.

Nolen, P. S. (1972). Reading nonstandard dialect materials: A study at grades two and four. *Child Development, 43*(3), 1092–1097.

Orazem, P. (1987). Black–White differences in schooling: Investment and human-capital production in segregated schools. *American Economic Review, 77,* 722.

Phillips, M., Crouse, J., & Ralph, J. (1998). Does the Black–White test score gap widen after children enter school? In C. Jencks & M. Phillips (Eds.), *The Black–White test score gap* (pp. 229–272). Washington, DC: Brookings Institute.

Riley, R. W. (1999). *Reauthorization of the elementary and secondary education act of 1965* (Statement to U.S. Senate Committee on Health Education Labor and Pensions). Washington, DC: U.S. Department of Education. Available: www.ed.gov/Speeches/990209.html

Rystrom, R. C. (1973–1974). Perceptions of vowel letter–sound relationships by first grade children. *Reading Research Quarterly, 9*(2), 170–185.

Seymour, H. N., Bland-Stewart, L., & Green, L. J. (1998). Difference versus deficit in child African American English. *Language, Speech & Hearing Services in Schools, 29*(2), 96–108.

Simons, H. D., & Johnson, K. R. (1974). Black English syntax and reading interference. *Research in the Teaching of English, 8*(3), 339–358.

Singham, M. (1998). The canary in the mine: The achievement gap between Black and White students. *Phi Delta Kappa, 80*(1), 8–15.

Slavin, R. E., Karweit, N. L., Wasik, B. A., Madden, N. A., & Dolan, L. J. (1994). A comprehensive approach to early intervention. In R. E. Slavin, N. L. Karweit, & B. A. Wasik (Eds.), *Preventing early school failure* (pp. 175–205). Boston: Allyn & Bacon.

Smith, J. P. (1984). Race and human capital. *American Economic Review, 74,* 685–698.

Snow, C. (1995). *Exposure to discourse and its impact on future reading skills.* Paper presented at the Language and Deafness Conference, Omaha, NE.

Snow, C. E., Burns, S. M., & Griffin, P. (Eds.). (1998). *Preventing reading difficulties in young children.* Washington, DC: National Academy Press.

Steffensen, M. S., Reynolds, R. E., McClure, E., & Guthrie, L. F. (1982). Black English Vernacular and reading comprehension: A cloze study of third, sixth, and ninth graders. *Journal of Reading Behavior, 14*(3), 285–298.

Torrey, J. W. (1983). Black children's knowledge of Standard English. *American Educational Research Journal, 20*(4), 627–643.

Troutman, D. E., & Falk, J. S. (1982). Speaking Black English and reading—Is there a problem of interference. *Journal of Negro Education, 51*(2), 123–133.

University of Michigan. (1989). *University of Michigan Detroit Area Study—Separate and unequal: The racial divide.* Ann Arbor: University of Michigan Institute for Social Research.

U.S. Department of Commerce & U.S. Bureau of the Census. (1997). *Statistical abstract of the United States* (116th ed.). Washington, DC: U.S. Department of Commerce, U.S. Bureau of the Census.

Washington, J. A. (1996). Issues in assessing the language abilities of African American children. In A. G. Kamhi, K. E. Pollock, & J. L. Harris (Eds.), *Communication development and disorders in African American children* (pp. 19–34). Baltimore: Brookes.

Washington, J. A., & Craig, H. K. (1994). Dialectal forms during discourse of poor, urban, African American preschoolers. *Journal of Speech and Hearing Research, 37,* 816–823.

Washington, J., & Craig, H. (1998). Socioeconomic status and gender influences on children's dialectal variations. *Journal of Speech and Hearing Research, 41,* 618–626.

Washington, J. A., & Craig, H. K. (1999). Performances of at-risk, African American preschoolers on the Peabody Picture Vocabulary Test–III. *Language, Speech, and Hearing Services in the Schools, 30*(1), 75–82.

Wiederholt, J. L., & Bryant, B. R. (1992). *Gray Oral Reading Test* (3rd ed.). Austin, TX: Pro-Ed.

Wolfram, W. (1971). Black and White speech differences revisited. In W. Wolfram & N. Clarke (Eds.), *Black–White speech relationships* (pp. 139–161). Washington, DC: Center for Applied Linguistics.

Wolfram, W., & Fasold, R. (1974). *The study of social dialects in American English.* Englewood Cliffs, NJ: Prentice-Hall.

Chapter 9

Language Variation and Literacy Acquisition in African American Students

Noma R. LeMoine
Los Angeles Unified School District

When non-English-speaking children first enter public schools in the United States, they must learn the language of school (English) in order to access the core curriculum, which in turn affects their ability to pursue postsecondary educational opportunities and various career options. To this end, many school districts make a valiant effort to assign these students to teachers who understand their language and culture and who know how to help these students acquire literacy in the new language. However, the effort to provide access is not made for all "language-different" students. African American standard English language learners are one such population. Language is one of the most widely acknowledged differences between African Americans and mainstream White Americans. Yet school curricula (including master plans for serving limited-English proficient students) routinely fail to acknowledge this difference and thereby fail to meet the instructional needs of many African American students.

Linguists agree that most African Americans speak a systematic rule-governed language that differs in significant ways from mainstream American English (Dillard, 1972; Labov, 1970; E. Smith, 1992; Smitherman, 1977; Williams, 1991). African American language differs from the school language, or mainstream Standard American English (SAE), in several ways. It differs phonologically (in how sounds are formed and used to construct words), morphosyntactically (in how words and sentences are formed to carry meaning), and pragmatically (in how language is used in social contexts; Baugh, 1983; Dillard, 1972; Labov, 1983; Smitherman,

169

1977; Williams, 1991). It has been called by many names: plantation Creole, Black dialect, Black English, Black English vernacular, African American Vernacular English, Black language, African American language, Ebonics, Nigritic Ebonics, Pan African languages, and African language systems. African American language represents the mother tongue of the great majority of African Americans, and 80% to 90% of African Americans speak the language at least some of the time (see Dillard, 1972; Smitherman, 1977). Teachers' views toward and understanding of this language affect the ability of African American children to acquire literacy and other skills necessary for success in American schools.

In this chapter, I examine the implications of language variation for teaching SAE and school literacy to African American children for whom standard English is not native. I briefly review several perspectives on the origin and historical development of African American language, but most of the chapter focuses on what educators can do to facilitate literacy and learning in linguistically different African American children.

BACKGROUND

When I was a child, my favorite pastime was reading. It was an escape from an otherwise "less than exciting" existence in a small segregated town in Texas. It was also one of the few leisure activities my mother allowed. "An idle mind is the devil's workshop" was her favorite saying, and idle children were immediately put to work pulling weeds from the yard, washing dishes, scrubbing floors, or some other such task. If you were reading a book, you weren't disturbed. So every Friday on my way home from school, I stopped at the library to check out books, 10 books to be exact, because that was the limit you could borrow.

I am the youngest of 11 children and by most financial standards we were poor. But we were rich in the things that really matter in life. Our father was full of humor and dearly loved his 11 children. He repeatedly told us we were geniuses and could achieve anything we put our hearts and minds to. My mother, well ahead of her time, was politically savvy and proud of her African heritage. She told us when we were very young (back in the early 1950s) that we were African, and that that was something to be proud of. My mother had, in the African tradition, a love for the word. She read everything she could get her hands on. She loved to read aloud newspaper or magazine articles she obtained from many sources, including the homes of Whites where she sometimes worked as a domestic. She would discuss each article with whoever was in earshot and almost always from a point of view that differed from that espoused in the article.

Other than the Bible, and what Mother brought in from other people's houses, we didn't own any books, probably because we couldn't afford them. But we had a rich tradition of storytelling. Stories filled the evenings of my childhood. In spring and summer, we would go outside after dinner and on a pallet on the grass listen to stories, and in the winter we snuggled together on blankets in the living room. My older sisters and brothers were the griots of the family. They passed on our rich history of African and African American folklore. Each night, we younger children listened carefully to as many as seven stories, complete with sound effects, and eagerly looked to the day when we, too, would become griots.

I don't remember learning to read, but as far back as I can remember, which is about age 6, I was a reader. I could hardly wait for Friday and Saturday when I could go to the library to get my 10 books, books that provided joyous excitement and fueled my dreams.

In this chapter I draw from my literacy experiences as an African American standard English language learner to provide guidelines for developing instructional programs that acknowledge African Americans as second language learners and that draw on nontraditional instructional methodologies to promote language, literacy, and learning. To help place these ideas in perspective, I first provide a brief overview of the origin of African American language.

THE ORIGIN OF AFRICAN AMERICAN LANGUAGE

The origin and historical development of the language of African Americans—African American language—has been the subject of research for more than 3 decades. Yet, in spite of vast amounts of research on the topic, a great majority of Americans, including educators, have distorted notions about the nature of this language form. More often than not, African American language is viewed as slang, defective, or a corrupt form of English. Linguists, however, generally agree that this language is systematic and rule-governed, and represents the communicative competence of the descendants of enslaved Africans in America (Alleyne, 1970; Baugh, 1983; Dillard, 1972; Labov, 1970; Smitherman, 1977; Williams, 1991). In January 1997, the Linguistic Society of America published a resolution that was unanimously adopted by the membership. It affirmed that African American language is systematic and rule-governed like all natural speech varieties, and that to refer to it as slang, mutant, lazy, defective, ungrammatical, or broken English is both incorrect and demeaning. The origin and historical development of African American language may be viewed from two perspectives, the deficit perspective and the difference perspectives.

Deficit Perspective

The *deficit perspective* dates back to the early 1900s, when the language of the descendants of enslaved Africans was viewed as substandard or inferior speech resulting from mental feebleness, inherent anatomical deviations, and, in general, the product of deficient language learners. Proponents of this perspective put forth two postulates to explain African Americans' inability to master the English language. First, they posited that slave descendants did not have enough brain mass to support the learning of a new language. Second, they argued that physiological deviations, such as thick tongues, broad noses, and oversized lips, impeded the ability of Africans to articulate the sounds of the English language (see Gonzales, 1964). Eurocentric bias and racism apparently underlay this perspective, because continental Africans who are multilingual articulate a wide range of complex sounds. Nevertheless, this deficit perspective on the origin of African American language still undergirds the thinking of many Americans and has considerable negative impact on the education of African American students.

My own experience provides an example of how the deficit perspective can pervade the contemporary classroom. When I was in junior high school, my family moved from the segregated South to California. What I remember most about my school experience in California is teachers commenting, in ways that still bring tears to my eyes, on my language and pronunciations. The language of my home was African American language, what some people call Ebonics. I didn't learn to use SAE fluently until I was in college, studying language and linguistics. However, my receptive acquisition of SAE may have begun during my senior year in high school, when I transferred to a predominantly White school where, for the first time in my life, I was surrounded by SAE speakers. My older siblings who had finished high school in the segregated South had a much better handle on SAE than I did. They had learned to switch back and forth from our home language to the school standard with relative ease.

I have no recollection of ever encountering direct teaching of phonics. In fact, my earliest explicit exposure to sound–symbol association was in a phonetics course I took as part of my master's degree in language and speech pathology. The phonetics course was an interesting experience, one that provided me with new rules for decoding some words I had been reading for some time with comprehension, but with a different pronunciation. Since I seldom read aloud, the significance of this new knowledge is debatable.

The language and literacy experiences I had as an African American child growing up in a African American language–dominant home environment raise important questions about literacy. For example, what impact do the culture, home language, and oral literacy experiences of children have on the acquisition of school literacy, and what role do parent and sibling interactions, storytelling, access to books, and literacy models play in this process?

Educators who accept the deficit perspective view African American language as a by-product or cause of poor cognitive functioning. As recently as 1977, in a book entitled *Good Reading for the Disadvantaged Reader* (Spache, 1977), speakers of African American language are described as language handicapped and the language itself as prolific in errors. For decades, educational programs designed to improve academic outcomes for African American students were based on this deficit perspective. In spite of much research that contradicts it, the deficit perspective continues to negatively impact African Americans in our schools and in our society.

Difference Perspectives

Following the early deficit views on the language of African Americans, other theories, referred to collectively as *difference theories* (see Williams, 1991), were put forth by sociolinguists to explain the origin and historical development of African American language. In general, difference theorists view the enslaved Africans' descendants' language as a product of historical, cultural, and linguistic influences, suggesting that the language of African Americans is not deficient, but simply different from SAE. Difference perspectives include those of the dialectologists, the pidgin/creolists, and the Africologists or African origin theorists.

Dialectologists assert that the language and culture Africans brought to America were wiped out by the practices of enslavement and that Black dialect is really no different from White dialect (see Davis, 1970; D'Eloia, 1973; McDavid, 1969; Schneider, 1989). Dillard (1972) soundly challenged the dialectologists' view. He argued that dialectologists, who focused much of their research on trying to trace features of "Black English" to British regional dialects, overlooked the obvious fact that African Americans are not descendants of English immigrants. "To proclaim that the English of Blacks is identical to that of whites," he wrote, "is to allow one's theories to deny the evidence of one's senses" (p. 5).

Creolists maintain that a linguistic phenomenon known as *pidgin English*, which enabled communication between Europeans and Africans, developed around the 17th century on the west coast of Africa, as well as on American and Caribbean plantations. Enslaved Africans adopted this simplified version of English as their primary mode of communication. Once this pidgin English became the native language of enslaved Africans' children, it creolized into what we now know as African American language, Gullah, Jamaican patois, and other Caribbean creoles (see Dillard, 1972; Rickford, 1997; Stewart, 1967).

Stewart (1970), an advocate of the creolist view, stated that "the American Negro dialects probably derived from a creolized form of English once spoken on American plantations by Negro slaves and seemingly related to creolized forms of English, which are still spoken by Negroes in Jamaica and other parts of the Caribbean" (p. 351). Dillard (1972) maintained that, at one time, Black English was fully creolized in the American South, but began decreolizing (approximating the standard language) at some point before the Civil War. Rickford (1998) acknowledged the possibility that some dialects of African American language may, themselves, be creoles and presents a convincing argument to support this hypothesis.

In general, creolists view the African American language as an English-based pidgin with origins in West Africa. Some creolists take a semi-creole perspective, and argue that the language of enslaved Africans resulted from a combination of imported creole speech and the regional speech of British settlers. Most creolists accept the notion of decreolization, and believe that over the past 300 years African American language has more closely approximated SAE. Mufwene (1991), however, has challenged this notion. He posited that African Americans may be utilizing two distinct linguistic codes based on situational appropriateness. Creolists generally acknowledge that African American language has retained some African linguistic features.

Africologists, or *African origin theorists*, hold that African American language has its origin in African languages. This view dates back to the early works of Black scholars such as Carter G. Woodson (1933/1990), who wrote in *The Mis-Education of the Negro*: "In the study of language in school pupils were made to scoff at the Negro dialect as some peculiar possession of the Negro which they should despise rather than directed to study the background of this language as a *broken-down African tongue*" (p. 19, italics added). Woodson's reference to the language of African Americans as a "broken-down African tongue" reflects the critical distinction between how Africologists view the language of the descendants of enslaved Africans versus how other theorists view it.

Africologists posit that the African American language has an African substratum with lexical borrowings from the English language (Alleyne, 1980; Asante, 1991; Blackshire-Belay, 1996; E. Smith, 1992; Williams, 1991). Much of the phonological, morphosyntactical, and semantic structure of African American language is derived from a West African linguistic base and represents linguistic continuity from Africa to America (Alleyne, 1980; Asante, 1991; Blackshire-Belay, 1996; Herskovits, 1941; E. Smith, 1977; Williams, 1991).

From the Africologist's perspective, African American language is not a dialect or vernacular of English. Rather, it is an African-based language that evolved among enslaved Africans on American plantations. According to Williams (1991), "It is accurate to say that the linguistic foundation and structural framework of African American language is African in origin and that much of the exterior (vocabulary) is English in origin" (p. 204). Africologists maintain that when African Americans communicate using African grammar with European words they are speaking a relatively new African language (see Blackshire-Belay, 1996).

All humans have a language, and the nature of that language is determined by the cultural, historical, and linguistic milieu of the people who speak it. African American language is an amalgamation of the cultural and linguistic experiences of Africans, enslaved in America, and their descendants. It is the voice of African American culture, the medium used for relating meaning in different contexts. It reflects the oral customs, cultural mores, and linguistic ingenuity of African people who were enslaved in America. For me, African American language invokes my grandmother gently chiding me in the comfort of her home, warmed by a pot-bellied stove and scented by peach cobbler and castile soap. It represents the love of my mother, the intelligence and humor of my dad. It is the language of my thoughts, the sounds of my community, the soul of my being. African American language is the voice of literary giants such as Langston Hughes, Zora Neal Hurston, Alice Walker, Toni Morrison, and August Wilson. To view this rich and beautiful code as anything less than a language is to ignore the rich linguistic contributions of generations of African people and to devalue African and African American history and culture. Teachers who reject the home language of African American students reject the child.

THE IMPACT OF LANGUAGE VARIATION ON LITERACY ACQUISITION IN AFRICAN AMERICAN STANDARD ENGLISH LANGUAGE LEARNERS (SELLs)

African American children, like all children, assimilate the home culture's ways of thinking and responding, and without effort they learn, during the first 4 years of life, the language or languages of the models in their environment. From 75% to 80% of African American children who arrive at America's inner-city schools during the kindergarten and first-grade years are fluent speakers of African American language. They use African American language as their primary mode of communication and generally possess limited facility in the language of school—SAE.

The research supports the fact that there is a strong connection between reading and oral language (Cazden, 1972; Goodman, 1986; Krashen, 1992; F. Smith, 1988) and that cultural and linguistic diversity has significant implications for the process of becoming literate (see Ferdman, 1990; Hilliard,

1992; Ladson-Billings, 1994; Lee, 1992). Students acquire school literacy more easily when their language matches the language of school or when they become proficient in the language of instruction. For students who arrive at school with limited proficiency in SAE, without appropriate intervention their acquisition of school literacy will suffer.

African American students, who must become literate in the forms of English that appear in newspapers, magazines, textbooks, voting materials, and consumer contracts, must master SAE—the base for school literacy development. Their needs are similar to those of the traditional second language learner. Teachers must have the skills to teach African American SELLs school language and literacy without devaluing the language and literacy experiences they bring from home. They must be able to create learning environments that establish continuity between the home and school cultures and where students are comfortable taking risks. Eradication of their home language or voice is not an option. As F. Smith (1988) asserted, "To try to change a person's language is to reject the very essence of that person" (p. 4). Instead, African American students must be provided opportunities to add SAE to their linguistic repertoire as a second language. An additive instructional model that builds on the home language to support second language learning is pedagogically sound and provides a foundation for the development of school literacy.

INSTRUCTIONAL PRACTICES THAT SUPPORT LITERACY ACQUISITION FOR AFRICAN AMERICAN SELLs

Teachers need more than mastery of the content area to ensure effective instruction of African American SELLs. They also must (a) have an understanding of the student's culture and language, (b) know how to modify traditional best practices to fit the learning needs of African American SELLs, and (c) be aware of effective nontraditional instructional methodologies (see LeMoine & Los Angeles Unified School District, 1999). In this section, I examine six nontraditional, research-based instructional strategies and attempt to tease out their advantages for facilitating literacy and learning in African American SELLs.

Effective teachers of African American SELLs:

1. Build their knowledge and understanding of nonstandard languages and the students who use them.
2. Integrate linguistic knowledge about nonstandard languages (African American language) into instruction.

3. Use second language acquisition methods to support student learning of school language and literacy.

4. Employ a balanced instructional approach to literacy that incorporates language experience, whole language/access to books, and phonics.

5. Infuse the history and culture of SELLs into the curriculum.

6. Consider the learning styles and strengths of SELLs in designing instruction.

Approach 1: Build Knowledge and Understanding of Nonstandard Languages and the Students Who Use Them

Labov (1972) wrote, "There is no reason to believe that any nonstandard vernacular is itself an obstacle to learning. The chief problem is ignorance of language on the part of all concerned" (p. 15). That American educational institutions produce so few bilingual, bicultural, literate African American students may result partly from the failure of educators to use the available linguistic knowledge. Many teachers have limited information about African American language, the learning profile of the children who use it, and its impact on instruction. The research cites teachers' low opinions and misunderstandings about nonstandard language as antecedents of the failure of SELLs to acquire literacy (Hoover, 1979). For too many minority-language children, school failure begins with poor reading skill development, and many of their problems result from the mismatch between their home language and the language of school. Snow (1983) maintained that if conversational interactions in children's homes and school do not parallel each other, the academic success of the child may be jeopardized. This view, known as the match–mismatch formulation of literacy, intimates a need for teachers to learn the language of students, and for students to learn the language of school.

The educational experiences of minority students are determined to a large degree by how teachers perceive their students and how they define themselves in relation to those students. Teachers who expect less of students typically demand less. Fairchild and Evans (1990) asserted that teachers with low expectations of students tend to engage in conscious and unconscious behaviors that produce failure in them. Teachers who have limited knowledge of, or who devalue, the language, culture, and experiences of SELLs convey messages that negatively impact classroom performance. This results in students' lowered aspiration and achievement. The best teachers are learners themselves. Teachers of African American SELLs must build their knowledge of the culture, language, learning styles, and strengths these stu-

dents bring to the classroom. Educating teachers on the cultural and linguistic differences of African American students thus becomes an important
strategy for combating negative perceptions, often held at a subconscious
level, about the ability of African American SELLs. In an article in the *Atlantic
Monthly*, Labov (1972) wrote:

> Teachers are now being told to ignore the language of black children as
> unworthy of attention and useless for learning. They are being taught to
> hear every natural utterance of the child as evidence of his mental inferior-
> ity. As linguists we are unanimous in condemning this view as bad observa-
> tion, bad theory, and bad practice. That educational psychology should be
> influenced by a theory so false to the facts of language is unfortunate; but
> that children should be the victims of this ignorance is intolerable. (p. 15)

Three decades of research provide information on the origin and historical development of the language of African Americans, as well as its characteristic linguistic features, style, use, and pedagogical implications. Teachers
must access this knowledge and use it to construct classroom learning environments that more effectively foster educational success in African American SELLs. Institutions of higher learning have an obligation to incorporate
the linguistic research on African American language into teacher training
programs. Such programs should include courses on language variation in
African American students, as well as opportunities for direct field experiences with African American SELLs. Such knowledge and experience will (a)
increase teachers' skills and comfort level in teaching language-different
African American students, (b) help them to identify effective methodologies
for facilitating their acquisition of school language, and (c) constitute a pre-
requisite for implementing an effective literacy acquisition program.

Approach 2: Integrate Linguistic Knowledge About African American Language Into Instruction

African American SELLs must understand that their home language and
the language of school differ. Moreover, for them to compete successfully in
mainstream language environments, they need to become bilingual and
bicultural and be able to use language appropriately in cross-cultural situations. The classroom teacher's knowledge and understanding of African
American language is a critical determinant of African American SELLs'
success in school. In order to facilitate language and literacy acquisition in
this population, teachers need to understand the process of first language
acquisition, the general principles of how languages are structured, and the
process of second language acquisition. They also need to know the linguistic features of African American language and how they differ from SAE.

Most important, teachers need to know how to infuse this knowledge into the instructional curriculum. Once SELLs understand the origin and development of their home language and how it differs from the language of school, the language of school becomes more comprehensible and their ability to use the target language—SAE—improves.

Taylor (1991) studied infusing linguistic knowledge into instruction through the use of contrastive analysis to support standard English language and literacy development in African American students. Teachers were trained in the use of contrastive analysis techniques, comparing and contrasting the linguistic structures of two languages. After employing these strategies over an 11-month period, their students showed a 59% reduction in the use of nonstandard language features in their written work. The teachers in the study who used traditional language arts approaches saw a slight increase (8.5%) in the use of nonstandard language features. As students learn to recognize the sometimes subtle differences between standard and nonstandard language forms, they become better able to edit their own work for differences in grammar, vocabulary, and syntax. Students also learn to use standard English structure proficiently in its oral and written forms, as they gain an appreciation of their home language and culture.

Approach 3: Use Second Language Acquisition Methods to Support Acquisition of School Language and Literacy

For African American SELLs, the widely held belief that African American language structure mirrors SAE is a misconception that contributes to school failure. The common vocabulary of African American language and SAE often veils the complex phonological, syntactical, and pragmatic differences between the two language systems and masks the difficulties that African American language speakers have with standard English forms. The language difficulties of these students may not be recognized until the demands for literacy and learning increase, around third or fourth grade. It is imperative that teachers understand that many of the literacy acquisition problems experienced by African American SELLs are related to issues of language difference. These language differences suggest the use of second language acquisition methods to support language, literacy, and learning in this population.

Children who are learning to read in a second language experience more problems than do those children whose home language matches school language. Many problems result from a lack of familiarity with the phonological, semantic, and grammatical constraints of school language, and from teachers' rejection of the home language.

African American students as second language readers need special help in vocabulary development, phonological and syntactic development, and cultural knowledge. Their lack of, or limited familiarity with, standard English syntax may impair their ability to identify important syntactic relationships in SAE, and their limited standard English vocabulary may cause difficulty using semantic cues for making predictions and comprehending what they read. Second language acquisition methods have been shown to be effective in facilitating mastery of standard English in African American SELLs, specifically in the acquisition of standard English grammar, syntax, and vocabulary (Hoover, 1979; Johnson, 1969)

African American SELLs need comprehensible input in SAE if they are to become proficient users of that language form. This input is best provided through daily opportunities to see, hear, and interact with more competent users of SAE. As students engage with oral and print models of the target language, their ability to intuit the structure of SAE is enhanced, and they become more proficient users of the new language form.

African American language has a significant impact on the development of written language. Taylor (1991) reported that the language of Black students often interferes with the standard English expectation of writing teachers and may be judged as "sloppy or wrong" or, worse yet, as linguistic distortions (p. 6). She maintained that African American language becomes a serious intrusion into classroom performance, often resulting in teachers' lowered expectations and condescension toward the students who speak it.

Children develop written language as they intuit rules and make sense of the literacy behaviors and routines in the context of their culture. Because the culture of African American SELLs is at variance with the school culture, traditional literacy activities may not yield the outcomes expected and instructional modifications may be required. Second language acquisition tools such as graphic organizers, diagrams, charts, graphs, and illustrations can provide support for African American SELLs in mastering SAE written discourse.

Approach 4: Use a Balanced Approach to Literacy Acquisition That Incorporates Language Experience, Whole Language/Access to Books, and Phonics

A holistic approach to learning and literacy acquisition, which provides opportunities for students to engage in authentic literacy experiences with teacher support, eliminates barriers created by cultural and linguistic differences. Krashen and Biber (1988) said that preschool learning experiences, which involve understanding messages and making sense out of print, are foundational for learning to read and write, much like understanding verbal messages aids in acquiring spoken language. Literacy is an extension of natural language learning and requires that readers draw on their personal knowledge about various topics. Therefore, instruction must be built around the child's home language. To assure that learning occurs, literacy instruction needs to be modified for non-mainstream-culture students who speak a different language and bring diverse literacy experiences to the classroom.

A meaning-construction view of reading balanced with contextual phonics—phonics tied to the context of the language the child uses—may be the best match for African American SELLs. Instruction should begin with meaningful units that engage students in the full process of reading and writing. It should take place in natural, authentic learning environments that welcome language and cultural variation and that draw from students' experiences to render learning relevant and meaningful (Cooper, 1997; Cummins, 1989; Flores, Teft, & Diaz, 1991; Goodman, 1986; Hale, 1995; Krashen, 1992; Larkin, 1993).

Access to Books. Many African American SELLs come from home environments where being read to is not part of the literacy routine. As was the case in my home, the literacy experience of these students is more likely to be storytelling. Reading to African American SELLs therefore must be part of daily instruction. Sulzby (1994) asserted that "young children who are read to before formal schooling are ushered into an understanding of the relationships between oral and written language" (p. 246). For SELLs who have not had exposure to books before school, classrooms must become the venue for building the relationship between oral and print language.

Increased reading results in improved literacy development. Students who read more perform better on tests of reading comprehension, vocabulary, writing, and grammar (Krashen, 1993). Harris (1995) reported that the benefits derived from increased reading include improved comprehension, increased vocabulary levels, enhanced critical-thinking skills, enjoyment of the creative uses of language and art, and exposure to a variety of linguistic models.

A culturally conscious classroom library and comfortable reading environment are important requirements for facilitating literacy acquisition in African American SELLs. However, teachers providing literature-based instruction in a whole-language context often are devoid of knowledge about culture as it relates to literacy and literature (Barrera, 1992). In a study of an elementary school located in a metropolitan center in the southwest United States, Barrera found that often the program's literature was dominated by themes and characters that did not reflect the faces, experiences, and histories of many of the school's children. According to Harris (1995), the literature infused into classrooms must be culturally conscious. When provided opportunities to engage with literature that reflects their own culture, language, and experiences, African American children are more motivated and their cultural identity is affirmed and validated. As they learn to appreciate literature in the context of their own culture, they are better able to appreciate the literature of other cultures. Books written by African American authors, Harris said, present real-world situations that enable students to use the knowledge they possess, transfer their knowledge to analogous situations, or create new knowledge and understanding. Introducing oral literature in the form of African folktales and storytelling in the classroom supports literacy acquisition by establishing important linkages between the home language and literacy experiences of African American SELLs and school.

Whole-Language and Language-Experience Approaches as Facilitators of Literacy Acquisition in African American SELLs. A whole-language approach to literacy instruction focuses on students constructing, comprehending, and expressing meaning in real learning environments. Whole language, according to Thompson (1997), evolved, at least in part, from language experience, an approach that considers reading to be an extension of the language skills a child has already acquired. Both approaches build on the language and literacy experiences children bring to school and may remove many of the barriers created by differences between the students' home language and culture and that of the school. McLaughlin (1994) concluded that because students, rather than teachers, define the context of the learning situation in whole-language classrooms, the cultural mismatch that frequently occurs with children from diverse backgrounds is reduced.

Another positive aspect of whole-language instruction when used with African American SELLs is its emphasis on interrelated learning experiences. This emphasis, according to some researchers, tends to curtail the use of workbooks, ditto sheets, and skill-and-drill orientations that often characterize classrooms of minority students (Flores et al., 1991; Goodman, 1986; Krashen, 1992; Larkin, 1993).

Phonics. Phonics instruction as part of a balanced approach to literacy acquisition for SAE language learners requires that the teacher have knowledge of the phonological linguistic features of the language the student is most proficient in (i.e., African American language). The "phonetic" method of teaching reading, which emphasizes auditory analysis of the correspondence between oral and written language, requires that learners be able to isolate and recognize the distinct phonemes of language and relate them to graphic signs (see Ferreiro & Teberosky, 1982). For African American SELLs, the ability to recognize some phonemes in the context of SAE may be impaired, creating phonological sources of reading problems. Labov

(1995) maintained that the differences between written language and spoken language are much greater for African American language than for other nonstandard languages. He stated that the most obvious linguistic contributors to reading problems involve sound–spelling relationships. Moreover, Labov asserted that the African American language rules that govern the articulation of final consonants can lead to "extreme growth of homonymy and great difficulty in recognizing distinctions that are obvious in classroom English" (p. 47). Speakers of African American language, Labov felt, use alphabetic skills only in attacking the first consonant and the first vowel, and abandon such efforts beyond this point. He maintained that "this loss of confidence in the alphabet is a direct result of the very abstract relationship between the alphabet and the surface realizations of words in [African American language]" (p. 48).

Berdan (1978) wrote that conventional phonics-based reading programs are inappropriate for speakers of African American language for several reasons. First, conventional phonics-based reading programs sequence late and give special attention to silent letters (e.g., the *b* of *dumb* and *lamb*). No such special treatment, however, is afforded comparable silent letters for African American language speakers (e.g., the *d* of *band* or the *k* of *mask*). Second, students typically receive additional practice in differentiating homophones for which pronunciation offers no spelling cues (e.g., *for, four, fore*). There is no such special practice for African American language homophones (e.g., *when, win, wind*). Finally, teaching procedures are considered to be most inappropriate when they attempt to use phonics instruction as articulation instruction for African American language speakers. When using a phonics approach with African American SELLs it must be applied in the context of the sound system the child hears and uses. This contextual phonics approach requires that teachers be knowledgeable of the phonological characteristics of African American language and SAE; it also provides opportunities for African American SELLs to acquire phonemic analysis, alphabetic, and phonic skills in the context of both the home and school languages.

Literacy acquisition for African American SELLs must build on the home language and literacy patterns, experiences, and funds of knowledge these students bring to the classroom. The teacher must infuse their culture and language into instruction, teach phonics skills in the context of their home language, read to them daily, and provide opportunities for free voluntary reading.

Approach 5: Infuse the History and Culture of SELLs Into the Curriculum

Culturally different students who experience high levels of academic failure generally benefit when their culture is integrated into the school curriculum. Learning about the cultural background of the child and incorporating that knowledge into instruction is a widely recommended intervention (see Asante, 1991; Cummins, 1989; Ladson-Billings, 1994; Ogbu, 1992). The cultural and linguistic differences of African American SELLs can result in school socialization and adaptation difficulties that lead to low achievement (see Cummins, 1989; Hale-Benson, 1986; Ogbu, 1992; Shade, 1982). The research confirms that in order for students to be academically successful, they must first be comfortable with themselves (Branch, Goodwin, & Gualtieri, 1993; Gay, 1993). Yet, many researchers agree that the traditional school culture reflects the dominant class (Barrera, 1992; Lee, 1992; Ogbu, 1992), and that not long after they start their formal schooling, minority students often become disadvantaged and lose their perceptions of personal competence (Gay, 1993). Students who have low self-esteem because they lack confidence in their potential will experience difficulty in school. Teachers must create comfortable learning environments that validate, affirm, and accommodate the cultural differences of African American SELLs.

Culturally Relevant Teaching. According to Ladson-Billings (1994), culturally relevant teaching—defined as pedagogy that empowers students intellectually, socially, emotionally, and politically by using cultural referents to impart knowledge, skills, and attitudes—is effective teaching for African American students. It transcends the negative effects of not seeing one's history, culture, or background represented in textbooks or curricula and allows African American students to choose academic excellence while still identifying with African and African American culture.

Cultural discontinuities in the classroom can exist in language, cognitive learning styles, work habits, and problem solving (see Gay, 1993; Hale, 1995; Vickers, 1994). These gaps represent significant obstacles to successful teaching and learning in culturally diverse classrooms. Studies show that when minority students have positive attitudes toward both their own culture and the dominant culture, school failure does not occur (Cummins, 1989). Ladson-Billings (1995) reported that teachers practicing culturally relevant teaching know how to support learning in African American students by consciously creating social interactions to help them meet the criteria of academic success, cultural competence, and critical consciousness. These teachers, she asserted, demonstrate a connectedness with students, develop a noncompetitive community of learners, encourage students to learn collaboratively, and extend interactions beyond the classroom and into the community.

African Americans are not culture-free, and the question of what elements are key in defining the cultural experience of Africans in America is one that has been pondered for decades. W. E. B. DuBois spoke years ago of a double consciousness that harries African Americans. More recently, Boykin (1997), who refers to this phenomenon as a "triple quandary" effect, asserted that African Americans must acknowledge and deal with an African consciousness, an American consciousness, and the effects of being oppressed and marginalized as descendants of enslaved Africans. Teachers of African American SELLs must critically examine themselves and their methods or "ways of doing" in the classroom. As Cummins (1989) said, "Minority students can become empowered *only* [italics added] through interactions with educators who have critically examined and, where necessary, challenged the educational (and social) structure within which they operate" (p. 6). Without being able to effectively communicate and understand a child, it is impossible to teach. Teachers must develop culturally consistent ways of interacting with students from cultures that are different from their own, and they must learn to adapt instruction so that learners from diverse cultures are accepted and accommodated in the classroom.

Approach 6: Consider the Learning Styles and Strengths of African American SELLs in Designing Instruction

Learning styles are an important dynamic in the classroom that impacts instruction. According to O'Neil (1990), learning style refers to characteristic cognitive, affective, and physiological behaviors that indicate how learners perceive, interact, and respond to the learning environment. The basic premise in learning-style theory is that cultural socialization can significantly influence how students with similar intellectual potential display their cognitive abilities. Much of the research reports that African Americans, as a group, have distinct ways of processing information, interacting, communicating, and learning (see Brandt, 1990; Dunn, 1990; Hale-Benson, 1986; Hilliard, 1976, 1992; Nelson-LeGall & Jones, 1991; O'Neil, 1990; Shade, 1982).

Hilliard (1992) contended that the high degree of within-group socialization that exists among African Americans, in general, derives from a long and continuing history of racial segregation and economic discrimination. In a study conducted in California, Hilliard (1976) contrasted African and African American culture with European and European American culture. He concluded that a unique African American core culture could be empirically described and that cultural behavioral style distinctions exist, and that traditional American schools are encapsulated in a style that mimics the cultural style of most European Americans. Hilliard found that African Americans view their environment as a whole rather than in isolated parts; prefer intuitive rather than deductive or inductive reasoning; approximate concepts of space, number, and time; attend to people stimuli rather than object stimuli; and rely on nonverbal as well as verbal communication. As humans, our culture is a reflection of our lives as we experience and understand it.

Boykin (1997) identified nine dimensions of African American culture and maintained that effective learning environments for African American students should reflect these dimensions. His research revealed that African American children's highest performance in comprehension and recall emerges when high-movement expressive content is presented in a high-movement expressive context. European American children, in his studies, scored highest when low-movement expressive content was presented in a low-movement expressive context. Boykin also examined the influence of learning conditions on students' critical thinking. His preliminary findings suggest that "learning in more culturally salient communal environments, may enhance the critical thinking abilities and facilitate the employment of advanced cognitive strategies of low-income African American elementary children" (p. 13).

Ogbu (1992) asserted that the school learning of minority students is influenced by complex social, economic, historical, and cultural factors, including minority status. He targeted the nature of the relationship between the minority culture and the dominant White American culture as the explanation for why "involuntary" or "caste-like" minorities such as African Americans, Native Americans, Native Hawaiians, and Mexican Americans find it harder to cross cultural and language boundaries to academic success. Involuntary minorities, he asserted, display "secondary cultural behaviors" that include characteristic cognitive, communication, interaction, and learning styles that work in opposition to the teaching styles that predominate in American schools. He posited that cultural differences in style explain why African Americans, among other involuntary immigrants, have greater difficulty crossing cultural barriers to achieve academic success.

Shade (1982) conducted a comprehensive theoretical review of the research to examine the notion that variance in academic competence results from differences in culturally induced psychological, cognitive, and behavioral strategies. She looked at cultural foundations of Afro-American thought, Afro-American social cognition, socialization influences on cognition, Afro-American style of knowing, perceptual style, conceptual style, personality style, and cognitive style. She found differences between White and Black students in perceptual style, social cognition, and personality style. Shade concluded that individuals may not learn in the same manner and may develop diverse cognitive strategies for processing information. Further, she concluded that African Americans' well-developed social cognition may be disadvantageous in object-oriented school settings. In traditional classrooms where low-movement expressive and individual-competitive environments are the norm, and where field-independent, analytical, or objective-oriented cognitive strategies are prerequisites to achievement,

African American children who bring a different learning style to the classroom are clearly at a disadvantage.

Many researchers feel that accommodating students' distinct learning and communication styles in instruction can make a difference in their learning (see Asante, 1991; Gonzalez, 1993; Hale, 1995; Viadero, 1996). Dunn (1990) wrote that when students cannot learn the way we teach them, we have an obligation to teach them the way they learn. Teachers who instruct African American SELLs need an understanding of the learning styles and strengths these students bring to the classroom.

Hilliard (1992) believed that the overriding issue in teaching practices in American schools is less a matter of style influencing learning and more one of style influencing teaching and teaching influencing learning. He maintained that students with diverse styles of learning can master any style of instruction provided they are given the opportunity to develop a new repertoire of behaviors and skills. African American SELLs need to learn new ways of interacting with and relating to stimuli in school settings. In other words, they need to become bilingual, biliterate, and bicultural, and teachers who have an understanding of learning-style differences are clearly in a better position to support this transition.

DESIGNING CLASSROOM INSTRUCTION FOR LITERACY ACQUISITION IN AFRICAN AMERICAN SELLs

In summary, instructional approaches that move African American SELLs toward mastery of school language and literacy include traditional instructional approaches (modified and unmodified) and nontraditional instructional approaches. African American SELLs need opportunities to engage in, see demonstrated, and learn to value school literacy practices while their home culture and literacies are valued and validated. As they approximate school or conventional literacy behaviors, their efforts should be celebrated and their reading miscues expanded on and treated as literacy attempts. The instructional approach to literacy development must embody language experience, access to books, and phonics.

The classroom environment that facilitates school literacy acquisition in African American SELLs should include the following:

- Classroom libraries that contain culturally conscious literature, magazines, and newspapers that reflect the students' home life, personal interests, cultural background, and language.

- Listening centers that include African and African American folklore, storytelling videos, books on tape, and literature that provide opportunities for students to hear the language of school modeled.
- Cultural art and artifacts, games, pictorial histories, family trees, and achievers who validate the importance of contributions of people of African descent to our world.
- Technology—computers, audio cassette recorders, headphones, overhead projectors, TV/VCR, video cameras, electronic thesauruses—as tools in language and literacy acquisition.
- A print-rich environment that includes writing centers, teacher- and student-generated lists, word walls, message boards, songs, chants, big books, and journals.
- Student desks grouped to encourage social interaction and collaborative learning.

The following instructional strategies foster literacy acquisition in African American SELLs:

Employ a balanced instructional approach to literacy that incorporates language experience, access to books, and phonics.

- Model and provide daily opportunities for silent sustained and/or free voluntary reading.
- Read to students daily from books that reflect their experiences and openly discuss content to help students make linkages between the spoken word and print.
- Provide opportunities for consistent exposure to the oral and written discourse patterns of standard English.
- Provide opportunities for students to write every day. Use journals, writing prompts, and other resources.
- Provide opportunities (through listening centers and other activities) for students to listen actively, gather information, and respond appropriately.
- Match print with oral language experiences by incorporating language-experience activities into instruction.
- Use multiple reading strategies and approaches (guided reading, partner reading, independent reading, etc.) to enhance students' ability to read with accuracy, fluency, and comprehension.
- Integrate listening, speaking, reading, and writing into the daily curriculum.
- Use the writing process.

Phonemic awareness/phonics.

- Provide opportunities for students to listen to, read, and recite poetry, rhymes, and songs.
- Compare and contrast poetry, songs, and stories written in African American language and SAE.
- Address homophones created in the context of the home language (African American language) usage.
- Begin phonics instruction with word-final consonant clusters.
- Build alphabetic and phonic skills in the context of the home and school languages.
- Introduce contrastive analysis of sound and spelling patterns to support phonetic analysis.

Expand the student's personal thesaurus of conceptually coded words.

- Encourage vocabulary development in the context of communicating ideas.
- Focus on vocabulary development with an emphasis on synonyms, antonyms, prefixes, and suffixes.
- Motivate students to appreciate literature and the role it plays in developing personal vocabularies.
- Emphasize vocabulary development around authentic events and student lives balanced with dictionary use.

Incorporate second language acquisition methodologies into instruction.

- Activate and use student's background knowledge.
- Integrate oral language into all curricular areas by engaging students in instructional conversations.
- Provide opportunities for students to speak for a variety of audiences and purposes.
- Use graphic organizers (Venn diagrams, T charts, outlines) and manipulatives to enhance meaning.
- Use manipulatives and realia to explain concepts.
- Question appropriately using referential questions, wait time, and comprehension checks.
- Negotiate and clarify meaning throughout lessons.

Integrate linguistic knowledge about standard and nonstandard languages into instruction.

- Understand the general principals of how languages are structured.
- Know the process of first and second language development.
- Use literature and samples of students' daily oral and written language to engage in contrastive analysis and to support the acquisition of SAE.
- Use the editing phase of the writing process as a vehicle for analyzing and identifying African American language and standard English structure.
- Provide opportunities for students to compare and contrast poetry and songs written in African American language and SAE.
- Use literature written in African American language and SAE to compare and contrast the two language forms.

Build on the learning styles and strengths of African American SELLs to develop critical thinking skills and enhance reading comprehension and recall.

- Emphasize small-group activities to encourage language development and the sharing of ideas.
- Infuse reading material with high-movement content (i.e., stories about skating, jump rope, swimming, basketball, racing, etc.).
- Incorporate music and movement to create a high-movement context for listening to literature.
- Create communal learning environments that encourage knowledge sharing.
- Use cooperative learning groups for instructional activities.
- Infuse storytelling into the curriculum and include wordless books and picture stories.
- Provide opportunities for role-playing, recited speeches, debates, and script reading.

Infuse the language, history, culture, and experiences of African American students into the curriculum to increase achievement.

- Know general aspects and values of African and African American culture.
- Convey knowledge on ancient Africa—its culture, history, impact on the contemporary world, and its contribution to the forward flow of human history.

- Validate students' home language in positive, affirming ways.
- Create a positive classroom environment that acknowledges, respects, affirms, and accommodates diversity.
- Match print with cultural/community activities (e.g., trips to the grocery store or mall, playground activities and popular physical movement games, church and Sunday school experiences).

The learning profile of African American SELLs differs in many ways from the profile of students whose home language and culture match the language and culture of school. It is the responsibility of teachers to learn about the culture, language, learning styles, and strengths of the students they teach and to incorporate into instruction approaches and methodologies that build on who they are and what they bring to school to support language, literacy, and learning.

RECOMMENDED READINGS

Adger, C. T., Christian, D., & Taylor, O. (Eds.). (1999). *Making the connection: Language and academic achievement among African American students*. McHenry, IL: Center for Applied Linguistics.

Au, K. (1993). *Literacy instruction in multicultural settings*. Orlando, FL: Holt, Rinehart & Winston.

Cummins, J. (1989). *Empowering minority students*. Sacramento: California Association for Bilingual Education.

Gadsden, L., & Wagner, D. (Eds.). (1995). *Literacy among African-American youth: Issues in learning, teaching, and schooling*. Cresskill, NJ: Hampton Press.

LeMoine, N., & Los Angeles Unified School District. (1999). *English for your success: A language development program for African American students*. Maywood, NJ: Peoples Publishing Group.

McLeod, B. (Ed.). (1994). *Language and learning: Educating linguistically diverse students*. Albany: State University of New York Press.

Tharp, R., & Gallimore, R. (1988). *Rousing minds to life: Teaching, learning, and schooling in social context*. Cambridge, England: Cambridge University Press.

REFERENCES

Alleyne, M. (1970). The linguistic continuity of Africa in the Caribbean. In H. Richards (Ed.), *Topics in Afro-American studies* (pp. 119–134). Buffalo, NY: Black Academy Press.

Alleyne, M. C. (1980). *Comparative Afro-American: An historical-comparative study of English-based Afro-American dialects*. Ann Arbor: University of Michigan Press.

Asante, M. (1991). Afrocentric curriculum. *Educational Leadership, 49*, 28–31.

Barrera, R. (1992). The cultural gap in literature-based instruction. *Education and Urban Society, 24*, 227–243.

Baugh, J. (1983). *Black street speech: Its history, structure, and survival*. Austin: University of Texas Press.

Berdan, R. (1978). *Dialect fair reading instruction for speakers of Black English*. Paper prepared for the Sociolinguistics of Reading session, Sociolinguistics Research Program, Ninth

World Congress of Sociology. Department of Health, Education, and Welfare, National Institute of Education, Uppsala, Sweden.

Blackshire-Belay, A. (1996). The location of Ebonics within the framework of the Africological paradigm. *Journal of Black Studies, 27*, 5–23.

Boykin, W. (1997, October). *Cultural factors in school-relevant cognitive functioning.* Paper presented at the Congressional Black Caucus Education Forum, Washington, DC.

Branch, R., Goodwin, Y., & Gualtieri, J. (1993). Making classroom instruction culturally pluralistic. *The Education Forum, 58*, 57–70.

Brandt, R. (1990). On learning styles: A conversation with Pat Guild. *Educational Leadership, 48*, 10–14.

Cazden, C. (1972). *Child language and education.* New York: Holt, Rinehart & Winston.

Cooper, J. (1997). *Literacy: Helping children construct meaning* (3rd ed.). Boston: Houghton Mifflin.

Cummins, J. (1989). *Empowering minority students.* Sacramento: California Association for Bilingual Education.

Davis, L. M. (1970). Social dialectology in America: A critical survey. *Journal of English Linguistics, 4*, 46–56.

D'Eloia, S. G. (1973). Issues in the analysis of nonstandard Negro English: A review of J. L. Dillard's Black English: Its history and usage in the United States. *Journal of English Linguistics, 7*, 87–106.

Dillard, J. L. (1972). *Black English: Its history and usage in the United States.* New York: Random House.

Dunn, R. (1990). Rita Dunn answers questions on learning styles. *Educational Leadership, 42*, 15–18.

Fairchild, H., & Evans, S. (1990). African American dialects and schooling: A review. In A. Padilla (Ed.), *Bilingual education: Issues and strategies* (pp. 75–86). Newbury Park, CA: Sage.

Ferdman, B. M. (1990). Literacy and cultural identity. *Harvard Educational Review, 60*, 181–204.

Ferreiro, E., & Teberosky, A. (1982). *Literacy before schooling.* Portsmouth, NH: Heinemann.

Flores, B., Teft, P., & Diaz, E. (1991). Transforming deficit myths about learning, language, and culture. *Language Arts, 68*, 369–378.

Gay, G. (1993). Building cultural bridges: A bold proposal for teacher education. *Education and Urban Society, 20*, 285–299.

Gonzales, A. (1964). *The black border: Gullah stories of the Carolina coast.* Columbia, SC: State Print Company.

Gonzalez, J. M. (1993). School meanings and cultural bias. *Education and Urban Society, 25*, 254–269.

Goodman, K. (1986). *What's whole in whole language.* Ontario, Canada: Scholastic.

Hale, J. (1995, September). *Best practices in early childhood programs serving African American children.* Working paper presented at the annual conference of the National Black Child Development Institute–Child Development Issues Forum, Washington, DC.

Hale-Benson, J. (1986). *Black children, their roots, culture and learning styles.* Baltimore: Johns Hopkins University Press.

Harris, V. (1995). Using African American literature in the classroom. In V. Gadsden & D. Wagner (Eds.), *Literacy among African-American youth* (pp. 229–259). Cresskill, NJ: Hampton Press.

Herskovits, M. (1941). *Myth of the Negro past.* Boston: Beacon Press.

Hilliard, A. G. (1976). *Alternatives to IQ testing: An approach to the identification of gifted minority children.* Sacramento: California State Department of Education.

Hilliard, A. G. (1992). Behavioral style, culture, and teaching and learning. *Journal of Negro Education, 61*, 370–377.

Hoover, M. R. (1979). A semiforeign language approach to teaching reading to bidialectal children. In R. Shafer (Ed.), *Applied linguistics and reading* (pp. 63–71). Newark, DE: International Reading Association.

Johnson, K. (1969). *A comparison of traditional techniques and second language techniques for teaching grammatical structures of standard oral English to tenth-grade Negro students who speak a nonstandard dialect.* Unpublished doctoral dissertation, University of Southern California, Los Angeles.

Krashen, S. (1992). *Fundamentals of language education.* Torrance, CA: Laredo.

Krashen, S. D. (1993). *The power of reading: Insights from the research.* Englewood, CO: Libraries Unlimited.

Krashen, S., & Biber, D. (1988). *On course: Bilingual education's success in California.* Ontario, CA: California Association for Bilingual Education.

Labov, W. (1970). *The study of nonstandard English.* Champaign, IL: National Council of Teachers of English.

Labov, W. (1972, June). Academic ignorance and Black intelligence. *The Atlantic Monthly, 229,* 14–17.

Labov, W. (1983). Recognizing Black English in the classroom. In J. W. Chambers (Ed.), *Black English educational equity and the law* (pp. 29–55). Ann Arbor, MI: Karoma.

Labov, W. (1995). Can reading failure be reversed: A linguistic approach to the question. In L. Gadsden & D. Wagner (Eds.), *Literacy among African-American youth: Issues in learning, teaching, and schooling* (pp. 39–68). Cresskill, NJ: Hampton Press.

Ladson-Billings, G. (1994). *The dreamkeepers: Successful teachers of African American children.* San Francisco: Jossey-Bass.

Ladson-Billings, G. (1995, Fall). Toward a theory of culturally relevant pedagogy. *American Educational Research Journal, 32*(3), 465–491.

Larkin, J. (1993). Rethinking basic skills instruction with urban students. *The Educational Forum, 57,* 412–419.

Lee, C. D. (1992). Literacy, cultural diversity, and instruction. *Education and Urban Society, 24,* 279–291.

LeMoine, N., & Los Angeles Unified School District. (1999). *English for your success: A language development program for African American students.* Maywood, NJ: Peoples Publishing Group.

McDavid, R. I. (1969). Dialects: British and American standard and nonstandard. In A. A. Hill (Ed.), *Linguistics today* (pp. 79–88). New York: Basic Books.

McLaughlin, B. (1994). First and second language literacy in the late elementary grades. In B. McLeod (Ed.), *Language and learning: Educating linguistically diverse students* (pp. 179–198). Albany: State University of New York Press.

Mufwene, S. (1991). Is Gullah decreolizing? A comparison of a speech sample of the 1930s with a sample of the 1980s. In G. Bailey, N. Maynor, & P. Cukor-Avila (Eds.), *The emergence of Black English, text and commentary* (pp. 213–230). Philadelphia: John Benjamins.

Nelson-LeGall, S., & Jones, E. (1991). Classroom help-seeking behavior of African American children. *Education and Urban Society, 24,* 27–40.

Ogbu, J. (1992). Understanding cultural diversity and learning. *Educational Researcher, 21,* 5–14.

O'Neil, J. (1990). Making sense of style. *Educational Leadership, 42,* 4–9.

Rickford, J. (1997). Suite for ebony and phonics. *Discover Magazine, 2,* 82–87.

Rickford, J. (1998). The creole origins of African American vernacular English: Evidence from copula absence. In S. Mufwene, J. R. Rickford, G. Bailey, & J. Baugh (Eds.), *African American English: Structure, history and use* (pp. 154–200). New York: Routledge.

Schneider, E. W. (1989). *American earlier Black English, morphological and syntactic variables.* Tuscaloosa: University of Alabama Press.

Shade, B. J. (1982). Afro-American cognitive style: A variable in school success? *Review of Educational Research, 52*(2), 219–244.

Smith, E. (1977). *The historical development of Ebonics: An examination and analysis of three linguistic views and ideological perspectives*. Unpublished manuscript, California State University at Fullerton.

Smith, E. (1992). African American language behavior: A world of difference. In P. H. Dreyer (Ed.), *Reading the world: Multimedia and multicultural learning in today's classrooms. Proceedings of the Claremont Reading Conference* (pp. 38–52). Claremont, CA: Claremont Graduate School.

Smith, F. (1988). *Joining the literacy club: Further essays into education*. Portsmouth, NH: Heinemann.

Smitherman, G. (1977). *Talkin' and testifyin': The language of Black America*. Boston: Houghton Mifflin.

Snow, C. (1983). Literacy and language: Relationships during the preschool years. *Harvard Educational Review, 53*(2), 165–189.

Spache, G. (1977). *Good reading for the disadvantaged reader*. Champaign, IL: Garrard.

Stewart, W. (1967, Spring). Sociolinguistic factors in the history of American Negro dialects. *Florida FL Reporter, 5*, 11–30.

Stewart, W. (1970). Toward a history of American Negro dialect. In F. Williams (Ed.), *Language and poverty: Perspectives on a theme* (pp. 351–379). Chicago: Markham.

Sulzby, E. (1994). Children's emergent reading of favorite storybooks: A developmental study. In B. Ruddell, M. Ruddell, & H. Singer (Eds.), *Theoretical models and processes of reading* (4th ed., pp. 244–280). Newark, DE: International Reading Association.

Taylor, H. (1991). *Standard English, Black English, and bidialectalism: A controversy*. New York: Peter Lang.

Thompson, B. (1997). The teaching of reading. In V. Edwards & D. Corson (Eds.), *Encyclopedia of language education: Vol. 2. Literacy* (pp. 9–17). Norwell, MA: Kluwer Academic.

Viadero, D. (1996, April 10). Culture clash. *Education Week*, 39–42.

Vickers, H. (1994). Young children at risk: Differences in family functioning. *Journal of Education Research, 87*, 262–270.

Williams, S. (1991). Classroom use of African American language: Educational tool or social weapon? In C. Sleeter (Ed.), *Empowering through multicultural education* (pp. 199–215). New York: State University of New York Press.

Woodson, C. G. (1990). *The mis-education of the Negro*. Trenton, NJ: Africa World Press. (Original work published 1933)

Chapter 10

From the Pews to the Classrooms: Influences of the African American Church on Academic Literacy

Beverly J. Moss
Ohio State University

It is fairly common knowledge that the African American church is the most powerful and long-standing institution within African American communities. This power can be measured in the number of politicians, African American and White, who parade through Sunday services at African American churches while on the campaign trail. They do so because the church is the most important vehicle, next to television and urban radio, for reaching large groups of African Americans. The implication is that by showing up in these churches, the politician has recognized the importance of African American communities to the political process. The church's influence is also evident in the number of African American politicians and social activists, from former presidential candidate Jesse Jackson to Republican Congressman J. C. Watts, who are ministers. The African American pulpit has proven to be a great training ground and launching pad for careers in public service. Yet, the influence of the African American church is more widespread and far-reaching than the political arena. Its influence can be seen on a more fundamental level among community members, namely, in how we come to understand and practice literacy. More specifically, how many African Americans define and negotiate major literacy events[1] has much to do with the way that language and literacy operate in contemporary African American churches.

---

[1]I use Heath's (1982) definition of *literacy event*: "Any activity involving one or more persons surrounding the comprehension of and/or production of print" (p. 92).

I focus, in this chapter, on the powerful ways that literacy is practiced and promoted in African American churches, particularly three churches in the Chicago area. These models of literacy are then discussed within the context of models of school literacy.

A HISTORICAL MOMENT

In the past, African American churches had a distinct role in the education, particularly the literacy education, of their people (Anderson, 1988). That role, quite literally, was to teach them how to read and write, something that was against the law during slavery. During that period, literacy instruction was confined generally to encoding and decoding, mostly reading the Bible, but also for the purpose of gaining freedom. Many a forged note or pass was written by slaves who had learned to read and write and who used such skills under the name of their owners to escape their imprisonment. Frederick Douglass, of course, is the most well-known example. However, just after slavery, African American churches played an even more prominent role in the literacy education of African Americans through their sponsorship and offering of Sabbath (and Sunday) schools. Royster (2000) explains that Sabbath schools, "run predominantly by African Americans themselves . . . operated in the evenings and on weekends and reached thousands of students who did not have the option of attending week-day schools" (p. 173). James D. Anderson (1988) states that:

> Sabbath schools continued to grow in the black community long after Reconstruction. In 1868, the African Methodist Episcopal (AME) church, for example, enrolled 40,000 pupils in its Sabbath schools. By 1885, the AME church reported having "200,000 children in Sunday schools" for "intellectual and moral" instruction. (p. 13)

Today, literacy instruction within African American churches takes on an even broader and more complex definition than in the past. No longer confined to encoding, decoding, and "moral" lessons, literacy instruction also encompasses understanding the relation between oral and written language, the nature of literacy events that are commonplace within African American churches, and the values and beliefs that surround those literacy events. And at the center of this instruction is the example that the minister sets, as a literate person whose literacy practices and literate behavior influence the majority of the congregation. For the purposes of this chapter I am most concerned with literacy events as defined and practiced in African American churches and their relations with academic literacy events (namely, academic essays and other academic literate practices). I am particularly interested in the models of literacy that many African American youths carry from African American churches, a home community institution, into their academic communities. How do these models intersect, match, or clash with models of literacy promoted by the academy? What can educators learn from what students bring into the classroom from their home communities that will move these students more quickly toward acquiring academic literacy and, thus, multiliteracy?

The data for this chapter come from an ethnographic study of three African American churches in the Chicago area and, in addition, Columbus, Ohio, where one of the ministers from the original study was a guest minister. I collected data through a participant-observer role as a regular parishioner in each church. The data consist of fieldnotes, interviews, and artifacts (e.g., church bulletins, transcripts, and audio recordings of the sermons).

THE CHURCH COMMUNITIES

The three churches[2] in which I conducted fieldwork represent three distinct church communities with different personalities; yet, these churches, distinctly different in their worship styles, are remarkably similar in that they can easily be marked as typical African American churches. They are also remarkably similar in the way they define and use literacy.

Of the three churches in Chicago, the first church site in which I collected data is the largest predominantly African American church in its majority White denomination, as well as in the Midwest, with well over 6,000 members. The size of this church is important because, as the youngest of the three churches at barely 50 years old, this church made great strides quickly. When the current minister came to this South Side church some 30 years ago, it had 100 members. Since I completed the study, this congregation has moved into a new $10-million complex (just a few blocks from the previous structure) that houses a sanctuary, restaurant and cafeteria, credit union, and educational complex. This church sees its mission as serving not only the needs of its own congregation but also the needs of the broader African American community in Chicago. A church as large as this one has a diverse congregation from all walks of life, but many identify it as a predominantly middle-class church. The minister is an internationally renowned theologian who travels around the world to preach. As a well-educated preacher's son, this minister, whom I

---

[2]For a more detailed description of the churches, see Moss (1994, in press).

refer to as the *manuscript minister,*[3] often assigns a book for the entire congregation to read (and later discuss within smaller groups, such as the trustees or the legal ministry). In addition to size and denomination, this church differed from the other churches in the study because the minister assigned books and discussed, within his sermons, books that he read.

The second church in which I conducted fieldwork is a middle-class Baptist church in a suburban community of Chicago. The minister of this church, the *nonmanuscript minister,* had been a theology professor at a nearby university and was an active member and leader in social and political organizations such as the NAACP and Operation PUSH. He describes himself as a "race preacher" who wants to lead his African American congregation forward spiritually, socially, and economically. This church's motto, printed on the Sunday bulletin, is "The Church of Faith and Freedom." This church promotes the idea that with stronger faith comes freedom from political, social, and economic bondage. This self-described race preacher emphasized repeatedly that strong faith, combined with education, is the means by which African Americans can improve their lives and their communities, concerns that were always in the forefront. This church congregation, with about 500 active members, had a large professional segment. Many of its members are associated with the nearby university or have professional careers in the Chicago area. The North Chicago suburb in which it is located is a predominantly White, middle-class suburb.

The third church, a member of the Pentecostal Holiness denomination, was located on the South Side of Chicago in a predominantly working-class, African American community. With approximately 500 on its membership rolls but only 100 who attended Sunday services, this church had the smallest membership and least active attendance of the three churches. Although this church fits within the tradition of African American worship—using call-and-response and having the sermon as the center of the service—it is the most conservative of the three in terms of doctrine and behavior. It also has the oldest congregation. Unlike the other two churches, men hold all the decision-making positions, the service is less vocally expressive, and sociopolitical topics rarely find their way into the minister's sermons. This *partial manuscript minister* is less well known outside his own congregation and church community than the other two pastors; yet,

---

[3]*Manuscript minister* and *nonmanuscript minister* are labels that were introduced to me by the minister of the first church where I conducted fieldwork, who described himself as a manuscript minister because he preached from a written manuscript. The nonmanuscript minister does not preach from a written text. *Partial manuscript* is a term that I (rather than the ministers) used to describe the preacher who writes one fourth to one half of his sermon. For an explanation of the importance of the role of writing in each minister's sermon, see Moss (1994).

his assignment as pastor of the Chicago church represents a major achievement because it is one of the more prestigious churches within the Pentecostal Holiness denomination in the Midwest. This minister sees his role as helping his congregation grow spiritually. The teachings of the Bible are the most important lessons that his congregation can learn. To that end, most of his sermons are explications of Biblical scripture, conducted much the way literature teachers instruct their students to do "close readings" or explications of literary texts. This model is quite different from the previous two ministers who, while using Biblical scripture as integral parts of the sermon, often structure sermons around pressing community issues and use scriptures to illustrate concepts. The manuscript and nonmanuscript ministers are more likely to preach about issues of the day like AIDS in the African American community or the large dropout rate of African American high school students, and to illustrate how specific Biblical scriptures apply to these issues.

The differences that I have pointed out among the ministers and three church communities signal the range of possibilities within the larger African American church community. I emphasize the range of possibilities because they point to individual African American churches as sites where different kinds of texts are emphasized at different times by the people within those churches, where a variety of experiences and issues are valued differently within the three churches, where the ministers' strengths and interests become those of the congregation. Members of these congregations receive many messages, implicit and explicit, about what literacy is, how it functions in these churches and in their daily lives, and how to integrate these notions of literacy with those from other communities.

LITERACY EVENTS WITHIN AFRICAN AMERICAN CHURCHES

The brief introduction to the church communities and pastors just provided adds a contextual backdrop and complexity to the discussion that follows about literacy within these churches. African American churches, like other churches, engage in numerous and varied literacy events. These events involve the congregation in a variety of literate practices and behaviors, from reading and memorizing Bible verses to reading, in the case of the manuscript minister's church, 30-page church bulletins. Some of the literacy events involve reading only, and some involve oral participation such as reciting memorized scripture. That there are a number of literacy events present in African American churches may be a revelation to those who assume that print literacy is not a major component of African American churches, because they are perceived as oral-based communities. In fact, although African American church worship services appear to be dominated by oral events—such as singing, preaching, and talking back (call-and-response)—print literacy is an integral part of the community.

As in most Protestant churches, particularly African American ones, the two major literacy events center on the Bible and the sermon. Most would argue that in African American churches the sermon occupies the spot as the most prominent literacy event. In my study, the sermon was as important to its community as the academic essay is to the academy. To do each well marks the speaker/writer as a skillful and successful person in his or her respective community.

The Bible as a Literate Text

Many would argue that the sermon, particularly in African American churches, is an oral event only and, therefore, does not meet Heath's (1982) definition of a literacy event (i.e., comprehension and production of print). However, with each of these ministers, print played a major role in the production of sermons. First, each minister, as well as most members of the congregation, saw the Bible, the most visible written text, as the source of most sermons. Even if the topic for a sermon was drawn from a secular event (e.g., the manuscript minister, in particular, discussed getting ideas for sermons from a variety of secular sources), each minister always looked to the Bible to support and shape the topic. Thus, a great deal of authority rests in the Bible. That authority, and consequently the text where the authority resides, is hardly ever questioned or challenged in African American churches. What kind of message does that send about the sacredness of the written text? What is appropriate literate behavior surrounding an important written text, if the Bible is used as a model?

Many members of African American churches see the Bible as a text that fills a unique function in their culture, and they understand that the Bible is not representative of all written texts. Nevertheless, these members' notions of the way texts, particularly written texts, function in our society may be influenced to varying degrees by the way the Bible functions in their churches. It is here that community rules of literate behavior clash with those of the academy. If, in many denominations, churchgoers view the dominant written text as one that has a fixed, uncontestable meaning, then that is an attitude that does clash with views held by those in the academy, where questioning texts and challenging assumptions are valued.

While the written word is highly valued in the academy, we most often view it as *a* truth rather than *the* truth. In academic settings, the authority that rests in a written text, even the Bible, is under constant negotiation.

Meaning is generally influenced not only by the words on the page but also by the "baggage" that the reader brings to the text and the context in which the words are read. In the three churches that I studied, it was rarely the case that the authority in the written text, especially the Bible, was negotiable. If anything, Biblical texts were used as illustrations of points in the sermons, Biblical characters were held up as examples, and the Bible was used as the ultimate persuasive evidence. Generally, in academic classrooms, there is rarely "ultimate persuasive evidence." Evidence can always be questioned. It is this example that reminds me of Bizzell's (1986) discussion of how the worldview promoted in the academy is often in conflict with the worldviews that many of our students bring into the academy.

More than once, I have tried to find a way to respect a student's religious views while at the same time helping that student understand that, in an academic essay, citing the Bible as the ultimate authority is not always the most appropriate strategy in an academic setting. I had this discussion most recently in an advanced composition course last Spring with a young African American man. In his essay, this young man argued that W. E. B. Du Bois, in *The Souls of Black Folk*, was anti-Christian because he discussed the church from a sociological standpoint rather than laying out his personal Christian beliefs and quoting scriptures throughout the book. It was a challenge to help this student understand that Du Bois was a sociologist who examined issues, such as race and religion, from the particular perspective of his discipline, and that in academic essays, it is inappropriate to rely solely on Biblical scripture as the only evidence or explanation of a point. Helping students understand that the academy resists the view that ultimate authority rests in any one text, even the Bible, often means asking students to think in a manner that differs significantly from the ways they've been taught to think in their home community. It was up to me as the teacher to show the young man that I was not questioning his values, a practice that many teachers engage in when confronted with such a dilemma.

However, I am certainly not suggesting that every student who belongs to an African American church, or any religious institution, will face a cultural clash like the one just described. Neither am I suggesting that African American children who attend these churches will not know how to use "academic literacy." Indeed, I know many African American scholars (and students) who have succeeded in academic circles while maintaining an active membership in African American churches. The point I want to emphasize here is that the way that the Bible (or the Koran in mosques or the Book of Mormon in Mormon churches) functions could have consequences for how literate practices are understood and displayed in school.

While the previous discussion points to a possible clash between literate practices in the church and the academy, there are practices in the two communities that match. For example, one way that the Bible serves as an important literacy event in the three churches is through the *responsive reading* that takes place in the beginning of each service. The responsive reading involves the minister and congregation taking turns reading an assigned set of Bible verses that presumably help to set the context for the sermon. The minister begins by reading one verse (or part of a verse), and the congregation responds by reading the next verse. The responsive readings are written in the church bulletin, as in the manuscript minister's church, or in the front or back of the hymnal, as in the nonmanuscript and partial manuscript ministers' churches. The importance of the responsive readings is that they engage the congregation in oral reading. By participating in the responsive readings, members of the congregation are subtly being taught the importance of reading. That the congregation reads aloud as a group means that members who are not good readers will not be singled out, but the very act of this reading ritual each Sunday places value on reading and thus reinforces a value promoted in the schools.

Another common practice in each of the three churches was the emphasis on memorizing Biblical scripture. Every Sunday in the manuscript and partial manuscript ministers' churches, the congregation had to recite a memory verse, and a new memory verse was printed in the church bulletin on the first Sunday of each month. Clearly, the major purpose for the memory verses was to teach the congregation the Bible. That each of the churches chose the strategy of memorization as the most effective way to teach the most people simply means that these churches called on a very traditional and conservative pedagogical tool. Memorization is a long-standing, though not always approved of, strategy in many classrooms across the country. It is a tool that has a long history in African American churches as well. Historically, people who could not read would memorize important information, such as Bible verses.

The Sermon

Though the Bible is quite clearly the most important written text in the three African American churches (but not the only one), it is not even the dominant literacy event. The sermon holds that place of honor. Like sermons in most Protestant churches, these ministers began with a scripture and saw the sermon as illustrating that scripture. How this illustration was carried out is where the cultural markers of the African American worship tradition and the diversity of preaching styles become important. The African American sermon is most noted for its dialogic features known as call-and-response, the process by which the congregation responds to the preacher throughout the sermon. Consider the following examples of call-and-response from the manuscript minister as he preaches in two different churches:

Example 1 (the manuscript minister preaching at his own church).

Minister: Faith is

Minister and Congregation: the substance of things hoped for and the evidence of things not seen

Example 2 (the manuscript minister preaching at a revival in a guest church). The parenthetical boldface statements are responses from the congregation. They are not on separate lines because they occur with little or no pause between the minister's statement and the congregation's.

Minister: When you shout before the battle is over **(Preach!)**
It puts things in a proper perspective **(Yeah!)**
It puts you in a posture of obedience **(Yeah!)**
And it puts things in a proper perspective
But finally
When you shout before the battle is fought
It puts the enemy in confusion **(Yeah! That's right!)**

In Example 1, the minister is quoting a Bible verse (Hebrews 11:1) and the congregation joins him. Many members of the congregation may have memorized this verse when it was in the bulletin as a memory verse. In Example 2, the congregation is providing constant feedback to the minister throughout the sermon. They are talking back. The responses in the second example are those most common in traditional African American churches. These responses encourage the preacher, affirm the preacher's statement, and/or indicate the congregation's involvement in the sermon.

A Community Text.   While call-and-response marks the sermon as a dialogue and not a monologue or speech, what is most important about the sermon is that in this cultural site that we call the African American church, this literacy event relies on active audience participation to complete the text. I refer to this text as a *community text*,[4] a text that exists as a creation of a community of participants. The ministers, as they are preparing their sermons, want to leave room for the congregation to enter the text. If the congregation does not enter the text as collaborators, the text remains incomplete. As the manuscript minister explained to me, to have a silent congregation in a mainstream African American church means that the minister and his or her sermon have failed.[5] Active participation can be any-

---

[4]For further explanation of the concept of a community text, refer to Moss (in press), where I examine, in detail, the attributes of the African American sermon as a community text.

[5]"Mainstream" here refers to the traditional African American denominations (e.g., Baptist, Methodist, African Methodist Episcopal), which operate within a traditional African American worship style where the sermon and music are easily identified as fitting within the tradition.

thing from members of the congregation responding with an "amen" or "preach," as in Example 2, to a more explicit call-and-response kind of exchange as in Example 1, or as in the following examples which occurred between the nonmanuscript minister and his congregation:

Example 3.

Minister: God said "I have come that you may have life" and have it how?

Congregation: Abundantly!

Example 4.

Minister: I'm glad today that God has given me a mission that is larger than [inaudible] Because where there is no vision the people do what?

Congregation: Perish!

What differs between the first two examples from the manuscript minister and the third and fourth from the nonmanuscript minister is that in the latter two, the nonmanuscript minister gives explicit markers through question words like *what* and *how* that he is inviting, maybe even requesting, response. Yet, each minister spoke of expecting either kind of response, both the affirmations or the completing of a statement, as part of the tradition of African American sermons. These kinds of audience response are what make the African American sermon unique.

Why is this kind of audience participation important to a discussion of literacy? One of the major consequences of the kind of give-and-take between the minister and the congregation is that meaning-making events occur between the participants sharing in the literacy event during the process of the sermon being delivered. In other words, if in an African American church the preacher stood up and read a sermon that required that the congregation sit silently listening to a "speech," then the sermon is not a meaning-making event. Members of African American congregations develop certain expectations about the features of a formal text, based on their experiences with a "good sermon." One tenet of this community text, the good sermon, is that it invites, either implicitly or explicitly, a dialogue to take place within the sermon. When the congregation is an active participant in producing this community text, then the boundaries between speaker/writer and audience are blurred. Although the preacher is clearly the leader in the dialogue, there is really no fixed notion of speaker/writer or listener/audience. Hence, by implication, what is also called into question is the ownership of ideas and words, a concept that is so important in the academy.[6] The notion of a community text is something that some members of African American church communities carry into school with them. Many members of the African American church community, particularly those who are not as familiar with discourse conventions in academic fields, do not operate under the same guidelines and beliefs about what counts as an original idea, or consequently what constitutes plagiarism, as members of the academy.[7] That some students, once they have entered the academy, still operate under the rules of literate behavior of a home community institution like the African American church and, subsequently, violate academic plagiarism rules, is a prime example of when models of literacy from two communities clash. This kind of clashing generally results in the students' receiving negative labels in school. Of course, the irony here is that when many of these same students enter the workforce, they will be expected to collaborate in the producing of literacy events. The issue for them is, when is it permissible to participate in the making of a text and when is it not?

Shared Knowledge

By viewing the African American sermon as a community text that can only be collaboratively constructed, I am suggesting that in order for the minister and congregation to participate in the literacy event and exhibit the appropriate literate behavior, these community participants must have a strong community identity. And the sermon is an important site for constructing this community identity. So not only is the sermon a literate text that functions as a dialogue, it is also a text that functions as a community-building construct. Thus, the ministers must use the sermons as opportunities to establish bonds with the congregation so that the congregation will actively participate in the making of the sermon. Although there are several rhetorical strategies that the three ministers used, such as consistent use of first-person plural pronouns and of representational "I," what most signaled the community identification was each minister's reliance on shared cultural knowledge within their sermons. This shared

---

[6]Of course, this concept is already called into question in this church community because of its belief that the Word (and most other words) come from God.

[7]The controversy that erupted over whether Martin Luther King, Jr., was a plagiarist may be explained by this belief that God gives us words; they do not originate from humans, and therefore we cannot own them. While King had acquired academic literacy, given his educational background and credentials, he seems to have been far more influenced by the Black Baptist worship tradition that he grew up in than the formal educational training he received. He adopted discourse rules from each community; yet, it is clear that the African American church community was far more outwardly influential.

cultural knowledge covered everything from content and language use to expected behavior. The manuscript minister suggests that, "to be successful at using shared knowledge as a strategy, the ministers must know their congregations well, they must make judgments about what their congregations know, what their congregations' expectations are" (Moss, in press). Practically everything that fits under the label of shared cultural knowledge was related in some way to the sermon as a literacy event.

Three of the four examples of the call-and-response pattern of audience participation highlighted earlier illustrate the importance of shared information between congregation and minister. In the cases where the minister begins a statement and the congregation finishes that statement, both the minister and the congregation see the sermon as a site where shared information allows the congregation to become part of the making of the text. That each minister assumed that the congregation could and would respond to each call in an appropriate manner, whether that call was implicit or explicit, signals that not only is there a reliance on shared knowledge of content—knowing what to respond—but there is also a reliance on shared knowledge of literate behavior—knowing when and how to respond. To respond inappropriately with the wrong answer or in the wrong form would signal that a participant has yet to become part of the community.

"Sounding Black." One way that ministers signal appropriate literate behavior and knowledge is through their thoughtful manipulation of language. These ministers were literate if they preached the kind of sermon that not only invited participation from the congregation but that also didn't sound like a written speech. In addition, the minister needed to be able to skillfully move between standard edited English and African American Vernacular English to connect to their congregations. In this instance, "sounding Black" is significant because it shows that the minister is still in touch with his people and that he is still one of them. Also, it provides the minister and the congregation the opportunity to, as one minister put it, "use English in a way that makes it their own."

Sounding Black is tied to cultural expectations that speaker and listener hold in this church setting. One expectation is the use of what is commonly associated with African American language features (Vernacular Black English, another term for Ebonics) in the sermons. Each minister in this study made use of these features to varying degrees. While these three ministers are excellent speakers/writers of standard English, having been trained at White schools and having succeeded in the Western academic tradition and language, they have, simultaneously, remained steeped in their own Black culture and have found the need to make use of the broad range of language features that identify these ministers as part of the African American community and church. They understand the social messages that language conventions carry, that certain discourse conventions gain validity when used by the powerful in the community, as these ministers are, and that language builds community. Thus, when the manuscript minister preaches, "That means that there's a king somewhere. This ain't no democracy. God ain't nobody you vote into office and if he don't perform like you think he ought to perform . . . then you vote him out. This ain't no democracy. This is theocracy," he demonstrates that even with his considerable education and broad level of knowledge, he is still one of the people. His decision to code-switch in his sermons is a rhetorical act, that is, a meaningful use of nonstandard English dialect. Valdes-Fallis (1978) reported that "code switching has been found to be neither random nor meaningless. Rather, it is a device that conveys important social information ranging from role relationships between speakers to feelings of solidarity, intimacy, and so forth" (p. 7). By peppering their sermons with instances of nonstandard dialect features, these ministers give an added value to the dialect. What is important to note about how dialects are used by these ministers is that these ministers, because of their abilities to understand their audiences' needs, know when to code-switch and what form that code-switching should take. Of course, these ministers are in a setting where code-switching is expected. Such expectations are rare in college classrooms, unless one is including dialogue in an essay. That there are so few opportunities for students to do the kind of code-switching in the academic community that is expected in their church communities points to another potential space where literate behaviors and values may clash.

The congregations in this study want their ministers to be educated, to have academic credentials. They want their ministers to be good with language. Verbal agility is highly valued in this community (Kochman, 1972). However, being good with language includes not only being able to manipulate standard English, but it also includes being able to use features of Black English, to sound Black. In this respect, sounding Black is integrally tied to shared knowledge. Both the congregations and the ministers share certain expectations about how African American preachers should preach and how they should use language to identify with and establish themselves as community members.

IMPLICATIONS FOR LITERACY LEARNING

Sites of Negotiation

The previous discussion points to several key issues that, when examined in light of how those same issues are viewed in academic settings—namely, settings where essayist literacy is valued as the norm—can be labeled *sites of negotiation*. These sites are important for those students who must negotiate their way through them in order to maintain their literacy in their home communities and master essayist literacy in a particular academic community. These sites of negotiation can become sites of conflict that present obstacles for students, or they can become sites of common ground on which students may build. *Sites of conflict* are those sites where the practices associated with and valued in the African American sermon model are in conflict with the practices commonly associated with and valued in the academic essayist model. *Sites of common ground* are those sites where the practices and values commonly associated with each model are similar.

The most important potential sites of conflict that are highlighted in this chapter include:

- Shifting boundaries between writer/speaker and reader/listener.
- Shifting ideas concerning ownership of text.
- Shifting boundaries between oral and written language.

This list is by no means exhaustive, as there can be numerous potential sites of conflict as students attempt to become multiply literate. For instance, Balester (1993), in discussing the "ritualized, formal language" her student Max uses in his essay, points to types of language and phrasing as potential concerns for students whose prose models that of the African American sermon (p. 83).

It is important to note, however, that these sites are not fixed. What becomes a site of conflict or common ground depends on the participants, types of text, and the context in which the literacy event occurs. Nevertheless, examining just a few potential sites of conflict for students who have the African American sermon as their primary model of a literate text, and are attempting to master the essayist academic model of a literate text, should prove useful.

1. *An alternative written academic text?* A major probable site of conflict to be negotiated is what the academic essay should look and sound like. Clearly, the sermon, with its dialogic quality, its multiple voices, and its blurred boundaries, does not look or sound like the academic expository essay.

As the analysis in this chapter demonstrates, however, the alternative literate model that the African American sermon provides would require that students who have the sermon as their primary model find ways to build on what they know about the sermon as a text to compose academic texts. For example, the boundaries of an academic essay are more distinct, the form more rigid, the voice more monologic than in a sermon. Students may take major risks in trying to produce a written text that tries to incorporate oral or rhythmical qualities in their essays. The repetition of words, phrases, sentences, or sounds, which are necessary parts of the sermon, may be deemed unnecessary distractions by an academic audience.

2. *Reconceiving writer and audience.* In most academic settings, the roles of writer/speaker or composer remain separate from that of audience except when writers write for themselves (journals, diaries) or when writers are revising their own texts. Rarely does the audience participate in the composing of the text.[8] They certainly do not take over the text. Many students who are influenced by the way the writer and audience switch roles within the sermon may have a difficult time negotiating the changing concepts of a writer's role within different discourse communities. In an academic discourse community, these students must negotiate the demands of composing a single-voiced, monologic text. As writers, they may make assumptions about the roles of their audience that are erroneous in an academic setting. In short, they may assume a type of active participation on the part of the audience in supplying parts of the written text that is deemed inappropriate in an academic context.

Sites of Common Ground

Just as there are potential sites of conflict, potential sites of common ground can act as bridges that aid students in their negotiation between differing models. These sites of common ground allow students to make use of the strategies they bring into the classroom from their home communities. Courage (1993) said of his student Janette, an African American woman who was also a preacher:

> Janette had acquired language abilities, attitudes, and conceptions about reading, writing, and communication in general that facilitated her initial encounters with academic literacy. In her essays, comments during class discussions, and answers to my many questions, she exhibited a conception of speaking and writing as public acts, a sense of her own sermons as spoken texts with distinct forms and purposes, a desire to use forums such as the church and classroom to communicate useful information to other people, respect for textual authority, and awareness of an audience's need for evidence and persuasive language. (p. 486)

Clearly, the type of literacy promoted in Janette's African American church provided her with a foundation for acquiring academic literacy. Courage described the way that Janette adapted her strategies for composing her

---

[8]The exception occurs through activities like peer response, when students engage in discussions about each other's texts, and brainstorming exercises where students get ideas from each other. Even though these activities take place in many writing classes, they are rarely recognized by teachers or students as moments when the audience becomes composer.

sermons to composing an essay, which required that she analyze a literary text. These strategies were quite similar to the ways that the ministers in my study composed sermons. Janette identified a key passage in the literature, interpreted it, and then illustrated its relevance to people in her community. The ministers in my study treated Biblical scriptures in much the same way. Although in their planning of a sermon they may have begun with an issue and then moved toward a key Biblical passage, the actual performed sermon always began with the key scriptural passage and then proceeded with illustration and interpretation. Sometimes the illustration of a passage's applicability to the community and its interpretation occurred simultaneously. The point is, however, that the strategies were complementary.

The ministers and congregations recognize that for the ministers to be persuasive, they must understand and meet the expectations of their audience and community. They must use rhetorical devices that will be meaningful to the audience. This same principle holds true for students learning academic written literacy. While some of the rhetorical devices that the rhetor has at his or her disposal may change based on the different community expectations, what does not change is the rhetor's need to analyze and understand his or her audience and then to use the appropriate strategies. In other words, each model recognizes the communicative purposes of its texts and participants.

The greatest problem faced by many students whose primary model of a literate text does not match that of the primary model in academic literacy is finding the tools to help them recognize the sites of negotiation, be they sites of conflict or common ground. The next problem they face is having the proper strategies to turn these sites into resources that can make them multiliterate. These tools and strategies must be taught in the classrooms if literacy and language learning are to take place.

Bloome (1987) reminded us that "literacy and literacy instruction always occur within a context (or, perhaps more accurately, within multiple contexts)" and that "literacy is a dynamic concept with shifting definitions and shifting contexts of literacy activity" (p. xviii). Rethinking literacy as a dynamic concept also reinforces the social nature of literacy. This study demonstrates that literacy in these African American churches is a process involving multiple participants in a dynamic setting who use shared cultural knowledge and literacy skills to create a community text, a text which itself is not fixed. Like literacy in so many other settings, literacy in these churches cannot be separated from the cultural expectations of the community. What constitutes a literate text, who can create it, and how that text functions are all tied to the values attached to reading, writing, and speaking within the churches and the broader African American communities.

REFERENCES

Anderson, J. D. (1988). *The education of Blacks in the South: 1860–1935*. Chapel Hill: University of North Carolina Press.

Balester, V. (1993). *Cultural divide: A study of African American college-level writers*. Portsmouth, NH: Boynton-Cook.

Bizzell, P. (1986). What happens when basic writers come to college? *College Composition and Communication, 37*, 294–301.

Bloome, D. (1987). Introduction. In D. Bloome (Ed.), *Literacy and schooling* (pp. xiii–xxiii). Norwood, NJ: Ablex.

Courage, R. (1993). The interaction of public and private literacies. *College Composition and Communication, 44*, 484–496.

Heath, S. (1982). Protean shapes in literacy events: Evershifting oral and literate traditions. In D. Tannen (Ed.), *Spoken and written language: Exploring orality and literacy* (pp. 91–117). Norwood, NJ: Ablex.

Kochman, T. (1972). Toward an ethnography of Black American speech behavior. In T. Kochman (Ed.), *Rappin' and stylin' out* (pp. 241–264). Chicago: University of Illinois Press.

Moss, B. (1994). Creating a community: Literacy events in African American churches. In B. Moss (Ed.), *Literacy across communities* (pp. 147–178). Cresskill, NJ: Hampton Press.

Moss, B. (in press). *A community text arises: A literate text and literacy traditions in African American churches*. Cresskill, NJ: Hampton Press.

Royster, J. J. (2000). *Traces of a stream: Literacy and social change among African American women*. Pittsburgh, PA: University of Pittsburgh Press.

Valdes-Fallis, G. (1978). Code switching and the classroom teacher. *Language in Education: Theory and Practice, 4*, 1–21.

Chapter 11

Design and Delivery Issues for Literacy Programs Serving African American Adults

Thomas A. Crowe
University of Mississippi

Marie E. Byrne
Mississippi University for Women

Sue T. Hale
University of Mississippi

Literacy issues in the adult African American population are difficult to assess for a variety of reasons. The issues are complex and are not easily defined either for individuals with poor literacy skills or for programs designed to address adult literacy. The very definitions of literacy and illiteracy have often been the greatest barriers to understanding the scope of the literacy problem and discerning reasonable solutions.

Early definitions of literacy for adults were based on grade-level achievement measures comparable to those used for children, measures that provided little insight into abilities or disabilities relative to challenges in the adult world. Only recently have national literacy surveys, devised to examine the scope of the problem in adult populations, used functional definitions of literacy. Revised definitions of literacy have moved beyond the summing of basic skills for word recognition and comprehension to assessing effective application of the knowledge of written language. The IEA Reading Literacy Study (U.S. Department of Education, 1996) defined *literacy* as "the ability to understand and use those written language forms required by society and/or valued by the individual" (p. 17). This definition placed adult literacy skills in the context of functional abilities such as job-related reading, financial management skills, and the understanding of print media. According to Chisman (1990), when definitions of functional literacy or basic skills are used as the criterion, it is evident that 20 to 30 million adult Americans have not mastered basic literacy skills.

Attempts to address the literacy problem have often been ineffective. The myriad of programs available are insufficient and often inefficient. It is estimated that over $700 million per year are invested in programs that reach only 3 to 4 million adults. Another 1 million young people leave school annually with deficient basic skills, and an additional 1 million adults enter the country annually with less than proficient English literacy (Chisman, 1990). These numbers suggest that while the march toward literacy is going forward to meet the country's present need, an almost equal amount of need develops annually.

While the ability to effectively meet the literacy needs of the adult population is elusive, the issues surrounding literacy in relation to racial and ethnic variables are even less understood. Every major literacy survey has identified an achievement gap between White Americans and those from other ethnic/linguistic backgrounds. The IEA Reading Literacy Study (U.S. Department of Education, 1996), seeking to control the influence of racial/ethnic variables on survey results, examined outcomes in relation to family structure, family wealth, and parents' education. When these confounding variables were eliminated, the gaps in literacy achievement among racial/ethnic groups were much less significant. The obvious conclusion is that adult illiteracy is not easily predicated on racial and ethnic background but involves a complex interplay of home, school, and social influences. Low-income families often experience the stressors of limited financial resources, inadequate housing, dangerous neighborhoods, unemployment, and a lack of realistic expectations that life will improve (Snow, Barnes, Chandler, Goodman, & Hemphill, 1991). This economic and social distress can be reasonably related to a lack of basic skills (Chisman, 1990).

The recognition that social and economic issues strongly influence the individuals enrolled in adult literacy programs has resulted in considerable effort directed at determining factors that cause individuals to enroll in, drop out of, or continue in literacy programs. Factors which influence successful achievement in literacy programs include personal motivation, family support, and the ability to foresee the attainment of goals (Fitzsimmons, 1991). Even then, it is estimated that 50% to 70% of those who enroll in literacy programs drop out before completion (Harman, 1987). The scope of this chapter focuses primarily on the issues directly pertaining to the structure, objectives, and delivery of various literacy training programs in the state of Mississippi. The programs discussed are illustrative of literacy training programs in similar settings nationally. Curricular issues are not addressed in this chapter.

ISSUES IN ADULT LITERACY TRAINING

We recently took part in the assessment of participants in a statewide literacy training program sponsored by the Mississippi Department of Human Services, the Governor's Office on Literacy, and the University of Mississippi (Byrne, Crowe, Hale, Meek, & Epps, 1996). Project LEAP (Learn, Earn, and Prosper) established a statewide 20-hour-per-week basic skills educational program for JOBS (Job Opportunities and Basic Skills) participants. Of the 3,586 participants in the first 2 project years, 84.16% were African American (2,956 females and 62 males). Project LEAP's innovative program provided educational programs at 80 sites in 60 Mississippi counties. The program combined interactive television and on-site instruction by certified teachers and aides. The on-air instruction, originating at the University of Mississippi, was transmitted by satellite to remote training sites. The use of technology provided for participant and teacher interaction by one-way video (participants saw the on-air teachers) and two-way audio (participants and on-air teachers talked to each other by telephone). On-site teachers provided a variety of classroom activities that enriched the on-air instruction. Site teachers and aides received intensive initial and ongoing training through programs televised monthly.

Local teachers and aides provided individualized instruction for each student based on that student's educational assessment. Two mobile laboratories were also used to enhance the students' learning. Each laboratory was equipped with 12 computer stations and instructional software and was moved from site to site for use by students and teachers. After 2 years, 216 of the 3,586 individuals who participated in Project LEAP received General Educational Development (GED) certificates, 310 obtained employment, 755 transferred to other JOBS program components, and 1,130 continued in Project LEAP. Funding for LEAP was discontinued after 3 years because of concerns about the program's cost-effectiveness.

As a result of participation in the Project LEAP study, a number of issues led to an investigation of the factors that may have had appreciable influence on outcomes in literacy training programs. Following is a general discussion of these issues and of literacy training programs currently underway in Mississippi.

Personnel Issues

A number of factors affect the recruitment of qualified, dedicated personnel for literacy training programs. Literacy programs are often funded through "soft" money and are often temporary. Some programs occur outside normal work hours in order to accommodate participants' work schedules. Some programs are in the inner city or in other locations that are judged unsafe. Many programs are staffed by volunteers rather than by professionals. Programs may not be monitored by supervisory personnel and therefore must be self-directing. These factors combine to make qualified, motivated, and dependable personnel difficult to obtain, affecting program quality and outcome.

In Project LEAP, despite a goal of program consistency from site to site, the motivation and skills of individual teachers were judged to be important factors in the achievement of participants. Even though all teachers had college degrees, factors such as classroom organizational skills, lesson plan structure, and the maturity and motivation of the teacher influenced teacher effectiveness. The instructor's personality was often directly related to a classroom environment that fostered achievement instead of chaos. Bingman (1998) underscored the importance of teachers in literacy programs by reporting that in a literacy study, participants credited their literacy teachers as being the most important factor in their success.

Demographic characteristics may be another consideration when recruiting literacy program personnel. Matching the demographic characteristics of teachers with those of participants may be important to the success of a program. Some of these characteristics may include age, gender, ethnicity, and geographic identity (e.g., rural vs. urban, region of the country, etc.). The success of Project LEAP may have been hindered by a high turnover of teachers in the program. In one year, 45 of the 85 sites had teacher turnovers involving 75 different teachers. Problems in teacher retention may have been related to insufficient consideration of demographic factors at the onset of the program.

If literacy programs are to be successful, they must incorporate the most qualified, experienced, and dedicated personnel possible. Stable funding and continuity of programs would serve to enhance recruitment of personnel who have the skills for achieving program success. Financial and other incentives may prove necessary to ensure retention of qualified staff. For volunteers or those who are modestly paid, incentives other than financial ones may be necessary. While the incentives of volunteers may be internally generated initially (e.g., pride, feelings of worth, etc.), they may not be sustained over time without additional incentives from students or supervisors within the program. These externally generated incentives may take the form of praise, trust, awards, public recognition, or subsidies for materials or travel.

Recruitment of Participants

Issues related to the recruitment of program participants may ultimately influence the participants' performance as well as the basic design of the program offered. Recruitment issues should be addressed at the outset in order to place them in the context of program outcomes. General factors associated with recruiting program participants include provision of transportation, accessibility of the location of the program within the participants' communities, and child care considerations. Several of the more critical participant recruitment issues are discussed next.

Attendance/Motivation.   Literacy program participants enroll in training due to intrinsic and extrinsic motivation. Intrinsic motivation includes factors such as meeting educational goals, advancing vocationally, becoming more effective as a parent, increasing independent participation in the social or environmental milieu, and enhancing personal and social skills. Fitzsimmons (1991) identified four general categories of self-motivating reasons why African American women enroll in literacy programs: career/work related, self-improvement, service oriented, and long-range goals. External motivation for enrollment in literacy programs typically stems from the requirements of a governmental agency to maintain funding in a program such as public assistance. Participants in Project LEAP, for instance, were required by the state of Mississippi to attend classes as a condition for receiving Aid to Dependent Children.

More effective literacy programs for African American participants would include activities that develop internal motivation. For example, counseling regarding the importance of completing the program and achieving personal literacy goals might serve to increase motivation. Opportunities to hear from former program participants from similar cultural/ethnic backgrounds, whose lives have been meaningfully changed by newly developed literacy skills, and the provision of mentoring programs are also ways to foster personal motivation. According to Lazar, Bean, and Van Horn (1998), literacy program teachers suggest that the personal motivation of program participants increases when the participants perceive positive changes in their lives as a likely result of improved literacy.

Retention/Dropout Rate.   It has been estimated that 50% to 70% of adults who enroll in literacy programs drop out (Harman, 1987). According to Purcell-Gates, Degener, and Jacobson (1998), an important factor in retention relates to the contextualization (i.e., relevance), versus decontextualization (i.e., irrelevance), of the curriculum to participants' lives outside the classroom. Purcell-Gates et al. assessed 271 literacy programs, of which 73% were judged to consist of activities and materials that were somewhat or highly decontextualized.

Effective literacy programs are relevant to the social, cultural, and environmental milieu of participants. Programs should also recognize the different learning styles among cultures. Curricula, materials, and external assignments that match the learning styles of African American participants are necessary to improve retention and achievement of meaningful goals. Regardless of program location or its funding source, program design will be enhanced by including consultants who have knowledge of multicultural issues that have the potential to impact program effectiveness.

Individuals With Special Needs.   The special needs of the participants in literacy training programs have a direct bearing on program outcomes. Programs may have three foci in regard to learners with special needs: (a) programs that target a single type of learning difficulty, for instance, visual limitations or problems of chemical dependency; (b) programs that screen out individuals with special needs but counsel them into programs that do meet their needs, or place them in programs that reduce the effect of the limiting factor on the person's ability to benefit from the literacy program; and (c) programs that are designed to accommodate learners with various special needs and which individually structure the learning program as necessary.

Approximately one third of the participants in the LEAP program were judged to be individuals with special learning needs. Before the termination of the program, this group was targeted for testing to determine the nature of the learning problems and a means for accommodating those problems. The testing, however, was not completed. The addition of an identification/remediation component during the initial phases of a literacy program could enhance the program's success and increase the retention of participants with special needs.

In addition to learning disabilities, program participants may have physically limiting conditions, psychological problems, a history of behavioral disorders or criminal conduct, chemical dependencies, and so forth. Studies of prison populations indicate a large percentage of inmates to be African American with histories of early academic failure and low literacy levels (Haigler, Harlow, O'Connor, & Campbell, 1994). Literacy programs in adolescent and adult correctional facilities have positive outcomes for those who complete them. There are indications that improved literacy decreases recidivism (Barton & Coley, 1996; Porporino & Robinson, 1992).

When addressing learners with special needs, it is essential to have a functional cross-disciplinary team for referrals, counseling, ancillary services, and problem management. This component can enhance the success of individuals with both global and subtle special needs.

Effect on Family/Significant Others.   Enrollment in literacy programs has both positive and negative effects on participants' family members. These effects should be discussed with participants during the recruitment process or at the outset of the program. Participants will thus be aware of potential benefits and problems, and can develop strategies for dealing with these effects at the outset of program participation.

Program participants who achieve higher levels of literacy can expect a number of potential positive effects on the family. The participating adult who acquires literacy skills may have improved opportunities for advancement in the workplace, further education, and improved socioeconomic status. A second positive effect might include improved parenting skills and the expectation of allowing facilitation of improved language and literacy skills for children in the home. A parent who is a reader sets an example for the children's literacy achievement, thus breaking the cycle and lessening the effects of illiteracy in the family.

When a parent participates in a literacy program, it is also reasonable to expect negative effects on the family. Although the negative effects are temporary, they may still determine whether or not the parent stays in the program. African Americans are overrepresented among single-parent families, which heightens the potential negative effects of their participation in literacy programs. Single-parent program participants, if employed, will necessarily spend even more time away from their children and, without the provision of child care by the program, their participation may be precluded. Other negative effects of program enrollment may include a lack of family support by significant others, jealousy, goal conflicts with significant others, and unfulfilled expectations on the part of the participant.

When planning literacy programs, recognition of potential positive and negative influences on participants' families and significant others should be considered in order to lessen their impact. Pre-enrollment counseling to inform participants of potential positive and negative outcomes, as well as ways to address them, is an essential component of program design. Social stressors can potentially affect individuals' performance in the program.

Long-Term Follow-up.   Long-term follow-up of participants in literacy programs is perhaps the most critical issue in determining the effectiveness of program design and training. Many literacy programs specify functional outcomes as an objective of the literacy training received by program participants. These outcomes can be stated in regard to the individual needs of program participants (e.g., finding a job, completing the GED, starting a new life after prison, etc.) or in broader societal terms (e.g., reducing unemployment, reducing the number of persons receiving welfare, reducing criminal recidivism, etc.).

Regardless of the targeted outcome as a result of literacy training, a substantial degree of a literacy training program's efficacy and ultimate viability is linked to the program's ability to achieve, demonstrate, and sustain functional outcomes secondary to literacy training. These goals may be met by building ancillary services into the delivery design of literacy programs, such as training in preparing of job applications and job interview strategies; assistance with applications for school admission and financial assistance; family, vocational, or psychological counseling; occupational, physical, or speech-language therapy—to name only a few possible types of services and training that might be appropriately provided to ensure that the stated functional outcomes of literacy training are achieved.

The most telling measure of the success of a literacy training program in achieving the outcomes presented in its mission statement is not in the statistics of participant completion/dropout or in the immediate results of newly acquired literacy—getting a job, for instance. Rather, program success is most meaningfully measured through long-term follow-up of program participants, well after the consequences of literacy training emerge through employment, entrance into an educational program, and so forth. Long-term follow-up study of the outcomes of literacy training should examine the far-reaching personal and societal effects of the training. This might prove difficult to determine, given the logistic and fiscal constraints of maintaining contact with program participants and conducting studies of their lives after they have completed the literacy program. It might also prove difficult to conclude with any certainty what positive and productive changes in the lives of participants are directly or indirectly attributable to newly acquired literacy skills, as opposed to other life opportunities and changes. And, of course, there is the inherent difficulty with longitudinal study design, of when to accept that an effect has been demonstrated. When, for instance, could one assume that literacy training had served effectively to break a participant's cycle of criminal recidivism?

The practicality of conducting a long-term follow-up study is relative to the use to which its results are put. If program designs are modified when long-term results indicate less-than-optimal outcomes or when long-term results are carefully monitored to ensure that optimal outcomes are maintained, then the investment of time and resources into long-term follow-up is justified. If, on the other hand, long-term follow-up results are not used for quality control in recruitment, training, and posttraining aspects of literacy programs, then the practicality of the long-term follow-up (as it relates to continuing training programs) is of questionable value.

An issue that is related to long-term follow-up of literacy training is whether or not literacy training for a particular participant will serve to break the cycle of illiteracy in his or her family/home constellation. This generalization effect of literacy training is one of the issues most germane to the societal impact of literacy training and one of the strongest justifications for continued funding and development of creative delivery strategies for literacy training. Literacy training programs might include breaking the cycle of illiteracy as a desired outcome of training and include assessment of this outcome in long-term follow-up plans.

Robinson and Crowe (1998) noted that a client's cultural system, environment, identity, and assimilation might appreciably influence the nature of the client–clinician relationship and the outcomes of clinical intervention for assessment and treatment of communicative disorders. The social and cultural contexts of participants in literacy training programs might similarly affect the teacher–student relationship and the outcomes achieved (Haigler, 1989). This issue could be addressed in pretraining counseling designed to identify participant beliefs, attitudes, and values that are culture-based and have the potential to interfere with optimal outcomes of training. Long-term follow-up after training might also be informative as to the role culture-based factors play in successful completion of literacy training programs and in the use of generalization of newly acquired literacy skills by participants. Specifically, long-term follow-up might be designed to determine if participants' cultural system, environment, identity, and assimilation influence the nature of use (employment, education, etc.) and generalization (breaking the cycle of illiteracy) of newly acquired literacy skills. The reverse effect also would be of potential value to assess through long-term follow-up study of participants; that is, does the acquisition of literacy skills by program participants effect change, deliberate or not, in their cultural system, environment, identity, or assimilation?

Ancillary Communication Skills. Instruction in oral language is usually considered to be a major part of literacy programs for those speaking English as a second language, but it is generally not addressed for African American participants in these programs. Proficient oral communication skills are generally considered to be an important factor in a person's attainment of vocational goals. Although there has been little research on the relation between oral communication skills and employment opportunities for economically disadvantaged adults, this relationship has been demonstrated for adults who are learning disabled or mentally retarded (Auty, Goodman, & Foss, 1987; Siegelman & Davis, 1978; Trent, 1987). When social communication problems have been identified, training to improve performance in this area has had positive results for adults in vocational rehabilitation programs (Farley & Hinman, 1986).

Although the recognition of African American Vernacular English as a legitimate dialect may be appropriate and beneficial for society as a whole, it may lead to the erroneous assumption that all differences in oral language proficiency are dialectal in nature. Problems in communication may be overlooked which would hinder a person's ability to attain or maintain employment as well as interfere with social interaction. As part of our participation in Project LEAP, we assessed the word-knowledge and social communication skills of project participants. A total of 92 women and 5 men participated in the study. Participants were predominantly African American (88.3%). The reciprocal relation between oral and written language had been established in the research on early childhood literacy development (Miller & Gildea, 1987; Scholes & Willis, 1987; van Kleeck & Schuele, 1987), but this has not been shown to be true for adult learners. We assessed the semantic language skills of the project participants to determine if they had adequate knowledge of word meaning to bring to the literacy learning task. The results indicate that, as a group, the adults enrolled in this literacy program demonstrated difficulty in word knowledge on tasks requiring them to define words, provide multiple meanings for words, and provide synonyms for words. The results of the study also indicate a significant correlation between reading level and word knowledge. Although all of the participants were identified as having problems with written language, those with higher reading levels had better word knowledge whereas participants with lower reading levels had poorer semantic language skills. Literacy programs may need to focus on enhancing oral language skills as they seek to improve written language.

In addition to assessing semantic language skills, we assessed the pragmatic language skills of Project LEAP participants. The pragmatic language skills assessed were those that we judged to be important to workplace communication. Interviews with each participant were videotaped and analyzed for linguistic, nonlinguistic, and paralinguistic behaviors. A 10-item pragmatic checklist based on the Pragmatic Protocol developed by Prutting and Kirchner (1987) was used to assess each participant's conversational skills. The results of this assessment indicated that a mean of 9% of observed behaviors on the pragmatic checklist were judged to be inappropriate. Behaviors most often found to be inappropriate included body movement (33.8%), eye gaze (19.5%), and vocal intensity (16.9%). These nonlinguistic and paralinguistic behaviors were judged to have a negative effect on participants' communicative effectiveness and were judged to be detrimental to the communicative interaction necessary for effective job interviewing. Additionally, turn-taking initiation was rated as inappropriate for nearly 10% of the participants, indicating another skill that could be perceived as negative when they participated in job interviews. Although the Project LEAP curriculum did not originally contain goals for developing pragmatic skills in the participants, the results of the pretesting were used to encourage the project coordinators to include such a component in the program. To assure that the examiner's racial/ethnic background did not unduly influence the results, the interviews that included both African American examiners and participants (13%) were analyzed separately. Similar levels of the aforementioned inappropriate communicative behaviors were found.

EXAMPLES OF LITERACY PROGRAMS IN RELATION TO DESIGN AND DELIVERY METHODS

We surveyed extant literacy programs within the state of Mississippi in order to present information regarding contemporary designs of programs. Four examples are given which represent a sampling of different program designs or different target populations. These programs are exemplary of programs in similar settings nationwide. The descriptions of the programs are given in the context of the factors identified previously as relevant to the effectiveness of the program for the participants. Information on all programs sampled was obtained through the distribution of a questionnaire to program directors.

Of the four programs surveyed, two had a majority of African American enrollees and in one, approximately one half of the participants were African American. The fourth program had predominantly White enrollees. Similarities in goals, outcomes, perceived problems, and solutions indicated that cultural/linguistic background was not an overarching factor in the success or failure of the programs or for the participants. This underscores the concept that adult illiteracy involves a complex interplay of home, school, and social influences and is not easily predicated on racial and/or ethnic background.

Family Literacy Program

An Even Start family literacy program was included in our survey. Family literacy programs such as Even Start attempt to break the cycle of illiteracy. These programs focus on the parents but also target their children. As Purcell-Gates (1995) stated, the maxim that the rich get richer and the poor get poorer is very true when applied to literacy. Children in homes where parents read are more likely to read than are children in homes where parents do not read. Benjamin (1993) reviewed the research on family literacy and concluded that low-literacy parents, particularly mothers, are more likely to exert a positive influence on their children's academic achievement when they are able to enhance their own literacy skills. Families eligible for Even Start must have at least one child 7 years old or younger and at least one parent who is in need of adult education services. Home visits are viewed as an important component in the Even Start program. An educator visits the home for 90 minutes each week. Lesson plans include goals for both parent and child. The educator checks out instructional material from a resource center for parents and children to use at home. In addition to improving literacy, the goals of an Even Start program may include improved career guidance, vocational training, computer skills, and parenting skills.

The Even Start family literacy program was administered through a school district. The school district was asked to identify 75 of the most-at-risk families. All adult participants were parents judged to be most in need of services as indicated by low income, low literacy, or low English language proficiency. Those in need of basic literacy skills were referred to existing adult literacy programs within the school district. Since its inception in 1997, a total of 90 families, 47% African American, have participated in the training program. Of these, 15 families have successfully completed the program and 25 families have dropped out. It is interesting to note that this program had the highest dropout rate of the programs surveyed. This may be due in part to the problems faced by any new program, but may also be related to problems unique to family literacy programs. Parents may be wary of adults who do not share the same cultural background providing guidance in parenting and child development. If parents feel that their child-rearing beliefs and goals for their children are being disregarded, they may be reluctant to participate. Modifications made in this Even Start program to increase successful completion included improved matching of educators to the participating families and custom-designed services provided in the home. These modifications were designed to allow parents to bring their own values and beliefs to the learning task rather than having the values and beliefs of the dominant culture imposed on them.

Other factors cited as interfering with successful participation in this literacy program included lack of time for participation and/or child-care scheduling conflicts. To address these issues, the program began offering flexible scheduling of services, transportation, and child-care services.

Factors cited as being important to success included the participants' ability to develop goals for themselves, parents' desires to help their children, and participants' family and peer support systems. Some of the incentives for successfully participating in the program included GED completion, the gratification participants felt in bonding with their children, and the free materials such as books and instructional items that participants could use in their homes. Indices that the program was succeeding in meeting its goals were reported to be improved achievement test scores, GED completion, employment, acquisition of computer skills, improved parenting practices, and an increase in children's success in school. Follow-through services were provided as needed, which might include college preparation or job-skills training.

An important feature of Even Start is its focus on the participant in the context of family and community. It has been suggested that family literacy programs should not be judged by short-term outcomes such as GED completion but by long-term outcomes that can only be measured years after a person's participation in the program. Hayes (1996) stated that although family literacy programs may show less effects than traditional literacy programs when compared on criteria such as GED production, job placements, or other direct adult-education goals, it is expected that the combined effects of the family literacy program services will be greater in the long term. It is, therefore, too soon to determine if family literacy in general and the responding Even Start program in particular will be judged as successful. The long-term functional outcomes for parents, their children, and the children of future generations will be the best indication of the success of family literacy programs.

Intergenerational Literacy Program

This program addresses literacy needs of adult participants ages 18 to 65; current participants are approximately 66% African American. The participants include preschool children, court-ordered/at-risk youth, and adults desiring GED, basic skills, and literacy instruction. The goals of the program are to assist participants through individualized instruction to acquire the literacy skills necessary to complete primary or secondary education, complete high school equivalency, and gain employment or job advancement. Overriding purposes of the program include serving industry and the community through a basic skills literacy initiative, preparing employed and unemployed adults for GED completion, assisting public schools in the prevention of student dropout, reducing the number of recipients of public assistance, reducing criminal recidivism, and improving life skills. The three major components of the program are adult education, alternative education, and child development. Although 72% of the program participants successfully complete the program, approximately 28% drop out annually.

Program personnel identified factors that contributed to participants' success, including self-motivation, family support, and the rewards of employment and self-sufficiency. Low self-esteem, unrealistic expectations of the time required for program completion, transportation difficulties, lack of child-care availability, the presence of learning disabilities, and job/family responsibilities that precluded continued enrollment were factors associated with failure to complete the program. In an effort to minimize these factors, the program was modified to include flexible class scheduling, on-site child care, addition of a curriculum for those with specific learning disabilities, enrollment orientation, and multimedia instruction. These modifications were beneficial for the majority of the participants. Those participants with severe learning disabilities, health problems, job scheduling difficulties, or high family demands did not benefit from the modifications.

Several incentives existed for participants who successfully completed the literacy coursework. These included qualifying for enrollment in college or military enlistment, completion of probation requirements, employment or job promotion, and self-satisfaction. Indices that the program was succeeding in meeting its goals included a measurable increase in participants' academic scores; an increase in the number of participants who obtained gainful employment or promotions, exited the public assistance rolls, and moved into higher education or vocational training programs; and a decrease in repeat criminal offenders.

Program participants received various types of training in addition to literacy education. These included training in job interview skills, completing applications for school or jobs, personal financial management, household management, job responsibility, work ethics, interpersonal/life skills, parenting skills, and study skills.

This program seemed to successfully include most of the features discussed earlier in this chapter as being critical to achieving successful program outcomes. The effort to modify the program in response to those who dropped out of the program increased retention and program effectiveness. The clearly identified outcomes as well as the ancillary areas of education provided to participants were the program's strengths. While the program targeted many of the issues associated with the individual participants as part of their environment, it did not appear to include goals that were pertinent to the participant in the context of family, neighborhood, and community.

Community College–Based Adult Basic Education Program

This project, funded by the National Literacy Act, offers adult basic education and GED preparation. It serves approximately 2,000 participants annually, of which 20% are African American. The goals of the program are identified as GED completion, employment and job advancement, and reduction in the number of recipients of public assistance. Approximately 32% of program participants dropped out of the program during the most recent reporting period, and the remainder completed the program goals.

Factors identified by program participants as fostering success included high basic skills at the time of enrollment as well as readily available transportation to classes. Participants who were already employed or who had employment available to them at program completion were also judged to have a greater likelihood of success in the program.

Negative factors cited by those who failed to complete the program included lack of child care, lack of access to transportation, initial low reading skills, and lack of family and peer support. Program modifications to address these and other issues associated with program retention included placing more emphasis on the context of the workplace within the program activities as well as greater use of technology. Whether or not these modifications will be effective has not been determined, in that the modifications have only recently been put into place.

Program participants are not provided with stated or tangible incentives for program participation. The program is voluntary for most participants, with the exception of those who are under an agency mandate to participate. Program administrators have judged the program to be successful, in that they report a high pass rate for those who have taken the GED, but specific data were not given. In addition, unemployment among the participants is judged to be very low. The success of the current participants in the program has caused new participants to enroll who have lower basic skills than previous enrollees.

The program is primarily focused on adult basic skills and education. Participants can expect additional assistance, however, with completing job and school applications and applying for financial aid from educational institutions. Participants also have access to career centers in each of the district offices associated with the program.

This program differs from the others described in this section in that it is more narrowly targeted and does not deliver literacy training beyond the individual participant level, as family services are not included. While high rates of passing scores on the GED and low unemployment are reported, literacy within the context of family and community is not addressed, nor is the impact of the participants' achievement on the cycle of illiteracy. This is an example of a very traditional program, one which has important, measurable short-term gains but which may not have the long-term positive effects that may be seen in the broader based intergenerational or family literacy programs previously discussed.

Prerelease Adult Literacy Program— State Penitentiary Based

This literacy training program is conducted in the state penitentiary at Parchman, Mississippi. The Parchman facility is located in west-central Mississippi and is a maximum-security facility spreading over 20,000 acres in a rural, agricultural setting. Over 4,600 inmates are housed in multiple units at Parchman; they are male, predominantly African American (70%), and predominantly from rural and low socioeconomic environments. The average age of inmates at the penitentiary is 31 years, and the average length of incarceration is 3.5 years.

The present literacy training effort was initiated in the Mississippi Department of Corrections in 1988. It is available to inmates as a prerelease opportunity to prepare for completion of primary or secondary education after release from prison, completion of GED requirements while incarcerated or after release, and possible eventual postsecondary matriculation. Long-term functional outcomes of literacy training for this specific population include gainful, steady employment by inmates upon release from prison and reduction of criminal recidivism.

Inmates learn of the program through an inmate handbook issued to all inmates, and they may self-refer or may be referred for literacy training by the correctional staff, parole board, or releasing authorities. Program participants range in age from 18 years to over 65 years and are 100% male (the Parchman facility is a male-only prison) and approximately 70% African American, which parallels general inmate population demographics.

Data reported by the project director indicate a high rate of program success; approximately 95% of participants complete the program and 5% drop out prior to completion. Project personnel have observed that successful participants are self-motivated, have a genuine desire to remain free after release from prison, wish to return to and remain with family members, and would like to have the skills to support themselves and their family upon release from prison. Reported reasons for participants failing to complete the program successfully are mostly disciplinary in nature—receipt of rule violation reports, receipt of additional time to serve on their sentences, denial of parole, and so forth.

The present high level of successful completion of this program by participants is reportedly due in part to modifications in project design implemented early in the project's operation. These modifications included the addition of more teachers to provide for individual attention to participants and restructuring of the curriculum and classes by school-grade levels. Other reported reasons for successful program completion include the award of meritorious earned time by inmates successfully completing literacy training—this time can be applied to time served on their sentence (10 days a month off the sentence up to a total of 180 days)—and inclusion in an appreciation program for inmates who complete their GED.

Program data reported for the fiscal year July 1997 to July 1998 indicate that the program was successful in meeting specific goals of increased education skills, GED completion, and job placement. During this period, 428 inmates were enrolled in the program. A random sample of their standardized test performance indicated a 1.5 school-grade-level increase in reading skills and a 2.4 school-grade-level increase in math skills. Fifty-four participants completed their GED training, and 75% were placed in jobs on release from prison.

In addition to literacy training, inmates participating in this program receive training in job interview skills, completion of job applications, personal financial management, household management, job responsibility, work ethics, and interpersonal skills. They also receive job guarantees and placement, employability skills training, help with school application, assistance with setting up job interviews, assistance with residence development, vocational counseling, and group counseling.

This program is judged to be exemplary in addressing the literacy issues in this particular population. The setting of a correctional facility raises issues of program design for literacy training not identified earlier in this chapter and minimizes relevance of some of the issues that were identified. Personnel recruitment, participant recruitment, participant attendance and motivation, and the relevance of literacy training to family and community all take on a different or moot relevance in the prison setting. But the personnel directing this project appear to have worked through the issues pertaining to their setting and, with willingness to modify their program design, have demonstrated successful literacy training outcomes for a sustained period of time. The effect of this program on the rate of criminal recidivism for participants was not reported; this would seem to be the chief measure of success for literacy training programs housed in correctional facilities.

CONCLUSIONS

The issues related to adult literacy are many and varied. This chapter examined some of the issues related to the design and objectives of adult literacy programs and factors perceived to be important to the success or failure of program participants. These issues are relevant for all populations but have special significance for African American adults. In 1991, a report to the Mississippi Employment Commission and the Governor's Office for Literacy estimated that 35% of adults in the state had low literacy skills (Cosby, Howell, Carr, & Miller, 1991). The report further concluded that African American adults were at greater risk for low literacy skills even when educational attainment levels were similar to White adults. The IEA Reading Literacy Study (U.S. Department of Education, 1996) noted that income differences between racial groups tend to disappear when literacy factors are held constant. The recognition of the relation between economic well-being and literacy has led to the establishment of numerous programs throughout the state. A sample of those programs was described in this chapter.

This chapter did not attempt to examine curricular issues in adult literacy programs. Discussion of which approach or approaches are most effective in facilitating the acquisition of reading and writing and mathematical ability would undoubtedly yield sufficient material for a separate text. Issues we believed to be relevant to the success and failure of adult literacy programs were described and related to programs that represented a cross-sample of programs within the state. In the programs described in this chapter, there was generally a recognition of the need to recruit prospective participants, individualize programs of instruction, and make the content relevant to the participants' lives. Many of the participants in these programs were unemployed and were attempting to improve literacy skills to improve their chances of gaining employment. It is interesting to note that we were unable to locate literacy programs in the state designed specifically for residents who were already employed. Individual corporations in the state may provide literacy instruction to employees to improve their productivity and opportunities for promotion, but apparently they have not publicized this information. Adults in low-paying jobs are those who most often have the greatest time restrictions, prohibiting them from enrolling in literacy programs. Workplace literacy programs may be an effective way to develop those literacy skills that would have the most relevance for this population. The IEA Reading Literacy Study (U.S. Department of Education, 1996) revealed that only a small fraction (perhaps as low as 10%) of adults in need of training in basic skills areas receive that training. The survey also found that half of those who enroll in such programs leave before they have made significant gains. To improve these statistics in the new century, adult literacy programs must address issues of recruitment and retention before the programs begin.

REFERENCES

Auty, W., Goodman, J., & Foss, G. (1987). The relationship between interpersonal competence and work adjustment. *Vocational Evaluation and Work Adjustment Bulletin, 20*, 49–52.

Barton, P. E., & Coley, R. J. (1996). *Captive students: Education and training in America's prisons. Policy information report*. Princeton, NJ: Educational Testing Service.

Benjamin, L. A. (1993). *Parent's literacy and their children's success in school: Recent research, promising practices, and research implication*. Washington, DC: U.S. Department of Education.

Bingman, M. B. (1998). *Learner-identified aspects of participation in adult literacy education*. Knoxville, TN: Center for Literacy Studies.

Byrne, M. E., Crowe, T. A., Hale, S. T., Meek, E. E., & Epps, D. (1996). Metalinguistic and pragmatic abilities of participants in adult literacy programs. *Journal of Communication Disorders, 29*, 37–49.

Chisman, F. P. (1990). *Leadership for literacy*. San Francisco: Jossey-Bass.

Cosby, A. G., Howell, F. M., Carr, J. C., & Miller, L. A. (1991). *The Mississippi literacy assessment: A report to the Mississippi Employment Commission and the Governor's Office for Literacy*. Jackson: State of Mississippi.

Farley, R. C., & Hinman, S. (1986). Enhancing job interview and job retention behavior with relationship training. *Vocational Evaluation and Word Adjustment Bulletin, 19*, 55–60.

Fitzsimmons, K. A. (1991). African American women who persist in literacy programs: An exploratory study. *The Urban Review, 23*, 231–250.

Haigler, K. O. (1989). *Building bridges of meaning: The role of contextual literacy* (Report No. CE057316). Jackson, MS: Adult, Career, and Vocational Education. (ERIC Document Reproduction Service No. ED 329 752)

Haigler, K. O., Harlow, C., O'Connor, P., & Campbell, A. (1994). *Literacy behind prison walls: Profiles of the prison population from the National Adult Literacy Survey.* Washington, DC: Adult, Career, and Vocational Education. (ERIC Document Reproduction Service No. ED 377 325)

Harman, D. (1987). *Illiteracy: A national dilemma.* New York: Cambridge University Press.

Hayes, A. (1996, January). Longitudinal study of family literacy program outcomes. In L. A. Benjamin & J. Lord (Eds.), *Family literacy: Directions in research and implications for practice.* Washington, DC: U.S. Government Printing Office.

Lazar, M. K., Bean, R. M., & Van Horn, B. (1998). Linking the success of a basic skills program to workplace practices and productivity: An evaluation. *Journal of Adolescent and Adult Literature, 41*, 352–363.

Miller, G. A., & Gildea, P. M. (1987). How children learn words. *Scientific American, 257*, 94–99.

Porporino, F. J., & Robinson, D. (1992). The correctional benefits of education. *Journal of Correctional Education, 43*(2), 92–98.

Prutting, C. A., & Kirchner, D. M. (1987). A clinical appraisal of the pragmatic aspects of language. *Journal of Speech and Hearing Disorders, 52*, 105–119.

Purcell-Gates, V. (1995). *Other people's words: The cycle of low literacy.* London: Harvard University Press.

Purcell-Gates, V., Degener, S., & Jacobson, E. (1998, July). *U.S. adult literacy program practice: A typology across dimensions of life—contextualized/decontextualized and dialogic/monologic* (NCSALL Rep. No. 2). Cambridge, MA: National Center for the Study of Adult Learning and Literacy, Harvard Graduate School of Education.

Robinson, T. L., Jr., & Crowe, T. A. (1998). Culture-based considerations in programming for stuttering intervention with African American clients and their families. *Language, Speech, and Hearing Services in Schools, 29*, 172–179.

Scholes, R. J., & Willis, B. J. (1987). Age and education in oral language skills. *Developmental Neuropsychology, 3*, 239–253.

Siegelman, C. K., & Davis, P. J. (1978). Habilitation. *Education and Training of the Mentally Retarded, 2*, 71–76.

Snow, C. E., Barnes, W. S., Chandler, J., Goodman, I. F., & Hemphill, L. (1991). *Unfulfilled expectations: Home and school influences on literacy.* Cambridge, MA: Harvard University Press.

Trent, S. D. (1987). The importance of social skills in the employment interview. *Education of the Visually Handicapped, 19*, 7–18.

U.S. Department of Education, National Center for Education Statistics. (1996). *Reading literacy in the United States: Findings from the IEA Reading Literacy Study.* Washington, DC: Author.

van Kleeck, A., & Schuele, C. M. (1987). Precursors to literacy: Normal development. *Topics in Language Disorders, 7*, 13–31.

Chapter 12

Effects of Structure Strategy Instruction on Text Recall in Older African American Adults

Bonnie J. F. Meyer
Andrew P. Talbot
The Pennsylvania State University

Leonard W. Poon
Melissa M. Johnson
University of Georgia

The number of adults over age 65 is increasing. Never in the history of the United States have so many adults lived so long and remained so active, productive, and healthy (Cooley et al., 1998). Reading comprehension is an important skill for older adults to employ in maintaining functional independence and quality of life. Understanding and remembering written information is useful in health maintenance and management as well as in continued learning in a variety of areas. Reading comprehension also plays an important role in managing finances and enjoying leisure and recreational activities. For many older adults, reading itself is a favorite leisure activity (e.g., Meyer, Poon, & Talbot, 1999).

Learning, remembering, and using information from expository texts are important skills for adult learners. Effective use of reading strategies in everyday life is one way that older adults can compensate for some of the cognitive declines associated with aging, such as slowing (Salthouse, 1985) and reduction in working memory (Light & Anderson, 1985). Adults with high verbal skills retain text-recall ability particularly well across the life span (Hultsch, Hertzog, Dixon, & Small, 1998; Meyer & Rice, 1983). This chapter investigates whether a reading comprehension strategy can be taught to older adults who do not have strong reading skills, with the expectation that strategy training would enable them to better cope with normal age-associated changes.

Building a system to organize information is important for success in reading and remembering (Britton & Graesser, 1996; Gernsbacher, 1996;

Kintsch, 1998). One way is to utilize the text's own structure for encoding and retrieving the main ideas (Grimes, 1975; Mann & Thompson, 1988; Meyer, 1975; Meyer & Rice, 1984; Sanders, Spooren, & Noordman, 1992). Readers who employ the text structure strategy approach reading with the knowledge that authors organize texts in predictable ways, allowing readers to build mental representations similar to the text's hierarchical organization of important ideas (Meyer, 1985a; Meyer, Brandt, & Bluth, 1980; Rickards, Fajen, Sullivan, & Gillespie, 1997).

Past research (Meyer, Young, & Bartlett, 1989) indicated that training young and old adults with the structure strategy doubled their recall of text information 2 days after instruction and 2 weeks later. In training, participants learn to identify and utilize five basic top-level structures (problem/ solution, comparison, description, sequence, and cause/effect) used by authors to organize their ideas. Participants also learn to recognize these structures in everyday reading materials and use these structures as a framework for acquiring new information. Guided by the text's structure, participants conduct a systematic memory search in order to organize, write, or retell what they remember. Performance is monitored closely and feedback is provided to allow everyone an opportunity to master the strategy.

THE STRUCTURE STRATEGY

The structure strategy involves two steps. In reading, the learner finds the overall structure used by the writer and the main idea(s) organized by that structure. In recalling, the learner uses the same organization as a strategy to improve memory. A key motto of the training program is "choose it, use it, or lose it." We explain that to find and choose the organizational structure or plan in text is the key to getting the writer's main ideas or message and that this strategy is a good one to use under certain conditions, but not others. Participants are encouraged to use the strategy when they want to know what a writer is trying to tell them. In addition, they are encouraged to use the recall step of the strategy when they want to tell someone about what they read in an article. However, the structure strategy is not useful merely to find a particular detail, such as the percentage of older adults attending church regularly, or when readers are not interested in the topic. Likewise, the structure strategy probably would not be used when reading for enjoyment or about familiar topics, where prior knowledge is available for the assimilation of new information (Meyer, 1984, 1987; Voss & Silfies, 1996).

In the first sessions of our training programs, we employ everyday texts (e.g., advertisements, magazine articles, books, and newspapers) that can be clearly classified into one of the five structures and corresponding signaling words identified in Table 12.1 (Meyer et al., 1989). Participants have no trouble finding similar examples in their everyday reading.

We stress the organizational components of various text structures for aiding retrieval from memory. For example, the contrastive pattern of the comparison structure is that different points of view are shown in the passage. One view might tell what happened while the other tells what did not happen, or each part might present opposing arguments. The comparison structure is frequently used in political articles to persuade. Often when opposing views are compared, they are compared on the same issues, for example, two political candidates' views on abortion, taxes, government spending, and defense. Recall is improved by remembering that a comparison structure was used to expound on a particular issue or group of issues.

We also emphasize the usefulness of structure in a problem/solution text to aid encoding and retrieval. As shown in Table 12.1 this structure is often used in scientific articles and frequently for the writer's goal of persuasion. The pattern of the problem/solution structure is that there is part of the passage that tells about a problem (question, puzzle, concern) and another that tells about its solution (answer, reply). In the problem/solution structure, the causes and effects of the problem are often discussed first, followed by a solution. When reading a problem/solution text we encourage readers to look for possible causes of the problems and descriptions of the effects of these causes, the problem itself. Next, readers are encouraged to look for a proposed solution, or solutions. When recalling the text, readers are encouraged to write *problem/solution* at the top of their recall sheet, followed by a main idea sentence that incorporates both the problem part and solution.

Next, the readers organize their written or oral recall using the problem/solution structure. First, they start off a paragraph by stating, "The problem is . . ." Then, they write about the problem or group of problems, remembering to include causes, effects, and descriptions of the problem. After recalling everything they can remember, they explicitly signal the solution, stating, "The solution is . . ." Paragraphs about the solution include a description of the solution and an explanation of how it attempts to eliminate causes of the problem. Readers check that the organizing structure for recall matches the structure identified during encoding. Finally, they add anything else they remember.

Through our strategy training program, we have been able to increase the communication between an author and a reader by helping readers follow the overall text structure or the thread of a discourse (Grimes, 1975). Once the readers understand the main points of the text, we ask them to evaluate the message from their own personal perspective. For example, in the sixth session of the training program, we explain that the structure

TABLE 12.1
Five Basic Organizational Structures and Their Signals

Writing Plan and Definition	Signals

Description

Descriptive ideas that give attributes, specifics, or setting information about a topic. The main idea is that attributes of a topic are discussed. (E.g., newspaper article describing who, where, when, and how.)

for example, which was one, this particular, for instance, specifically, such as, attributes of, that is, namely, properties of, characteristics are, qualities are, marks of, in describing, _____

Sequence

Ideas grouped on the basis of order or time. The main idea is the procedure or history related. (E.g., recipe procedures, history of Civil War battles, growth from birth to 12 months.)

afterwards, later, finally, last, early, following, to begin with, to start with, then, as time passed, continuing on, to end, years ago, in the first place, before, after, soon, more recently, _____

Causation

Presents causal or cause-and-effect-like relations between ideas. The main is organized into cause and effect parts. (E.g., directions: **if** you want to take good pictures, **then** you must . . . ; explanations: the idea explained is the effect and the explanation is its cause.)

as a result, because, since, for the purpose of, caused, led to, consequence, thus, in order to, this is why, if/then, the reason, so, in explanation, therefore, _____

Problem/Solution

The main ideas are organized into two parts: a *problem* part and a *solution* part that responds to the problem by trying to eliminate it, or a *question* part and an *answer* part that responds to the question by trying to answer it. (E.g., scientific articles often first raise a question or problem and then seek to give an answer or solution.)

Problem: problem, question, puzzle, perplexity, enigma, riddle, issue, query, need to prevent, the trouble, _____

Solution: solution, answer, response, reply, rejoinder, return, comeback, to satisfy the problem, to set the issue at rest, to solve these problems, _____

Comparison

Relates ideas on the basis of differences and similarities. The main idea is organized in parts that provide a comparison, contrast, or alternative perspective on a topic. (E.g., political speeches, particularly where one view is clearly favored over the other.)

not everyone, but, in contrast, all but, instead, act like, however, in comparison, on the other hand, whereas, in opposition, unlike, alike, have in common, share, resemble, the same as, different, difference, differentiate, compared to, while, although, despite, _____

Listing can occur with any of the five writing plans. (E.g., listing can occur when groups of descriptions, causes, problems, solutions, views, etc., are presented.)

Common signals include: and, in addition, also, include, moreover, besides, first, second, third, etc., subsequent, furthermore, at the same time, another, _____

Note. From Meyer et al. (1989).

strategy can be helpful in taking notes about articles related to health issues and then using these notes to gather more information about a health issue. "A Drug for Fragile Bones," an article that appeared in the November 6, 1995, issue of *U.S. News & World Report*, was used to teach this skill. Participants were encouraged to organize their notes by using a problem/solution structure, one commonly used in health-related materials. The goal of the author was to increase awareness about osteoporosis and to offer alternative solutions, with an emphasis on the new drug Fosamax. The desirability of each alternative varies according to the needs of the reader. We explained that once the information is understood, readers could use this information to make medical decisions. For example, if a reader had been previously diagnosed with breast cancer, she might decide to use Fosamax instead of estrogen, as this would protect her from osteoporosis without the danger related to reoccurring breast cancer. However, if a reader had no personal or family history of breast cancer, but a strong family history of heart disease and osteoporosis, she might want to take estrogen in order to protect herself from both diseases.

We have found that the structure strategy helps readers to remember more of what they read (e.g., Meyer et al., 1980), remember more of the important information in what they read (e.g., Meyer et al., 1989), and remember this information longer (Meyer et al., 1989). Due to limited processing capacity, readers cannot remember and learn everything in a text, so some information must be selected for deeper encoding, more cycles of processing or elaboration, than other information. The overall structure or plan of the text can help readers select the most important information for thorough encoding. In addition, the structure can help the reader retrieve this information from memory over time.

The original structure strategy program (Meyer et al., 1989) involved five 1½-hour sessions spread over 2 weeks. In more recent programs (Meyer et al., 1999), we added a sixth session designed to promote skill transfer to other everyday activities (TV viewing, medical decision making). The six training sessions are spread over 3 weeks. Participants are expected to practice the strategy at home after each day of training. Homework for the second session involves reading 15 passages taken from magazine articles and sorting them evenly into five groups, representing each of the five organizational structures. Also, the homework packet includes short paragraphs, taken primarily from the "News You Can Use" section of *U.S. News & World Report*; participants identify the overall structure of each paragraph and underline signaling words. Other homework activities are less formal and involve finding these structures in their everyday reading, identifying signaling words, and sharing these materials with others in the class.

COHORT AND CULTURAL DIFFERENCES
IN TEXT RECALL

In past research, we did not expect differences in the effectiveness of structure strategy instruction as a function of ethnic group. The basis for this expectation was that structure strategy training programs have yielded positive effects with persons from a wide variety of age groups (e.g., 14-year-olds: B. J. Bartlett, 1978; young and old adults: Meyer et al., 1989), educational backgrounds (Meyer et al., 1999), and cultures (e.g., English as a Second Language: Carrell, 1985). However, such differences are possible because cultural or cohort differences (e.g., Hultsch & Dixon, 1983) can interact with different topics of texts.

Hultsch and Dixon's (1983) findings point to the presence or absence of age differences depending on the level of pre-experimental knowledge about text topics. Participants in their study read biographical sketches about famous entertainment figures varying in datedness (e.g., Mary Pickford [old], Steve Martin [young]). Older participants recalled more information from the *old* biography than from the *young* biography. Younger participants recalled more information than older adults from the *young* biography, whereas older participants recalled slightly, but not significantly, more information from the *old* biography than younger adults and significantly more than middle-aged adults.

Meyer, Talbot, Stubblefield, and Poon (1998) also found that different interests of younger and older adults in passage topics related to text recall. Older adults expressed greater interest in the topic of trusts (financial vehicles), whereas younger adults expressed greater interest in the topic of schizophrenia. A significant interaction resulted between age group and passage topic for the amount of information recalled. Older adults remembered more information from the text about trusts than younger adults, but younger adults remembered more information from the schizophrenia than older adults. Such findings suggest that age groups who vary in their familiarity with or interest in passage topics will perform differentially on text-recall tasks.

Cultural effects, similar to these cohort effects for the different age groups, also would be expected to affect performance on prose recall tasks. More culturally familiar topics would provide relevant prior knowledge structures for integration with the text material and boost learning and retention (F. C. Bartlett, 1932; Rice, 1980). Also, more culturally interesting topics would be expected to increase motivation and subsequent learning and performance.

Meyer et al. (1999) examined the effects of training in the structure strategy with different types of young and older learners. One sample from that study, a group of older African Americans with a range of 7 to

18 years of education and an average of 11 years, is examined more closely in this chapter.

AFRICAN AMERICAN SAMPLES FROM GEORGIA

Recruiting the Samples

Rural participants were recruited through two predominantly African American churches and were mostly community dwelling. A presentation on the study was given at each church. Additionally, a representative from each church was selected to assist with scheduling and to make sure the participants would attend the sessions held at the church. The study began with 15 African American participants; however, only 10 completed the study. In an attempt to increase the number of older African Americans in the study and to enroll African Americans with higher levels of education, we worked with a social coordinator for a retirement community in Atlanta, Georgia. All of the participants from the urban sample lived in a housing development. The social coordinator for the housing development assisted with scheduling the participants. The study began with 14 participants; however, only 12 completed the study.

The education levels of the rural and urban African Americans were not significantly different (see Table 12.2). There were only two high school graduates in the rural sample; there were seven who had finished high school in the urban sample. In the rural sample, there were no college graduates; there were two in the urban sample. Education level ranged from 7 to 12 years in the rural sample; it ranged from 9 to 18 years in the urban sample. Thus, there was a great deal of variance in participant characteristics, but particularly in the urban sample, as can be seen in the large variances for this sample on some of the characteristics listed in Table 12.2. Former occupations for the rural group included farm and domestic laborer, beautician, cook, factory and post office worker, driver, and insurance salesman; former occupations listed by the urban group included product quality inspector, teacher's assistant, housewife, farm laborer, hospital worker, cook, "helping others help themselves," nurse, minister, social worker, and domestic laborer.

Materials, Procedure, and Scoring

The materials, procedure, and scoring of tasks are specified in detail in Meyer et al. (1999). Briefly, vocabulary was measured by the Quick Word Test (Borgatta & Corsini, 1964), a 100-item multiple-choice test of word synonyms. Five working-memory tests were administered: reading span

TABLE 12.2
Characteristics of Older African American Participants From Rural and Urban Communities

Variable	Rural[a] M	(SD)	Urban[b] M	(SD)	t	(df)	p
Age	71.44	(6.89)	70.17	(3.19)	0.57	(19)	n.s.
Education level	10.30	(1.70)	12.33	(3.06)	1.87	(20)	n.s.
Quick Word Test	22.42	(5.60)	30.42	(15.48)	1.69	(14.3)	n.s.*
MMSE	27.80	(1.48)	27.17	(1.19)	1.11	(20)	n.s.
Davis Reading Test							
Timed	3.60	(2.37)	2.17	(3.01)	1.22	(20)	n.s.
Untimed	8.00	(3.40)	2.75	(3.84)	3.36	(20)	.003
Pretest recall performance							
Pre-Creation/Evolution	13.10	(14.88)	11.17	(8.80)	0.38	(20)	n.s.
Pretest Schizophrenia	12.13	(9.46)	18.00	(15.62)	0.95	(18)	n.s.
Pretest Trust passage	10.44	(3.05)	26.50	(23.08)	2.06	(19)	n.s.*
Working-memory measures							
Reading span	1.25	(0.59)	1.58	(0.63)	1.27	(20)	n.s.
Computation span	1.45	(0.76)	1.71	(0.69)	0.84	(20)	n.s.
Short-term memory measures							
Digits forwards	4.95	(0.55)	5.29	(1.05)	0.92	(20)	n.s.
Digits backwards	3.30	(0.48)	3.50	(1.02)	0.57	(20)	n.s.
Word span	4.05	(0.64)	4.04	(0.84)	0.03	(20)	n.s.

[a]$n = 10$. [b]$n = 12$.
*Group variances for these measures were significantly different.

(RSPAN; Babcock & Salthouse, 1990), computation span (CSPAN; Babcock & Salthouse, 1990), Wechsler Adult Intelligence Scale–Revised (WAIS–R) Digits Backwards (Wechsler, 1981), WAIS–R Digits Forwards (Wechsler, 1981), and word span (Johnson et al., 1997).

Two measures were used to assess mental status: the Folstein Mini Mental State Exam (MMSE; Folstein, 1983) and the Functional Assessment Staging Test (FAST; Reisberg et al., 1984). Criteria for inclusion in the study were a score of 24 or higher on the MMSE and Stage 3 or lower on the FAST. A subset of items from the Duke Older Americans Resource and Services (OARS; Fillenbaum, 1988) survey made up the health inventory. Reading comprehension was assessed with the first half of the Davis Reading Test, Form 1B (Davis, 1944). The Davis Reading Test has previously been found to be predictive of prose recall in aging studies (Hartley, 1986, 1988). This portion of the Davis Reading Test is made up of 40 multiple-choice questions designed to measure reading comprehension of several short passages. Forty points are possible, with a correction for guessing subtracted from the total number correct. Two measures of performance on the Davis Reading Test were obtained: one with the original 20-minute time constraint and one with no time constraint.

Each participant rated her knowledge of and interest in a total of 24 topics, including the topics of the passages used in this study. Each knowledge rating was made on a 7-point Likert scale from 1 (*nothing*) to 4 (*average*) to 7 (*a great deal*). The question posed on the questionnaire asked, "Which topics do you know nothing to little about and which do you know a great deal about?" Similarly, each interest rating was made on a 7-point Likert scale from 1 (*no interest*) to 4 (*average*) to 7 (*extreme interest*). The question posed to the participants was, "Which topics would you be very interested in reading more about in the future and which would you rather not read about at all?" Questions were asked regarding biographical information as well as information about reading and memory habits, as well as strategy-use prior to training. Questions were asked at the final posttest about changes in reading and remembering noted since the beginning of the research project.

Texts read and recalled included the Creation Versus Evolution set of passages (Coal Mine [see the Appendix] or Archaeopteryx—265 words and 129 scorable idea units each; Meyer et al., 1989). Each participant read a different comparison (Creation/Evolution) passage on the pretest and posttest, and their presentation was counterbalanced. For the Creation/Evolution set, half the participants read about different interpretations of a coal mine in Australia and half read about different interpretations of the fossil Archaeopteryx on the pretest; then these groups received the other passage on the posttest. This procedure of counterbalancing sets of passages has been our usual method for evaluating training effects (Meyer et al., 1989). Due to concerns about variability in passages and problems involved in designing equivalent passages, such as differences in topic interest (see Meyer et al., 1998), and the long span of 2½ months between the pretest and posttest, some of the passages were read and recalled both on the pretest and posttest by the all the participants. Participants read both the Schizophrenia and Trusts passages twice, once on the pretest and once on the posttest. The problem/solution texts on Schizophrenia and Trusts (504 words and 191 scorable idea units each; Meyer et al., 1989) had identical structures presenting three problems and one solution with its explanation and description. A comparison text was read between these two problem/solution texts to prevent possible facilitation from consecutively reading two passages with the same structure.

Participants attended four testing sessions and six training sessions over a period of approximately 4 months; each session lasted approximately 90 minutes. During the first testing session, the Quick Word Test, MMSE, and FAST were administered along with the working-memory tasks. During the second testing session, participants filled out a series of questionnaires including the biographical questionnaire, interest/knowledge questionnaire, and the Davis Reading Test. The third testing consisted of a series of reading and recall tasks and is identified as the pretest. These three sessions occurred prior to training; within 2 days of the completion of training, the final testing session (referred to as the posttest) was conducted; it was very similar to the pretest. At the end of the posttest, participants evaluated any changes in their reading during the project on the reading questionnaire.

The prose analysis system of Meyer (1975, 1985b) was used to score recall and top-level structure (how a protocol was organized, scored 1–9; Meyer, 1985b). Scores of 6 and above on the 9-point scale for top-level structure indicate use of the same top-level structure as was found in the text (7–9 simply have increasing amounts of signaling, e.g., "the problem is" added by the participant). For example, if the text presents a problem and a solution, a recall protocol using the same top-level structure and scoring 6 and above would need to organize all the problem information together and then present the solution. The scale was broken into a dichotomy based on use or lack of use of the text's top-level organization (6 and above on the scale indicating use of the text's top-level structure and below 6 indicating no use); use of the top-level structure was taken as evidence for use of the structure strategy on a particular passage. A reliability check of a random sample of 10% of the data indicated high reliability ($r = .88$ for 9-point top-level structure score and $r = .96$ for total recall). The average agreement in scoring specific idea units was 94% for recall.

Comparison of Rural and Urban Samples

Interest in Text Topics.   Table 12.3 shows that the only differences in self-ratings of knowledge between the rural and urban samples were about schizophrenia, nutrition, and osteoporosis. Topics read on various tasks were the first eight listed in Table 12.3. Overall, these topics held very little interest for either the rural or the urban participants, and they did not differ significantly in their interests on these or any of the topics they rated (see Table 12.3). However, the topic of Trusts held above-average interest for both groups of older African Americans. Death is supposed to be a topic of interest to most people, but it did not seem too intriguing to these older African Americans, where health, nutrition, finances, aging, and exercise seemed to hold more interest.

TABLE 12.3
Ratings of Passage Topics by Older Adults From Rural and Urban Areas

| | Interest in Topic of Passages | | | | Topic Knowledge | | | |
| | Rural[a] | | Urban[b] | | Rural | | Urban | |
Topics	M	(SD)	M	(SD)	M	(SD)	M	(SD)
Supertankers	1.50	(1.07)	1.70	(1.06)	1.20	(0.42)	1.70	(1.06)
Schizophrenia	2.00	(2.07)	2.25	(1.44)	1.30	(0.95)	3.00	(2.16)*
Creation	2.50	(2.14)	4.10	(2.13)	2.60	(1.84)	4.30	(2.21)
Evolution	1.50	(1.07)	2.78	(1.99)	1.33	(0.50)	2.56	(1.81)
Airlines	2.38	(1.51)	2.00	(1.32)	3.10	(2.18)	3.00	(1.87)
Railroads	1.25	(0.46)	2.18	(1.25)	2.20	(1.55)	3.20	(1.81)
Trusts	5.00	(2.00)	5.00	(1.55)	4.11	(1.69)	4.10	(2.03)
Coal mines	1.13	(0.35)	1.64	(1.03)	1.22	(0.44)	1.60	(0.97)
Finance	5.25	(1.28)	4.70	(1.57)	4.40	(1.71)	4.36	(1.21)
Cancer	3.88	(2.30)	3.46	(1.75)	2.60	(1.84)	4.30	(2.21)
Nutrition	5.00	(1.51)	5.33	(1.41)	4.20	(1.32)	5.60	(1.27)*
Cars	3.25	(1.91)	3.46	(2.21)	4.20	(2.04)	2.82	(1.47)
Animals	2.75	(2.05)	3.27	(2.24)	3.70	(1.69)	4.10	(2.03)
Health	5.25	(1.28)	5.89	(1.45)	4.25	(2.38)	5.33	(1.37)
Osteoporosis	3.57	(2.57)	4.69	(1.75)	2.10	(1.29)	4.44	(1.88)*
Nuclear reactors	1.63	(0.92)	2.94	(2.15)	1.11	(0.33)	2.25	(1.58)
Exercise	4.86	(1.22)	5.73	(1.10)	4.50	(1.58)	5.67	(1.16)
Aging	0.88	(1.36)	5.00	(1.33)	4.60	(1.35)	4.73	(1.42)
Cooking	4.38	(2.07)	5.32	(1.89)	6.00	(1.23)	5.92	(1.08)
Death	3.00	(1.77)	4.00	(2.06)	4.90	(1.66)	5.00	(2.16)

Note.   Interest: $1 = no\ interest$, $4 = average$, $7 = extreme\ interest$; Knowledge: $1 = nothing$, $4 = average$, $7 = a\ great\ deal$.
[a]$n = 10$. [b]$n = 12$.
*Significant difference between Rural and Urban groups at $p < .05$.

Reading Habits. Table 12.4 presents the everyday reading activities and strategies of the rural and urban samples. They differ significantly only on claiming reading to be their favorite activity, with none of the rural sample making this claim and 33% of the urban sample claiming reading as their favorite activity. For an open-ended question concerning the types of materials usually read, about two thirds of both the rural and urban participants included the Bible. Table 12.5 shows self-appraisal of memory functioning; the rural and urban groups are equivalent, except that the urban sample rates their memory better and does not use calendars as much for memory aids. It is interesting that an important memory strategy of relating information to learn to what you know (lots of relating in Table 12.5) was used twice as often by older White adults (Meyer et al., 1999) as by the older African American adults.

Appraisal of Effectiveness of the Structure Strategy Training. As seen in Table 12.6, there were no significant differences between the two older African American groups on their self-appraisal of the effectiveness of the structure strategy training program for them. Most claimed to be reading more and to experience more interest and enjoyment in reading than

TABLE 12.4
Everyday Reading Activities and Strategies of Older Participants
From Rural and Urban Communities

	Rural[a]		*Urban*[b]				
Variable	*M*	*(SD)*	*M*	*(SD)*	*t (df) or* χ^2 *(df)*		*p*
Hours/day reading	2.11	(1.45)	2.36	(1.07)	0.46	(18)	n.s.
Percentages reporting:							
Reading is favorite activity	0%		33%		4.07	(1)	.04
Read every day	70%		58%		0.32	(1)	n.s.
Better reader than others	10%		33%		1.69	(1)	n.s.
Hours of reading/week							
Newspapers	2.90	(2.27)	2.96	(3.17)	0.05	(19)	n.s.
Magazines	1.23	(1.19)	1.55	(1.21)	0.58	(18)	n.s.
Textbooks/technical	0.29	(0.75)	0.36	(0.67)	0.23	(16)	n.s.
Stories or novels	0.38	(1.06)	0.50	(0.74)	0.30	(17)	n.s.
Need information	1.33	(0.75)	3.67	(3.08)	1.80	(10)	n.s.
Interest/curiosity	1.58	(1.43)	1.83	(2.32)	0.23	(10)	n.s.
Relax/"escape"	2.71	(3.68)	1.33	(2.34)	0.79	(11)	n.s.
Reading strategies							
Argue lots with author	0%		8%		0.86	(2)	n.s.
Outline rarely	60%		33%		1.33	(2)	n.s.
Never taught outlining	44%		17%		1.94	(1)	n.s.

[a]$n = 10$. [b]$n = 12$.

TABLE 12.5

Self-Appraisal of Memory Functioning and Strategies by Older Participants From Rural and Urban Areas

Variable	Rural[a] M	(SD)	Urban[b] M	(SD)	t (df) or χ^2 (df)	p
Memory						
Better memory than others	22%		17%		0.07 (2)	n.s.
Think as age memory worse	22%		42%		3.26 (3)	n.s.
Memory better 5 years prior	60%		63%		1.18 (2)	n.s.
Memory[c]	3.40	(0.70)	4.25	(1.14)	2.06 (18.6)	.05
Names	2.89	(1.45)	3.42	(1.83)	0.71 (19)	n.s.
Faces	3.89	(1.36)	4.83	(1.79)	1.34 (19)	n.s.
Addresses	3.10	(1.20)	3.33	(1.37)	0.42 (20)	n.s.
Phone numbers	3.67	(1.23)	3.54	(1.41)	0.21 (19)	n.s.
Trivia	2.75	(1.17)	3.77	(1.75)	1.43 (17)	n.s.
Memory strategies						
Lots use of lists	25%		22%		0.78 (3)	n.s.
Lots use calendars	63%		22%		2.84 (2)	.092
Lots notes	11%		36%		1.68 (1)	n.s.
Lots repeating	11%		17%		2.46 (3)	n.s.
Lots relating	11%		9%		2.57 (3)	n.s.
Prefer debate to learn	70%		72%		0.02 (3)	n.s.

[a] $n = 10$. [b] $n = 12$. [c] $1 = poor$, $4 = average$, $7 = excellent$.

TABLE 12.6
Self-Appraisal of Changes in Reading Over the Duration of the Study
by Older Participants From Rural and Urban Communities

Question	Rural	Urban	χ^2 (df)	p
Have you been reading more since you began working with us?				
Yes	90%	73%	1.01 (1)	n.s.
Do you feel that you remembered more from your reading in everyday life than you did before you volunteered for this project?				
Yes	40%	50%		
Somewhat	60%	50%	0.20 (1)	n.s.
No	0%	0%		
Has your interest in reading increased since you began this project?				
Yes	90%	82%	0.29 (1)	n.s.
Has your enjoyment of reading increased since you began this project?				
Yes	90%	100%	1.05 (1)	n.s.
Do you feel that you remembered different kinds of information from your reading in today's session (posttest) than you did during the last testing session (pretest)?				
Yes	80%	91%	0.51 (1)	n.s.
Do you feel that you remember different kinds of information from your reading in everyday life than you did before you volunteered for this project?				
Yes	80%	91%	0.51 (1)	n.s.
When you read in this testing session did you try to figure out how a passage was organized?				
Yes	100%	91%	0.86 (1)	n.s.

before starting the project; these findings are similar to the reports of Meyer et al.'s (1989) high school–educated older adults in Arizona, but not Meyer et al.'s (1999) highly educated older adults in Pennsylvania, who were avid, proficient readers prior to training. As seen in Table 12.6, most felt that they now remembered different kinds of information in their everyday lives and at least somewhat more information than before the training. Open-ended questions asked participants about any changes they had observed in their reading in the testing sessions and everyday life. Responses to observed changes in the testing session included "I now look for the main idea," "The five plan [text structures were called plans in the training materials] help me a lot, because I really didn't no [sic] about these plan before now," "I can do better," "Recognize the plan," "I attempt to determine the plan, the main idea and something key about the data," and "I learn to read faster." Statements about changes they have observed in everyday life included "I check for the plan," "Look for problem, question, puzzle, trouble, issue, need, solution, answer, return, comeback, to solve," "It have been good in the TV viewing," "Observe, follow instruction, pay attension [*sic*], listen," "I am conscious of an organizational structure of information given," "I have tried to outline the 5 plain [*sic*]," and "Paying more attention to what I am look at reading and seeing on TV."

Changes in Text Recall. Table 12.7 depicts the improvements in recall performance on the main dependent measures administered to assess training effects with the structure strategy. On the posttest, half of the rural sample used the structure strategy to organize their recall, while greater use of the strategy was found for the urban sample, particularly on the schizophrenia passage. In terms of pretest-to-posttest gains in amount of information recalled, both groups made substantial improvement.

Predictors of Use of the Structure Strategy. In examining the rural and urban samples of older adults, we ran some exploratory regression analyses to see if some of the individual differences variables predicted use of the strategy prior to instruction and then after instruction. Predictor variables considered were age, education, and performance on various tests (MMSE, RSPAN, Davis Reading Test, and Quick Word Test). Interestingly, education and performance on the MMSE appeared to be the best predictors, but their strength of prediction varied with time of testing, before or after instruction. Top-level structure scores for each of the three passages (Creation/Evolution, Schizophrenia, and Trusts) were added together to give a measure of strategy usage. On the pretest, education predicted 46% of the variance on this measure of strategy usage, $t(df = 18) = 3.8$, $p < .001$, with scores on the Quick Word Test, RSPAN,

TABLE 12.7
Improvements in Recall Performance of Older Adults
From Rural and Urban Areas After Training

| Passages | Gains in Total Recall | | | | Posttest Use of Top-Level Structure | |
| | Rural[a] | | Urban[b] | | Rural | Urban |
	M	(SD)	M	(SD)	% Use	% Use
Creation/Evolution	7.22	(11.38)	17.25	(19.17)	50%	50%
Schizophrenia	4.86	(6.12)	17.50	(22.96)	50%	92%*
Trusts	10.29	(11.03)	11.33	(12.20)	50%	75%

[a]$n = 10$. [b]$n = 12$.
*Significant difference between Rural and Urban groups, $\chi^2(1) = 4.77$, $p < .03$.

and MMSE explaining no further variance. This finding makes sense in that more schooling is associated with more opportunities for learning effective reading and memory strategies.

However, after instruction with the structure strategy, the MMSE was the only significant predictor, $t(df = 19) = 2.43$, $p < .03$, explaining 26% of the variance. An additional 9% of the variance was explained by the addition of Quick Word Test scores, although this factor was not a significant predictor, $t(df = 19) = 1.51$, $p = .15$. For difference scores between the pretest and posttest measures of structure use, only the MMSE was a significant predictor, $t(df = 17) = 3.48$, $p < .003$, accounting for 43% of the variance. Thus, it appears that use of the strategy before instruction is related to the opportunity for instruction afforded by more education, whereas use after instruction with the strategy appears to equalize out the effects of prior education for those with sufficient cognitive functioning to learn the strategy. The MMSE was used in our study to screen for possible dementia; 24 on the MMSE was our cutoff for inclusion in the study. Participants with high scores on the MMSE (e.g., 30) made substantial improvement in learning the strategy, but those with low scores (e.g., 26) tended to make little improvement. The MMSE tests basic functional skills that focus on orientation (e.g., year, town), memory, language, attention, calculation, drawing, and following directions; a score of 23 on the MMSE is associated with mild Alzheimer's disease. Performance on the MMSE was the best predictor in this older sample of African Americans for identifying who could learn and apply the structure strategy.

Overall, the structure strategy instruction appeared to improve performance. Although the rural group did not differ statistically on many measures from the urban group, they did appear to be a more homogeneous group, with only two completing 12 years of school and none attending college. The next section of this chapter looks at some of the individuals from this group in more depth. This is a special group of participants with characteristics not often found in prose recall studies. People with low verbal skill, as measured by the Quick Word Test and Davis Reading Test, do not often volunteer for research projects involving reading and recalling text, so we were privileged to work with this group and gather insight about their reading and interaction with the strategy instruction.

A CLOSER LOOK AT THE OLDER ADULTS
FROM THE RURAL COMMUNITY

First we look at a participant we call Alveretta. Alveretta was 82 years old, had 11 years of education, read 4 hours a day, and rated her memory as average. She reported usually reading the newspaper and the Bible. She rated her knowledge of creation, evolution, and schizophrenia as extremely limited (*nothing* on the Likert scale) but her knowledge of trusts as *average*. In contrast, her interest in creation was more than average, and it was minimal for evolution and schizophrenia and average for trusts. She received 4 out of 40 possible points on the Davis Reading Test, 17 out of 100 possible points on the Quick Word Test, 0.5 on the RSPAN, 1 on the CSPAN, and 26 on the MMSE. She showed no evidence for using the structure strategy on any of the pretest measures.

During the first sessions of the instructional program, Alveretta appeared to have difficulty in both understanding and displaying her knowledge of the information. She had physical difficulty writing, making the writing process long and painstaking. Alveretta appeared very content to go along with whatever someone in the training group said was the correct answer. She often looked on the page of her neighbors to get the right answer. This pattern of "community reliance" continued through the other sessions. She would often wait until someone said the right answer before she would write an answer. After five instructional sessions she still did not show a true understanding of the structure strategy. Her writing was disjointed at times, though if helped she could use the plan to write a small amount of information from the passage.

After instruction Alveretta reported more reading, better memory of her reading in everyday life, and more interest, but not enjoyment of reading. Following is a copy of her recall of the schizophrenia passage on the pretest and posttest, 2½ months after the pretest, but a few days after completion of training.

Pretest:

This is cause off [*sic*] insane at brain. Reflect the mine make the person nervis [*sic*] and need attention.

Posttest:

Probelm [*sic*] with the ideal strange behavior of adult and children in mental hospital. Adult need to learn to aprove [*sic*] their albility [*sic*].
Children need to treated for there life off [*sic*] responsible.

Although Alveretta did not employ the problem/solution structure on the posttest, she did see that there was a problem and attempted to develop it. Her recall on the pretest is very disjointed with little correspondence to the passage read. She was credited with 7 ideas recalled on the pretest and 12 on the posttest. We found no evidence that Alveretta had mastered the structure strategy after instruction. When asked to write about any changes she observed in her reading and remembering in the testing sessions, Alveretta responded, "It was good to be together enjoyed it poor thinking I tried." When asked to report any changes she observed in her everyday life, she wrote, "Reading was OK But remembering was very very unusual poor." These statements are a good indication of the effectiveness of the program for Alveretta. Basically, she enjoyed the time together with her friends, but did not get much out of the training, perhaps due to possible beginnings of Alzheimer's disease; her MMSE score was one of the lowest in the rural sample and over 1 standard deviation below the group's average MMSE performance ($M = 27.80$, $SD = 1.48$). Her recalls of some short and easier passages read at various stages during the training sessions also suggest some memory problems. Prior to the first instructional session, she was asked to read and recall a short text comparing the advantages of dwarf and semidwarf fruit trees. Her recall only produced her prior knowledge about apple trees, as shown here:

> Apple trees can Grow any place you put them But to bear fruit is problem They need to cared you such as furherliz [sic] with. Good Ground & water at all time season.

However, some aid of the strategy instruction can be seen in Alveretta's writing by looking at her recalls after Sessions 1 and 5 of a short passage about rat allergies. The actual passage is produced next, followed by Alveretta's recalls.

Text:

> An occupational hazard for researchers who work with animals is that they often become allergic to the rats and mice used for experiments.
> New evidence, presented at a recent meeting in Washington sponsored by the National Institutes of Health, suggests that it is not the fur or skin of these animals that is most to blame, but protein substances in urine.
> Dr. Andrew J. M. Slovak, a British physician who spoke at the meeting, said that kindness to the animals may help. Workers who soothe their charges when picking them up to examine them are less exposed to the proteins that can trigger allergies.

Alveretta's recall after Session 1:

> The Rats is no Bet for me I am afraid off [sic] them, they afraid off [sic] me. You can always tell where Rat Been, even his order [sic] he leaves, an oder [sic] Smell, also a path where they Been.

After the first session, before any explanation of how to use the five structures in recalling and writing, we see again that Alveretta merely recalled some of the things she knew about rats, the topic of the text, without recalling anything from the actual text. However, as can be seen in her recall of this same text after five instructional sessions, Alveretta attempted to use the text structure and recall some ideas from the text, but she was confused about the content of the text. As she reported herself, "poor thinking" is evident in her recalls.

Alveretta's recall after Session 5:

Problem/Solution When picking up rat, should Be handle careful. To keep the allergrie [*sic*] from spreading

The fur skin off [*sic*] these animal is Blame when handle the Rats cause them to urinate most quickly. that will stop problem.

Alveretta attempted to apply the strategy after Training Session 5, but her difficulties in thinking and memory were greater than the aid available through the training program. Although participants with education levels below high school and high MMSE scores clearly showed evidence for learning and applying the strategy, many participants, such as Alveretta, with similar education levels but lower MMSE scores showed minimal benefits from training.

Bonita's progress is examined next. Bonita was Alveretta's partner in the training sessions and was also 82 years old. Bonita had 8 years of education, rated her memory as slightly below average, and her knowledge of creation, evolution, and schizophrenia as *nothing*, but her knowledge of trusts as slightly below average. In contrast, her interest in creation and trusts was very high, and she expressed no interest in evolution and schizophrenia. Bonita received a 9 on the Davis Reading Test (4 for timed), 25 on the Quick Word Test, 2 on the RSPAN and also on the CSPAN, and 30 on the MMSE. She also showed no evidence of using the structure strategy on the pretest measures. During the first instructional session, Bonita appeared similar in performance to Alveretta. With only an eighth-grade education, she appeared to have difficulty with the amount of information provided in the first instructional session.

However, by Session 2 we realized that Bonita was quite capable. In that session, when she came up with a different answer for a short passage, she clearly understood the teacher's answer but explained that she read it a little bit differently, and as a result another structure seemed correct. She was extremely motivated to do well in the instructional program. She diligently followed the homework assignments of finding examples of the text structure or plans in everyday life. She spent a long time at home writing examples for each of the five structures so that she could learn them; she produced 5 pages' worth of summaries and examples from the first three training sessions. Bonita's understanding of the main ideas and all of the information presented in the instructional sessions was very good. Despite working more slowly than the other participants, she progressed very well. Bonita was verbal and active, and in terms of the group dynamics, she was more of a leader than a follower. Her development over the training sessions was quite dramatic, as shown by her recall of the rat allergies text after Sessions 1 and 5, shown here:

Bonita's recall after Session 1:

I have never worked in a place to test or work with rats but I always felt like keeping things clean and destroying what they leave behind would be good for health sake.

Bonita's recall after Session 5:

Problem/Solution. The problem is the allergies this come when the rats are handle real rough which will distrub [*sic*] the rat and make them urinate more frenquently [*sic*].

To prevent this is to be real gentel [*sic*] to the rats when you handle them this will be a solution to the problem of the allergies.

After instruction, Bonita reported more reading, better memory of her reading during testing sessions and in everyday life, and more interest and enjoyment in reading. In addition, she stated that she remembered different kinds of information in the testing sessions and everyday life after training and tried to figure out how a passage was organized and whether she was interested in it. Following are her pretest and posttest recalls from the major passages in the study, the creation/evolution set, schizophrenia, and trusts. On the pretests for each of the passages, Bonita was not following the structure strategy, but she showed good use of the structure strategy to organize her recall on the posttests (comparison for creation/evolution, and problem/solution for schizophrenia and trusts). Even though she still shows some confusion of content, her strategy use is good.

Pretest: (recall score = 7)

Evolution is a fossil of man's ideas.
Creation is of God.
in making every thing in his own image
I do not believe bird and reptiles are alike in to [*sic*] many ways
there are flying snakes that would be some what resembles of bird by wings

Posttest: (recall score = 21)

A comparison of different views about a coal mines scienties [*sic*] have on creation and evolution. There was a thick clay of clean soil these was buired [*sic*] there were layer of different. They seem to think that the heat was responisable [*sic*].

And this is the way the creationist thought it to be.

Evolutionist interperted [*sic*] it to be a big swamp with to [*sic*] kind of mud - there was a white clay. And there was a clean darker clay that covered over years ago that ran through the swamp.

Pretest: (recall score = 0)

You may help by showing great love. And most of all Prayer.

Posttest: (recall score = 14)

Problem/solution. Problem with the brain not being in control. the abnormal brain have corkscrew shape. Normal brain accordion.

the solution is to see a doctor they use the anti-s-protein. which help to control the brain.

Pretest: (recall score = 6)

how to have your property at death.
leave a will and trust to a trustee

Posttest: (recall score = 20)

Problem/solution. Talking about property and taxes.

You should always make a will nameing [*sic*] who you want to have the property.

This will keep you from having to spend lots of money on lawyer fee.

Solution is to have a trust funds for the ones you want to leave it to.

Bonita showed a 14-point gain from pretest to posttest on each of the passages and went from not using the structure strategy to organize recall to using the strategy to organize recall and providing her own signals to keep herself organized. Although some difficulties in her writing are quite noticeable, probably due to her limited education of only 8 years, her diligent work in the instructional program yielded excellent improvement for only 9 hours of instruction.

Grace was 74 years old with 11 years of education, a Davis Reading Test score of 6 (timed = 1), Quick score of 13, RSPAN of 1, CSPAN of 2, and MMSE of 26. She reported usually reading the Bible, numerous devotional booklets and magazines, and the newspaper. She reported reading 4 hours a day, and rated her memory as somewhat poor and her knowledge and interest in creation, evolution, schizophrenia, and trusts as *none*. Grace was slow in her work during the training sessions, but seemed to understand the information. For extra assistance, in the fourth instructional session a student helper took Grace through the five structural plans with examples from cooking, something about which Grace knew a great deal; Grace did well with this exercise about familiar ideas. Although she got confused with new ideas and tasks, she did seem to understand the basic idea about the structure strategy. She was very confused when working on homework.

Grace reported after instruction more reading, somewhat better memory of her reading during testing sessions and in everyday life, more interest and enjoyment in reading, memory for different kinds of information in testing sessions and everyday life, and trying to figure out how a passage was organized and whether she was interested in it. Grace showed no evidence of using the structure strategy prior to instruction, but used it after instruction. She did not even attempt to write anything on the pretest for either the schizophrenia or trust passages, but recalled 23 and 15 ideas of the posttests, respectively, and used the same top-level structure as the author to organize her recall protocols. Her recalls are shown next for the pretest and posttest of the creation/evolution set. On the pretest, she gave no evidence of using the comparison structure to organize her recall and literally used a list, but she did use the structure strategy to organize her recall with a comparison top-level structure on the posttest.

Pretest: (recall score = 5)

feather
claws
Creath.
Eelv. by man
Crea. by God

Posttest: (recall score = 22)

Main idea is about creationist and evolution also about coal. Coal came from when the creation of world or Noah's time when it rain 40 days and nit [*sic*] say creationists. Creationists say foodling [*sic*] (flooding) and that where coal from.

Evolution thinks coal come from old swap where white clay and peat over billions of years ago. I believe in creationists.

Thus, although Grace had the same education level and MMSE score as Alveretta, Grace did improve substantially after instruction. Thus, simply eliminating people on the basis of MMSE scores would have precluded Grace's success.

Roberta, though younger (65) than the previously mentioned participants, appeared to have less language proficiency than did Bonita. Roberta reported usually reading the newspaper. Roberta had 12 years of education, reported reading an hour a day, and rated her memory and knowledge of trusts as average, but her knowledge of creation, evolution, and schizophrenia as *nothing*. She did not fill out the topic interest inventory. She received 6 points on the Davis Reading Test (3 for timed), 28 points on the Quick, RSPAN of 2 and CSPAN of 1, and MMSE of 27.

Roberta's ability to recall information from text was extremely limited. When she read a passage and then tried telling us the main idea, she lost the information. Even when she chose or guessed the right plan (given a choice limited by the instructor to only two plans), she often could not come up with the correct content to fit the plan. She often forgot about the ideas in the passage before she could write anything. During the first few training sessions, she had a pronounced tendency to rely on the social support of the group. She would mimic the answers of other people within proximity to her. During the later sessions, she seemed to do less of the repeating of others' ideas, but she still was not very confident in her use of the structure strategy, and for a good reason, because she was usually unable to find the overall structure. Some language deficits appeared to play a large factor in her trouble learning the structure strategy, and, perhaps, her motivation was low, too.

After instruction, Roberta noted more reading, somewhat better memory of her reading during testing sessions and in everyday life, more interest and enjoyment in reading, memory for different kinds of information in testing sessions but not everyday life, and trying to figure out how a passage was organized and her interest. In evaluating her performance, she wrote, "Since we met I remember things much better. I listening most than I did before. I also read most." However, Roberta showed no evidence of using the structure strategy on the pretests or the posttests. Thus, the instruction appeared to have little measurable effect on her reading performance.

Phyllis was an interesting person with stronger verbal skills than most of the participants in the rural sample; she was 68 years old with 12 years of education, a Davis Reading Test score of 15 (8 timed), a 30 on the Quick Word Test, RSPAN of 1 and CSPAN of 2, and MMSE of 27. She claimed to read 1 hour a day, mainly newspapers and books, and rated her memory as average and knowledge of schizophrenia and creation as minimal, evolution as slightly more, and knowledge of trusts as average.

Phyllis was very outspoken and tended to want to lead the group in answers and suggestions. She often only considered a portion of the text when making her decision about the plan or top-level structure of a text. In Session 2 we worried that she was never going to do well in the strategy because she dwelt so much on her own knowledge that was only tangentially related to the texts; she tended to infer so much information from the text that it became difficult to talk about a "correct" structure for each passage. We originally thought that this would hamper her ability to use the strategy and it may have. Actively relating prior knowledge to topic content is important for tying information you read into the knowledge you already have, but taken to an extreme, it makes selecting the top-level structure of a text difficult. When confronted with an answer different from what she selected, she was much like Bonita in responding that it depends on how you read it. Phyllis was quite amenable to change her answer to what the instructor recommended as the "right" one.

Phyllis' recall coming into the training was relatively good. During the training sessions, her recall was high, and in the later training sessions, she was good at selecting the overall structure and organizing the information in the text according to that structure. For example, see her recall that follows the comparison text about semidwarf and dwarf fruit trees written at the beginning of Session 1 and during Session 5.

Text:

Semidwarf apple trees grow 12 to 15 feet tall and bear fruit four or five years after planting. They require more space than dwarf tress, but produce larger harvests. Semidwarf trees look terrific on a front lawn, next to a deck, or as a tall screen. Space semidwarf apple trees 12 feet apart.

Dwarf apple trees reach heights of only 8 to 10 feet. Because of their diminutive size, they are easier to harvest than semidwarfs and may develop fruit a year or two earlier. You can squeeze dwarf apple trees into an unused garden corner, or grow them in containers on a patio or deck. Space dwarf apple trees 8 feet apart.

Phyllis' recall at beginning of Session 1:

Semidwarf and Dwarf Trees

Semidwarf trees grow about 12 to 15 feet tall. They bare [*sic*] fruit in 5 to 6 years. For best results they should be spaced from 10 to 12 feet apart.

The Dwarf trees will bear in about 3 years and can be spaced about 6 to 8 feet apart. The Dwarf tree makes a pretty fence or can be used in corner to make it more attractive.

Phyllis' recall during Session 5:

> Comparison The difference between the Semidwarf and the Dwarf
> Apple tree

The semidwarf should be planted about 12 feet apart. They bear fruit in 5 years. Semidwarf trees make a beauity [*sic*] fence or to enhance a deck or fill in a space in the garden.

The dwarf tree will bear in about 3 years. They are Easy to Harvest because of the small size. They can be grown in pots and used as suberity [*sic*]. Dwarf trees should be planted 8 feet apart.

However, Phyllis still had some difficulty being distracted by inferences and smaller pieces of text that displayed a definite organization, but not the overall organization for the text. She had trouble completing the homework and writing some of the main idea sentences.

After instruction, Phyllis voiced no change in amount of reading, greater memory of her reading during testing sessions and in everyday life, no change in interest in reading, but more enjoyment of reading, memory for different kinds of information in testing sessions and everyday life, and trying to figure out how a passage was organized. On the posttests there was only evidence for her using the structure strategy on the creation/evolution set, but total ideas recalled were boosted considerably from pretest to posttest on all passages. Her pretest and posttest for the creation/evolution set are reproduced here:

Pretest: (recall score = 16, without use of the comparison top-level structure)

> It take millions of years for trees and bones to stay together in the soil to produce coal. However, it can be produced in one day in the laboratory today.
>
> The is proof the Great Flood did take place
>
> The white clay that surrounded 300 meters of coal indicates some great proshure [*sic*] was present at this location at this time

Posttest: (recall score = 27, evidence for use of the comparison top-level structure)

> Evolutionists hold that birds evolved from reptils [*sic*]. They found wings with claws. Some of these folciss [*sic*] (fossils) were 130 millions years old.
>
> Creationist believe difference. They states that feather and claws together does not mean they were evolution but some other reason.

The final participant considered will be called Susan. She was 64 years old, had 11 years of education, a Davis Reading Test score of 8 (7 timed), a Quick Word Test of 27, RSPAN of 1 and CSPAN of 2, and MMSE of 30. She reported reading 4 hours a day, primarily the Bible, newpapers, and magazines, and rated her memory as slightly below average and thought she knew nothing about schizophrenia and evolution but thought she had average knowledge about trusts and slightly below-average knowledge about creation. She had high interest for trusts, but no interest in creation or evolution and only slight interest in schizophrenia.

Susan was a quiet and thoughtful woman who was never the first to speak. However, she was not a follower. She took her time in deciding on the top-level structure for a text and then she would stick by her choice, because she had a good reason for each choice. It sometimes took her longer to read a passage, but probably because of her deliberate use of the structure strategy. During the instructional sessions, she would often read a passage and then look up as if in deep thought about the organization of the passage; she never just started writing information without planning.

Susan was very good at organizing her recall, even though she did not always use a main idea statement. She was usually right in selecting the best top-level structure from all five structures taught. She recalled quite a good deal from each passage during the training sessions. For example, reproduced next are her recalls after Sessions 1 and 5 of the passage about rat allergies; both recalls are basically accurate, quite good, and show evidence for use of the strategy (problem/solution structure followed), but the final recall more explicitly and clearly uses the structure strategy to organize the recall protocol.

Susan's recall after Session 1:

An occupational [*sic*] hazard for workers that work with mice and rats is that they becom [*sic*] allegic [*sic*] to them. It is not the skin or hair but the urin [*sic*] that have a protein that they are allegic [*sic*] to. A British scientist Dr. Salrui said kindness to the animal was one way the help, those that stroked them were less likely to become effected.

Susan's recall after Session 5:

The Plan is Problem Solution. The main idea is to prevent allegic [*sic*].

An occupational [*sic*] hazzard [*sic*] that workers had working with rats was allegic [*sic*]. Scientiest [*sic*] found that is was not the hair or skin that caused the alleg. [*sic*] but a protein subtance [*sic*] found in the urin [*sic*] that caused the alleg. [*sic*].

The solution that the scientiest [*sic*] found was being kind to the animal. When picking it up it would help to sooth [*sic*] them.

Her self-appraisal of changes resulting from training indicated more reading, greater memory during testing sessions and everyday life, and a greater interest in reading but no greater enjoyment of reading. She also reported working to remember different kinds of information in testing sessions and everyday life and trying to figure out how a passage was organized and whether she was interested in it.

On the pretest, Susan's performance showed no evidence for use of the structure strategy, but on all the posttests she clearly utilized the structure strategy, liberally adding signaling words (e.g., "problem," "important"; Meyer, 1975) to keep herself organized. As an example, her recall protocols for the trust passage are reproduced here:

Pretest: (recall score = 14, without use of the problem/solution top-level structure)

The passage is about making a will before you die to prevent the court cost and delays. You can be tied up in court for years without a will. And it may not be distributed like you want it.

Posttest: (recall score = 48, clear evidence for use of the problem/solution top-level structure)

It is very important to make a will while you are in your sound mind. You can control who you want your belongings to go to before and after death. It is also important what kind of will you make, going through Probate Court can cost a lot of money plus tie up your belongings for years.

However, a trust can solve a lot of problems without going through court. And it does not have a life span. A beneficary [*sic*] can control the property such as living on a farm without cost. A trust transfers ownership at death to the person you desire it does not die

Overall for the rural sample, there seemed to be a large effect of community on the learning in the instructional sessions. This was reflected in the way the participants shared answers to the exercises in their instructional booklets as a group, rather than as cooperative partners exchanging, discussing, and debating their individual work. The more highly verbal older participants, Phyllis and Susan, did not seem subject to this effect to such an extent as most of the others. Phyllis and Susan would stick with their own analyses of the passages and ideas rather than going along with the more vocal members of the groups who shared their ideas orally.

Due to this apparent relationship with verbal skills (as measured by the Quick Word Test and Davis Reading Test), we wonder if this observed community effect is cultural or just due to low education, low self-efficacy, or fear of failure. We did not observe it at all in young African American college students (Meyer et al., 1999), who had higher levels of education and verbal abilities as well as recent experiences in university classrooms and studies. Perhaps the observed community effect was, in part, the result of our attempt to make the participants feel comfortable. There may have been a misinterpretation of what was expected of them, in terms of working independently instead of collaboratively. The younger African Americans (Meyer et al., 1999) were clear about their role as participants in a study, whereas the older participants were probably more or less "hanging out" with their friends. For many of the older participants, the collaborative effort may have been an adaptive strategy to accomplish tasks that could not be adequately accomplished alone.

CONCLUSIONS

A number of investigations (Meyer et al., 1989, 1999) have indicated that structure strategy training is helpful for participants regardless of the capabilities they bring to the training. That is, although training is not effective for everyone, we have not been able to predict from numerous individual difference characteristics who will benefit most from training. The identification of the MMSE as a good predictor for success with the sample of older African Americans is the first time we have been able to identify such a predictor. Our in-depth look at some of the older African American participants indicated that training with the structure strategy can be quite helpful for some learners with very low verbal skills as measured by standardized tests. However, it did not help all readers, and those readers had lower scores on the MMSE. Good candidates for dramatic success in the strategy training program from the group of older African Americans were those participants with low levels of education but high scores on the MMSE. For the group of readers with lower scores on the MMSE, there seemed to be a mixed group comprised of people who could benefit from training and those whose memory functioning bordered mild Alzheimer's symptoms who seemed unable to benefit from training.

Our understanding of the strategy training program and testing materials has been increased by working with these low-literacy adults. We expect that comparable findings would have resulted from working with White adults with similar literacy levels. As can be seen in the writing samples shown earlier for some of the more able students, such as Susan, Bonita, and Phyllis, their writing and recall protocols were much better on the easier, more familiar, and shorter training materials than on the more complex, less familiar, and longer testing materials. Suggestions for modifying the instructional approach to better meet the needs of low-literacy adults similar to the older African Americans in this sample include (a) using materials more relevant to their everyday lives (e.g., Bible stories with comparison plans, such as Jacob vs. Esau, and problem/solution plans, such as the problem of sin and the solution of Jesus) and examples from more familiar domains, such as childrearing and cooking (refer to Table 12.3 to examine the more familiar and interesting topics for our sample); (b) using shorter passages during testing and training; (c) presenting one or two structures per session instead of all five at once; (d) presenting smaller instructional units with more practice; and (e) individualizing the instruction for some of the participants with lower MMSE scores. In addition, it would be of interest to see how much improvement could be made with continued instruction for students like Bonita, who was highly motivated and made such excellent progress in only 9 hours of instruction.

ACKNOWLEDGMENT

The research reported in this chapter was supported in part by National Institute of Aging Grant AG09957.

REFERENCES

Babcock, R., & Salthouse, T. A. (1990). Effects of increased processing demands on age differences in working memory. *Psychology and Aging, 5,* 421–428.

Bartlett, B. J. (1978). *Top-level structure as an organizational strategy for recall of classroom text.* Unpublished doctoral dissertation, Arizona State University.

Bartlett, F. C. (1932). *Remembering.* Cambridge, England: Cambridge University Press.

Borgatta, E. F., & Corsini, R. J. (1964). *Manual for the Quick Word Test.* New York: Harcourt, Brace, & World.

Britton, B. K., & Graesser, A. C. (1996). Five metaphors for text understanding. In B. K. Britton & A. C. Graesser (Eds.), *Models of understanding text* (pp. 341–351). Mahwah, NJ: Lawrence Erlbaum Associates.

Carrell, P. L. (1985). Facilitating ESL reading by teaching text structure. *TESOL Quarterly, 19,* 727–752.

Cook, L. K., & Mayer, R. E. (1988). Teaching readers about the structure of scientific text. *Journal of Educational Psychology, 80,* 448–456.

Cooley, S., Deitch, I. M., Harper, M. S., Hinrichsen, G., Lopez, M. A., & Molinari, V. A. (1998). What practitioners should know about working with older adults. *Professional Psychology: Research and Practice, 29,* 413–427.

Davis, F. B. (1944). Fundamental factors in reading. *Psychometrica, 9,* 185–197.

A drug for fragile bones. (1995, November 6). *U.S. News & World Report,* 89–90.

Fillenbaum, B. (1988). *Multidimensional functional assessment of older adults: The Duke Older Americans Resources and Services procedures.* Hillsdale, NJ: Lawrence Erlbaum Associates.

Folstein, M. (1983). The Mini-Mental State Exam. In T. Crook, S. Farris, & R. Bartus (Eds.), *Assessment in geriatric psychopharmacology* (pp. 47–51). New Canaan, CT: Mark Powley.

Gernsbacher, M. A. (1996). The structure-building framework: What it is, what it might also be, and why. In B. K. Britton & A. C. Graesser (Eds.), *Models of understanding text* (pp. 289–312). Mahwah, NJ: Lawrence Erlbaum Associates.

Grimes, J. E. (1975). *The thread of discourse*. The Hague, Netherlands: Mouton.

Hartley, J. T. (1986). Reader and text variables as determinants of discourse memory in adulthood. *Psychology and Aging, 1,* 150–158.

Hartley, J. T. (1988). Aging and individual differences in discourse memory. In L. L. Light & D. M. Burke (Eds.), *Language, memory, and aging* (pp. 36–57). New York: Cambridge University Press.

Hultsch, D. F., & Dixon, R. A. (1983). The role of pre-experimental knowledge in text processing in adulthood. *Experimental Aging Research, 9,* 17–22.

Hultsch, D. F., Hertzog, C., Dixon, R. A., & Small, B. J. (1998). *Memory change in the aged.* Cambridge, England: Cambridge University Press.

Johnson, M. M., Elsner, R. J. F., Poon, L. W., Meyer, B. J. F., Yang, B., Smith, G., Noble, C. A., Talbot, A. P., Hetrick, C. J., Stubblefield, R. A., Puskar, D., Edmondson, J., & Shaffer, S. C. (1997). Building a model to test the capacity-speed hypotheses. In C. A. Noble & R. J. F. Elsner (Eds.), *An odyssey in aging* (pp. 123–141). Rural, GA: University of Georgia Gerontology Center.

Kintsch, W. (1998). *Comprehension: A paradigm for cognition.* New York: Cambridge University Press.

Light, L. L., & Anderson, P. A. (1985). Working memory capacity, age, and memory for discourse. *Journal of Gerontology, 40,* 737–747.

Mann, W. C., & Thompson, S. A. (1988). Rhetorical structure theory: Toward a functional theory of text organization. *Text, 8,* 243–281.

Meyer, B. J. F. (1975). *The organization of prose and its effects on memory.* Amsterdam: North-Holland.

Meyer, B. J. F. (1984). Organizational aspects of text: Effects on reading comprehension and applications for the classroom. In J. Flood (Ed.), *Promoting reading comprehension* (pp. 113–138). Newark, DE: International Reading Association.

Meyer, B. J. F. (1985a). Signaling the structure of text. In D. H. Jonassen (Ed.), *The technology of text* (Vol. 2, pp. 64–89). Englewood Cliffs, NJ: Educational Technology Publications.

Meyer, B. J. F. (1985b). Prose analysis: Purposes, procedures, and problems. In B. K. Britton & J. Black (Eds.), *Analyzing and understanding expository text* (pp. 11–64, 269–304). Hillsdale, NJ: Lawrence Erlbaum Associates.

Meyer, B. J. F. (1987). Following the author's top-level organization: An important skill for reading comprehension. In R. J. Tierney, P. L. Anders, & J. N. Mitchell (Eds.), *Understanding readers understanding* (pp. 59–76). Hillsdale, NJ: Lawrence Erlbaum Associates.

Meyer, B. J. F., Brandt, D. M., & Bluth, G. J. (1980). Use of the top-level structure in text: Key for reading comprehension of ninth-grade students. *Reading Research Quarterly, 16,* 72–103.

Meyer, B. J. F., Poon, L. W., & Talbot, A. P. (1999). *Examining the generalizability of structure strategy training to different types of readers and tasks.* Manuscript submitted for publication.

Meyer, B. J. F., & Rice, G. E. (1983). Learning and memory from text across the adult life span. In J. Fine & R. O. Freedle (Eds.), *Developmental studies in discourse* (pp. 291–306). Norwood, NJ: Ablex.

Meyer, B. J. F., & Rice, G. E. (1984). The structure of text. In P. D. Pearson (Ed.), *Handbook of reading research* (pp. 319–352). New York: Longman.

Meyer, B. J. F., Talbot, A. P., Stubblefield, R. A., & Poon, L. W. (1998). Interest and strategies of young and old readers differentially interact with characteristics of texts. *Educational Gerontology, 24,* 747–771.

Meyer, B. J. F., Young, C. J., & Bartlett, B. J. (1989). *Memory improved: Enhanced reading comprehension and memory across the life span through strategic text structure.* Hillsdale, NJ: Lawrence Erlbaum Associates.

Reisberg, B., Ferris, S. H., Anand, R., de Leon, M. J., Schneck, M. K., Buttinger, C., & Borenstein, J. (1984). Functional staging of dementia of the Alzheimer's type. *Annals of the New York Academy of Sciences, 435*, 481–483.

Rice, G. E. (1980). On cultural schema. *American Ethnologist, 7*, 152–171.

Rickards, J. P., Fajen, B. R., Sullivan, J. F., & Gillespie, G. (1997). Signaling, notetaking, and field independence–dependence in text comprehension and recall. *Journal of Educational Psychology, 89*, 508–517.

Salthouse, T. A. (1985). Speed of behavior and its implications for cognition. In J. E. Birren & K. W. Schaie (Eds.), *Handbook of the psychology of aging* (pp. 400–426). New York: Van Nostrand Reinhold.

Sanders, T. J. M., Spooren, W. P. M., & Noordman, L. G. M. (1992). Towards a taxonomy of coherence relations. *Discourse Processes, 15*, 1–35.

Voss, J. F., & Silfies, L. N. (1996). Learning from history text: The interaction of knowledge and comprehension skill with text structure. *Cognition and Instruction, 14*, 45–68.

Wechsler, D. (1981). *WAIS–R manual: Wechsler Adult Intelligence Scale–Revised*. New York: Psychological Corporation.

APPENDIX

Coal Mine Text From the Creation/
Evolution Set of Passages

Different views about a coal mine in Australia result from different beliefs held by scientists supporting the creation model and those supporting the evolution model. Creationists interpret the coal mine as evidence of the catastrophic, Biblical flood. One reason for the creationists' interpretation is that the right pressure conditions and right heat conditions have been shown to make coal in the laboratory in one day. The Yallourn, Australia coal mine has no soil in it or near it; the mine contains 1000 cubic kilometers of brown coal. Pine logs at all angles and fossilized sea creatures are mixed together in the coal mine. The 300 meter thick seam of coal sits on clean clay; this flat layer of white clay underlies the coal. The clay is without fossilized roots. Since the creation model states that fossil graveyards were created rapidly by a worldwide flood in Noah's time, the model can easily account for the coal on top of the clean clay.

In contrast, evolutionists interpret the huge mine as an old swamp that stood at the same spot and existed years ago. However, additional theories are required to deal with the lack of soil and the clean clay bottom. Evolutionists explain that the swamp's soil must have washed away and the clean, white clay must have washed in under the coal. The evolution model states that coal was formed from peat over billions of years. As a result, evolutionists state that change must have occurred over billions of years in both the swamp and the movement of the soil and clay under the coal mine.

Chapter 13

An Age-Related View of Computer Literacy for Adult African Americans

Monica M. Huff
University of Georgia

Wendy A. Rogers
Georgia Institute of Technology

Literacy is being redefined to incorporate cultural components of literacy as well as computer knowledge (Fisher, 1997–1998; Hawkins & Paris, 1997; Newman & Beverstock, 1990). In this way, computer literacy is becoming an integral part of how literacy in general is defined. The focus of this chapter is on computer literacy rather than more traditional types of reading literacy. In addition, we take an adult life-span developmental perspective in reviewing computer literacy research of African Americans from high school age to older adults. Our focus is on young adults through older adults who have transitioned or are having to transition to using technology and computers in the home and workplace. The structure of the chapter is as follows: First we define computer literacy. Then we discuss the lifelong value of knowing how to use technology and the importance of computer access in different environments (specifically, at school, in the home, and at work). We then briefly describe research considerations for this domain, and conclude by providing direction for future work.

What is meant by *computer literacy*? Perhaps the best place to start is by parsing the term into its components. A *computer* is defined as a high-speed electronic device that stores, processes, and retrieves information. *Traditional literacy*, as has been discussed throughout this book, is often defined as being able to read and write, or as being educated. According to these definitions then, *computer literacy* is having the ability or being educated to perform tasks using a high-speed electronic device that processes, retrieves, and stores programmed information. This chapter reviews literature on the computer literacy of high school age through older adult African Americans. Potential solutions to differences in computer literacy are discussed at the end of the chapter.

LIFELONG VALUE OF USING TECHNOLOGY

What is the value of using technology? And why is it important to include computer literacy in a general definition of literacy? In response to the first question, technology may be a source of power such that a lack of computer knowledge is viewed as a barrier to success, social mobility, and as potentially being responsible for the creation of a "technological underclass" (Badagliacco, 1990; Carver, 1994; Leggon, 1995; Novak & Hoffman, 1998; Resta, 1992). This belief suggests that those without technological savvy are in danger of being left behind in terms of job opportunities and access to information. Another factor has to do with the pervasiveness of technology in modern society. Computers are not just the traditional monitor, keyboard, and central processing unit. Instead, we encounter many types of computers on a daily basis, for example, electronic alarm clocks, microwave ovens, fax machines, and telephone systems. All of these are "computers" with storage, processing, and information-retrieving capabilities.

The pervasiveness of computers makes operational know-how important throughout the lifetime. The lifelong value of learning different types of technology takes on more meaning in light of the fact that we are an aging population. It is anticipated that by 2030 approximately 20% (70 million) of the U.S. population will be 65 years and older (U.S. Bureau of the Census, 1998). As the number of older adults in the workforce increases, the need to train or retrain employees on how to use computers is estimated to grow steadily (Czaja & Sharit, 1993). New technologies, new software programs, and new tools will require training or retraining for most employees (Gist, Rosen, & Schwoerer, 1988; Kelley & Charness, 1995). Many tasks are already computerized (e.g., banking and library card-catalog systems), and older adults are often required to use these systems (Kelley & Charness, 1995; Rogers, Meyer, Walker, & Fisk, 1998). In addition, older adults could enhance their lives and independence by using computers for communicating with family members, planning trips, and even more everyday tasks such as grocery shopping (Czaja, Guerrier, Nair, & Landauer, 1993; Kelley & Charness, 1995; Morrell & Echt, 1997).

In the current information age, it is a necessity, not an option, to learn different types of technology for functioning in daily life. Given that computer literacy is important for everyone, we now examine research that suggests there may be race or ethnicity differences in computer literacy.

LEARNING TO USE COMPUTERS

The literature considering African Americans and human–computer interaction has focused primarily on how people learn to use computers and why there may be differences in African Americans' usage of computers. How people learn to use computers is closely linked to the question of where people learn to use computers. By examining differences in how and where people learn to use computers, we may gain insight into how to create more effective learning environments. For this reason, it is important to consider if there are differences in African Americans' usage of computers and access to computers. People learn to use computers at school, at home, or at work and are either taught or teach themselves. Each of these issues is discussed in more detail in the following sections.

School—High School and College

Many of today's youth learn to use computers in their schools. An important issue is whether there are differences in the availability and use of computers based on the ethnicity or socioeconomic composition of the school. Research suggests that there are fewer computers available in less affluent schools, which often have larger African American student populations. The students have less access to computers and, consequently, less computer experience. For the computers that are available, students often are required to share them. There are also differences in the types of computer tasks performed. African American students are more likely to use computers for rote drills such as multiplication tables as opposed to programming or more elaborate problem solving tasks (Carver, 1994; Clayborne & Seefeldt, 1991; Leggon, 1995; Resta, 1992; Robinson, 1998; Rosen & Weil, 1995).

Rosen and Weil (1995) found that many teachers do not make use of technology in their classrooms because of their own anxiety and negative attitudes about computers. Moreover, African American teachers were found to have significantly more computer anxiety than all other teacher groups. Yet, evidence suggests that as many as 75% of African American males learn about computers from their teachers (Carver, 1994). What happens when the teachers in the classroom are not comfortable using computers?

Before focusing on this specific issue, there are a few general findings that are relevant about people who have no prior computer experience, regardless of ethnicity. In general, people with less computer experience have more anxiety and negative attitudes about computers (Badagliacco, 1990; Rosen & Weil, 1995). People with less experience are also more likely to overestimate the difficulties of using a computer (Gilroy & Desai, 1986).

These differences in attitudes may affect teachers' overall desire to learn to use computers and their ability to teach their students. Liu and Johnson (1998) found that computer achievement is a function of enjoyment, motivation, and freedom from anxiety. Not surprisingly, Levine and Donitsa-Schmidt (1998) found that computer experience has a positive effect on computer attitudes and computer confidence toward computers. More training is needed to ensure that teachers are comfortable using and teaching others to use computers in the classroom. In addition, teachers need to communicate more on how to incorporate computer skills into the daily curriculum and design appropriate lessons that use technology (Fisher, 1997–1998; Lowther, Bassoppo-Moyo, & Morrison, 1998). Resta (1992) suggested providing training for teachers in predominantly minority schools and recruiting more minority teachers who are computer literate and competent to serve as role models for students.

A lack of African American computer users as role models in the schools may contribute further to African American students having less computer experience. For example, many schools have separate computer labs run by a computer coordinator. Most computer coordinators are European American, further contributing to the lack of African American role models (Resta, 1992). None of the African American male students in the Carver (1994) study had computers in their classroom; rather, usage was restricted to the computer lab. Resta suggested implementing programs that expose African American students to computer-literate African American role models in the schools, as well as at summer camps and university programs (see Bos &Wisnudel, 1996, for an example of a computer camp).

What happens when these students with less computer experience in high school go to college? Do differences in African American high school students' computer usage and access translate to differences in college usage? The answer is rather complicated. Resta (1992) suggested that African American students lacking computer knowledge find that they have an additional barrier in their college academic success. Similarly, Badagliacco (1990) found that African Americans who had no experience with computers before college continued to have less experience and lagged behind in terms of computer knowledge and computer usage in college. Not surprisingly then, it seems high school computer experience influences college experience.

Hawkins and Paris (1997) also found that African American students entered college with less computer experience and skills and that these differences were not minimized in college, but may have even increased. They found that while computer usage in general is increasing for everyone in college, the type of use and frequency of use differs between African Americans and European Americans. While the majority of students were found to use a computer for some purpose (e.g., library searches), using a computer did not necessarily equate with computer literacy. The European American students were found to be more computer literate, using computers for a wider variety of computer applications than the African American students. Hawkins and Paris concluded that colleges and universities need to recognize these skill differences and do more than just make computers available to students. Classes and programs need to be implemented that eliminate the differences between student groups' computer skills.

The good news is that positive experiences in high school are also influential in college. In fact, African American students with precollege computer experience surpassed the European American students in terms of computer experience. According to Badagliacco (1990) this finding remains to be explained, but she suggested the possibility that African American students who used computers in high school view computing as a vehicle for upward social mobility. Lack of high school computer experience impedes college success, but experience in high school seems particularly beneficial for African American students. Thus, the benefits of learning computers in high school can be long lasting.

Home

What effect does having a computer at home have on computer literacy? Having home access to a computer appears to increase usage of computers and contribute to computer learning. Levine and Donitsa-Schmidt (1998) found that school-based computer learning and home use had a cumulative effect on students' confidence, attitudes, and knowledge toward computers. Based on their findings, they recommended that teachers advise parents to buy a home computer and encourage their children to use it often. A home computer provides constant availability to a computer and is believed to foster role-modeling of computer use. The parents' beliefs, attitudes, and expectations about computers can shape their children's attitudes and beliefs about computers. For example, Clayborne and Seefeldt (1991) found that junior high students and their mothers had similar attitudes toward computers. This is important because Carver (1994) found that learning from family members about computers was more common than learning about computers from peers. This signifies the importance that family members can have as computer role models for African American children.

Hoffman and Novak (1998) and Novak and Hoffman (1998) found that European Americans are significantly more likely to have a home computer (44.2% vs. 29.0%) than are African Americans. In general, increasing levels of income explained owning a home computer, regardless of race, whereby people with higher income levels were more likely to own a home computer. However, they found that computer ownership varied depending on household income. In households with incomes below $40,000, European Americans were more likely to own a computer, but in households with incomes of $40,000 or greater, a larger percentage of African Americans owned computers. Although these income–computer patterns were not statistically significant, they still indicate an interesting trend.

Computers in the home also have important implications in terms of computer literacy in African American older adults. Research suggests that African American grandparents often care for their grandchildren. The importance of learning to use computers and technology throughout the lifetime takes on new significance when factoring in the number of grandparents that care for their grandchildren. Fuller-Thomson, Minkler, and Driver (1997) found that 1 in 10 grandparents have raised a grandchild for at least 6 months. For African American grandparents, the odds of being a caregiver were 83% more likely than respondents from other races. This means that African American grandparents often care for and serve as role models for their grandchildren. Watson (1997) found that African American grandparents were more interested in taking a grandparenting class than European American grandparents. Grandparents have an opportunity to serve as computer-using role models by using different types of technology in front of their grandchildren. Grandparenting classes could provide training on how to use computers so grandparents could teach their grandchildren at home and at school (grandparents comprise the majority of elementary classroom volunteers). To date, there has been no research on computer use and technology between grandparents and their grandchildren. The effect of older adult African Americans using computers and new types of technology and the direct influence on their grandchildren's access, attitudes, and behaviors will be an interesting area for future research.

Grandparents can also increase their own life satisfaction by using different types of technology. Studies have found that the family role involvement and participation in church activities of the older adult African American are significant life satisfaction predictors (Coke, 1992; Coke & Twaite, 1995). Computers and technology (e.g., e-mail and Internet) can be used to communicate with family members who live far away, develop new hobbies, learn new information, or to participate in church activities. By using computers to foster these activities, the life satisfaction of African American older adults may be increased.

Work

Technology and automation can be viewed as both creating jobs for and taking jobs from African Americans (Carver, 1994). For example, automation in a factory can create a monitoring or supervisory position, but at the same time it also takes away manufacturing jobs. Similar issues arise in other occupations such as office work, aeronautics, and communication businesses. Thus, technology can increase the existing inequality for those people who do not have the required skills, in that they may lose their position or their job may become obsolete. Technology can also increase social mobility whereby people who have experience and expertise in computers are more likely to benefit from changes in technology. Technology is capable of increasing or reinforcing existing inequality, but it also can be seen as a means for social mobility (Badagliacco, 1990; Leggon, 1995). In this way, automation can be seen as both friend and foe.

Novak and Hoffman (1998) found that European Americans are somewhat more likely to have a computer at work (38.5% vs. 33.8%) than African Americans, but this difference was not statistically significant. They found that regardless of race, education explains access to a computer at work, such that people with increasing levels of education are more likely to have a computer. Badagliacco (1990) suggested that computer-related jobs and activities are viewed as primarily being European American and male, so that minorities are discouraged academically from seeking careers that require high-technology skills. Who is using computers at work, what type of training or computer background the person has, and exactly how computers are being used need to be studied in more detail.

Access

Do African Americans have less access to computers? Are there differences in computer access for African Americans at school, in the home, and at work? The answers seem to be yes. As previously stated, research suggests that minority urban schools have fewer computers, require students to share the available computers more, and even differ in the types of computer tasks that are performed (Carver, 1994; Clayborne & Seefeldt, 1991; Leggon, 1995; Resta, 1992; Rosen & Weil, 1995). All of these differences in access seem to result in differences in usage, and computer usage may translate into better jobs.

One component to computer access that is often raised is the issue of socioeconomic status (SES; Clayborne & Seefeldt, 1991; Resta, 1992; Rosen & Weil, 1995). Do African Americans have less access to computers because they have less money to buy computers? Based on the Clayborne and Seefeldt (1991), Resta (1992), and Rosen and Weil (1995) studies, the answer would be yes, lower SES African Americans have less money to buy computers. Resta (1992) and Novak and Hoffman (1998) suggested implementing programs to aid lower SES African Americans in buying their own computers with the idea that computer access translates into usage.

Socioeconomic status is probably just one component of the access problem, and other factors should and need to be explored. For example, advertisements and commercials that are focused on a European American market may affect African Americans' choice not to buy a computer (Clayborne & Seefeldt, 1991). Another relevant area is the effect of attitudes and beliefs regarding computers on actual usage and proficiency of interacting with computers. Many other implicit and explicit factors such as education, marketing, role models, peers, and so on, may be adding to the computer access problems of some African Americans, and these other factors should be investigated further.

OTHER TYPES OF TECHNOLOGY

The focus of the chapter thus far has been on traditional forms of desktop computing. However, as described earlier, computers are pervasive and are found in a wide variety of everyday tasks. This section reviews literature concerning other everyday types of computing.

Other Types of Technology

One question relevant to the present focus is whether there are race-related differences in other types of technologies that incorporate computers. Rogers, Cabrera, Walker, Gilbert, and Fisk (1996) conducted a survey of technology usage across the adult life span (a subset of their data is presented in Table 13.1). The survey included 1,562 people in the Memphis

TABLE 13.1
Other Types of Computer Technology Used

	Race	
Computer Technology	*African American*	*European American*
Answering machine	84.0%	87.1%
Automatic teller machine	65.4%	64.0%
Cellular phone	57.3%	57.2%
Compact disc player	57.3%	57.3%
Cruise control*	71.0%	90.1%
Fax machine*	53.4%	63.9%
Microwave oven*	93.9%	98.1%
Photocopier*	87.8%	93.6%
Telephone banking	40.5%	35.7%
Video camera	54.2%	59.9%
Video cassette recorder*	79.4%	87.2%
Voice mail	49.6%	56.1%

Note. These data are a regrouping of the data reported by Rogers, Cabrera, Walker, Gilbert, and Fisk (1996).

*Group differences are significant.

and Atlanta metropolitan areas. Rogers et al. found that there were no differences between African Americans ($n = 47$) and European Americans ($n = 440$) in the use of automatic teller machines (ATMs), cellular phones, telephone banking, answering machines, compact disc players, video cameras, or voice mail. They did find small but statistically significant race differences in the use of fax machines, photocopiers, videocassette recorders (VCRs), microwave ovens, and cruise control, such that the European Americans were more likely to use the technology. However, the overall pattern of data suggests that for this sample of individuals (ages 18–82) there was no real evidence that African Americans did not want to use or avoided using different types of technology.

Respondents in the Rogers et al. (1996) survey were also queried about their willingness to participate in a training program for learning to use ATMs. African Americans indicated being more willing than European Americans to participate in training programs (40% vs. 11%). Thus, it does not appear to be the case that African Americans are not interested in using different types of technology or in being trained in how to use them (Rogers et al., 1996; also see Qualls, chap. 1, this volume).

Another study that focused on use of various types of technology was conducted in a focus-group format that allowed discussion with the participants (Rogers et al., 1998). Interviews with both African American and European American older adults revealed that they were interacting with many different types of technology and encountering a number of different problems with technology on a daily basis. The sample size was relatively small for this study, with only 21 African Americans and 35 European Americans. Nonetheless, the patterns of reported problems were similar across race.

The results of these interviews about the older adults' difficulties and concerns with using everyday types of technology are descriptive of the types of problems they have. For example, there were complaints about phone menus, such as one woman who remarked, "Almost everything you call, you get machines." The bottom line is that older adults, just like everyone else, are being confronted with different types of technology on a daily basis, regardless of their desire to interact with the technology.

Other types of technology that were discussed in the interviews included microwave ovens, VCRs, and ATMs. Microwave ovens were viewed both positively as saving time cooking and negatively as potentially causing cancer. Several older adults described VCRs as being difficult to operate because they have too many functions. An older adult made the following illustrative remark when talking about the number of bank cards sent to her house encouraging her to use an ATM card: "I do it the same old way. They want me to do it all sorts of ways and give me all sorts of cards and I just file them away." As seen in these attitudes and comments, technology is pervasive in older adults' lives. Through training (such as educating about microwave ovens) and redesign (e.g., shortening telephone menu lists), older adults can learn to benefit from and perhaps even enjoy using many different types of technology.

DISCUSSION

We have considered how computer literacy is defined, how there is life-long value in using technology, and how there may be differences in access to computers and technology for African Americans. This chapter has primarily focused on differences throughout the adult life span in using technology in terms of access to computers at school, at home, and at work. Our review of the literature also revealed several issues that should be regarded with caution, and that should be addressed in future research.

One critical research issue is how ethnicity or race has been defined in these studies. Many of the studies relied on self-reports, where people might define themselves differently depending on how race is categorized. Depending on the number of categories and the level of ethnic detail, a person can easily fit into more than one category. For example, persons of Jamaican descent may describe themselves as African American or Black if Jamaican or Caribbean descent is not listed as an option (see Horner, chap. 5, this volume). Phinney (1996) described how ethnic categories and labels vary over time, context, and individuals and how such labels may have different meanings for members versus nonmembers.

Another problem with the existing research relevant to race differences in computer literacy is the fact that sample sizes are not reported, or the samples are relatively small and may not be representative. Consequently, it is not clear if these findings are based on real differences in race and access to computers and technology. Larger scale studies need to be conducted to determine the extent of race differences and the source of such differences.

Another potential problem that was raised in the Access section is that socioeconomic status is often blamed for differences in computer literacy. However, there may be other factors contributing to computer literacy of African Americans that are being mistakenly overlooked, such as differences in advertisements, education, and technology role models. These other factors should be and need to be examined further.

With these caveats in mind, where do we go from here? Training and access opportunities should be better advertised. There are many camps, university programs, libraries, and senior centers that already provide training and access to computers. Awareness of these existing programs needs to be increased. Creative ways to use computers in the classrooms need to be explored such that computers are used in different contexts rather than simply for basic rote math drills. Creative design of computer technology also needs to be explored. Technology can always be improved so that it is more usable and inviting to more users.

In summary, this chapter highlights some of the issues in computer literacy for African Americans ranging in age from teenagers, to college students, to working adults, to grandparents. Clearly computer technology has a major impact on all our lives. There is a need to focus our resources on understanding race-related differences in computer literacy, on trying to minimize them, and on providing better access, training, and design of different types of technology.

ACKNOWLEDGMENTS

This research was supported in part by National Institutes of Health (National Institute on Aging) Grant P50 AG11715, under the auspices of the Center for Applied Cognitive Research on Aging (one of the Edward R. Roybal Centers for Research on Applied Gerontology). This chapter is based on a presentation made at the Memphis Research Symposium Focus on Communication and Literacy in African Americans (June 1998). We thank Joyce Harris and Constance Dean Qualls for their suggestions and constructive criticisms of the chapter.

REFERENCES

Badagliacco, J. M. (1990). Gender and race differences in computing attitudes and experience. *Social Science Computer Review, 8*, 42–63.

Bos, N., & Wisnudel, M. (1996, April). Summer computer camps—Developing appropriate educational goals. *Learning and Leading With Technology,* 6–9.

Carver, B. A. (1994). Defining the context of early computer learning for African American males in urban elementary schools. *Journal of Negro Education, 63*, 532–545.

Clayborne, B. M., & Seefeldt, C. (1991). The relationship between the attitudes of urban students and mothers toward computers. *Journal of Negro Education, 60*, 78–84.

Coke, M. M. (1992). Correlates of life satisfaction among elderly African Americans. *Journal of Gerontology: Psychological Sciences, 47*, 316–320.

Coke, M. M., & Twaite, J. A. (1995). *The Black elderly satisfaction and quality of later life.* New York: Haworth.

Czaja, S. J., Guerrier, J. H., Nair, S. N., & Landauer, T. K. (1993). Computer communication as an aid to independence for older adults. *Behavior and Information Technology, 12,* 197–207.

Czaja, S. J., & Sharit, J. (1993). Age differences in the performance of computer-based work. *Psychology and Aging, 8*, 59–67.

Fisher, M. M. (1997–1998). Design your future: Technology literacy competency recommendations for K–12 education. *Journal of Educational Technology Systems, 26*(1), 27–34.

Fuller-Thomson, E., Minkler, M., & Driver, D. (1997). A profile of grandparents raising grandchildren in the United States. *The Gerontologist, 37*, 406–411.

Gilroy, F. D., & Desai, H. B. (1986). Computer anxiety: Sex, race, and age. *International Journal of Man–Machine Studies, 25*, 711–719.

Gist, M., Rosen, B., & Schwoerer, C. (1988). The influence of training method and trainee age on the acquisition of computer skills. *Personnel Psychology, 41*, 255–265.

Hawkins, R., & Paris, A. E. (1997). Computer literacy and computer use among college students: Differences in black and white. *Journal of Negro Education, 66*(2), 147–158.

Hoffman, D. L., & Novak, T. P. (1998). Bridging the racial divide on the Internet. *Science, 280*, 390–391.

Kelley, C. L., & Charness, N. (1995). Issues in training older adults to use computers. *Behavior and Information Technology, 14*, 107–120.

Leggon, C. B. (1995). The impact of science and technology on African Americans. *Humboldt Journal of Social Relations, 21*, 35–53.

Levine, T., & Donitsa-Schmidt, S. (1998). Computer use, confidence, attitudes, and knowledge: A causal analysis. *Computers in Human Behavior, 14*(1), 125–146.

Liu, L., & Johnson, D. L. (1998). A computer achievement model: Computer attitude and computer achievement. *Computers in the Schools, 14*(3/4), 33–53.

Lowther, D. L., Bassoppo-Moyo, T., & Morrison, G. R. (1998). Moving from computer literate to technologically competent: The next educational reform. *Computers in Human Behavior, 14*(1), 93–109.

Morrell, R. W., & Echt, K. V. (1997). Designing written instructions for older adults: Learning to use computers. In A. D. Fisk & W. A. Rogers (Eds.), *Handbook of human factors and the older adult* (pp. 335–361). New York: Academic Press.

Newman, A. P., & Beverstock, C. (1990). *Adult literacy contexts and challenges*. Newark, DE: International Reading Association.

Novak, T. P., & Hoffman, D. L. (1998). *Bridging the digital divide: The impact of race on computer access and Internet use* [On-line]. Available: http://www2000.ogsm.vanderbilt.edu/papers/race/science.html

Phinney, J. S. (1996). When we talk about American ethnic groups what do we mean? *American Psychologist, 51*, 918–927.

Resta, P. (1992). Organizing education for minorities: Enhancing minority access and use of the new information technologies in higher education. *Education & Computing, 8*, 119–127.

Robinson, P. (1998). Equity and access to computer technology for grades K–12. In B. Ebo (Ed.), *Cyberghetto or cybertopia? Race, class, and gender on the Internet* (pp. 137–151). Westport, CT: Praeger.

Rogers, W. A., Cabrera, E. F., Walker, N., Gilbert, D. K., & Fisk, A. D. (1996). A survey of automatic teller machine usage across the adult life span. *Human Factors, 38*, 156–166.

Rogers, W. A., Meyer, B., Walker, N., & Fisk, A. D. (1998). Functional limitations to daily living tasks in the aged. *Human Factors, 40*, 111–125.

Rosen, L. D., & Weil, M. M. (1995). Computer availability, computer experience and technophobia among public school teachers. *Computers in Human Behavior, 11*, 9–31.

U.S. Bureau of the Census. (1998). *Growth of the 65+ population, by age group: 1900–2050* [On-line]. Available: http://www.aoa.dhhs.gov/aoa/stats/growthchart97.gif

Watson, J. A. (1997). Factors associated with African American grandparents' interest in grandparent education. *Journal of Negro Education, 66*(1), 73–82.

Chapter 14

Coming Full Circle: Some Circumstances Pertaining to Low Literacy Achievement Among African Americans

John Baugh
Stanford University

ORIENTATION

This discussion draws on different sources of evidence in support of a conclusion that is simultaneously obvious and elusive. The personal and professional prospects of anyone living in an advanced industrialized society are enhanced by literacy, but access to literacy differs for many reasons in different communities throughout the world. Our collective focus on literacy among African Americans amplifies this fact. Each contribution to this volume confirms, either directly or implicitly, that African Americans have yet to attain full educational equality. Our collective efforts seek to awaken all Americans from the slumber of Dr. King's deferred dream to the dawn of a new era in which we no longer can point to race-based discrepancies in literacy, college admissions, or professional prospects that unfairly discriminate against anyone.

Controversies surrounding the linguistic legacy of American slavery have confused issues so that many people conclude that low levels of literacy in African American communities result from laziness, diminished personal volition, or reluctance to embrace mainstream U.S. English (see Lippi-Green, 1997). Seeking to complement the significant contributions provided herein by my colleagues, I begin with a brief historical survey of American slave descendants' unique linguistic history, which includes the incontrovertible consequences of laws, spawned by slavery, intended to deny literacy to slaves and their descendants and of educational apartheid. I next

consider the lingering consequences of diminished educational opportunities for the vast majority of African Americans.

Although my remarks do not dwell on the efforts to dismantle affirmative action or eliminate school busing and other programs that
forced affluent schools to admit students of color, it would be wrong to
ignore the history of overt racism and the social dislocation that such
efforts have imposed on the majority of African Americans. Whereas
contemporary criticism of affirmative action grows from the sentiment
that "reverse discrimination" and "racial quotas" constitute an unfair
burden against Whites, there was no such concern among the advocates
of slavery, who denied liberties to enslaved Africans at the same
moment that they demanded independence from European monarchs.
Kozol (1991) documented the *Savage Inequalities* that continue to taint
the hallowed national ethos that every child in America should be given
equal educational opportunities. That ethos embraces the quest for a
colorblind society where every child may be judged by the content of
their character—regardless of race, sex, social class, or other demographics.

THE UNIQUE LINGUISTIC HISTORY
OF AMERICAN SLAVE DESCENDANTS

In the wake of the 1997 controversy over Ebonics, a term that suffers from
multiple definitions,[1] many scholars and pundits failed to acknowledge
that, because of the African slave trade, the linguistic legacy of African
Americans differed—substantially and fundamentally—from that of every
other immigrant group. Several, including well-known African American
critics of affirmative action such as Sowell (1972) and Steele (1990), were
quick to draw comparisons between the African American experience and
that of other immigrant groups. In fact, slaves and their descendants do

---

[1]*Ebonics* was first coined by Professor Robert Williams in 1973, and is described in his
1975 book, *Ebonics: The True Language of Black Folks*. Williams' definition focused on the linguistic and paralinguistic behavior of African slave descendants in West Africa, the
Caribbean, and the United States. However, most people became aware of the term in 1996,
when the Oakland School Board passed a controversial resolution declaring Ebonics to be
the official language of African American students within that school district. Their definition differed from Williams', claiming that Ebonics was not related to English. The Oakland
School Board later revised their resolution in favor of an alternative definition, claiming that
Ebonics is "not merely a dialect of English." Presently, most people equate Ebonics with
African American vernacular English; however, multiple definitions of the term are common
(see Baugh, 2000).

not share comparable sociolinguistic histories with other immigrants, be they from Europe, Asia, or elsewhere.

Ogbu (1992) sought to view these differences without invoking race, preferring instead to ponder the castelike nature of the social stratification of American society (see Horner, chap. 5, this volume). He noted that the Africans who first came to America did so in bondage and against their free will. During the Atlantic crossing, some Africans, unaware of Patrick Henry's famous remark, chose death at sea rather than the loss of personal liberty. However, the vast majority of enslaved Africans became chattel and the victims of dehumanizing exploitation at the hands of this nation's otherwise venerable leaders. We now know that at least one of the most revered national forefathers also fathered children who, like their mother, became his legal property.

Born of slavery, social pathology lies at the root of diminished prospects for fully realized literacy and social opportunities for a vast majority of African slave descendants. With the passage of time, some tend to dismiss the effects of social dislocation and chastise the victims of racial discrimination for not yet closing the educational and social divide that—for so many years—has been fertilized by racial bigotry and legally sanctioned before and after the Emancipation Proclamation.

As we come full circle on matters of African American literacy, readers of this text should never forget the unique linguistic history resulting from the African slave trade, which many linguists have confirmed through identifying pidginization and creolization processes that limited African exposure to educated varieties of American English (Baugh, 1983, 1999; Dillard, 1972; Labov, 1972; Mufwene, Rickford, Bailey, & Baugh, 1998; Rickford, 1996; Stewart, 1970; Winford, 1991).

Other sources of independent evidence confirm the unique linguistic history of which I speak. For example, all of the voluntary immigrants to the United States brought their language (and dimensions of their native culture) with them to this land. The import of languages other than English, on the tongues of newly arrived immigrants, remains a hallmark of the American experience, and yet we find that slave descendants are the only U.S. citizens who were unable to bring their heritage language with them to these shores. The fact that no indigenous African language survived the Atlantic crossing speaks volumes to those of us who actively seek educational equality. One must conclude that those among us who dismiss or diminish the long-lasting effects of the slave traders' efforts to cut off communication among slaves do so out of ignorance or ideological zeal. The readers of this volume would do well to correct the false linguistic impressions of others who do not fully appreciate the unique linguistic consequences of the African slave trade, or the ensuing literacy blockade that existed for centuries under slave law.

SOME CONSEQUENCES OF EDUCATIONAL
APARTHEID ON AFRICAN AMERICAN LITERACY

During the early stages of the controversy over Ebonics in 1997, I had mixed emotions during several television, radio, and news interviews regarding the linguistic consequences of slavery. On one hand, I was gratified to know that attention was being devoted to the linguistic legacy and educational consequences of American slavery. On the other hand, I was dismayed that Oakland's educators were compelled to reinvent linguistic history in their efforts to confront low levels of academic performance, literacy, and diminished standard English proficiency by the vast majority of Black students within the Oakland Unified School District (Baugh, 1999).

The seeds of the Ebonics debate were also germinated during slavery, at a time when Blacks in slave states were not allowed to attend schools. Or when, following slavery, they attended inferior, racially segregated schools. The gap in educational opportunities has gradually declined, but it is far from being eliminated, with educators throughout the country seeking innovative solutions to overcome the glaring differences in educational achievement between African Americans and others (Ball, 1996; Foster, 1991; Gadsden & Wagner, 1995; Hollins, 1996).

Most of the preceding historical facts are not in dispute. There were no schools for slaves, and those Whites who dared to teach slaves to read and write did so at their personal peril, in direct violation of laws intended to restrict slaves. As time passed, and the post–Civil War era gave birth to schools for Black children, these schools were always inferior to those serving affluent students. Indeed, it was partially due to the existence of entrenched racial segregation that Booker T. Washington began the wonderful legacy of historically Black colleges and universities, created because, at that time, the doors to predominantly White institutions of higher learning were closed to African Americans.

In much the same manner that the Emancipation Proclamation did not eliminate racial bigotry, the 1954 Supreme Court ruling (i.e., *Brown v. Board of Education*) did not eliminate educational inequities. Readers of this text have lived through other social experiments, such as school busing and court-ordered school desegregation, that have yet to achieve the desired goal of providing African Americans with equal educational opportunities. Many courts naively assumed that the educational consequences of racial bigotry would somehow wash away if schools were no longer racially segregated. By this thinking, low levels of literacy would also disappear once Black children were taught in the same classrooms with White children. But, the massive gap in literacy, education, and test performance prevails despite all of the efforts to eradicate racial barriers to educational equality. My orientation toward these problems grows not only from my own history as an African American student who attended inner-city schools in Philadelphia and Los Angeles, but is also shaped by my linguistic knowledge that access to mainstream U.S. English has been thwarted by racially motivated residential segregation.

Whereas the South had overt Jim Crow laws to navigate Black and White social relations, other states beyond the South maintained racial segregation through less overt means that were more directly tied to socioeconomic status and covert racial discrimination. It is partially for this reason that African American adults whom I have interviewed over the past 30 years share different impressions of how best to improve African American literacy and education.

Two anecdotes illustrate the point. The first comes from an elderly man who moved from Louisiana to California during the 1930s, and his memory of toiling in the fields in preference to academic pursuits points to his early recognition of racial and educational inequities.

John: How would you describe your education in Louisiana?

Leroi: I got to tell you; it was awful. Not 'cause the teachers didn't care. Y'know, we had Black teachers who was from the community, and we treated them with a lot of respect, but down to Louisiana where I come from we didn't get to go to school 'til after all the crops got picked.

See? We had to work in the fields, and we be working when they come by with the White children in a school bus taking them to school. And . . . I can remember this just like it was yesterday, . . . I'm thinking to myself, . . . "Why I gots to be working like a dog in these fields when the White children get to ride a bus to school?" Even when we did get to go to school we had to walk; ain't no bus come to get us. And then, once you got to school they didn't have nothing for you to work with, just some benches and some old books that they didn't want no more at the White school, and we didn't even have enough of them to go 'round.

Yes indeed; I remember that jus' like it was yesterday.

The next anecdote was produced by a husband and wife during an interview where I also asked them to describe their educational experiences and their impressions of how best to improve education. In this instance, it is important to know that the man attended racially segregated schools during the 1940s. His wife attended affluent public schools in Rhode Island, also during the 1940s, where she was one of two African American girls in a school that served wealthy families in Providence. Unlike

Leroi,[2] both Gregory and Betty had graduated from college and were working as successful professionals at the time of the following discussion:

> Gregory: I must admit that I have mixed feelings about school busing and racial integration in schools, because I received a good education in Texas, and I doubt that anyone would have cared about my education had I attended a White school, because . . .
>
> Betty: I disagree . . . I strongly disagree . . . My mother worked in Providence, and I was able to attend an excellent public school—which is why I probably still have this strong New England accent—and most of my friends were other White girls at the school, and we would talk and help each other with our homework. I think I would have received an inferior education had I gone . . . attended a Black . . . a school just teaching Blacks, and
>
> Gregory: But do you think they really accepted you?
>
> Betty: Yes . . . well at least some of the girls . . . you know, the ones that were trying to be friendly . . . The ones who "wouldn't care" wouldn't care about race . . . I think . . . I think . . . they were just . . . just . . . only thinking about themselves. Race didn't matter. They weren't even nice to the other White girls.
>
> Gregory: Maybe it was . . . no, it must have been different for you because there was no way on earth that White Texans would allow us to even be in the same neighborhood . . . let alone go to the same school. and even . . .
>
> Betty: Yes . . . the North was different . . . well, at least for me it was because Mama . . .
>
> Gregory: . . . wait . . . wait a minute . . . I think I received more attention from my Black teachers because I went to a Black school, and then on to Tuskegee. I stood out in the all-Black school . . . there was no way I could have been noticed in a White school.
>
> Betty: Right . . . I know that was true for many kids in our neighborhood
>
> John: (directing a question to Betty) But you said there were only two Black girls in the school.
>
> Betty: Yes . . . I didn't go to school in my neighborhood. Mama made arrangements for me to go to school in the neighborhood where she worked, which was a rich White neighborhood. She cleaned houses and the lady who she worked for helped me get into the school.
>
> John: Oh . . . Okay. I just didn't understand how . . .

---

[2]All names are pseudonyms.

Betty: Right . . . my situation wasn't typical, but it makes me feel that Blacks can get a good education in a White school, at least that's been my experience.

At the conclusion of this interview, both parties acknowledged that they had not previously discussed their differences of opinion regarding the relative advantages, or disadvantages, of racially integrated education. Their opinions, which are echoed by many other African Americans whom I have known through fieldwork around the country, differ. However, there can be no doubt that common ground exists regarding a shared recognition of the importance of a good education.

John: Okay . . . so . . . even though you have different educational experiences, you both went to college and clearly value higher education

Betty: Oh yes . . . we feel strongly that education is the key to Black success. I know that Greg's childhood was very, very, different from mine, but we share . . . we both believe that a good education is the most important thing you can have.

Gregory: Absolutely. A good education is essential, regardless of how you get to it. Betty was treated all right by those people in her school, and I was given lots of attention from my Black teachers who knew my parents and wanted to see me succeed. We've ended up in the same place but we push education, which is why we work so hard to help our own kids get ahead in school.

SOME RELEVANT CONSEQUENCES
OF HISTORICAL LINGUISTIC DISLOCATION

During the Ebonics controversy, one question that was repeatedly asked was: "Is it a language or a dialect?" Linguists equivocated on this point, trying to walk a judicious tightrope between overwhelming hostility toward the suggestion that Ebonics, and the language of African Americans, was not English, and that the vernacular dialects spoken by African Americans were linguistically coherent, grammatical, and logical (O'Neil, 1998). Many reacted with considerable skepticism to this professional linguistic caution, concluding that linguists were seeking to be "politically correct." Others were quick to note that the Linguistic Society of America is not a hotbed of liberalism; many members are quite conservative in their political and/or linguistic views. The fact that a resolution in support of the linguistic legitimacy of African American English (or Ebonics) received unanimous support reflects how professional linguists strongly consider all languages and dialects to be equally worthy—that is, from a linguistic point of view.

As a sociolinguist, I also recognize that various dialects and languages are either valued or devalued by those who speak them. It is within this more pragmatic realm that we come to realize that the descendants of American slaves were dislocated from their heritage languages (Cummins, 1991) in ways that resulted in pidginization and creolization wherever African slaves were sold. Within the United States, the consequence has been one where the speech of slaves and their descendants survived due to racial isolation and, as previously mentioned, racially motivated educational apartheid.

Whereas most other immigrants can trace their linguistic heritage with relative ease (particularly those who have lived in the United States for three generations or less), descendants of African slaves were intentionally dislocated from their heritage languages. Therein lies part of the reason why many linguists were reluctant to split terminological hairs over whether Ebonics should be considered a language or a dialect.

Elsewhere, the 1979 Black English trial is discussed at considerable length (Smitherman, 1981), and Judge Charles Joiner, who ruled in favor of 11 African American plaintiffs who sued their local school district for *not* teaching them standard English, did so based on laws that were intended to help students for whom English is not native. Most linguists would agree that Africans Americans speak English, albeit through a broad range of socially stratified and geographically dispersed dialects. However, most linguists would also agree that many African American children do not speak mainstream U.S. English. We also recognize—as do the contributors to this volume—that by increasing literacy among African American students, we also improve their future prospects of becoming productive citizens who will contribute to our collective welfare.

SOME PROSPECTS FOR FUTURE RESEARCH

Scholars from different research disciplines have advanced our collective knowledge of African American language, and, in every instance, we have moved from deficit hypotheses to informed studies that acknowledge the special linguistic circumstances that apply to descendants of African slaves. The editors of this volume are perhaps most noteworthy for their individual and collective contributions to advances in studies of normal and abnormal language development among African American children. In the volume *Language Development and Disorders in African American Children: Research, Assessment, and Intervention* (Kamhi, Pollock, & Harris, 1996), Wyatt (1996) and others confirmed that, at one time, the dialect of many Black children was believed to result from personal pathologies, rather than the social pathology that was embodied in slavery. Seymour and Seymour (1979), Stockman (1996), and Vaughn-Cooke (1986) have all produced major studies that have helped speech pathologists and educators better understand the linguistic behavior of Black children. In so doing, they have advanced the cause of linguistic tolerance that is necessary to advancing the educational prospects of African American students. Educators, many of whom have devoted their research to advancing literacy among Black students, have devised innovative strategies to help improve literacy for African American students. Ball (1996, 1997), Foster (1991), Gadsden and Wagner (1995), Hollins, King, and Haymen (1994), and Smitherman (1980) have been most notable in this regard.

Linguists, like myself, have often neglected the significant medical and educational problems that our colleagues were unable to avoid. Nevertheless, we find new and exciting studies of the linguistic behavior of African Americans, and a host of technical analyses that provide vivid insight into the evolution and structure of socially diverse African American dialects. Some of my fellow linguists, including Bailey (1993), Fasold (1972), Green (1995), Labov (1972), Mufwene et al. (1998), Rickford (1999), Weldon (1994), Winford (1991), and Wolfram (1994), have provided detailed studies that emphatically shatter myths that portray Black speech as being linguistically deprived, and Lippi-Green (1997) provided an excellent synthesis of these results in her observations about American English more broadly.

Although studies of African American language have been broached from different scholarly perspectives, each discipline has addressed the false linguistic impressions born of racial bigotry. These studies continue to swim against the tide of uninformed linguistic prejudice and reinvented stereotypes. The timeliness of this volume, *Literacy in African American Communities*, is precisely because so many people have yet to fully comprehend the circumstances surrounding issues of Black language and literacy.

SUMMARY AND CONCLUSION

The historical circumstances surrounding the birth and evolution of African American language has been reviewed in the hope that readers will more fully comprehend the lingering legacy of slavery and educational apartheid on the education and literacy development of many African American children. Whereas many people assume that African Americans are no different, in a social or linguistic sense, from other groups of poor, voluntary American immigrants, the fact that no indigenous African language survived the Atlantic crossing speaks volumes to scholars who recognize that such evidence confirms the unique linguistic history of slave descendants. Moreover, the ensuing linguistic dislocation from their indigenous language community, combined with laws that were designed to prevent Black literacy, only serve to compound the educational divide that continues to serve as a stark reminder that America has yet to achieve the colorblind status that most Americans value.

Until such time that those who are responsible for the education of students from low-income families demonstrate the political will to devote the necessary resources, including overt acknowledgment of the special educational needs of students who do not employ mainstream U.S. English, glaring gaps in literacy and educational performance will continue. In addition, because of the undeniable racial tenor of this discussion, those who continue to place exclusive blame for this problem at the feet of children whose ancestors were not only enslaved, but then denied the basic liberties that allowed other immigrants with lighter shades of skin to melt more rapidly into mainstream American culture, we shall not overcome the racial abyss that inhibits prospects for children who are most in need of help.

Despite facts that might otherwise lead one to a pessimistic forecast, those who have contributed to this volume, and numerous others in communities throughout the country, continue to make exceptional progress against strong—if not overwhelming—odds. It is because of their efforts that I pray that future generations of African Americans may be allowed to receive educational training that is sensitive to their past, while preparing them to become productive and successful members of society in the future. I continue to see the glass as "half full." Readers of this volume are likely to be among those who will fill the vessel of unfulfilled promises and, by so doing, eventually eliminate the vestiges of racial bigotry and linguistic ignorance that are confirmed by other chapters in this book.

REFERENCES

Bailey, G. (1993). A perspective on African American English. In D. Preston (Ed.), *American dialect research* (pp. 287–318). Philadelphia: John Benjamins.

Ball, A. (1996). Expository writing patterns of African-American students. *English Journal, 85*(1), 27–36.

Ball, A. (1997). Expanding the dialogue on culture as a critical component when assessing writing. *Assessing Writing, 4*(2), 169–202.

Baugh, J. (1983). *Black street speech: Its history, structure, and survival.* Austin: University of Texas Press.

Baugh, J. (1999). *Out of the mouths of slaves: African American language and educational malpractice.* Austin: University of Texas Press.

Baugh, J. (2000). *Beyond Ebonics: Linguistic pride and racial prejudice.* New York: Oxford University Press.

Cummins, J. (1991). Introduction. *Canadian Modern Language Review, 47*(4), 601–605.

Dillard, J. L. (1972). *Black English*. New York: Random House.

Fasold, R. (1972). *Tense marking in Black English*. Washington, DC: Center for Applied Linguistics.

Foster, M. (1991). Constancy, connectedness, and constraints in the lives of African American women teachers. *National Association of Women's Studies Journal, 3*, 70–97.

Gadsden, V. L., & Wagner, D. A. (Eds.). (1995). *Literacy among African American youth: Issues in learning, teaching, and schooling*. Cresskill, NJ: Hampton Press.

Green, L. (1995). Study of verb classes in African American English. *Linguistics and Education, 7*, 65–82.

Hollins, E., King, J., & Haymen, W. C. (Eds.). (1994). *Teaching diverse populations: Formulating a knowledge base*. Albany: State University of New York Press.

Hollins, E. (1996). *Culture in school learning: Revealing the deep meaning*. Mahwah, NJ: Lawrence Erlbaum Associates.

Kamhi, A. G., Pollock, K. E., & Harris, J. L. (Eds.). (1996). *Communication development and disorders in African American children: Research, asessment and intervention*. Baltimore: Brookes.

Kozol, J. (1991). *Savage inequalities*. New York: Crown.

Labov, W. (1972). *Language in the inner-city: Studies in the Black English Vernacular*. Philadelphia: University of Pennsylvania Press.

Lippi-Green, R. (1997). *English with an accent: Language, ideology, and discrimination in the United States*. London: Routledge.

Mufwene, S., Rickford, J., Bailey, G., & Baugh, J. (Eds.). (1998). *African American English: History, structure, and usage*. London: Routledge.

Ogbu, J. (1992, November). Understanding cultural diversity and learning. *Educational Researcher*, 5–14.

O'Neil, W. (1998). If Ebonics isn't a language, then tell me, what is? In T. Perry & L. Delpit (Eds.), *The real Ebonics debate: Power, language, and the education of African American children* (pp. 38–48). Boston: Beacon Press.

Rickford, J. (1996). Copula variability in Jamaican Creole and African American Vernacular English: A reanalysis of DeCamp's texts. In G. R. Guy, C. Feagin, D. Schiffrin, & J. Baugh (Eds.), *Towards a social science of language: Papers in honor of William Labov. Vol. 1. Variation and change in language and society* (pp. 357–372). Amsterdam: John Benjamins.

Rickford, J. (1999). *African American Vernacular English*. Oxford, England: Blackwell.

Seymour, H., & Seymour, C. (1979). The symbolism of Ebonics: "I'd rather switch than fight." *Journal of Black Studies, 9*, 397–410.

Smitherman, G. (Ed.). (1981). *Black English and the education of Black children and youth: Proceedings of the National Invitational Symposium on the King Decision*. Detroit: Wayne State University Press.

Sowell, T. (1972). *Black education: Myths and tragedies*. New York: McKay.

Steele, S. (1990). *The content of our character*. New York: St. Martin's Press.

Stewart, W. (1970). Toward a history of Negro dialect. In F. Williams (Ed.), *Language and poverty: Perspectives on a theme* (pp. 351–379). Chicago: Markham.

Stockman, I. (1996). Phonological development and disorders in African American children. In A. G. Kamhi, K. E. Pollock, & J. L. Harris (Eds.), *Communication development and disorders in African American children: Research, assessment and intervention* (pp. 117–154). Baltimore: Brookes.

Vaughn-Cooke, F. B. (1986). The challenge of assessing the language of nonmainstream speakers. In O. L. Taylor (Ed.), *Treatment of communication disorders in culturally and linguistically diverse populations* (pp. 23–48). Boston: College-Hill Press.

Weldon, T. (1994). Variability in negation in African American Vernacular English. *Language Variation and Change, 6*, 359–397.

Williams, R. (Ed.). (1975). *Ebonics: The true language of Black folks*. St. Louis, MO: Robert Williams & Associates.

Winford, D. (1991). Another look at the copula in Black English and Caribbean creoles. *American Speech, 67*, 21–60.

Wolfram, W. (1991). *Dialects and American English*. Englewood Cliffs, NJ: Prentice-Hall.

Wyatt, T. A. (1996). Acquisition of the African American English copula. In A. G. Kamhi, K. E. Pollock, & J. L. Harris (Eds.), *Communication development and disorders in African American children: Research, assessment and intervention* (pp. 95–116). Baltimore: Brookes.

Author Index

A

Adams, M., 131
Alexander, K. L., 148, 149, 151, 155
Allen, B. A., 153
Alleyne, M., 171, 174
Allingtion, R. L., 148
Ames, W. A., 157
Anand, R., 241
Anderson, J. D., 17, 196
Anderson, P. A., 233
Anderson, R., 82, 83
Anderson-Yockel, J., 22, 41
Applebee, A., 49
Asante, M., 171, 184, 187
Atkinson, P., 48
Aucella, A. F., 119
Auty, W., 221
Axelrod, J., 157, 162

B

Babcock, R., 241
Badagliacco, J. M., 266, 267, 268, 269, 271
Bailey, G., 279, 285
Baker, C., 51
Baker, D. W., 13, 14–15
Bakhtin, M., 48, 49

Baldwin, L. E., 151, 152, 154, 155, 159
Balester, V., 208
Ball, A., 280, 285
Bankston, C. L., III, 148
Baratz, J. C., 156, 157, 163
Baratz-Snowden, J., 148, 149, 162
Barnes, W. S., 214
Barnitz, J. G., 155
Barrera, R., 181, 184
Bartel, N. R., 157, 162
Bartlett, B. J., 234, 235, 236, 237, 238, 241, 242, 246
Bartlett, F. C., 238
Barton, P. E., 218
Baskin, J. H., 148, 151
Bassoppo-Moyo, T., 268
Bates, E., 41
Baugh, J., 84, 169, 171, 278(n), 279, 280, 285
Bauman, R., 46, 47, 48
Beach, R., 48
Bean, R. M., 217
Benjamin, L. A., 223
Benjamin, W., 47
Berdan, R., 183
Bereiter, C., 156
Bernstein, B., 78
Beverstock, C., 265

Biber, D., 180
Bingman, M. B., 216
Bizzell, P., 201
Blachman, B., 131
Blackshire-Belay, A., 174, 175
Bland-Stewart, L., 163
Bloome, D., 47, 48, 49(n), 51, 69, 78, 210
Bluth, G. J., 234, 237
Borgatta, E. F., 239
Bos, N., 268
Boykin, A. W., 153
Boykin, W., 185, 186
Branch, R., 184
Brandt, D. M., 234, 237
Brandt, R., 185
Bretherton, I., 41
Briggs, C., 46
Britton, B. K., 233
Broda, L., 21, 40
Broenstein, J., 241
Brooks-Gunn, J., 149, 151
Brown, H., 13
Brown, R., 111
Bruner, J., 21, 22, 41
Bryant, B. R., 157
Buck, C., 155, 158
Burke, S. M., 163
Burnhill, P., 122
Burns, S. M., 147, 159
Bus, A., 39, 130
Buttinger, C., 241
Byrne, M. E., 215

C

Cabrera, E. R., 272, 273
Caldas, S. J., 148
Campbell, A., 5, 13, 218
Campbell, F. A., 10
Campbell, L., 78, 80, 84, 86
Carnine, D., 141
Carr, J. C., 229
Carrell, P. L., 238
Carver, B. A., 266, 267, 268, 269, 270, 271
Catts, H., 132
Cazden, C., 78, 81, 175
Chall, J. S., 151, 152, 154, 155, 159
Champion, T., 45, 49, 56, 71, 72
Chandler, J., 214
Chaney, C., 136, 137
Charness, N., 266

Chisman, F. P., 213, 214
Clayborne, B. M., 267, 269, 271, 272
Coates, W. C., 14–15
Coke, M. M., 270
Cole, M., 100
Coley, R. J., 218
Collins, J., 49
Comer, J., 85
Commission on Reading, 128
Connell, P. J., 152
Connors, L. J., 10
Cook-Gumperz, J., 158
Cooley, S., 233
Cooper, D., 45
Cooper, J., 77, 181
Cornell, E., 21, 40
Corno, L., 78
Corsini, R. J., 239
Cortazzi, M., 47(n), 48
Cosby, A. G., 229
Courage, R., 209
Covington, M., 124
Craig, H. K., 152, 155, 159(n), 160, 161, 162, 163
Crouse, J., 150
Crowe, T. A., 215, 221
Cummins, J., 181, 184, 185, 284
Cunningham, P. M., 155, 156
Czaja, S. J., 266

D

Daley, K., 137
Davies, L., 122
Davis, F. B., 241
Davis, L. M., 173
Davis, P. J., 221
DeBaryshe, B., 139
DeBose, C. E., 8, 9, 10
Debruin-Parecki, A., 124
Degener, S., 217
Deitch, I. M., 233
Delain, M., 83
De La Paz, S., 45
de Leon, M. J., 241
DeLoache, J., 22, 40, 41
D'Eloia, S. G., 173
Delpit, L., 148, 158, 159
DeMendoza, O., 22, 40, 41
Dervarics, C., 104
Desai, H. B., 267

Diaz, E., 181, 182
Dillard, J. L., 169, 170, 171, 173, 174, 279
Dixon, R. A., 233, 238
Doak, C. C., 113, 118
Doak, L. G., 113, 118
Dobrich, W., 129–131
Dodds, J., 25
Dolan, L. J., 147
Dombey, H., 45
Donitsa-Schmidt, S., 268, 269
Dorsey-Gaines, C., 82, 133
Driver, D., 270
Dummett, L., 158
Duncan, G. J., 149, 151
Dunn, R., 185, 187
Dwyer, F. M., 117
Dyson, A., 45, 66

E

Echt, K. V., 266
Edmondson, J., 241
Edwards, P., 139, 141
Ellis, D. B., 118
Elsner, R. J. F., 241
Entwisle, D. R., 148, 149, 151, 155
Epps, D., 215
Evans, S., 177

F

Fairchild, H., 177
Fairclough, N., 57
Fajen, B. R., 234
Falk, J. S., 158
Farley, R. C., 221
Fasold, R., 156, 285
Fazio, B. B., 152
Ferdman, B. M., 100, 175
Ferguson, R. F., 155, 160
Ferreiro, E., 66, 182
Ferris, S. H., 241
Fey, M., 27, 132
Fillenbaum, B., 241
Fishback, P. V., 148, 151
Fisher, M. M., 265
Fisk, A. D., 266, 272, 273
Fitzsimmons, K. A., 214, 217
Flanagan, A., 149, 150
Flores, B., 181, 182

Folstein, M., 241
Foner, N., 100
Foss, G., 221
Foster, M., 285
Frankenburg, W., 25
Frederiksen, C., 47
Freire, P., 93
Froma, P., 45
Fuller-Thomson, E., 270

G

Gadsden, V., 13, 139, 280, 285
Garrett, D., 78
Gay, G., 184
Gee, J., 46, 72
Gemake, J. S., 157
Gernsbacher, M. A., 233
Gibson, M. A., 101
Gilbert, D. K., 272, 273
Gildea, P. M., 222
Gillespie, G., 234
Gilroy, F. D., 267
Gist, M., 266
Godman, K. S., 155, 156, 158, 163
Goldfield, B., 128, 129
Gonzales, A., 172
Gonzalez, J. M., 187
Goodman, I. F., 214
Goodman, J., 221
Goodman, K., 79, 175, 181, 182
Goodwin, Y., 184
Gough, P., 132
Grabowski, B. L., 111
Graesser, A. C., 233
Green, J., 51, 73
Green, L., 163, 285
Griffin, P., 147, 159
Grimes, J. E., 234, 235
Grissmer, D., 149, 150
Gualtieri, J., 184
Guerrier, J. H., 266
Gumperz, J., 46, 158
Guthrie, H. T., 157
Guthrie, L. R., 157
Gutierrez-Clellen, V. F., 72

H

Haigler, K. O., 5, 218, 221
Hale, J., 181, 184, 187

Hale, S. T., 215
Hale-Benson, J., 184, 185
Hamill, D., 162
Hammer, C. S., 23, 26, 42
Harber, J. R., 157
Harley, J., 112, 113, 114, 115, 116, 117,
    119, 120, 124
Harlow, C., 5, 218
Harman, D., 214, 217
Harper, M. S., 233
Harris, J. L., 2, 4, 15, 138, 284
Harris, V., 181, 182
Harrison, C., 113
Hart, J. T., 157
Hartley, J., 122, 241
Hawkins, R., 265, 268
Hayes, A., 225
Haymen, W. C., 285
Haynes, W., 22, 41
Heath, S. B., 22, 41, 69, 72, 80, 82, 100,
    129, 195, 200
Hedges, L. V., 152, 153
Hedrick, D., 25
Hemphill, L., 214
Herrnstein, R. J., 11, 153
Hershberger, W. A., 118
Herskovits, M., 174
Hertzog, C., 233
Hetrick, C. J., 241
Hiebert, E., 82
Hilliard, A. G., 175, 185, 187
Hinman, S., 221
Hinrichsen, G., 233
Hirsch, E., 78, 142
Hoffman, D. L., 266, 269, 271
Hohnson, K., 180
Hollingshead, A., 23
Hollins, E., 280, 285
Hoover, M. R., 177, 180
Hoover, W., 132
Howell, F. M., 229
Huey, E. B., 110
Hultsch, D. R., 233, 238
Hymes, D., 46
Hyon, S., 49

I, J

Inman, W. E., 119
Irvine, J., 78, 85, 87
Jacobs, B., 13

Jacobs, V. A., 151, 152, 154, 155, 159
Jacobson, E., 217
Jakobson, R., 47
Jefferson, G., 47
Jencks, C., 148, 150, 153, 159, 162, 163
Johannesen, L., 118
Johnson, D. L., 268
Johnson, K. R., 158
Johnson, M. M., 241
Johnson, N., 47
Jonassen, D. H., 111
Jones, E., 185
Jorm, A. F., 130

K

Kameeniu, E., 141
Kamhi, A., 138, 284
Karweit, N. L., 147
Kasinitz, P., 100, 101
Kato, Y., 66
Kearns, K., 31, 33, 35, 38
Kelley, C. L., 266
Kernell, S., 4
Keys, E., 118
King, J., 285
Kintsch, W., 234
Kirchner, D. M., 222
Klebanov, P. K., 149, 151
Knafle, J. D., 163
Kochman, T., 207
Koretz, D., 147
Kozol, J., 7, 278
Kraly, E. P., 101
Krashen, S., 175, 180, 181, 182

L

Labov, W., 46, 47, 48, 80, 138, 156, 169,
    171, 177, 178, 182–183, 279, 285
Ladson, Billings, G., 176, 184
L'Allier, S., 133
Landauer, T. K., 266
Larkin, J., 181, 182
LaSpina, J. A., 118
Lazar, M. K., 217
Lee, C. D., 176, 184
LeFevre, J., 137
Leggon, C. B., 266, 267, 271
LeMahieu, P. G., 147

LeMoine, N., 176
Levenstein, P., 83
Levine, T., 268, 269
Lewis, C., 113
Light, L. L., 233
Lindamood, P., 141
Lippi-Green, R., 277, 285
Liu, L., 268
Loeber, R., 147
Lonigan, C., 130
Lopez, M. A., 233
Lorch, E. P., 119
Lorch, R. F., 119
Los Angeles Unified School District, 176
Lowther, D. L., 268
Luke, A., 51
Lyon, G. R., 133, 136, 137, 138, 140, 142

M

Maclean, R., 130
Madden, N. A., 147
Maguin, E., 147
Mandler, J., 47
Manguel, A., 17, 110, 111
Mann, W. C., 234
Marcus, C., 78, 85, 91
Mardell, B., 45
Margo, R., 150–151, 152
Markham, L., 155
Marks, C., 3
Marshall, D., 100, 101
Martin, L., 22, 41
Matthews, R., 130
McCabe, A., 49
McClure, E., 157
McDavid, R. I., 173
McGillip, J., 87
McGlone, C., 119
McLance, J., 22, 42
McLaughlin, B., 182
McMillen, N. R., 18
McNamee, G., 22, 42
Meek, E. E., 215
Melmed, P. J., 157
Meyer, B., 266, 273
Meyer, B. J. F., 233, 234, 235, 236, 237,
    238, 239, 241, 242, 244, 246, 259,
    260
Michael, M., 87
Michael, S., 103, 105

Michaels, S., 49, 81
Miller, G. A., 222
Miller, L. A., 229
Minkler, M., 270
Molinari, V. A., 233
Moore, P. J., 116
Morrell, R. W., 266
Morris, C. D. J., 113
Morrison, G. R., 268
Morrow, L., 79, 80, 139
Moss, B., 78, 94, 197(n), 198(n), 203(n), 206
Mufwene, S., 174, 279, 285
Mukaigawa, Y., 66
Murray, C., 11, 153
Murray, J. D., 119

N

Nair, S. N., 266
Naremore, R. C., 152
National Assessment of Educational
    Progress, 148, 149
National Center for Educational Statistics,
    4, 6
National Center on Education and the
    Economy, 5
Nelson-LeGall, S., 185
Nettles, M. T., 147, 149, 151
Newman, A. P., 265
Nichols, P. C., 154
Ninio, A., 21, 22, 41
Nisbett, R. E., 153
Noble, C. A., 241
Nolen, P. S., 157
Noordman, L. G. M., 234
Novak, T. P., 266, 269, 271
Nowell, A., 152, 153
Nurss, J. R., 13, 14–15

O

Ochs, E., 42, 46, 48, 72, 73
O'Connor, E. M., 139
O'Connor, P., 5
O'Connor, R., 218
Ogbu, J. U., 100, 101, 102, 103, 104, 105,
    184, 186, 279
O'Hare, W. P., 101
Olson, A. V., 157
Olson, L. S., 149, 151

O'Neil, J., 185
O'Neil, W., 283
Orazem, P., 151
Ozaki, K., 66

P

Panofsky, C., 41
Parikh, N. S., 13, 14–15
Paris, A. E., 265, 268
Parker, R. M., 13, 14–15
Pearson, P., 83
Pelligrini, A., 39, 130
Peralta de Mendoza, O., 41
Perna, L. W., 147, 149, 151
Pessar, P. R., 101
Peterson, C., 49
Pflaum, S. W., 163
Phillips, M., 148, 150, 153, 159, 162
Phillips, S., 82
Phinney, J. S., 274
Phinney, M., 48
Pitkin, K., 14–15
Pollock, K., 138, 284
Poon, L. W., 233, 237, 238, 239, 241, 242, 244, 246, 260
Porporino, F. J., 218
Potter, S. S., 118
Prather, E., 25
Preece, A., 49
Preissle, J., 104, 105
Pressley, M., 111
Prisuta, R., 13
Prutting, C. A., 222
Purcell-Gates, V., 133, 135, 136, 217, 223
Puskar, D., 241

Q, R

Qualls, C. D., 2, 4, 8, 15
Quinn, R., 72
Ralph, J., 150
Rashotte, C. A., 131
Reder, S. M., 100
Redlich, F., 23
Reisberg, B., 241
Rescorla, L., 25
Resta, P., 266, 267, 268, 271
Reynolds, R. E., 157
Rice, G. E., 233, 234, 238
Rickards, J. P., 234

Rickford, J., 173, 174, 279, 285
Riley, R. W., 154–155
Robinson, D., 218
Robinson, P., 267
Robinson, T. L., Jr., 221
Rogers, L., 80
Rogers, W. A., 266, 272, 273
Rong, X. L., 104, 105
Rooks, D., 45
Root, J. H., 113, 118
Rosen, B., 266
Rosen, C. L., 157
Rosen, H., 47(n)
Rosen, L. D., 267, 271
Roth, S., 45
Rowe, D., 46
Royster, J. J., 196
Rystrom, R. C., 157

S

Sacks, H., 47
Salthouse, T. A., 233, 241
Sanders, T. J. M., 234
Sassoon, R., 122
Scarborough, H., 129–131
Scevak, J., 116
Schieffelin, B. B., 42, 46, 72, 73
Schneider, E. W., 173
Scholes, R. J., 222
Schriver, K. A., 111, 112, 113, 114
Schuele, C., 128, 132, 222
Schwoerer, C., 266
Scollon, R., 72
Scott, C., 80
Scott, J., 79, 80, 82, 83
Scribner, S., 100
Seefeldt, C., 267, 269, 271, 272
Segal, A., 99
Senechal, M., 21, 40, 137
Seymour, C., 285
Seymour, H., 45, 71, 163, 285
Shade, B. J., 184, 185, 186
Shaffer, S. C., 241
Share, D. L., 130
Sharit, J., 266
Sheridan, D., 49(n)
Sherzer, J., 46
Siegelman, C. K., 221
Silbert, J., 141
Silfies, L. N., 234

Simons, H. D., 158
Singham, J., 147, 148, 152, 159, 160
Slavin, R. E., 147
Small, B. J., 233
Smith, D., 133
Smith, E., 169, 174
Smith, F., 175, 176
Smith, G., 241
Smith, J. K., 139
Smith, J. P., 147
Smith, S. L., 119
Smitherman, G., 8, 9, 81, 170, 171, 179, 284, 285
Snow, C., 147, 159, 177, 214
Snow, D., 128, 129
Snyder, L., 41
Snyder, T., 6
Solsken, J., 47, 48
Sowell, T., 278
Spache, G., 173
Speece, D., 45
Spooren, W. P. M., 234
Steele, S., 278
Steffensen, M. S., 157
Stewart, W., 173, 174, 279
Stockman, I., 285
Street, B., 46, 49, 49(n), 50, 51, 70(n)
Street, J., 70(n)
Strickland, D., 87, 140, 141
Stubblefield, R. A., 238, 241, 242, 260
Sullivan, J. F., 234
Sulzby, E., 21, 49, 79, 181

T

Talbot, A. P., 233, 237, 238, 239, 241, 242, 244, 246, 260
Tallant, C., 45
Taylor, D., 82, 105, 133
Taylor, H., 179, 180
Taylor, O., 78
Teale, W. H., 21, 23, 40, 42, 105, 133
Teberosky, A., 66, 182
Teel, K. M., 124
Teft, P., 181, 182
Terry, D. F., 118
Tharp, R., 83
Thomas, E., 137
Thompson, B., 182
Thompson, S. A., 234
Thompson-Porter, C., 159(n)

Tobin, A., 25
Tomblin, B., 132
Toolan, M., 47(n)
Torgesen, J. K., 131, 136
Torrey, J. W., 156
Trent, S. D., 221
Troutman, D. E., 158
Trueman, M., 119
Twaite, J. A., 270

U

Ueda, A., 66
University of Michigan, 148
U.S. Bureau of the Census, 147, 266
U.S. Department of Commerce, 147
U.S. Department of Education, 213, 214
U.S. News and World Report, 241

V

Valdes-Fallis, G., 207
Van Horn, B., 217
van Ijzendorn, M., 39, 130
Van Keulen, J. E., 8, 9, 10
van Kleeck, A., 85, 128, 129, 132, 222
Vaughn-Cooke, F. B., 285
Vernon-Feagans, L., 42
Viaderon, D., 187
Vickers, H., 184
Voss, J. F., 234

W

Wagner, D. A., 280, 285
Wagner, R. K., 131
Walker, A., 3
Walker, N., 266, 272, 273
Walker, P., 113
Wallat, C., 73
Waller, R. H. W., 118, 119
Walmsley, S. A., 148
Washington, J. A., 152, 155, 159(n), 160, 161, 162
Wasik, B. A., 147
Waters, M. C., 104, 105
Watson, J. A., 270
Wechsler, D., 241
Weddington, G. T., 8, 9, 10

Weil, M. M., 267, 271
Weldon, T., 285
Wells, G., 46, 131
Westby, C., 22, 42
Wiederholt, J. L., 157, 162
Wilhite, S. C., 119
Wilkinson, I., 82
Williams, M. V., 13, 14–15
Williams, R., 278(n)
Williams, S., 169, 170, 171, 173, 174,
    175
Williamson, S., 149, 150
Willis, B. J., 222
Winfield, L., 157

Winford, D., 279, 285
Wisnudel, M., 268
Wolfram, W., 78, 156, 285
Woods, D. D., 118
Woodson, C. G., 174
Wyatt, T. A., 284

Y, Z

Yang, B., 241
Young, C. J., 234, 235, 236, 237, 238, 241,
    242, 246
Zhang, X., 132

Subject Index

A

Academic achievement, reading skills and, 147, 181

Academic essays, African American sermons and, 208–209

Academic literacy
literacy events of African American churches and, 196–197
code-switching, 207
community texts, 204–205
implications for literacy learning, 207–210
textual authority, 200–201
plagiarism and, 205

Access structures
headings, 119
lists, 119–120
numbering systems, 119
overview of, 118–119
summaries, 119

Adaptation, in narrative development, 49–50

Adoption, in narrative development, 49–50

Adult literacy, 214
definitions of, 213
prison population, 5

Adult literacy programs, *see also* Project LEAP
ancillary communication skills and, 221–222
attendance/motivation in, 217
breaking the cycle of illiteracy, 220
community college–based, 226–227
effect on families, 218–219
Even Start family program, 223–225
functional outcomes and, 219–220
intergenerational, 225–226
long-term follow-up, 219–221
need for, 214
personnel issues, 215–216
pre-enrollment counseling and, 219
for prisoners, 218, 227–229
recruitment of participants, 216–222
retention of participants, 214, 217–218
special needs individuals and, 218
survey of design and delivery methods in, 223–229
the unemployed and, 230
in the workplace, 230

Adults, *see* African American adults; Older adults; Parents

Affirmative action, 278

African American adults, *see also* Adult literacy programs; Older adults; Parents
functional health literacy, 13–15

African American adults (*cont.*)
  illiteracy rates, 6
  intergenerational literacy issues, 13
  literacy needs and, 214, 229
  reading practices, 15–17
African American children, *see also* Standard
    English Language Learners
  African American English and, 175
    code-switching, 161–162, 163–164
    dialect density, 159–160
    dialect interference, 156–159
  Black–White achievement gap
    contributing factors, 150–159
    historical trends, 148–150
    research issues, 159–164
  book reading interaction study, 23–41
  cognitive tests and, 153
  computer literacy and
    at home, 269–270
    in schools, 267–269
  early literacy experiences of, 133–138
  home literacy environment and, 10, 29,
    153–154, 181
  home–school literacy connections, 22,
    42; *see also* Home–school literacy
    connections
  learning styles, 185–187
  low teacher expectations and, 154–155,
    160
  reading difficulties and, 136–138, 148
  reading studies and, 163–164
  reading tests and, 162–163
  school desegregation and, 150–151
  socioeconomic status and, 151–153
  spoken and written narrative develop-
    ment in
    construction of social identities and
      relationships, 62–66
    differentiating stories and non-narra-
      tive writing, 70
    literacy development and, 45, 50–51,
      66–70
    repertoire acquisition, 49–50, 72
    textual structure of narratives, 54–56
    theoretical perspectives on, 46–51
    uptake and transformation of narra-
      tives, 56–59
    use of uptake and hybridization in
      written stories, 69–70
    use of writing objects and static repre-
      sentations, 67–69

using and transforming other children's
    stories, 59–62
African American churches
  field studies of, 197–199
  literacy education and, 196
  literacy events and, 195–196, 199–207
    Bible as literate text, 200–202
    community text, 203–205
    implications for academic literacy,
      196–197, 200–201, 204–205, 207
    implications for literacy learning,
      207–210
    memorization of Scripture, 202
    notions of shared knowledge,
      205–207
    responsive reading, 202
    sermons, 202–205
  political influence of, 195
African American English
  alternative names for, 170
  in church sermons, 206–207
  code-switching by schoolchildren,
    161–162, 163–164
  communication problems and, 221
  compared to Standard American English,
    169
  confounding with low socioeconomic stat-
    us, 162
  deficit hypothesis and, 172–173
  dialect density of schoolchildren and,
    159–160
  dialect interference hypothesis and, 79,
    156–159
  difference hypothesis and, 173–175
  history of research on, 78
  home–school discontinuities and, 79–82,
    83
  improving teacher knowledge of,
    177–178
  linguistic legitimacy and, 283–284
  miscue analysis and, 163
  morphosyntactic features and, 157, 158,
    159–160
  narrative structures and, 49, 80–81
  negative attitudes toward, 84
  origins of, 171–175, 278–279
  phoneme awareness and, 158
  phonics and, 182–183
  phonology and, 157, 158
  prevalence of, 170, 175
  reading studies and, 163–164

research issues and, 159–160, 161–162, 284–285
teacher bias and, 155
African American literacy, *see also* Literacy
  Black–White achievement gap
    contributing factors, 150–159
    historical trends, 148–150
    research issues, 159–164
  history of, 17–18
  intergenerational issues in, 13
  meanings of, 2–4
  personal impact of, 10–15
  profile of, 4–6
  reading programs and, 18
  research in, 78
  unique characteristics of, 8–10
African American mother–infant dyads, book reading interaction study
  background to, 21–23
  child behavior and, 37–38, 41
  comparisons to White, middle-class dyads, 41
  description of play sessions, 25
  implications for education, 41–42
  interactions of low- vs. middle- socioeconomic-status dyads, 26–38, 39, 40–41
  mothers' educational level and, 39–40
  reading styles of mothers, 29–38, 40–41
  results from, 39–41
  socioeconomic status of dyads, 23–25
African Americans, *see also* African American adults; African American children; African American mother–infant dyads; Older adults; Southern Blacks
  Black–White achievement gap
    contributing factors, 150–159
    historical trends, 148–150
    research issues, 159–164
  computer literacy and, 267–272
  cultural–ecological theory and, 102, 103, 104
  dislocation from heritage languages, 279, 284
  educational inequality and, 277, 278, 280–283
  education profile of, 6–8
  home literacy environment and, 10, 29, 153–154, 181
  learning styles, 185–187

literacy profile of, 4–6
meanings of literacy to, 2–4
narrative structure employed by, 80–81
racism and, 278
school retention rates, 104
social cognition and, 186
technology usage and, 272–274
African American teachers, computer literacy and, 267–268
African origin theorists, 174–175
Africologists, 174–175
Age, literacy proficiency and, 5
Alphabetic principle/skills
  African American English users and, 183
  early reading ability and, 131
Ambiguity, 9
Apprenticeship learning, 82
Atlantic Monthly (magazine), 178
ATMs, *see* Automatic teller machines
Attendance, in adult literacy programs, 217
Audience
  call-and-response congregations, 202–205, 206
  community text and, 204–205
  notions of when writing, 209
  shared knowledge and, 205–207
Author books, 53
Automatic teller machines (ATMs), 6, 273

B

Baptist church, 198
Barney's Farm Animals (Kearns), 31, 33, 35, 38
Becoming a Nation of Readers (Anderson), 82
Behavior, in communication, 222
Bias
  in cognitive tests, 153
  in reading tests, 162–163
Bible, as a literate text, 200–202
Bibliographies, 120
Black Entertainment Television, 91–94
Black press, liberation of Southern Blacks and, 3–4
Black–White achievement gap
  cognitive tests and, 153
  contributing factors, 150–159
  dialect interference and, 156–159
  historical trends in, 148–150
  home literacy environment and, 153–154

Black–White achievement gap *(cont.)*
  low teacher expectations and, 154–155,
    160
  middle-income families and, 152–153,
    160–161
  research in
    future directions, 159–161
    methodology issues, 161–164
  socioeconomic status and, 151–153
  unequal opportunity and, 150–151
Body language, 9
Bold print, 116
Book reading, *see* Joint book reading;
    Reading ability/performance
Book reading styles, in mother–infant
    dyads, 29–38, 40–41
  different styles for different book genres,
    32–35, 40
  limited period of joint attention, 36–38,
    40–41
  modeling style, 30–32, 40
  text reading style, 36, 40
Books, classroom access to, 181–182
Brown v. Board of Education, 280

C

California
  Ebonics and, 278(n), 280
  reading ability of fourth graders, 133
Call-and-response, 202–205, 206
Capital letters, 116
Caribbean Americans
  acceleration in schools, 104
  areas for future research, 105–106
  Black American identity and, 104, 105
  cultural–ecological theory and, 101–
    105
  cultural identity and, 104–105
  dual frames of reference and, 102
  folk theories of getting ahead and, 102–
    103
  immigration and, 100–101
  primary cultural and language differ-
    ences, 103
  school retention rates, 104
Caribbean Creole, 173–174
Central African Republic, 100
Chicago, African American churches in,
    197–199

Children, *see also* African American children;
    Standard English Language Learners
  effect of home environment on reading
    skills, 10
  home–school literacy connections, 22,
    42; *see also* Home–school literacy
    connections
  mother–infant book reading interactions,
    21–23; *see also* African American
    mother–infant dyads
  from multicultural backgrounds, literacy
    experiences and, 22, 41–42
  storytelling and, 48, 73
Child vocalizations, in mother–infant book
    reading interactions, 28, 30, 39
Classroom relationships, in children's nar-
    ratives, 65–66
Classrooms, *see also* Education; Schools;
    Teachers
  access to books, 181–182
  desegregation and, 150–151
  recommendations to facilitate literacy
    acquisition, 187–188
Code-switching
  by African American children, 161–162,
    163–164
  by African American ministers, 207
Cognitive abilities, reading ability and, 132
Cognitive tests, 153
Collaborative learning, 82, 83
  barriers to, 84
Colleges, computer literacy and, 267–268
Color, in typographic cuing, 117–118
Color Purple, The (Walker), 3
Communication
  behaviors, 222
  in mother–infant book reading interac-
    tions, 26–29, 40–41
Community-based literacy programs, 18
Community college–based adult basic edu-
    cation, 226–227
Community literacy, effects of, 10
Community texts, 203–205
Comparison structure, 235
Comprehension strategies, reading ability
    and, 137–138
Computation span test, 241
Computer anxiety, 267
Computer literacy, *see also* Technology;
    Word processors
  acquiring, race-related differences

in access, 271–272
at home, 269–270
in schools, 267–269
at the workplace, 270–271
defined, 265
digital music recording, 6
levels of, 17
lifelong value of, 266
recommendations for expanding, 274–275
research issues, 274
Computer-related jobs, 271
Computer technology, classrooms and, 188
Condition of Education, The (National Center for Education Statistics), 149
Congregations, *see also* African American churches
call-and-response, 202–205, 206
community texts and, 203–205
notions of shared knowledge and, 205–207
Constructivist pedagogy, 82
Context, narrative performance and, 52(n)
Contextual phonics, 181
Contrastive linguistic analysis, 179
Cooperative learning, 82, 83
Correctional facilities, literacy programs and, 218, 227–229
Creolists, 173–174
Cultural artifacts, in classrooms, 188
Cultural aversion, 85
Cultural–ecological theory, 101–105
Cultural inversion, 85
Culturally relevant teaching, 183–185
Cultural synchronization, 85–86
Cyclical action, in children's narratives, 55–56

D

Davis Reading Test, 241, 242
Deficit hypothesis, of African American English, 156, 172–173
Deficit models, of literacy development, 51
Denver Developmental Screening Test II, 25
Desegregation, in schools, 150–151
Desk arrangements, 188
Dialect density, 159–160
Dialect interference, 79, 156–159
Dialectologists, 173
Difference hypothesis, 156, 173–175
Digital music, 6

Directives, in reading interactions with infants, 26, 28, 39
Discourse patterns, home–school discontinuities and, 80–82
Discrimination, perceived by voluntary and involuntary minorities, 103
Doaks, Rosaland, 91
Double-coded messages, 9
Double consciousness, 185
Douglass, Frederick, 196
Down syndrome, literacy and, 11–13
Dropout rates, *see also* Retention rates
in adult literacy programs, 214, 217, 224
DuBois, W. E. B., 184–185

E

Early literacy experiences, *see also* Emergent literacy
acquisition of specific literacy knowledge, 131–132
of African American children, 133–138
family literacy and, 127
in high-literacy homes, 128–133
joint book reading, 128–131
Ebonics, 278, 280, 283; *see also* African American English
Ebonics (Williams), 278(n)
Education, *see also* Classrooms; Home–school literacy connections; Instructional practices; Schools; Teachers
historical profile of African Americans, 6–8
inequality in, African Americans and, 277, 278, 280–283
instructional interference and, 79–80
literacy proficiency and, 5
of mothers, effect on reading interactions with children, 39–40
of parents, child literacy skills and, 152
Elderly, *see* Older adults
Electronic media, *see* Computer literacy; Technology
Emergent literacy, *see also* Early literacy experiences
defined, 77
family literacy and, 127
home–school connections and, 77–78
areas for future research, 94–95
bidirectional bridging, barriers to, 83–84

Emergent literacy *(cont.)*
  bidirectional bridging, models and
    programs for, 82–83, 85–94
  discontinuities, 78–83
  unidirectional models and, 85, 86
Employment, literacy proficiency and, 5
English, *see* African American English;
    Standard American English
Essays, African American sermons and,
    208–209
Ethnocentrism, 84
Even Start family literacy program, 223–
    225
Explicit naming, 66
External motivation, 217

F

Families
  affected by adult enrollment in literacy
    programs, 218–219
  in children's narratives, 62–63
  computer literacy and, 269–270
Family literacy, *see also* Home literacy envi-
    ronment
  early literacy experiences and, 127
  effects of, 10–13
  in high-literacy homes, 128–133,
    134–135
  in low-income homes, 133–136
  in low-literacy homes, 134
Family literacy programs, 139–140
  Even Start program, 223–225
FAST, *see* Functional Assessment Staging Test
Figurative literacy, 8–10
"Finger spaces," 122
Functional Assessment Staging Test (FAST),
    241, 242
Functional health literacy, 13–15

G

GED certification, adult literacy programs
    and, 215, 224, 225, 226, 227, 228
Gender, in children's narratives, 63–65
General Educational Development certifi-
    cation, *see* GED certification
Good Reading for the Disadvantaged Reader
    (Spache), 173
Gothic typeface, 113

Grandparents, *see also* Older adults
  in children's narratives, 62–63
  computer literacy and, 270
Graphic organizers, 189
Gray Oral Reading Tests, 157
Grid paper, 122, 123
Gutters, 114

H

Hart–Cellar Immigration Reform Act, 101
Hawaiian children, cooperative learning
    and, 82, 83
Headings, 116, 119
Health literacy, 13–15
Heritage languages, dislocation of African
    Americans from, 279, 284
High-literacy homes, early literacy experi-
    ences in, 128–133, 134–135
High schools, computer literacy and,
    267–268
Home literacy environment, *see also* Family
    literacy; Home–school literacy con-
    nections
  of African American children, 153–154,
    181
  computer literacy in, 269–270
  impact on children's reading skills, 10
  mother–infant reading interactions, 29
Home–school literacy connections, 22, 42
  areas for future research, 94–95
  bidirectional bridging, 82–83
    barriers to, 83–84
    cultural synchronization and, 85–86
    Parents as Expert Teachers (PET) pro-
      gram, 87–91
    television-based program, 91–95
  Black–White achievement gap and,
    153–154
  discontinuities
    in language functions, 80–82, 83
    in language structure, 79–80, 83
    in literacy functions, 82–83
    research in, 78, 95
  overview of, 77–78
  unidirectional bridging, 85, 86
Home visits, in family literacy programs, 223
Homework, 70
  television-based bidirectional literacy
    program and, 91–94

Homonymy, 183
Homophones, 183, 189
Horizontal justification, 114

I

Ideas, community vs. private ownership of,
    204–205
IEA Reading Literacy Study, 213, 214
"I Go to The Rock" (song), 9
Illiteracy rates, 6
Illustrations, color and, 117
Immigrants
    cultural–ecological theory and, 101–105
    dual frames of reference and, 102
    folk theories of getting ahead and,
        102–103
    perceptions of prejudice and discrimina-
        tion, 103
    primary cultural and language differ-
        ences, 103
Immigration, of Caribbean Americans,
    100–101
Immigration Act of 1924, 100–101
Indexes, 120
Instructional interference, 79–80
Instructional practices, for Standard English
        Language Learners
    access to books, 181–182
    African American learning styles and,
        185–187
    cultural relevance, 183–185, 190–191
    holistic approaches, 180–183
    improving teacher knowledge, 177–178
    integration of linguistic knowledge,
        178–179, 190
    overview of, 176–177, 188–191
    phonics instruction and, 182–183,
        189
    second language acquisition methods,
        179–180, 189
    whole-language approaches, 182
Intergenerational literacy programs,
    225–226
Interim summaries, 119
Intrinsic motivation, 217
Involuntary minorities
    cultural–ecological theory and, 102, 103,
        104
    defined, 101, 102

perceptions of prejudice and discrimina-
        tion, 103
    school learning and, 186
    secondary cultural and language differ-
        ences, 103
IQ tests, 153
Italics, 117

J, K

Jazz, 2
JOBS program, 215
Joint book reading
    African American mother–infant dyads
        study
        background to, 21–23
        child behavior and, 37–38, 41
        comparisons to White, middle-class
            dyads, 41
        description of play sessions, 25
        implications for education, 41–42
        interactions of low- vs. middle- socio-
            economic-status dyads, 26–38, 39,
            40–41
        mothers' educational level and, 39–40
        reading styles of mothers, 29–38,
            40–41
        results from, 39–41
        socioeconomic status of dyads, 23–25
    early reading ability and, 129–130
    in high-literacy families, 128–129
    negative effects and, 130–131
Justified text, 114
King, Martin Luther, Jr., 205(n)

L

Landscape layouts, 114
Language abilities, reading ability and, 132
Language acquisition, 178, 179–180
Language Development and Disorder in
        African American Children (Kamhi),
        284–285
Language Development Survey, 25
Language-experience instruction, 182
Language functions, home–school disconti-
        nuities and, 80–82, 83
Language practices concept, 46, 51
Language structure, home–school disconti-
        nuities and, 79–80, 83

Layout of texts
  page sizes, 113–114
  readers and, 113–115
  space and structure, 114–115
  text spacing, 114
  writing instruction and, 122
Learning disabilities, adult literacy pro-
    grams and, 218
Learning environments, 186
Learning styles
  adult literacy programs and, 217–218
  of African Americans, 185–187
Letter play, 67–68
Letter recognition, early reading ability
    and, 131
Letter spacing, 114
Limited literacy proficiency
  failure to admit, 13–14
  health care issues and, 14–15
  issues of family tolerance and, 14
Lined paper, 122–123
Line spacing, 114
Linguistic analysis, contrastive, 179
Linguistic knowledge, applying to literacy
    instruction, 178–179, 190
Linguistic Society of America, 171, 283
Listening centers, 188
Lists, in texts, 119–120
Literacy, *see also* African American literacy;
    Early literacy experiences; Emergent
    literacy; Family literacy; Home liter-
    acy environment; Limited literacy
    proficiency; Literacy acquisition; Lit-
    eracy events
  Black–White achievement gap
    contributing factors, 150–159
    historical trends in, 148–150
    research issues, 159–164
  definitions of, 1–2, 213
  language practices concept and, 46, 51
  meanings of, 1, 2–4, 99–100
  narrative development and, 45, 50–51,
    66–70
  participatory, 15
  Reading History and Habits Survey of,
    15–17
  scenarios of the future, 142–143
Literacy acquisition
  sites of common ground, 209–210
  sites of negotiation, 207–209
  by Standard English Language Learners
    classroom environment, 187–188

  impact of language variation on,
    175–176
  instructional strategies, 176–187,
    188–191
Literacy artifacts, 128
Literacy education, *see also* Education
  in African American churches, 196
Literacy events
  in African American churches, 195–196,
    199–207
    Bible as literate text, 200–202
    community text, 203–205
    implications for academic literacy,
      196–197, 200–201, 204–205, 207
    implications for literacy learning,
      207–210
    memorization of Scripture, 202
    notions of shared knowledge, 205–207
    responsive reading, 202
    sermons, 202–205
  defined, 195(n)
Literacy functions, home–school disconti-
    nuities and, 82–83
Literacy programs, *see also* Adult literacy
    programs; Family literacy programs;
    Reading programs
  to prevent reading failure, 139–140
  recommendations for, 141–142
  to reduce reading failure, 140–142
Literacy socialization, 128
Literacy tests, 18
Low-income families
  confounding African American English
    with, 162
  early literacy experiences in, 133–136
  joint book reading in, 130
  literacy skills and, 5–6, 151–152
Low-literacy adults, structure strategy and,
    260–261
  examples from a rural community, 248–
    260
Low-literacy families, early literacy experi-
    ences in, 134

M

Manuscript ministers, 198(n), 199
Maps, color and, 117
Margins, 114
Meaning, community vs. private ownership
    of, 204–205

Memorization, 202
Mental retardation, literacy and, 11–13
Message units, 73
Metalinguistic awareness, reading ability and, 137
Meyer's prose analysis system, 242
Microwave ovens, 273
Middle-income families
  Black–White achievement gap and, 152–153, 160–161
  book reading interaction study, 26–29, 32, 34–35, 36–38, 39, 40–41
MIDI (musical instrument digital interface), 6
Mini Mental State Exam (MMSE), 241, 242, 247, 248, 260
Ministers, *see also* African American churches
  code-switching and, 207
  manuscript, nonmanuscript, and partial manuscript ministers, 198(n), 199
  notions of shared knowledge and, 205–207
  responsive readings, 202
  sermons and, 202–205
  "sounding Black," 206–207
Minorities, *see also* Immigrants; Involuntary minorities
  cultural–ecological theory and, 101–105
  school learning and, 186
  voluntary and involuntary, 101–102
Miscue analysis, 163
Mis-Education of the Negro (Woodson), 174
Mississippi, adult literacy programs in, 213–230
MMSE, *see* Mini Mental State Exam
Modeling reading style, 30–32, 40
Modifiers, in reading interactions with infants, 28, 39
Moral themes, in children's narratives, 55, 56
Mothers, *see also* African American mother–infant dyads; Parents
  mother–infant book reading interactions, 21–23
Motivation
  in adult literacy programs, 217
  reading ability and, 138
Multiple meanings, 9
Music literacy, 2

N

NAdLitS, *see* National Adult Literacy Survey
Narrative development, *see also* Spoken and written narrative development study
  adoption and adaptation in, 49–50
  concepts of narrative as text and performance, 46–48
  construction of social identities and relationships, 62–66
  differentiating stories and non-narrative writing, 70
  language practices concept and, 46, 51
  literacy development and, 45, 50–51, 66–70
  repertoire acquisition, 49–50, 72
  research issues concerning performance and context, 52(n)
  textual structure of narratives, 54–56
  uptake and transformation of narratives, 56–59
  use of uptake and hybridization in written stories, 69–70
  use of writing objects and static representations, 67–69
  using and transforming other children's stories, 59–62
Narratives
  adapting and transforming stories by others, 59–62
  constructing social identities and relationships, 62–66
  cyclical action in, 55–56
  distinguished from stories, 47–48
  moral themes in, 55, 56
  repertoire acquisition, 49–50, 72
  stylizing in, 59
  as text and performance, 46–48
  textual structure, 54–56
  topic-centered and topic-associating, 81, 94
  uptake and transformation of, 56–59
Narrative structures
  acquisition of repertoire in, 49–50, 72
  African American English users and, 49, 80–81
  home–school discontinuities and, 80–81
  textual, 54–56
National Adult Literacy Survey (NAdLitS), 1–2, 4–6, 229, 230
National Assessment of Educational Progress, 133

National Center for Education Statistics, 149

National Institute of Child Health and
  Human Development, 139

National Literacy Act, 1, 226

Native Americans, 82

Newspapers, liberation of Southern Blacks
  and, 3–4

New York City, Caribbean Americans in,
  101–102

Nonlinguistic behavior, 222

Nonmanuscript ministers, 198(n), 199

Non-narrative writing, 70

Notebook layouts, 114

Numbering systems, in texts, 119

O

Oakland Unified School District (California),
  278(n), 280

OARS, *see* Older Americans Resource and
  Services survey

Older adults
  in children's narratives, 62–63
  computer literacy and, 266, 270
  reading comprehension and, 233
  reading habits of, 244
  reading strategies and, 233–234
  structure strategy and, 234–237
    examples from a rural community,
      248–260
    Georgia study, 239–260
    predictors for use, 247–248, 260
    self-appraisal, 244, 246–247
    text recall, 234, 235, 237, 238–239,
      247, 248–260
  usage of technology, 273–274

Older Americans Resource and Services
  (OARS) survey, 241

Oral language skills
  adult literacy programs and, 221–222
  predictors for, 137

Oral–verbal literacy
  of African Americans, 8–10
  television-based bidirectional literacy
    program and, 93

Overview summaries, 119

P

Page sizes, 113–114

Paper, lined, child writers and, 122–123

Paralinguistic behavior, 222

Parchman correctional facility (Mississippi),
  227–229

Parents
  bidirectional literacy projects and, 83,
    87–94
  computer literacy and, 269
  educational level, child literacy skills and,
    152
  involvement in child's literacy learning,
    135

Parents as Expert Teachers (PET) program,
  87–91

Partial manuscript ministers, 198(n)

Participatory literacy, 15

Peer review, 209(n)

Penitentiaries, *see* Correctional facilities;
    Prison population

Pentecostal Holiness church, 198–199

Performance
  in concepts of narrative development,
    46–48
  issues of context and, 52(n)

PET program, *see* Parents as Expert Teach-
    ers program

Phoneme awareness
  African American English and, 158
  reading ability and, 131–132, 136–137

Phonics
  African American English and, 182–183
  contextual, 181
  instructional interference and, 79
  instruction of Standard English Lan-
    guage Learners and, 182–183, 189

Phonics-based reading programs, 183

Phonology, African American English and,
  157, 158

Picture books
  color illustrations and, 117
  reading style of mothers, 30–31, 32–33,
    34–35, 40

Pidgin English, 173–174

Plagiarism, 205

Play-based utterances, in reading interac-
    tions with infants, 28

Points, in typesize, 112

Political refugees, 101

Portrait layouts, 114

Poverty, *see also* Low-income families;
    Socioeconomic status
  literacy proficiency and, 5

Pragmatic language skills, 222

Pragmatic Protocol, 222
Prejudice, perceived by voluntary and
    involuntary minorities, 103
Prerelease adult literacy programs, 227–
    229
Print literacy, *see also* Reading ability/per-
    formance
    African American churches and, 199–202
Prison population
    literacy proficiency and, 5
    literacy programs and, 218, 227–229
Problem/solution structure, 235
Project LEAP
    assessment of pragmatic language skills
        in, 222
    assessment of semantic language skills in,
        221–222
    motivation of participants in, 217
    overview of, 215
    personnel recruitment in, 216
    special needs individuals in, 218
Prose analysis system, 242

Q

Questions
    in early literacy experiences, 129
    home–school discontinuities and, 80, 81
    in reading interactions with infants, 26,
        28, 30, 31, 41
    in second language acquisition methods,
        189
Quick Word Test, 239, 242, 247, 248

R

Racism, 278
Reading ability/performance, *see also* Print
    literacy
    academic success and, 147, 181
    access to books and, 181
    alphabetic principle and, 131
    Black–White achievement gap
        cognitive tests and, 153
        contributing factors, 150–159
        dialect interference and, 156–159
        historical trends in, 148–150
        home literacy environment and,
            153–154
        low teacher expectations and, 154–155,
            160

research issues, 159–164
        socioeconomic status and, 151–153
        unequal opportunity and, 150–151
    comprehension strategies and, 137–138
    demographic disparities in, 147–148
    factors hindering, 136–138
    home literacy environment and, 10,
        153–154
    inadequate teacher preparation and, 138
    joint book reading and, 128–131
    and language and cognitive abilities, 132
    letter recognition and, 131
    metalinguistic awareness and, 137
    motivation and, 138
    negative attitude and, 131
    older adults and, 233
    phoneme awareness and, 131–132,
        136–137
    recommendations for improving, 142
    scenarios of the future, 142–143
    typographic conventions and
        access structures, 118–120
        overview of subject, 109–111, 124
        skilled readers, 110, 111
        text layout, 113–115
        typefaces, 113
        typesizes, 111–113
        typographic cuing, 115–118
        unconscious processing, 110
Reading comprehension strategies,
        137–138; *see also* Structure strategy
    older adults and, 233–234
Reading development
    factors hindering, 136–138
    narrative development and, 50–51
Reading failure
    Black–White achievement gap
        contributing factors, 150–159
        historical trends in, 148–150
        research issues, 159–164
    factors involved in, 136–138
    programs to prevent, 139–140
    programs to reduce, 140–142
Reading History and Habits Survey, 15–17
Reading practices, of African American
        adults, 15–17
Reading programs, 18; *see also* Structure
        strategy
    phonics-based, 183
    to prevent reading failure, 139–140
    recommendations for, 141–142
    to reduce reading failure, 140–142

Reading span test (RSPAN), 239, 241, 247
Reading studies/tests
    bias and, 162–163
    disadvantaging of African American students in, 163–164
Recall, *see* Text recall
Refugees, 101
Repetition, in children's narratives, 55–56
Residential segregation, 281
Responsive reading, 202
Retention rates
    in adult literacy programs
        of participants, 214, 217–218
        of teachers, 216
    in schools, 104
Review summaries, 119
RSPAN, *see* Reading span test

S

Sabbath schools, 196
SAE, *see* Standard American English
Sans serif typeface, 113
Sassoon Primary typeface, 121–122
School desegregation, 150–151
Schools, *see also* Classrooms; Education;
        Home–school literacy connections;
        Teachers
    computer literacy and, 267–269
    family literacy programs and, 224
    instructional interference and, 79–80
    low teacher expectations and, 154–155
    non-English-speaking children and, 169
    retention rates, 104
Scriptural authority, 200, 201
Second language acquisition, 179–180, 189
SELLs, *see* Standard English Language
        Learners
Semantic language skills, 221–222
Sequenced Inventory of Communication
        Development, 25
Serif typeface, 113, 121
Sermons
    call-and-response pattern, 202–205, 206
    as literacy events, 202–205
    modeling writing on, 208–209
    notions of shared knowledge and,
        205–207
    "sounding Black" in, 206–207
Shared knowledge, 205–207
Signifying, 8

Single-parent families, affected by adult
        enrollment in literacy programs, 219
Sites of common ground, 208, 209–210
Sites of conflict, 208
Sites of negotiation, 207–209
Slavery
    linguistic legacy of, 278–279
    nature of oral–verbal communication in, 9
    prohibitions on literacy and, 17
Social cognition, 186
Social identities and relationships, in children's narratives, 62–66
Socioeconomic status
    computer access and, 271
    confounding African American English
        with, 162
    literacy skills and, 5–6, 151–153
    mother–infant book reading interaction
        study, 23–25, 26–38, 39, 40–41
"Sometimes I Feel Like a Motherless Chile"
        (song), 9
Songs, communication under slavery and, 9
"Sounding Black," 206–207
Southern Blacks
    Black press and, 3–4
    historical profile of educational attainment, 7
Spacing, in text layouts
    impact on reading, 114–115
    impact on writing, 122
Spanish speakers, functional health literacy
        and, 14, 15
Special needs, adult literacy programs and,
        218
Spoken and written narrative development
        study project, *see also* Narrative
        development
    conclusions, 45, 71–73
    connecting storytelling and literacy,
        66–70
    data analysis, 53
    data collection, 52–53
    findings, 54–66
    project history, 52–53
    storytelling program context, 52–53
    theoretical basis, 46–51
Squared paper, 122, 123
Standard American English (SAE)
    African American English compared to,
        169
    dialect interference hypothesis and, 79

Standard English Language Learners
(SELLs)
  literacy acquisition and
    classroom environment, 187–188
    impact of language variation on,
      175–176
    instructional strategies, 176–187,
      188–191
  written language development, 180
Statements, in reading interactions with
  infants, 26, 28, 39
Static representations, 67–69
"Steal Away" (song), 9
Stereotyping, 84
Stories, distinguished from narratives, 47–48
Storytelling, *see also* Narrative develop-
    ment; Narratives
  in African American homes, 181
  children and, 48, 73
  concepts of narrative development and,
    46–48
  study program, 52–53
Storywriting, *see also* Narrative develop-
    ment; Narratives
  adapting and transforming stories by
    others, 59–62
  differentiating from non-narrative writ-
    ing, 70
  uptake and hybridization in, 69–70
  use of writing objects and static represen-
    tation in, 67–69
Structure strategy
  effectiveness of, 260
  Georgia study on
    comparison of rural and urban sam-
      ples, 243–248
    materials, procedure, and scoring, 239,
      241–243
    recruiting participants, 239
    text recall in rural community older
      adults, 248–260
  for low-literacy adults, 260–261
  overview of, 234–237
  predictors for use of, 247–248, 260
  self-appraisals of, 244, 246–247
  text recall and, 234, 235, 237
    cohort and cultural differences in,
      238–239
    examples from rural community older
      adults, 248–260
    improvements in, 247

Summaries, in texts, 119
Sunday schools, 196

T

Table of contents, 120
Teachers, *see also* Classrooms; Education;
    Instructional practices; Schools
  in adult literacy programs
    demographic issues, 216
    recruiting issues, 215–216
    retention, 216
  certification requirements and, 140
  in children's narratives, 65–66
  computer literacy and, 267–268
  improving preparation of, 140, 178
  inadequate preparation, 138
  instructional practices for Standard
    English Language Learners,
    176–187, 188–191
  low expectations of African American
    children, 154–155, 160
Teacher training programs, 178
Technology, *see also* Computer literacy
  classrooms and, 188
  grandparents and, 270
  lifelong value of, 266
  usage by African Americans, 272–274
Teen Summit (television show), 91–93
Television, bidirectional literacy program
    and, 91–95
Test of Functional Health Literacy in Adults
    (TOFHLA), 13–15
Text reading style, 36, 40
Text recall, structure strategy and, 234,
    235, 237
  cohort and cultural differences, 238–239
  examples from rural community older
    adults, 248–260
  improvements in, 247
Texts
  concepts of narrative development and,
    46–48
  layout considerations, 113–115; *see also*
    Typography
  reading style of mothers, 31–32, 33–34,
    35, 36, 40
Text structure strategy, *see* Structure strategy
Textual authority, 200–201
Times Roman typeface, 113

TOFHLA, *see* Test of Functional Health Literacy in Adults
Topic-associating narratives, 81, 94
Topic-centered narratives, 81, 94
"Triple quandary" effect, 185
Turn-taking, 222
Two-Factor Index of Social Position, 23
Typefaces, 113, 121–122
Typesizes, 111–112
Typographic cuing, 115–116
    capital letters, 116
    color, 117–118
    italics, 117
    multiple cuing, 118
Typography
    reading and
        access structures, 118–120
        layout, 113–115
        overview of subject, 109–111, 124
        skilled readers, 110, 111
        typefaces, 113
        typesizes, 111–113
        typographic cuing, 115–118
        unconscious processing, 110
    word processors and, 123, 124
    writing and, 120–124

U

U.S. Department of Education, 139
University of Mississippi, 215
Unjustified text, 114
Uppercase letters, 116
Urban schools, problems of, 7
U.S. News & World Report (magazine), 237

V

Vai people, 100
VCRs, 273
Verbal literacy, 8–10
Vertical justification, 114
Videocassette recorders, 273

Vocabulary development, 189
Voluntary minorities, *see also* Immigrants
    cultural–ecological theory and, 101–105
    defined, 101
Volunteers, in adult literacy programs, 216
Voting
    literacy proficiency and, 5
    literacy tests and, 18

W, Y

Wages, literacy proficiency and, 5
Washington, Booker T., 280
West Africa, 100, 174
White children, *see* Black–White achievement gap
White space, 115
Whole-language instruction, 182
Word processors, *see also* Computer literacy
    learning typographic conventions and, 123–124
Word spacing, 114
Workplace
    computer literacy and, 270–271
    literacy programs in, 230
Writing, *see also* Narrative development;
        Narratives; Storywriting
    audience and, 209
    language practices concept and, 46, 51
    models from African American church
        sermons and, 208–209
    non-narrative, 70
    notions of community text and, 204–205
    peer review and, 209(n)
    plagiarism and, 205
    textual authority and, 200–201
    typographic conventions and, 120–124
    word processors and, 123, 124
Writing objects, 67–69
Written language development
    narrative development and, 50–51
    Standard English Language Learners
        and, 180
Young Sisters and Brothers (magazine), 92